Social Theory

Social Theory

A Historical Introduction

Alex Callinicos

NEW YORK UNIVERSITY PRESS

Washington Square, New York

First published 1999 by Polity Press
in association with Blackwell Publishers Ltd.

First published in the U.S.A. in 1999 by
NEW YORK UNIVERSITY PRESS
Washington Square
New York, NY 10003

CIP data available from the Library of Congress

ISBN 0-8147-1593-1 (clothbound)
ISBN 0-8147-1594-X (paperbound)

Typeset in 10 on 12 pt Times
by Ace Filmsetting Ltd, Frome, Somerset
Printed in Great Britain by MPG Books Ltd, Victoria Square, Bodmin, Cornwall

This book is printed on acid-free paper.

In Memoriam

Aelda Callinicos
(1920–1994)

CONTENTS

Preface and Acknowledgements

I was lucky enough to become intellectually self-conscious and politically active at the end of the 1960s. This was a time when, among other things, interest in various heretical brands of social theory associated either with some version of Marxism or with an exotic species of Continental philosophy (or both) was exploding. The excitement I felt then has never left me. I hope that this book conveys a little at least of that excitement even in what is evidently a much less intellectually and politically invigorating climate.

Behind this book, then, is getting on for thirty years of reading, discussing, teaching, and writing social theory. During that time I have of course accumulated far too many debts possibly to acknowledge most here. I must, however, thank the successive generations of students who have listened to me with more patience than I deserved, forced me to state what I was trying to say more clearly, and helped to develop our discussions in stimulating and illuminating directions.

There are others who cannot go without more specific mention. David Held has been trying to coax me into writing this book ever since we taught together for a short while at the beginning of the 1980s. Since I finally cracked, he has been, as ever, an endlessly encouraging and helpful editor. Everyone else with whom I have dealt at Polity and Blackwell – Julia Harsant, Gill Motley, Jennifer Speake, and Janet Moth – have been equally supportive.

Sam Ashman was heroically kind and patient while I wrote this book. She has also, in the final stages of production, overcome her earlier (to my mind inexplicable) reluctance about actually reading the draft to help with the awful task of checking the proofs. For this, and for much else, I am eternally grateful.

I have however, left my greatest debt till last. My mother died very suddenly while I was in the early planning stages of this book. Her memory was never far away while I worked on and wrote it. I know very well how much I owe to her. It is therefore only natural that I should dedicate *Social Theory* to her.

Note to Readers

In order keep the scholarly apparatus supporting my text to the minimum only works directly cited appear in the footnotes to each chapter. 'Further Reading' at the end of the book has a section for each chapter in which books and articles on which I have drawn or which readers may find useful are listed. The footnotes also include brief biographical sketches of the thinkers I discuss. I have tried, as far as possible, to cite their texts in good, readily available editions, and to avoid using sources in languages other than English. Unless otherwise indicated, italics in quotations are in the original. It has rightly become unacceptable to use pronouns in a way that equates humanity with men: most of the thinkers I discuss, however, followed the old usage, and sometimes, in expounding their views, it would have distorted these not to have done likewise.

Introduction

Social theory, as it has developed over the past two centuries, has concerned itself more than anything else with the three main dimensions of social power – economic relations, which have reached their furthest development in the market system known as capitalism; the ideologies through which forms of special power are justified and the place in the world of those subject to them defined; and the various patterns of political domination. The leading social theorists – Marx, Durkheim, and Weber above all – have been concerned to understand the interrelations of these three kinds of social power, especially in the constitution of the modern world. Such an understanding would seem indispensable to anyone seeking to make sense of, or to improve that world. *Social Theory* traces the development of, and the variations and the conflicts in this understanding.

Yet to write an introduction to social theory may seem like a rather old-fashioned enterprise. After all, social theory is often seen in contemporary intellectual debates as an outdated form of understanding. In the rather apocalyptic style that has become common during the past couple of decades, the end of numerous institutions, practices, and traditions – even of history itself – has been announced. Though, as far as I know, no one has yet announced the end of social theory, someone is bound to get round to it sooner or later.

This book is in no sense an introduction to, or a history of, sociology as an academic discipline. Nevertheless, since certain themes in social theory have provided sociology with one of its main sources of legitimacy, the relative marginalization of sociology over the last twenty years was bound to have some impact on the standing of social theory. Sociology has been on the retreat in part for political reasons. The New Right, ascendant in the Western liberal democracies during the 1980s, effectively regarded sociology as a stalking horse for socialism. In Britain under the Thatcher government the relevant funding body for academic research was renamed in order to free it of any association with the idea of social science.

This kind of ideologically induced institutional pressure has been reinforced by shifts in intellectual fashion. Sociology has been thrown into the shade by the new boom subject of cultural studies. A visit to any academic bookshop usually reveals an etiolated sociology section dwarfed, or even swallowed up completely, by cultural studies. Of course, a great deal of repackaging of old material is involved in this reordering of disciplinary frontiers – quite a lot of what used to be called sociology is now pursued within the framework of cultural studies. Nevertheless, changes in academic taste have material consequences, since they can affect the flow of students, research funding, and book contracts.

In any case, there are deeper forces at work here. For better or worse, we live in an era where postmodernism has come to set the terms of intellectual and cultural debate. The most influential account of postmodernity was provided by Jean-François Lyotard. He defines '*postmodern* as incredulity towards metanarratives', contrasting it with the modern, that is, with 'any science that legitimates itself with reference to a metadiscourse . . . making an explicit appeal to some grand narrative, such as the dialectics of Spirit, the hermeneutics of meaning, the emancipation of the rational or working subject, or the creation of wealth'.[1] A grand narrative for Lyotard is an attempt to make sense of the totality of human history. He makes it clear that he regards this kind of philosophy of history as essentially a child of the eighteenth-century Enlightenment, and that its most important practitioners were Hegel, for whom history was the progress of the consciousness of freedom, and Marx, who saw in it the development of the productive forces and the class struggle. Postmodernity represents the collapse of these grand narratives, the abandonment of any attempt to cast the entire historical process into a single interpretive scheme.

Acceptance of some version of Lyotard's view is bound to have a negative impact on the status and influence of social theory. Social theory, as I argue in more detail in chapter 1 below, (1) seeks to understand society as a whole (as opposed to particular political forms); (2) distinguishes between and makes generalizations about different kinds of society; and (3) is concerned in particular to analyse modernity, the forms of social life which have come to prevail first in the West and increasingly in the rest of the world over the past couple of centuries. Simply to set out this definition is to indicate that any social theorist is likely to construct or to presuppose a grand narrative. Marx indeed is generally regarded as a major social theorist. Those usually also included in this company – for example, Tocqueville, Durkheim, and Weber – are, whatever their differences both with Marx and among each other in respect of political perspective, intellectual style, and substantive analysis, thinkers of comparable ambition and scope.

---

[1]   J.-F. Lyotard (1979), *The Postmodern Condition* (Manchester, 1984), pp. xxiii–iv.

More generally, social theory is best seen as one of the chief heirs of the Enlightenment: it has taken over, and acted out, both the aspirations and the contradictions of the Enlightenment. The influence of postmodernism has made fashionable the dismissal of the Enlightenment as an era of illusions when numerous forms of oppression were forged. This is a profoundly disabling view. It is undoubtedly true that the promise of universal knowledge and freedom offered by the eighteenth-century *philosophes* was falsified by the limitations and dilemmas inherent in their project. Nevertheless, as I try to show in this book, the very collapse of the Enlightenment project set an intellectual agenda which continues to provide the framework within which we struggle to make sense of the social world. The leading social theorists discussed here all grappled with the difficulties created by this collapse, neither completely abandoning the aspirations of the Enlightenment nor uncritically ignoring its weaknesses.

It does not follow that the history of modern social theory is simply that of competing grand narratives. For one thing, at least one leading character in our story – Weber – was extremely sceptical about the ability of scientific thought to come up with a totalizing account of human history (though, at least arguably, his writings nevertheless imply such an account). For another, some general theories of society are less compelling than others: for example, Comte, Spencer, and Parsons, all highly influential in their day, do not provide the insights offered by social theorists of the first rank.

A more important qualification is that the attempts to continue the Enlightenment project outlined in this book were constantly accompanied by, and often in dialogue with, root-and-branch rejections of that entire project. For this reason, there is little sense in considering the thought of what are generally regarded as the 'classic' social theorists – say, Tocqueville, Marx, Durkheim, and Weber – without some attempt to situate them with respect to the critics of modernity – for example, Maistre, Nietzsche, and Heidegger. One consequence of widening the context in this way is that it becomes clear that the postmodernist 'incredulity about metanarratives' is simply the latest episode in a much longer debate.

The foregoing should underline that my treatment of social theory is wider than traditional accounts of the 'Founders of Sociological Thought'. Few interesting thinkers fit easily within conventional disciplinary boundaries. Of the four 'classic' thinkers listed in the preceding paragraph, only Durkheim ever occupied a chair in sociology. Marx and Tocqueville never held any academic posts. As for Weber, Keith Tribe writes:

> Professionally Weber was an economist; his early training and qualification was in law, in which he had written a number of historical essays; he was a founding member of the German Sociological Society; he was active in a number of political issues and associations, so that his death was said to have robbed Germany of

one of its leading political figures . . . Although Weber today is commonly regarded as a 'founding father of sociological thought', this was neither his intention nor the understanding of his contemporaries.[2]

One virtue of widening the intellectual horizons within which social theory
is considered is that it may make it more difficult to sustain certain prejudices.
Thus three intellectual historians seeking to draw attention to some neglected
nineteenth-century British political thinkers echo the Thatcher government's
disdain for social science, which they associate with 'such sociological nabobs
as Comte, Durkheim, and Weber'. Indeed: 'the very category of "social science" has been construed in ways which make it unreceptive and even hostile
to the more traditional notions of the centrality and relative autonomy of politics entertained by our figures'.[3] This is a strange way of viewing Weber, for
example, an intensely political thinker who was concerned, among other things,
to vindicate 'the centrality and relative autonomy of politics'.

My treatment of social theory lays special emphasis on philosophy and
political economy. The problem of modernity which preoccupied
so many thinkers discussed here poses what is essentially a philosophical question: can human reason make sense of the social world and shape it for the
better? Answered generally in the affirmative by the Enlightenment, this question is explored far more profoundly by Hegel. As Jürgen Habermas has
argued, recognition that Hegel's solution could not be sustained set the terms
on which debate about modernity has continued to the present day. Hence
the treatment of the Hegelian synthesis in chapter 2 and hence also my inclusion of Nietzsche and Heidegger, whose forceful negative responses to the
same question are of great significance to, and have had some intermittent
influence on, social theory.

It was Marx who highlighted the significance of political economy to social
theory when he decided to focus on 'the material conditions of life, the totality
of which Hegel . . . embraces within the term "civil society" ', and went on to
argue that 'the anatomy of this civil society, however, has to be sought in political economy'.[4] The form of civil society which classical economists such as
Smith and Ricardo analysed was what we have come to call, since Marx, capitalism. His master-work, Capital, seeks to capture the dynamics of this mode of
production, which he argued was based on the exploitation of wage-labour.
Marx subtitled Capital 'A Critique of Political Economy'. The relationship
between their own work and what by then was the academic discipline of economics was also an important issue for both Durkheim and Weber, as was the
role played by capitalism in the constitution of modernity. It seems to me, however, that the significance of political economy cannot be reduced to these clas-

[2]   K. Tribe, translator's introduction to W. Hennis, Max Weber (London, 1988), p. 2.
[3]   S. Collini et al., That Noble Science of Politics (Cambridge, 1983), p. 10.
[4]   K. Marx, A Contribution to the Critique of Political Economy (London, 1971), p. 20.

sical debates. In particular, in chapter 10 below, I consider Keynes's attempt to show that the injustices and instabilities identified by Marx could be at least regulated and moderated within the framework of capitalism, as well as the criticisms of free-market economists, notably Hayek.

It should be clear enough by now that social theory is an irredeemably political form of thought. Weber was far from being the only major figure to have been actively involved in the politics of his day. As a revolutionary socialist, Marx sought to realize in his own life the unity of theory and practice which he defended philosophically. Tocqueville was an ambitious but frustrated participant in French parliamentary politics during the 1840s. Many other examples could be given. More fundamentally, however much Weber may have sought to resist this conclusion, social theories at least implicitly evaluate as well as analyse, and offer political solutions to what they describe.

This does not mean that, when we speak of the social world, there is no objective way of establishing the truth of a sentence, the validity of an argument, or the superiority of an explanation to its rivals. On the contrary, I think it is important to resist the idea (encouraged by postmodernism) that social theories are mutually incommensurable and equally valid perspectives. Nevertheless, as I suggest below, the thinkers discussed in this book are best assessed from the standpoint of the problems which implicitly constitute their theories. But the problems thus identified often concern political and ethical issues. Social theories consequently tend to weave together analytical and normative dimensions.

It follows that some consideration of the relationship between social theories and political ideologies is unavoidable. Such consideration is familiar enough in Marx's case. But, somewhat more than other treatments of social theory, I trace the connections between various thinkers and liberalism. Smith's *Wealth of Nations* did not, of course, simply provide Marx with one of his main analytical starting-points: it also gave nineteenth-century liberalism its economic programme. But Tocqueville and Weber in particular represent attempts to sustain a much more self-aware, embattled, and difficult liberalism than at least some of its earlier variants. Further, Keynes and Hayek embody one of the chief antinomies of twentieth-century liberalism – to regulate the market or set it free? I would have liked to have continued the story up to the present. The publication of John Rawls's *A Theory of Justice* in 1971 marked the beginnings of a remarkable renaissance in liberal political philosophy in the English-speaking world. But faced with a vast and complex literature, and the limits set by time, space, and my own competence, I decided not after all to broach a subject which is in any case covered by a number of good introductions.

The same limits explain many of the other exclusions in any case inevitable in any introductory work such as this one. I have, for example, not been able here to consider sufficiently the relationship between social theory and anthropology, despite the importance of Durkheim's later writings for the development of the latter discipline and the manner in which this process has dramatized the problem of the relationship between social theory, a product of the modern West, and the non-European 'other' of Western thought in Asia, Africa, and the Americas. Other exclusions are sometimes rather more arbitrarily based. Despite their importance for twentieth-century political sociology, I have never been able to escape the feeling that there is less to the so-called 'elite theorists' (Pareto, Mosca, and Michels) than meets the eye, and I accordingly largely ignore them in what follows. Such direct expressions of the author's subjectivity are unavoidable when selecting from so wide a range of thinkers as have contributed to modern social theory.

I have, on the other hand, paid more attention to the idea of social evolution and its relationship to biological concepts than has been usual in works of this nature for the past fifty years or so. Evolutionary biology, of course, provided many nineteenth-century social theorists – above all, Spencer – with their scientific model. Evolutionary social theory fell into discredit in part because of the influence of thinkers such as Weber, who stressed the intentional character of human action and therefore the fundamental difference between the social and the natural sciences, but also because of the role played by biological racism in the Nazi Holocaust. There has in recent years been a certain revival of interest in the concept of social evolution, influenced perhaps by the salience which modern biology (particularly as popularized by writers such as Steven Jay Gould and Richard Dawkins) has come once again to achieve in intellectual culture, at least in the English-speaking world. Moreover, biological reductionism did not die with Hitler, as contemporary debates about the relationship between social inequality and genetic differences show. Finally, considering the significance of evolutionary biology for social theory provides an opportunity to touch on the problem referred to in the preceding paragraph, that of how Western thought relates to its non-European 'other'.

This book's scope having thus been defined, what about its method? I attempt here a historical and critical treatment of social theory. 'Historical' does not simply imply that thinkers are treated in (roughly) chronological succession. Further, some attempt is made to reconstruct the context in which their theories were formulated. The problem of setting texts in their context has become a prime theme in the history of political thought as a result of the work of Quentin Skinner and those influenced by him. Skinner focuses on 'the more general social and intellectual matrix' from which texts emerge, and in particular on 'the intellectual context in which the major texts were conceived – the context of earlier writings and inherited assumptions about political society, and of more ephemeral contemporary contributions to social and political thought'.[5]

---

[5]   Q. Skinner, *The Foundations of Modern Political Thought* (2 vols, Cambridge, 1978), I, pp. x, xi.

Skinner's approach is undoubtedly a valuable corrective to attempts to identify certain timeless issues in social and political thought to which everyone from Plato to Habermas has contributed. But detailed textual reconstruction of the kind practised by the Skinner school is, however scholarly, quite out of the question in an introductory work of this nature. I have, rather, tended to follow Lord Acton's advice to historians: 'study problems in preference to periods'.[6] In other words, I seek to identify certain specific problems – often in the form of a set of questions tacitly or explicitly addressed – which underlie a particular thinker's work and tend to structure his writings. (Alas, almost all the theorists dealt with in this book are indeed male.) In doing so I have been influenced, albeit in a fairly loose and eclectic way, by some otherwise very different philosophers – Gaston Bachelard, R. G. Collingwood, Karl Popper, Louis Althusser, and Imre Lakatos – who all stressed the importance of identifying a theory by means of its 'problematic' or 'problem-situation'.

This focus on problems has certain merits. In the first place, it lets history in. The problems which give shape to one thinker's work are usually not the same as those which play the same role in another's. The reasons why certain questions are formulated rather than others are likely to have much to do with the specific intellectual and social context in which the thinker concerned operated. Highlighting the problems specific to an individual theory may also help to identify connections between different thinkers: one theorist may be best understood as responding to or reformulating questions left unanswered or unresolved by an earlier theorist.

It is worth noting here an important difference between this approach to intellectual history and Skinner's. The latter places great emphasis on reconstructing the intentions of a particular writer against the background of shared conventions and styles of reasoning: hence the reliance Skinner places on socalled 'speech-act theory' in the philosophy of language, which treats the meaning of an utterance as an expression of the speaker's intentions. By contrast, in saying that the identity of a theory is given by the questions it *tacitly* or explicitly addresses, I leave open the possibility that a theorist may not be in full command of his own writing. To adapt a famous saying of Marx's, human beings make theories not in circumstances of their own choosing – and this is reflected in the very construction of these theories. By going beyond the author's intentions, we run the risk of imposing purely arbitrary interpretations on texts. But this is a risk inherent in the very act of interpreting, since in doing so we always go beyond the available evidence. In making an author's intentions the bench-mark of his interpretations, Skinner is seeking to avoid anachronistic readings of particular texts which reduce them to 'anticipations' of later works. Anachronism is indeed to be avoided, but not at the price of denying the existence of affiliations and affinities between different theorists.

---

6   Lord Acton, *Lectures on Modern History* (London, 1960), p. 37.

Identifying the constellation of problems from which a theory starts also gives proper scope to criticism. I have already made clear my belief that every social theory implies a distinctive politics. The same is surely true of a historical overview of social theory. But such an account which continually counterposes to the theorists considered the truth of the matters under discussion as the author sees it is unlikely to be terribly interesting, unless perhaps these criticisms culminate in a reconstruction of social theory, as does Parsons's classic *The Structure of Social Action*. (Postmodernists, despite their hostility to the concept of objective truth, are just as liable to contrast the writers surveyed with what they believe to be the correct view of the subject.) On the other hand, a purportedly neutral, 'positive' account of successive thinkers will almost certainly be crashingly dull, as well as misleading, since the author's substantive views are likely to figure, albeit tacitly, for example, in the selection of the theorists discussed.

As far as possible, in what follows my criticisms concentrate on the theorist's relative success or failure in addressing the questions he posed to himself, or on the internal coherence of his answers. More 'external' criticism is often unavoidable – for one thing, time passes, and sometimes settles various questions (although *which* questions have been settled, and precisely *how*, are often themselves matters of great controversy). All the same, I try as much as possible to judge thinkers in their own terms, rather than mine. My own views obtrude, no doubt, more than I am aware, and emerge more explictly in chapter 12, but I have proceeded on the assumption that all the theorists discussed are worth taking seriously.

This assumption is, as I indicated above, currently disputed. Thus David Parker, for example, attacks the sociological canon with its 'familiar holy trinity of the founding fathers, Marx, Weber and Durkheim'. He protests:

> Paradoxically, a discipline which debunks everything else by socializing whatever it studies deifies and reifies a tiny number of individuals at the expense of an understanding of their historical and institutional conditions of emergence. The orthodox narrative is enshrined in teaching practices by a move from founders to classics, a mapping of persons to texts, short-circuiting historicization and inventing a canonical tradition of quasi-sacred writings most of which were written between 1840 and 1920.[7]

Nicos Mouzelis has responded to this complaint by arguing that, judged by the standards of '*cognitive rationality*', Marx, Weber, and Durkheim have produced both 'conceptual frameworks' and 'substantive theories' which are 'superior to other writings in terms of cognitive potency, analytical acuity, power of synthesis, imaginative reach and originality'.[8] This is a good answer, and one with

---

[7] D. Parker, 'Why Bother With Durkheim?', *Sociological Review*, 45 (1997), p. 124.

[8] N. Mouzelis, 'In Defence of the Sociological Canon', ibid., pp. 245, 246.

which I agree. Nevertheless, it does not sufficiently address the objection raised by critics of the sociological 'canon', which is that the 'classics' of social theory are not relevant, or only partially relevant, to the problems which concern a contemporary audience. Thus Parker argues that 'feminism, cultural and ethnic studies' constitute 'fresh sources of inspiration' which can be used 'to truly redefine the core of sociology' and thereby to resituate the 'classics' within 'a sharper critique of modernity'.[9]

In fact, Marx, Durkheim, and Weber were engaged in just the kind of debate about the nature of modernity into which their 'multicultural' critics now wish to draw them. Indeed, as I seek to demonstrate in this book, social theory has been constituted by precisely this debate, in which attempts to understand modernity are inseparable from the struggle among those who seek to defend, to reject, or to transform it. The interest of the 'holy trinity', and indeed of many of the other thinkers discussed here – for example, Hegel, Maistre, Tocqueville, Nietzsche, Simmel, Lukács, Heidegger, Adorno, Horkheimer, Foucault, Habermas, and Bourdieu – lies to a significant extent in the intellectual quality of their attempts to stake out, explore, and refine particular positions in the debate about modernity.

Keynes famously wrote: 'Practical men, who believe themselves to be quite exempt from any intellectual influences, are usually the slaves of some defunct economist.' [10] Analogously one might say that those who believe themselves to be staking out some novel contemporary (or even 'postcontemporary') position are all too often repeating familiar moves, concluding perhaps in frequently occupied dead-ends, in the debate about modernity. Attempts to counterpose the classics and the contemporary create a false dilemma. Social theory is indispensable to engaging with the present.

[9] Parker, 'Why Bother With Durkheim?', pp. 134, 141.
[10] J. M. Keynes, *The General Theory of Employment Interest and Money* (London, 1970), p. 383.

1

The Enlightenment

1.1 Prehistory

What is a social theory? I have suggested it has three identifying features:

1 It is concerned with society, which is conceived as being distinct from political institutions;
2 It distinguishes between and seeks to make generalizations about different kinds of society;
3 It is concerned in particular to analyse modernity – the form of society which emerged in the modern West over the past few centuries and has come to dominate the world as a whole.

Social theory thus understood is a historically novel phenomenon, and not merely because of condition (3). The great philosophers and historians of classical antiquity – Plato and Aristotle, Thucydides and Polybius – wrote compelling analyses of political life. They were, however, concerned with the inter-relationship between the constant features of human nature, as they saw them, and certain forms of government – monarchy, aristocracy, and democracy – each of which was liable to degenerate into, respectively, tyranny, oligarchy, and mob rule. The Greeks, in other words, did not conceptualize society as something distinct from the different kinds of political institution they discussed. This move had to await the eighteenth-century Enlightenment. Johan Heilbron suggests that 'Rousseau was probably one of the first to use *société* as a key concept and explicitly to reason in terms of "social" relations.'[1]

---

[1] J. Heilbron, *The Rise of Social Theory* (Cambridge, 1995), p. 88. Jean-Jacques Rousseau (1712–78): writer; born in Geneva, but active in France; according to Lord Acton, 'Rousseau produced more effect with his pen than Aristotle, or Cicero, or St Augustine, or St Thomas Aquinas, or any other man who ever lived'; probably a paranoid schizophrenic.

Of course, one may use a concept without explicitly formulating it. Thus the great medieval Muslim philosopher and historian Ibn Khaldûn argues that 'man is a child of the customs and the things he has become used to. He is not a product of his natural dispositions and temperament.' Further, 'differences of condition among people are the result of the different ways in which they make their living'.[2] On the basis of these claims Ibn Khaldûn develops a systematic contrast between two basic forms of human civilization – the sedentary, some-times luxurious, life of town-dwellers and the mobile, austere existence of desert nomads. In these respects, his *Muqaddimah* (Introduction to History) can be seen as a precursor of the kind of materialist historical sociology developed later by the Scottish Enlightenment (see §1.4 below) and by Marx.

Simply to view Ibn Khaldûn thus would, however, be misleading, for two reasons. First, his propositions about the varieties of human social organization are advanced within the framework of an essentially religious discourse, in-deed of a variant of Islamic theology that seeks to emphasize the limitations of human reason. Secondly, he conceives the relationship between the two main social forms he analyses as a cyclical one. The martial virtues of the nomads allow them to conquer the cities. The new rulers are, however, gradually cor-rupted by the social environment over which they now preside. In particular, luxurious living causes the former nomads to lose the 'group feeling' (*àsabîyah*) which gave them the cohesion and self-confidence required to conquer. The regime consequently declines until it succumbs to some new invasion from the desert. 'In this way, the life-span of a dynasty corresponds to the life (span) of an individual: it grows up and passes into an age of stagnation and thence into retrogression.'[3]

This cyclical view of history was not simply an empirical generalization from the experience of Islamic polities. Like all medieval Islamic and Christian in-tellectuals, Ibn Khaldûn was profoundly influenced by ancient Greek thought. The idea that human social and political life, like nature itself, moves in cycles was deeply entrenched in the thinking of classical antiquity. The historian Polybius, for example, argued that forms of government tended to follow a natural succession – vigorous invention, followed by maturity, degeneration, decline, death, and renewal. This way of thinking continues to shape Ibn Khaldûn's conception of history. Within its framework, it is impossible to for-mulate the idea of a radically novel form of society which breaks with prece-dent, and inaugurates a new pattern of development.

The same conception of history still informs much of the political thought of early modern Europe in the sixteenth and seventeenth centuries. *Historia magistra*

---

[2] Ibn Khaldûn, *The Muqaddimah* (3 vols, New York, 1958), I, pp. 258, 249. 'Abd-ar-Rahmân b. Muhammed b. Khaldûn al-Hadrami (1332–1406): leading statesman and intellectual of the Islamic West; wrote *The Muqadimmah* as part of a much larger *History of the Berbers* during the interludes in a stormy political career spent largely in the emirates of North Africa and Spain.

[3] Ibid., I, p. 345.

vitae – history the teacher of life – the Roman politician Cicero had written. This formula implied a direct continuity between present and past. It is possible to learn from history because the past has already revealed the full inventory of social and political forms. No fundamental innovation is possible. As the sixteenth-century political theorist Jean Bodin put it, 'while empires age, history remains eternally the same'.[4] The efforts of humanist intellectuals during the Renaissance accurately to recapture the literature of classical antiquity reflected their belief that these writings were of direct practical relevance to their own time.

This belief can be traced even in those thinkers who go beyond the ancient models. Machiavelli scandalized Europe with the frankness of his political advice to rulers in *The Prince* (1513). In a famous letter, he describes how, in conditions of impoverished rural exile, he composed the book:

> At nightfall I return home and seek my writing room, and, divesting myself at its threshold of my rustic garments, stained with mud and mire, I assume courtly attire, and thus suitably clothed, enter within the ancient courts of ancient men, by whom, being cordially welcomed, I am fed with the food that *alone* is mine, and for which I was born, and am not ashamed to hold discourse with them and inquire the motives of their actions; and these men in their humanity reply to me, and for the space of four hours I feel no weariness, remember no trouble, no longer fear poverty, no longer dread death, my whole being is absorbed in them.[5]

The same sense of being in direct communication with the ancients is evinced by Montaigne.[6] Commentators often stress Montaigne's modernity, his sense of himself as a particular individual subject: 'My aim is to reveal my own self', he writes. Starting from his own mutable and uncertain nature, Montaigne went on to explore the variety of human conduct, and in particular to stress the relativity of social practices to time and place. Nevertheless, his main reference-point, within the framework of Catholic orthodoxy, remains the accumulated wisdom of classical antiquity. Thus he writes of 'the Ancients': 'Our powers are no more able to compete with them in vice than in virtue, both of which derive from a vigour of mind which was incomparably greater in them than in us.' Montaigne constantly cites ancient precedents to guide contemporary practice, down to such details as to whether or not to wear heavy armour in battle.[7]

---

4   Quoted in R. Koselleck, *Futures Past* (Cambridge, Mass., 1985), p. 239.

5   Letter to Francesco Vettori, 10 Dec. 1513, quoted in P. Villari, *The Life and Times of Niccolò Machiavelli* (2 vols, London, n.d.), II, p. 159. Niccolò Machiavelli (1469–1527): Florentine politician and diplomat; head of the second chancery of the republic of Florence, 1498–1512; in 1513 imprisoned and tortured by the Medicis and then forced into exile, where he composed his chief works.

6   Michel Eyquem, Seigneur de Montaigne (1533–92): southern French gentleman who, after having fought on the Catholic side in the Wars of Religion, withdrew from public life to compose his *Essays*, successive editions of which were published in 1580, 1588, and 1595.

7   M. de Montaigne, *The Complete Essays* (Harmondsworth, 1991), I. 26, p. 167, I. 49, p. 334; II. 9, pp. 453–6.

Montaigne was writing towards the end of the sixteenth century when, as a result of colonial conquests and the formation of the modern world economy, empirical knowledge of societies often radically different from those in Europe was expanding vastly. He could register this information, using various non-European examples in his great essay 'On Habit', in order to establish that 'there is nothing that custom can and cannot do'.[8] In principle, this proposition implied that human nature was, to some extent at least, malleable, and liable to be shaped in divergent forms by different social institutions. But the nature of these institutions could not be properly examined as long as it was assumed that the writers of classical antiquity had already identified the limited range of social forms·

1.2   The concept of modernity

The significance of the Enlightenment lies in large part in the fact that it broke with this assumption. It did so by formulating the idea of a new age which no longer seeks to derive its legitimacy from principles derived from the past, but rather offers its own self-justification. In Jürgen Habermas's words: 'Modernity can and will no longer borrow the criteria by which it takes its orientation from the models supplied by another epoch: *it has to create its own normativity out of itself.*'[9]

This conception of modernity as a new epoch representing a radical rupture with the past gradually takes shape in the course of the eighteenth century. It implied a changed relationship to historical time. Whereas previously European intellectuals had oriented towards the classical past, now they turned towards the future. A critical stage in this reorientation came at the end of the seventeenth century in what came to be known as the *querelle des anciens et des modernes*. Various French and English writers argued that the 'new science' of physics developed by Galileo, Descartes, Boyle, and Newton was decisively superior to anything the ancients had written. In particular, Bernard de Fontenelle, secretary of the Académie des Sciences, argued that scientific knowledge had not simply progressed, but would continue to do so indefinitely into the future.

The idea that knowledge progressed was readily extended to the claim that the entire course of human history represented a more or less continuous forward movement. Turgot wrote of man in 1750:

> Possessor of the treasure-house of signs . . . he can assure himself of the possession of all his acquired ideas, communicate them to other men, and transmit them

---

[8]   Ibid., I. 23, pp. 122–39 (quotation from p. 129).
[9]   J. Habermas, *The Philosophical Discourse of Modernity* (Cambridge, 1987), p. 7.

to his successors as a heritage which is always being augmented. A continual combination of this progress with the passions, and with the events they have caused, constitutes the history of the human race, in which no man is more than one part of an immense whole which has, like him, its infancy and its advancement.[10]

Like Ibn Khaldûn, Turgot compares history to an individual life, but there is no longer any room for decline and retrogression: the future offers only further 'advancement'. From the start, then, the concept of modernity was indissociably allied to the idea of historical progress. It was precisely from the prospect of infinite future improvement that the new age sought its legitimacy. As Hans Blumenberg puts it, 'the idea of progress . . . is the continuous self-justification of the present, by means of the future that it gives itself, before the past, with which it compares itself'.[11]

What historical conditions provided the context within which the concept of a new age moving steadily forward into the future could be formulated? We tend to think of the modern world as the product of what Eric Hobsbawm calls 'the "dual revolution" – the French Revolution and the contemporaneous (British) Industrial Revolution'.[12] The ideas outlined above took shape well before 1789, when the French Revolution began (an event which they are indeed often held to have caused), let alone the much more gradual socio-economic transformation through which industrial capitalism began to establish itself in parts of north-western Europe.

Nevertheless, a number of developments in the eighteenth century helped to encourage European intellectuals to see the world anew. Greater political stability and domestic peace after the horrors of the sixteenth-century Wars of Religion and the Thirty Years War (1618–48) helped to induce a sense of 'improvement', as did the scientific revolution of the seventeenth century. The struggle for supremacy of the European powers increasingly took place on a global stage: the Seven Years War (1756–63), says Reinhart Koselleck, was 'the first world war of our planet', waged in India, the Caribbean, and North America, as well as in central Europe. The consolidation of a European-

---

[10]   *Turgot on Progress, Sociology and Economics*, ed. R. L. Meek (Cambridge, 1973), p. 63. Anne Robert Jacques Turgot, Baron de'Aulne (1727–81): French philosopher and economist; a leading member of the Physiocrat school, as Inspecteur des Finances in 1774–6 he attempted unsuccessfully to reform the regime of Louis XVI.

[11]   H. Blumenberg, *The Legitimacy of the Modern Age* (Cambridge, Mass., 1983), p. 32.

[12]   E. J. Hobsbawm, *The Age of Revolution* (London, 1973), p. 11. There is a silly fashion among economic historians for calling the British Industrial Revolution a myth. Michael Mann's sensible comments ought to dispose of the matter: 'By 1850, most labour and investment had switched to towns, commerce, and manufacturing. There had never been such a prolonged period of agrarian growth as over the previous three centuries; never such a commercial expansion as over two centuries; and never the emergence of an urban, manufacturing-centred economy. In world-historical terms, if this combination doesn't count as a social revolution, nothing can': *The Sources of Social Power*, II (Cambridge, 1993), pp. 93–4.

dominated world economy provided the framework within which certain advanced enclaves began to experience the process of capitalist industrialization. All these factors contributed to a feeling of what Koselleck calls 'the acceleration of history', of participating in a forward movement rapidly cutting European societies off from their past.[13]

Properly speaking, 'the Enlightenment' is the name given to the group of eighteenth-century intellectuals, mainly French and Scottish, who at once articulated and (often with strong reservations) championed this sense of a radical rupture into modernity. Conditions in the two countries in the vanguard of the Enlightenment were significantly different. The French *philosophes* were faced with the greatest of the Continental absolute monarchies. They occupied the increasingly large space provided by the court society for intellectual criticism – provided that it concentrated on the analysis of morals, which, in the tradition of *moralistes* inaugurated by Montaigne, consisted in the study of the interaction between human passions and social institutions. As the century went on, moral critique became an oblique way of highlighting the political defects of the *ancien régime*.

The Scottish Enlightenment, by contrast, developed in a country which since 1701 had been part of the first constitutional monarchy in history. Benefiting from one of the most advanced systems of schools and universities in Europe, its members had before their eyes a striking instance of what Trotsky would later call uneven and combined development. In south-western Scotland, around the city of Glasgow (at whose university Adam Smith occupied a chair), an industrial economy was developing, closely integrated into Britain's colonial plantations across the Atlantic.[14] But the Highland clans seemed to the *philosophes* of Edinburgh and Glasgow to belong to the same historical time as the Native American 'savages' rather than to that of European 'civil society': lowland Scotland joined enthusiastically in the repression of the rebellions of 1715 and 1745, when the Highlanders emerged as a threat to Great Britain's constitutional progress under the Hanoverians.

1.3   A moral science

Whatever these and other national variations, the Enlightenment thinkers had two decisive features in common. First, their model of rationality was provided by the principles they understood to have been at work in the seventeenth-century foundation of modern physics. Thus Voltaire's *Philosophical Letters* (1734) are, among other things, an attempt to present to a French readership the

---

[13]   Koselleck, *Futures Past*, pp. 120, 150.

[14]   Adam Smith (1712–90): Professor of Moral Philosophy at the University of Glasgow, 1752–63; the founder of modern economic thought.

new science and philosophy of Isaac Newton and John Locke that he had discovered in England.[15] Secondly, the *philosophes* sought to extend this scientific method to the systematic study of what they initially continued to think of as morals, understood broadly to embrace human passions and social institutions. Hence Hume's *Treatise of Human Nature* (1739–40) is subtitled 'An Attempt to introduce the experimental Method into Moral Subjects'. Studied today chiefly for its contribution to epistemology and metaphysics, it was intended by its author as a contribution to 'the science of man'.[16]

This science was explicitly modelled on Newtonian physics. Helvétius argued that 'we must make morals like an experimental physics'. More specifically, he wrote: 'The passions are in morals what movement is in physics; the latter creates, destroys, conserves, animates everything; and without it everything is dead. It is the former which gives life to the moral world.'[17] When the workings of the passions were analysed more closely, it was tempting to conceive these along lines analogous to Newton's law of universal gravitation. Comparing the tendency for the price level and the stock of money to come into equilibrium with one another with that of water to settle at one level, Hume writes: 'we need not have recourse to a physical attraction, in order to explain the necessity of this operation. There is a moral attraction, arising from the interests and passions of men, which is full as potent and infallible.'[18]

Here we see taking shape the conception of an objective social pattern which somehow emerges from the behaviour of individual actors. Its most famous formulation is by Smith, arguing (possibly against Rousseau) that the rich play a socially useful role:

> They consume little more than the poor, and in spite of their natural selfishness and rapacity, though they mean only their own conveniency, though the sole end they propose from the labour of all the thousands whom they employ be the gratification of their own vain and insatiable desires, they divide with the poor the produce of all their improvements. They are led by an invisible hand to make nearly the same distribution of the necessaries of life, which would have been made, had the earth been divided into equal portions among its inhabitants, and

---

[15]   François Marie Arouet, known as Voltaire (1694–1778): author of a vast body of writing – prose and poetry, history and fiction, drama and polemic, philosophy and satire; the central figure of the Enlightenment.

[16]   See the introduction to D. Hume, *A Treatise of Human Nature* (Harmondsworth, 1969), esp. pp. 42–3. David Hume (1711–76): his philosophical writings undervalued in his own day, and denied an academic position because of his religious scepticism, he nevertheless made a European reputation through his *Essays* (1741–2) and *History of England* (1754–62); secretary of the British embassy in Paris, 1762–5, where he made contact with the leading French *philosophes* (and had a stormy relationship with Rousseau).

[17]   C. A. Helvétius, *De l'esprit*, abr. edn (Paris, 1968), pp. 67–8, 40. Claude Adrien Helvétius (1715–71): tax farmer and philosopher.

[18]   D. Hume, *Essays Moral, Political, and Literary*, ed. E. F. Millar (Indianapolis, 1987), p. 313.

thus without intending it, without knowing it, advance the interest of the society, and afford means for the multiplication of the species. When Providence divided the earth among a few lordly masters, it neither forgot nor abandoned those who seemed to have been left out of the partition. These last too enjoy their share of all it produces.[19]

Smith here reflects one of the leading preoccupations of the Scottish Enlightenment. Did the development of modern 'commercial societies' such as eighteenth-century Britain and France, with their highly unequal distribution of property, represent progress over the more egalitarian but also poorer societies they supplanted? His reply in the affirmative involves developing what later came to be known as the principle that social structures are the unintended consequences of individual actions. The rich, through their self-seeking actions, 'without intending it, without knowing it, advance the interest of society'.

Kant would later express the same idea more generally when he argued that the mechanism through which historical progress takes place is men's '*unsocial sociability*':

Without these asocial qualities (far from admirable in themselves) which cause the resistance inevitably encountered by each individual as he furthers his self-seeking pretensions, man would live an Arcadian, pastoral existence of perfect concord, self-sufficiency and mutual love. But all human talents would remain hidden forever in a dormant state, and men, as good-natured as the sheep they tended, would scarcely render their existence more valuable than that of their animals. The end to which they were created, their rational nature, would be an unfilled void. Nature should thus be thanked for fostering social incompatibility, enviously competitive vanity, and insatiable desires for possession or even power. Without these desires, all man's excellent natural capacities would be roused to develop.[20]

More explicitly than Smith, Kant reveals the theological roots of the principle of unintended consequences. Christian thinkers such as St Augustine had developed a philosophy of history in which the selfish actions of individual humans unwittingly serve the purposes of God's secret plan for the world. Nevertheless, in two crucial respects Smith went decisively beyond this providential view of history. First, in *The Wealth of Nations* (1776), he turns the principle of unintended consequences into an analytical tool. Commercial society involves an increasingly complex division of labour which makes possible

[19]   A. Smith (1759), *The Theory of the Moral Sentiments* (Indianapolis, 1982), IV. 1. 10, pp. 184–5.
[20]   I. Kant, *Political Writings* (Cambridge, 1991), pp. 44–5. Immanuel Kant (1724–1804): philosopher; born in Königsberg (East Prussia), at whose university he spent most of his life teaching; his three great critiques – the *Critique of Pure Reason* (1781), *Critique of Practical Reason* (1788), and *Critique of Judgement* (1790) – represent the starting-point of Western philosophy since the French Revolution.

the rising output needed to support a growing population. The diverse activities of this economy are bound together by the purchase and sale of commodities on the market. Producers and consumers participate in the market purely out of a concern for their own individual advantage, yet the outcome is an equilibrium between supply and demand. The fluctuations of commodities' prices on the market tend to gravitate around their 'natural prices' at which landowners, wage-labourers, and capitalist entrepreneurs all receive an income reflecting their contribution to the productive process.

Smith's analysis of commercial society represented a theoretical breakthrough in a second respect. The economic patterns he identified represented a social objectivity which could not be equated either with political institutions and the actions of statesmen or with individual human beings and their self-conscious actions. Earlier economists – for example, Sir James Steuart – had argued that government intervention was necessary to bring supply and demand into balance at a level at which capitalists could expect to make a decent profit. Smith denied this: in *The Wealth of Nations*, he does not rule out all state interference in the market, but nevertheless insists that it is a self-regulating mechanism. This mechanism is, further, beyond the control and, to a large extent, the understanding of the individual actors whom it relates.

In thus conceiving a market economy as a self-regulating system tending – provided governments left it alone – towards a level where the main social classes are appropriately rewarded, Smith reflected one of the most widely shared assumptions of the Enlightenment. The *philosophes* commonly identified a natural course of events to which things would tend unless interfered with. In doing so, they were undoubtedly influenced by the principle of inertia in physics formulated by Galileo and Newton, according to which a body tends to move in a given direction unless acted on by another body. But they gave 'natural' a normative connotation, so that the natural course of events was also the right course. Thus François Quesnay, one of the French school of Physiocrat economists, offered the following definition of a natural physical law: '*the regular course of all physical events in the natural order which is self-evidently the most advantageous to the human race*'.[21] Appropriately enough it was Quesnay who coined the slogan of free-market economics: 'Laissez faire, laissez passer.'

Applied to society, this approach gave a privileged status to the concept of human nature. Identifying the natural course of social events depended on first establishing what were the dispositions and capabilities inherent in, and therefore common to, all human beings. Seeking to explain the division of labour, which he regards as the source of economic progress, Smith writes: 'It is the necessary, though very slow and gradual consequence of a certain propensity in human nature, which has in view no such extensive utility, the propensity to truck, barter, and exchange one thing for another.' However we may explain

---

[21]   R.L. Meek, ed., *The Economics of Physiocracy* (London, 1962), p. 53.

this propensity itself, he continues, '[i]t is common to all men, and to be found in no other race of animals.'[22]

There were, of course, precedents for thus trying to base concrete accounts of social institutions and behaviour on generalizations about human nature. Hobbes had opened his great work *Leviathan*, written during the English Revolution (1640–60) to justify absolute monarchy, with a first part entitled 'Of Man'.[23] He paints a bleak portrait of creatures driven endlessly to compete by fear, greed, and envy: 'life itself is but motion, and can never be without desire, nor without fear, no more than without sense'. Consequently, the state of nature, where government does not exist, is necessarily a state of war: 'during that time when men live without a common power to keep them all in awe, they are in that condition which is called war, as is of every man, against every man'. Hobbes then goes on to argue that the only way to avoid this war of all against all, in which 'the life of man' was famously 'solitary, poor, nasty, brutish, and short', was for men, through a convenant, 'to confer all their power and strength upon one man, or upon one assembly of men', the sovereign.[24]

Few *philosophes* accepted such grim premises as Hobbes, or drew such absolutist conclusions. Nevertheless, the model he offered was a powerful one. Like the Enlightenment thinkers Hobbes based his method on the new physics: he sought to develop his argument deductively starting from clear definitions, following the example of geometry ('the only science that it hath pleased God hitherto to bestow on mankind') and of his contemporaries Galileo and Descartes, who were using mathematical reasoning to open the book of nature.[25] Many Enlightenment thinkers followed Hobbes in believing that human nature can in principle be established by considering how people would behave in the absence of political and social institutions. Montesquieu, for example, argued that to know the laws of nature, which 'derive uniquely from the constitution of our being . . . one must consider a man before the establishment of societies. The laws he would receive in such a state would be the laws of nature.'[26]

This form of reasoning often went together with the view so ruthlessly stated by Hobbes that human beings in this state of nature would each consider their own individual interests: coercion or education would be required to persuade

---

[22]   A. Smith (1776), *An Inquiry into the Nature and Causes of the Wealth of Nations* (2 vols, Indianapolis, 1981), I. ii, p. 23.
[23]   Thomas Hobbes (1588–1679): a parson's son, lifelong dependent on the patronage of the great Cavendish family; despite the political turbulence of the age (Hobbes spent the 1640s in exile in France) and the notoriety of his doctrines (the Jesuits dubbed him 'the Demon of Malmesbury'), he survived into his nineties.
[24]   T. Hobbes (1651), *Leviathan* (Oxford, 1996), VI. 58, p. 41; XIII. 8 and 9, p. 84; XVIII. 13, p. 114.
[25]   Ibid., IV. 12, p. 23.
[26]   Charles de Secondat, Baron de La Brède et de Montesquieu (1748), *The Spirit of the Laws* (Cambridge, 1989), 1. 2, p. 6. Montesquieu (1689–1755): French nobleman; president of the Parlement of Bourdeaux.

them to consult the general interest. Would then the liberation of individual desires in commercial society be consistent with the maintenance of a stable and prosperous polity? Smith has no doubt that it would, in part because of the mechanism of 'the invisible hand'. Individuals pursuing their own interests would interact on the market in a manner devised by no one but nonetheless contriving to secure the welfare of the whole. Moreover, in *The Theory of the Moral Sentiments* Smith argues that our tendency towards self-love is controlled by our capacity sympathetically to identify with the emotional states of others: 'And hence it is, that to feel much for others and little for ourselves, that to restrain our selfish, and to indulge our benevolent affections, constitutes the perfection of human nature.'[27]

If sympathy and interest together form the bonds of social life, its goal is the general happiness. Bentham gave the most influential formulation of this idea in his principle of utility (or greatest happiness principle): 'An action then may be said to be conformable to the principle of utility . . . when the tendency it has is to augment the happiness of the community is greater than any it has to diminish it.'[28] But the founding doctrine of Bentham's utilitarianism expressed the general consensus among the *philosophes*. The priority given to happiness implied a commitment, not to atomistic individualism, but to the pursuit of social reform. It could also be used to justify revolutionary measures. 'Happiness is a new idea in Europe', declared the Jacobin leader Saint-Just when he presented to the Convention in March 1794 the *loi ventôse* redistributing the property of 'the enemies of the Revolution' to the poor.[29]

1.4   The development of social theory

Decisive though Smith's conception of a self-regulating economy was in articulating a concept of society distinct from political institutions, the formal development: of social theory began somewhat earlier, in the writings of Montesquieu. *The Spirit of the Laws* in one sense continues classical thinkers' concern with different political forms. Montesquieu identifies three basic kinds of government: republican, monarchic, and despotic. But his analysis does not focus primarily or exclusively on political institutions. He distinguishes between 'the nature of the government and its principles: its nature is that which makes it what it is, and its principles, that which makes it act. The one is its particular structure, and the other is the human passions that set it in motion.'[30]

[27]   Smith, *Theory*, I. i. 5. 5, p. 25.
[28]   J. Bentham (1789), *An Introduction to the Principles of Morals and Legislation* (London, 1982), pp. 12–13. Jeremy Bentham (1748–1832): Legal reformer and founder of Utilitarianism; his mummified body is on public display at University College London.
[29]   Quoted in A. Soboul, *La Révolution française* (Paris, 1988), p. 349.
[30]   Montesquieu, *Spirit*, 3. 1, p. 21.

Thus monarchies are animated by honour, republics by virtue, and despotisms by fear.

These passions, each associated with a specific form of government, in fact form part of a wider totality of interrelated conditions, institutions, practices, and beliefs which underlie and sustain that form. It is this totality which Montesquieu calls 'THE SPIRIT OF THE LAWS'. Thus he argues:

> They [laws] should be related to the *physical aspect* of the country; to the cli-
> mate, be it freezing, torrid, or temperate; to the properties of the terrain, its
> location and extent; to the way of life of the peoples, be they ploughmen, hunt-
> ers, or herdsmen; they should relate to the degree of liberty that the constitution
> can sustain, to the religion of the inhabitants, their inclinations, their wealth,
> their number, their commerce, their mores, their manners; finally, the laws are
> related to one another, to their origin, to the purpose of the legislator, and to the
> order of things on which they are established. They must be considered from all
> these points of view.[31]

Montesquieu thus widens political theory to encompass the study of *morale* – of what he calls 'mores [*moeurs*] and manners'- in relation to governmental forms. But, since 'the character of the spirit and passions of the heart are ex-tremely different in the various climates, *laws* should be relative to the differ-ences in these passions and to the differences in these characters'. He deploys this emphasis on climate most dramatically in his analysis of despotism, where '[m]an is a creature that obeys a creature that wants'. Asia's torrid climate means that 'despotism is, so to speak, naturalized there'.[32] Heat enervates men, mak-ing them submissive and fond of luxury. It also so incites desires that men and women cannot be left alone together, making harems and seraglios necessary. (As Louis Althusser observes, '[t]he spring of despotism could be said to be desire as much as fear.'[33]) These circumstances favour the concentration of power in the hands of a single, arbitrary ruler. Colder northern climes, by con-trast, favour the courage and vigour necessary to sustain republican and monar-chical forms of government.

Montesquieu had already sought to contrast Oriental and European *moeurs* in the *Persian Letters* (where it served chiefly as a device for throwing critical light on the France of his day). His approach had classical precedents: the an-cient Greeks used climatic theories to explain why their city-states were so different in structure and ideology from the Persian empire. The accumulation of contemporary European travellers' tales about the great monarchies of the Near East, India, and China provided Montesquieu with raw material for his portrait of despotism. Nevertheless, like many other European authors who have

---

[31]   Ibid., 1. 3, p. 9.
[32]   Ibid., 14. 1, p. 231; 3. 10, p. 29; 5. 14, p. 63.
[33]   L. Althusser, *Politics and History* (London, 1972), p. 81.

drawn such global contrasts between East and West, his concern was less to produce knowledge of Oriental societies than to deepen the self-understanding of the Occident.

This can be traced in the tensions detectable in Montesquieu's explanatory model. He asserts, on the one hand: 'The empire of climate is the first of all empires.' On the other hand, he offers more pluralistic versions of his theory: 'Many things govern men: climate, religion, laws, the maxims of the government, examples of past things, mores and manners; a general spirit is formed as a result.' A strict climatic determinism would imply that Europe was safe from despotism. Yet Montesquieu warns that 'if, by a long abuse of power or by a great conquest, despotism became established for a certain time, neither mores, nor climate would hold firm, and in this fine part of the world, human nature would suffer, at least for a while, the insults heaped on it in the other three'.[34]

Climate is thus not fate. Montesquieu's lurid portrait of despotism is at least in part a tacit critique of Bourbon absolutism, which had transformed the aristocracy into dependants of the monarchy, and denizens of a court society ruled by favourites and mistresses, as well as a warning of the future that awaited France unless 'moderate government' were reinstated. Montesquieu insists that '[i]ntermediate, subordinate and dependent powers constitute the nature of monarchical government', and the 'most natural' of these powers is the nobility, so that the 'fundamental maxim' of monarchy is *no monarch, no nobility: no nobility, no monarch*; rather, one has a despot'. 'Moderate government' is best secured through the separation of legislative, executive, and judicial powers which Montesquieu believed had happened in contemporary England. 'Among the Turks, where the three powers are united in the person of the sultan, an atrocious despotism reins.'[35] Althusser suggests that this famous doctrine, which influenced the framing of the Constitution of the United States, reflects less any political radicalism on Montesquieu's part than his defence of '*an outdated order*', his attempt to reinstate the proper powers of the feudal aristocracy under the French monarchy.[36]

Althusser also argues that Montesquieu was '*the first to propose a positive principle of a universal explanation for history*', arising from the tensions between a form of government's institutional structure and its underlying principle – the distinctive spirit of its laws.[37] Yet to the extent that Montesquieu accords climate a decisive role in shaping this spirit, he denies himself the possibility of identifying and explaining historical transformations. Since climatic differences are (relatively) constant, they can at best offer the basis of an account of the

[34]   Montesquieu, *Spirit*, 19. 14, p. 316; 19. 4, p. 310; 8. 8, p. 118.
[35]   Ibid., 2. 4, p. 18; 11. 6, p. 157.
[36]   Althusser, *Politics*, p. 106.
[37]   Ibid., p. 50.

permanent causes of social and political institutions. Though *The Spirit of the Laws* inspired eighteenth-century historians to relate political events to changes in mores and manners, its own theoretical framework is that of a static comparative sociology. John Millar, when setting forth the theory of history developed by the Scottish Enlightenment, bluntly declared in direct opposition to Montesquieu that 'national character depends very little upon the immediate operation of climate.'[38]

This theory was in fact more or less simultaneously formulated by Turgot and Smith around the year 1750, though its proper articulation was one of the main collective achievements of the Scottish Enlightenment. It has come to be known as 'the Four Stages Theory'. History is to be understood not as the actions and conflicts of rulers that are best captured through a political narrative, but as a progressive development through four distinct stages of society representing qualitatively different kinds of economic organization – hunting, pasturage, agriculture, and commerce. This classification implies that priority should be given in the study of society to economic relations. This view was expressed most succinctly by William Robertson in his *History of America* (1777): 'In every enquiry concerning the operations of men when united together in society, the first object of attention should be their mode of subsistence. Accordingly as that varies, their laws and policy must be different.'[39]

Millar similarly emphasizes the 'mode of subsistence'. He discerns 'in human history, a natural progress from ignorance to knowledge, and from rude to civilized manners, the several stages of which are usually accompanied with peculiar laws and customs'. Thus the improvement in the status of women which Millar claims is a feature of the 'refined and polished nations' of Europe is 'chiefly derived from the progress of mankind of the common arts of life'. The same progress is responsible for the gradual disappearance of slavery in Europe: 'little profit can be drawn from the labour of a slave, who has neither been encouraged to acquire that dexterity, nor those habits of application, which are essentially requisite in the finer and more difficult branches of manufacture'. Though, to Millar's regret, slavery continues to flourish in the American plantations and even to survive among the colliers and salters of Scotland, it cannot long survive the 'infallible tendency' which the 'introduction of personal liberty' has 'to render the inhabitants of a country more industrious; and, by producing greater plenty of provisions, must necessarily increase the populousness, as well as the strength and security of a nation'.[40]

[38]   J. Millar (1771), *The Origin of the Distinction of Ranks*, in W. C. Lehmann, *John Millar of Glasgow 1735–1801* (Cambridge, 1960), p. 180. John Millar (1735–1801): a pupil of Smith and Professor of Civil Law at the University of Glasgow 1761–1801; a follower of Charles James Fox, he advocated parliamentary reform and opposed the slave trade and the war with Revolutionary France.

[39]   Quoted in R. L. Meek, *Economics and Ideology and Other Essays* (London, 1967), p. 37.

[40]   Millar, *Origin*, pp. 176, 225, 228, 299, 317.

The historical pattern outlined by the Scottish *philosophes* is thus progressive not simply in the sense that it represents a movement from less to more complex and productive modes of subsistence, but in increasing political freedom. What is the motor of this process? Millar puts it down to the presence 'in man [of] a disposition for improving his condition, by the exertion of which he is carried from one degree of advancement to another; and the similarity of his wants, as well as of those faculties by which those wants are supplied, has everywhere produced a remarkable uniformity in the several stages of his progression.'[41] Stimulated by need, human capabilities develop: the breakthrough of agriculture in particular permits the proliferation of occupations, leading, over time, to the development of manufacture and commerce.

In his version of the theory, Turgot laid a greater emphasis on the role of human ambition and greed in blindly pushing history forward: 'The passions, tumultuous and dangerous as they are, become a mainspring of action and of progress.'[42] As we have seen, Smith used the same theory to account for the integration of individual interests in the final stage of the process, commercial society. By contrast, Condorcet's *Sketch for a Historical Picture of the Progress of the Human Mind* (1794) is perhaps more representative of the French Enlightenment in making, as the title of his essay suggests, intellectual advancement the source of more general social development: ideas are thus the motor of historical change.[43]

Rodney Meek, who has made a most important contribution to winning proper recognition of the significance of the Four Stages Theory, argues that 'in the latter half of the eighteenth century the Scottish Historical School developed this Classical sociology to a stage where it was becoming remarkably similar, at least in its broad outlines, to Marxist sociology'.[44] Such claims carry within them some danger of anachronism. The leading thinkers of the Scottish Enlightenment often took their questions and even their categories from ancient and early modern political thought. Nevertheless, in the answers they give to these questions, we see taking shape a theory which distinguishes sharply between society as such and the forms of government; which formulates a general account of the successive stages of social development; and which is particularly concerned to elucidate the nature of the 'commercial societies' of contemporary Europe, radically different as these were from past social forms. In other words, it is in the writings of the Scottish *philosophes* that we see modern social theory first emerge.

---

[41]   Ibid., p. 176.

[42]   Meek, ed., *Turgot on Progress*, p. 70.

[43]   Marie Jean Antoine de Caritat, Marquis de Condorcet (1743–94): sought to develop a 'social mathematics' anticipating modern game theory; a Girondin deputy during the French Revolution, he was arrested by the Jacobins and poisoned himself in prison.

[44]   Meek, *Economics and Ideology*, pp. 34–5.

1.5   Inner strains

It is customary to damn the Enlightenment for a naïve, rationalist optimism soon exploded by the experience of events. Examples of such optimism are not hard to find. Thus Condorcet opens his *Sketch* by promising 'to show by appeal to reason and fact that nature has set no term to the perfection of human faculties; that the perfectibility of man is truly indefinite; and that the progress of this perfectibility, from now onwards independent of any power that might wish to halt it, has no other limit than the duration of the globe'. He assures us: 'The moral goodness of man, the necessary consequence of his constitution, is capable of indefinite perfection, like all his other faculties . . . nature has linked together in a unbreakable chain truth, happiness and virtue.'[45] This faith in the future is all the more remarkable when one takes into account that Condorcet composed this essay while imprisoned by the Jacobins during the French Revolution.

Simply to identify the Enlightenment with such apparently blind optimism is, however, facile in the extreme. Voltaire's great novel *Candide* was prompted by the great Lisbon earthquake of 1 November 1755. This catastrophe, which destroyed two-thirds of the city and killed between 5,000 and 15,000 people, shocked European society. Voltaire used the earthquake, and man-made disasters such as the suffering caused in central Europe by the Seven Years War, systematically to lampoon all optimistic views, and in particular the philosopher Leibniz's metaphysical doctrine that 'all is for the best in this best of all possible worlds'.

Moreover, as we shall see, many *philosophes* expressed powerful reservations about the sustainability and even the desirability of the historical progress which Condorcet treated as an unalterable law. These doubts were simply one of a series of tensions internal to the system of ideas developed by Enlightenment thinkers. Briefly surveying these sources of difficulty will help to identify the agenda these thinkers defined for later social theorists.

(1) *Human nature and history.*   The concept of human nature frequently figures in the explanations framed by Enlightenment theorists. Think, for example, of Smith's 'propensity to truck, barter, and exchange', and of Millar's 'disposition [of man] to improve his condition'. But on what grounds could one claim to have identified characteristics genuinely common to all human beings? Reasoning about how humans would behave in the state of nature was often used to provide such grounds. But how plausible was the idea that men and women could somehow exist, as Montesquieu put it, 'before the establishment of

---

[45]   Marquis de Condorcet (1796), *A Sketch for a Historical Picture of the Progress of the Human Mind* (London, 1955), pp. 4, 193.

societies'? The more engaged *philosophes* became with the historical particularities of social life, the more doubtful the concept of the state of nature became.

Thus Adam Ferguson, one of the most influential figures of the Scottish Enlightenment, directly attacked the concept as it was used by Rousseau and Helvétius:

> If we would know him [man], we must attend to himself, to the course of his life, and to the tenor of his conduct. With him the society appears to be as old as the individual, and the use of the tongue as universal as that of the hand or the foot. If there was a time in which he had his acquaintance with his own species to make, and his faculties to acquire, it is a time of which we have no record, and in relation to which our opinions can serve no purpose, and are supported by no evidence.[46]

Rousseau himself, though he is widely presented as the author of a sentimentalized portrait of a virtuous 'natural man', expressed much the same difficulty at the start of the *Second Discourse*: 'how can man come to know himself as nature made him once he has undergone all the changes which the succession of time and things must have produced in his original constitution, and so distinguish that which belongs to his own essence from that which circumstances have added to, or altered in, his primitive state?' The answer he gives to this question, relying on 'hypothetical and conditional reasonings' rather than on anything purporting to be historical enquiry, depicts the original man as a mute, asocial, unreflecting animal, living in solitude and reproducing as a result of chance encounters with members of the opposite sex.[47] This zero degree of human existence serves Rousseau as a bench-mark by means of which to evaluate the historical development of the species, but, in highlighting the changes men have subsequently undergone, he opens the door to the suggestion that human nature is in fact historically variable, bearing the imprint of the social relations prevailing at any given time.

(2) *Sovereignty and liberty.*   These analytical difficulties did not prevent many *philosophes* counterposing an idealized image of society, which they conceived of as corresponding to human nature, to existing social and political institutions. Thus the Abbé Raynal wrote in 1770: 'Society is a product of the needs of people, and government a product of their shortcomings . . . society is in essence good; government can be evil, as we well know, and all too often is so.'[48]

---

[46]   A. Ferguson (1767), *An Essay on the History of Civil Society* (Farnborough, 1969), p. 9. Adam Ferguson (1723–1816): principal chaplain of the Black Watch regiment, 1746–54; Professor of Pneumatics and Moral Philosophy, Edinburgh University, 1764–85; the *Essay* was translated into French and German and widely read throughout Europe.
[47]   J.-J. Rousseau (1755), *Discourse on the Origins and Foundations of Inequality among Men* (Harmondsworth, 1984), pp. 67, 78.
[48]   Quoted in Heilbron, *Rise*, p. 92.

In the later decades of the eighteenth century, as the difficulties of the Bourbon regime grew more acute, the criticism of the French Enlightenment became more explicitly hostile to the Catholic Church, and more oriented towards political reform. While the Scottish *philosophes* did not have to confront what turned out to be a pre-revolutionary crisis, demands for parliamentary reform to make the Hanoverian state more representative became a running theme in British politics. In the early nineteenth century, among the strongest advocates of reform were Bentham and his followers, the Philosophical Radicals, many of whom were strongly influenced by the Scottish Enlightenment.

What direction should political reform take? One of the great achievements of early modern political thought, in the writings of Hobbes, Bodin, and others, had been to formulate the modern concept of sovereignty, according to which the state is conceived as a distinct entity from which all legitimate political power derives. At least initially, this line of thought provided a justification for the centralization of power in the great Continental absolutist states. It coexisted, however, with another powerful strand in early modern thought, what historians have come to call the classical republican tradition. Drawing inspiration from the political theory of the ancient Roman republic which had been rediscovered by Renaissance humanists, this tradition asserted that political liberty consisted in participating as a citizen in a self-governing republican community. A flourishing polity thus depended on the virtue of the citizens. As Bolingbroke put it, '[a] wise and brave people will neither be cozened nor bullied out of their liberties.'[49] The most important exponent of classical republicanism was Machiavelli, whose originality lay in arguing that civic virtue (*virtù*) did not necessarily consist in observing the ordinary canons of individual conduct, but in being willing to do whatever was required to maintain the state, however brutal or dishonest this might be.

Montesquieu spoke for many *philosophes* in expressing doubts about the viability of republican government in the relatively large and complex states of early modern Europe. Yet the republican tradition found a powerful exponent in Rousseau. In *The Social Contract* (1762), he takes over the concept of sovereignty elaborated by Hobbes and Bodin, but relocates it in the people. Legitimate government is created when individuals come together and agree to form themselves into 'an artificial and collective body', the sovereign. The people thus constituted alone has the right to make laws, which may not be delegated to elected representatives: 'the sovereign, which is simply a collective being, cannot be represented by anyone but itself – power may be delegated, but the will itself may not'. This arrangement realizes the republican ideal of liberty as self-government: 'man acquires with civil society, moral freedom, which alone

---

[49]   Lord Bolingbroke, *Political Writings* (Cambridge, 1997), p. 111. Henry St John, Viscount Bolingbroke (1678–1751): British politician, whose practical failures were compensated for by the influence of his writings on eighteenth-century political thought.

makes man the master of himself; for to be governed by appetite alone is slavery, while obedience to a law one prescribes to oneself is freedom'.[50]

Rousseau's vesting of sovereignty in the people constituted one of the main starting-points of modern democratic thought. But the exercise of sovereignty involves the assertion of the sovereign's will. How do the people express their will, according to Rousseau? He distinguishes between the private wills of individual citizens, which reflect their particular interests, and the general will, which articulates the common interest of society. Laws are the declaration of the general will. But this general will is not necessarily expressed through the majority vote of the citizens gathered together in assembly. Rousseau famously declares: 'There is often a great difference between the will of all and the general will; the general will studies only the common interest while the will of all studies only the private interest, and indeed is no more than the sum of individual desires.' This drives him to propose a variety of devices – for example, a lawgiver to devise the initial constitution, the suppression of factions articulating sectional interests, and state-instituted civil religion – which will inculcate in the citizens republican virtue and encourage them to consult the common interest rather than their private desires. He also advocates minimizing social inequality: 'Do you want coherence in the state? Then bring the two extremes as close together as possible; have neither rich men nor beggars, for these two estates, naturally inseparable, are equally fatal to the common good; from one class come friends of tyranny, from the other tyrants.'[51]

Such a solution would hardly commend itself to those *philosophes* such as Smith and Hume, who believed that modern commercial societies, despite the growth in social inequality they involved, were producing a generally beneficial increase in living standards. Rousseau's struggle to subordinate the assertion of individual interests to the requirements of republican citizenship in any case involved more than conceptual tensions internal to his political theory. The radical Jacobin regime which held power at the climax of the French Revolution in 1792–4 explicitly appealed to Rousseau's ideals of republican virtue to justify the Terror to which it subjected its opponents. Benjamin Constant wrote of the Jacobins: 'They believed that everything should give way before collective will, and that all restrictions on individual rights would be amply compensated for by participation in social power.'[52]

Liberalism as it began to take shape in the aftermath of the Revolution could draw on older sources. As John Rawls has emphasized, this tradition's origins can be traced to the sixteenth-century Wars of Religion, and the developing

---

[50]   J.-J. Rousseau, *The Social Contract* (Harmondsworth, 1968), I. 6, p. 61; II. 1, p. 69; I. 8, p. 65.

[51]   Ibid., II. 3, p. 72; II. 11, p. 96 n.

[52]   B. Constant, *Political Writings* (Cambridge, 1988), p. 320. Benjamin Constant (1767–1830): of Protestant Swiss origins, but active chiefly in France; a critic of Napoleon's regime, he became a leader of the liberal opposition under the Bourbon Restoration.

understanding that religious toleration represented the only acceptable solution to the historically novel coexistence of rival versions of the same 'salvationist' religion each demanding unconditional commitment.[53] But it was the experience of the Jacobin Terror which encouraged post-Revolutionary liberals directly to attack the republican idea that political freedom is the property of a collective agent.

Thus Constant systematically contrasts two kinds of liberty, those of the ancients and the moderns. The active public life of the citizens of the Greek and Roman city-states presupposed a narrow and confined private life, reflecting the very limited role of commerce in antiquity. In modern times, however, commerce is 'the normal state of things, the only aim, the universal tendency, the true life of nations', filling individuals' private lives with hopes, projects, and activities. Consequently, 'we can no longer enjoy the liberty of the ancients, which consisted in an active and constant participation in collective power. Our freedom must consist of peaceful enjoyment and private independence', that is, of individual liberty guaranteed by political rights. Rousseau's attempt to rehabilitate ancient liberty merely 'furnished deadly pretexts for more than one kind of tyranny'.[54]

Yet, while thus championing individual freedom against the republican tradition, Constant acknowledged: 'The danger of modern liberty is that, absorbed in the enjoyment of our private independence, we should surrender our right to share in political power too easily.'[55] Rousseau's liberal critics therefore continued to grapple with the problem that had confronted him of how to reconcile what they would increasingly acknowledge as democratic citizenship with the assertion of private interests encouraged by commercial society.

(3) *Rationality and subjectivity.*   Rousseau's political theory posed a further problem. His distinction between slavery to appetite and the freedom that comes from self-mastery, from 'obedience to a law one prescribes to oneself', suggested that the self was a complex entity. Part of me is ruled by the private will, and driven by selfish desires; but in another aspect I partake of the general will, at once sharing in law-making and ruling myself. Rousseau's critics were quick to detect here a doctrine of a 'higher self' in whose name (and that of the collective liberty in which it participated) the actual self could legitimately be repressed. But the problem raised here of how to conceptualize the self raised much larger difficulties for the Enlightenment.

The human individual was not simply, for the *philosophes*, the object of social analysis and the subject of political life; it provided the underpinning of their claim to knowledge. At the beginning of the seventeenth-century scientific

[53]   J. Rawls, *Political Liberalism* (expanded edn, New York, 1996), pp. xxvii ff.
[54]   Constant, *Political Writings*, pp. 314, 316, 318.
[55]   Ibid., p. 326.

revolution René Descartes imagined the subject isolated from all its physical and social circumstances. In what Charles Taylor calls this ' "punctual" or "neutral" conception of the self', 'the self is defined in abstraction from any constitutive concerns and hence from any identity . . . Its only constitutive property is self-awareness.'[56] The self thus conceived, Descartes argued, would be certain at least of the contents of its own consciousness. From this secure resting-point, the entire edifice of scientific knowledge could gradually be constructed. John Locke offered a more empirical version of the same idea, arguing that sense-experience as well as rational reflection was the source of knowledge. But empiricists and rationalists alike tended to treat the individual subject, with the self-certainty which derived from its secure access to its own conscious states, as the foundation of all knowledge.

This secure resting-point did not survive Hume's subversion in the *Treatise of Human Nature*. Beneath all the apparently secure structures of both the social and the physical worlds he discovered the effects of the human mind. It was our mental activity, and in particular our tendency to project regular patterns onto the world even where their existence could not be rationally demonstrated, that was responsible for most of what we took to be natural laws. Even the self, supposedly the pivot of knowledge, turned out to be 'nothing but a bundle or collection of different perceptions, which succeed each other with an inconceivable rapidity and are in a perpetual flux or movement'.[57]

Kant's response in the *Critique of Pure Reason* was not to deny that the world we experience is the product of our mental activity. But he identified as the source of this activity, not the empirical self which under Hume's examination had disintegrated into a mass of sense-impressions, but a transcendental subject underlying these impressions. The very possibility of conscious experience, Kant argued, required that we presuppose a 'transcendental unity of apperception' to which our sense-impressions could be attributed but which was not itself present in experience. Presupposing this unity further implied that certain categories inherent in the human understanding were applied to organize and give structure to our sense-experience. The world of ordinary life and Newtonian physics, with its bodies and causal relations, was the result of the application of these categories to sense-experience. Kant further extended the role of the transcendental subject in his moral and political writings, which were heavily influenced by Rousseau. This 'noumenal self', beyond but presupposed by sense-experience, was the source of the universal moral laws which regulated individual conduct and provided the foundations of political life.

Kant's critical philosophy represented the pinnacle of the Enlightenment's intellectual achievement. But his vindication of the rationality and objectivity

[56]   C. Taylor, *Sources of the Self* (Cambridge, 1989), p. 49.
[57]   Hume, *Treatise*, I. iv. v, p. 300.

of human knowledge against Hume's challenge involved a high price. In making the structure of the world of everyday experience dependent on the activities of the transcendental subject, Kant opened the door to the idealist doctrine that the world is the creation of mind, or consists in ideas. He resisted this implication, distinguishing between the world of appearances, formed by the application of the categories to sense-impressions, and that of things in themselves, beyond the limits of experience, and therefore of human knowledge. But by making ultimate realities unknowable Kant seemed to many to have unacceptably restricted the scope of human reason.

(4) *Universality and the other.* Kant's philosophy also highlights the Enlightenment's preoccupation with the universal. Thus, his doctrine of the categorical imperative requires as a necessary condition of any moral principle that it is strictly universal in its application. The *philosophes* concerned themselves with the conditions and prospects of humankind as a whole. But was this concern genuinely universal?

One of the great documents of the Enlightenment is the American Declaration of Independence of 4 July 1776. Drafted by Thomas Jefferson, it is impregnated with the ideas especially of the Scottish *philosophes*.[58] The universal claims they made have never been better stated than in the Declaration's opening lines: 'We hold these truths to be self-evident: that all men are created equal; that they are endowed by their creator with certain inalienable rights; that among these rights are life, liberty, & the pursuit of happiness.' Yet Jefferson himself was a Virginia gentleman who throughout his life owned black slaves. Indeed, in the *Notes on the State of Virginia* (1787), originally written to present the newly independent American republic to an enlightened French audience, he went as far as to express the 'suspicion' that 'the blacks, whether originally a distinct race, or made distinct by time and circumstances, are inferior to the whites in the endowments both of body and mind'.[59]

Jefferson was far from being the only Enlightenment figure to express racist 'suspicions'. Hume, for example, declared: 'I am apt to suspect the negroes, and in general all the other species of men (for there are four or five different kinds) to be naturally inferior to the whites.'[60] Despite such views, the *philosophes* were generally strongly critical of both the institution of slavery and the Atlantic slave trade, which during the eighteenth century tore millions from their homes in Africa to toil in the plantations of the New World. Jefferson himself took up

---

[58]   Thomas Jefferson (1743–1826): Governor of Virginia, 1779–81; American minister to France, 1784–9; US Secretary of State, 1790–4; Vice-President, 1797–1801; President, 1801–9: an extraordinary combination of gentleman planter, intellectual polymath, crankish inventor, and astute politician.

[59]   T. Jefferson, *Writings*, ed. M. D. Peterson (New York, 1984), pp. 19, 270.

[60]   Hume, *Essays*, pp. 629–30.

a highly ambivalent attitude towards the issue. On the one hand, he advocated the abolition of slavery; on the other, he quailed at the disruptive economic and political consequences of freeing the slaves. A famous letter well expressed this attitude: 'we have the wolf by the ears, and we can neither hold him, nor safely let him go. Justice is in one scale, and self-preservation in the other.'[61]

The case of racial slavery raises the question of the extent to which the proclaimed universality of Enlightenment thought was qualified by tacit limitations. Were rationality and liberty the property of all human beings, or were the majority of humankind in fact excluded by their race, their gender, or their class? This question highlights three other issues. First, how could a body of thought developed by a narrow group of European intellectuals claim genuine universality? Could, indeed, any theory achieve the objectivity on which such universality might be thought to depend? Might not thought be necessarily parochial, the expression of the time, place, and circumstances of those expressing it?

The second issue concerns the elitism of the *philosophes*, within Europe as well as without. On the face of it, their writings were addressed to everyone. Typically, however, their audience was a much narrower one, comprising those in the upper ranks of society who were at least potentially capable of becoming enlightened. 'What does it matter', Voltaire wrote to Helvétius in 1763, 'that our tailor and our cobbler should be ruled by Father Kroust and by Father Berthier? The main point is that those with whom you live should lower their eyes before the philosopher. It is in the interest of the king, that is, of the State, that the philosophers should rule society.'[62]

Probably the closest that Enlightenment philosophers came actually to ruling society was in India as it was incorporated into the British empire. Bentham's close collaborator James Mill was a senior official, and ultimately examiner (chief executive) of the East India Company, which ruled British India till 1858.[63] Mill was perhaps the first leading European intellectual explicitly to advocate democracy, in his *Essay on Government* (see §3.1 below). Yet he believed Indians incapable of ruling themselves, and sought to impose on them Bentham's legal and political doctrines and Ricardo's political economy on the basis of what amounted to the dictatorship of a handful of suitably enlightened officials backed by British military power.[64] 'Mill will be the living executive – I shall be the dead legislative of British India', the ageing Bentham declared.[65] The

---

[61]   Letter to John Holmes, 22 Apr. 1820, in Jefferson, *Writings*, p. 1434.

[62]   Quoted in G. Besse, introduction to Helvétius, *De l'esprit*, p. 30.

[63]   James Mill (1773–1836): assistant examiner of the East India Company, 1819; examiner, 1830; a key link between the Philosophical Radicals and the Scottish Enlightenment, whose influence is evident in his most influential work, the *History of British India* (1817); other important works include *Elements of Political Economy* (1821).

[64]   David Ricardo (1772–1823): successful London stockbroker (of Dutch Jewish origin); self-educated economist; Member of Parliament, 1819–23.

[65]   Quoted as the epigraph to E. Stokes, *The English Utilitarians and India* (Delhi, 1989).

Indians' 'backwardness' apparently made them an appropriate object of such social engineering.

Finally, racial slavery as it developed in the Atlantic economy in the seventeenth and eighteenth centuries challenged any simple understanding of historical progress. Robin Blackburn has pointed out:

> Its [i.e. American slavery's] development was associated with several of those processes which have been held to define modernity: the growth of instrumental rationality, the rise of national sentiment and the nation-state, racialized perceptions of identity, the spread of market relations and wage-labour, the development of administrative bureaucracies and modern tax systems, the growing sophistication of commerce and communication, the birth of consumer societies, the publication of newspapers and the beginnings of press advertising, 'action at a distance', and individualist sensibility.[66]

(5) *The ambiguities of progress.*   Many Enlightenment thinkers were themselves willing to cast doubt on the meaning of the progressive development depicted by their theories of history. The most radical challenge came from Rousseau. In the *Second Discourse* he portrays the evolution of civil society, rooting the process, in a manner not dissimilar to Millar's account, in *'the faculty of self-improvement* – a faculty which, with the help of circumstance, progressively develops all our other faculties, and which in man is inherent in the species as in the individual'. Yet, Rousseau argues, 'this distinguishing and almost unlimited faculty of man is the source of all his misfortunes'.[67] The expansion of productive powers made possible by man's innate capabilities creates the circumstances in which the institution of private property and growing divisions between rich and poor take shape: established forms of government serve to sanction and reinforce these social inequalities. Out of this process there emerges in contemporary Europe a profoundly inauthentic society, in which men are governed not by their own sense of self-worth but rather by others' judgements of them. Artificiality and luxury reign supreme, and the primitive innocence of the original undeveloped man is lost beyond recall.

More moderate versions of this critique found a resonance among other *philosophes*. The influence of classical models continued to make itself felt on many Enlightenment thinkers: many were still influenced by the idea of a historical cycle of birth, youth, maturity, and decline. The hold that the collapse of classical antiquity exercised on the eighteenth-century imagination – expressed most powerfully in the Enlightenment's greatest historical narrative, Edward Gibbon's *Decline and Fall of the Roman Empire* – reflected in part the fear that modern Europe would also cease to advance and sink into decadence.

Such fears were expressed, for example, by some of the leading figures of the

[66]   R. Blackburn, *The Making of New World Slavery* (London, 1997), p. 4.
[67]   Rousseau, *Discourse*, p. 88.

Scottish Enlightenment. Thus Ferguson writes: 'We observe among nations a kind of spontaneous return to absurdity and weakness.' He argues that to the traditional causes of the decadence of states identified by classical thinkers (luxury, corruption, political faction, etc.), the development of commercial society adds new dangers. His particular concern is with the effects of the division of labour, which Smith treated as the motor of economic progress:

> The separation of the professions, while it seems to promise improvement of skill and is actually the cause why the productions of art become more perfect as commerce advances; yet in its terminations, and ultimate effects, serves, in some measure, to break the bonds of society, to substitute mere forms and rules of art in place of ingenuity, and withdraw individuals from the common scene of occupation, on which the sentiments of the heart, and of the mind, are most happily engaged.[68]

More specifically, the division of labour may erode the kind of civic commitment which healthy states demand of their citizens. 'Commercial nations' tend to separate the roles of 'the senator, the statesman, and the soldier', Ferguson argues, and 'to place every branch of administration behind the counter, and come to employ, instead of the statesman and warrior, the mere clerk and accountant'. Reliance on a purely professional army, common in 'polished and mercantile states', makes 'a cowardly and undisciplined people' vulnerable to invasion or insurrection.[69] Behind such concerns, we see the classical republican ideal of the ancient *polis*, of an active, armed citizenry as the basis of the state. This ideal helps to explain the hold which the image of Sparta, the most martial of the Greek city-states, whose warrior elite practised a sort of crude communism and subjected themselves to a rigorous moral code, had on eighteenth-century thinkers as different as Rousseau and Ferguson, as well as on the Jacobin leader Robespierre.

The further development of the Scottish Enlightenment's most important creation, political economy, involved the destruction of this ideal. A key step in this process is taken by Malthus in his *Essay on the Principle of Population*.[70] First published in 1798 (and subsequently much revised), the *Essay* is a powerful polemic against the democratic egalitarianism of the French Revolution, as expressed in particular by Condorcet and by the English radical utilitarian William Godwin. Malthus argues that Godwin's 'attributing of almost all the vices and misery that prevail in civil society to human institutions' ignores 'those deeper-seated causes of evil, which result from the laws of nature and the passions of

---

[68] Ferguson, *Essay*, pp. 347, 364.
[69] Ibid., pp. 366–7, 380–1.
[70] Thomas Robert Malthus (1766–1834): Anglican clergyman; Professor of Political Economy at the East India College at Haileybury, 1805–34; his correspondence with his friendly opponent Ricardo is one of the richest treasure-troves of classical political economy.

mankind'. Even if the *philosophes* were to found a society 'with benevolence for its moving principle', it 'would, from the inevitable laws of nature, and not from any original depravity of man or of human institutions, degenerate in a very short period into a society constructed upon a plan not essentially different from that which prevails in every known state at present; a society divided into a class of proprietors and a class of labourers, and with self-love for the main-spring of the great machine'.[71]

The most important of these 'inevitable laws' Malthus claimed to have discovered himself. Population tends to rise in a geometric ratio (i.e. doubling every twenty-five years), while the production of food only grows arithmetically. While human desire is unlimited, investment in agriculture is subject to what later economists would call the law of diminishing returns: given unchanged technique, each additional unit of investment applied to a unit of land will produce a smaller quantity of output. The interaction of these factors produces a constant 'oscillation' whereby periods of prosperity and high wages encourage poor households to have more children, thus causing population to increase at a rate which soon overtakes the rate of growth of agricultural production. The increase in population lowers wages and increases food prices, thereby temporarily reducing fertility rates, but encouraging higher levels of investment which recreate the conditions of prosperity which started the cycle off in the first place. This 'constant effort in the population to increase beyond the means of subsistence . . . as constantly tends to subject the lower classes of society to distress and to prevent any great permanent melioration of their condition'.[72]

Where Rousseau had treated inequality as a consequence of particular social institutions, Malthus thus argued that it arose from the laws of nature itself; where Condorcet conceived human perfectibility as infinite, Malthus sought to demonstrate the necessary physical limits to which progress was subject. In the process, he sought to demolish the model of antique republican virtue, dismissing '[t]he preposterous system of Spartan discipline, and that unnatural absorption of every private feeling in concern for the public' as a 'strong indication of the miserable and almost savage stage of Sparta, and of Greece in general at that time'.[73] Similarly, where Ferguson had worried that the division of labour would undermine citizens' martial virtues, Constant argued in *The Spirit of Conquest and Usurpation* (1814) that modern commerce drew nations into so close a network of mutually beneficial relations as to make war a dangerous and unprofitable disruption which could only benefit those (above all Napoleon) who wished to reintroduce the anachronism of despotism to Europe.

---

[71] T. R. Malthus, *An Essay on the Principle of Population* (2 vols, Cambridge, 1989), I, pp. 317 n. 5, 325–6.

[72] Ibid., I, p. 20.

[73] Ibid., I, pp. 58–9.

(6) *The limits of civil society.*   Malthus's attempt to naturalize social inequality raised sharply the question of the character of the societies taking shape in the West at the end of the eighteenth century. The emergence of this issue can be traced by the transformation of the concept of civil society. Enlightenment thinkers, like their early modern predecessors, regarded civil society as coextensive with the state. Thus, for those of them who believed that governments were created by a social contract, what this contract established was civil society. It was Hegel who first contrasted civil society with the state. For him, 'the creation of civil society is a product of the modern world': it is the outcome of a historical process, not something that arises whenever men come together to form a government. 'In civil society, each individual is his own end, and all else means nothing to him.' But since the individual needs others, he has to cooperate with them to achieve his goals: 'through its reference to others, the particular end takes on the form of universality, and gains satisfaction by similarly satisfying the welfare of others'.[74]

Hegel's civil society is thus Smith's commercial society, where '[i]t is not from the benevolence of the butcher, the brewer, or the baker, that we expect our dinner, but from their regard to their own interest.'[75] In thus isolating the distinctive socio-economic structure analysed by the political economists (whom he read attentively), and contrasting it with the political forms of the state, Hegel highlights the novelty of the social logic at work in this structure. This logic has two features worth noting here. First, as we have already seen, this society is integrated less through self-conscious political regulation than as a result of the interactions of self-interested actors on the market. Secondly, these relations give rise to a distinctive set of class relations. In identifying three main forms of income of which the 'natural price' of a commodity is composed – rent, profit, and wages – Smith was isolating a specific class-structure. In particular, he was the first political economist systematically to treat capitalist entrepreneurs as a specific economic grouping who could expect, in the normal workings of a market economy, their own distinctive income in the shape of profits.

The next generation of political economists concerned themselves with the relationship between capitalists and the other main classes of commercial society, landowners and wage-labourers. Proposals to repeal the Corn Laws protecting British agriculture from competition from imports provoked intense debate at the end of the Napoleonic Wars in 1815, and led to more general discussion of the impact of changes in relative prices and taxes on the price level and the distribution of income. The key figure in these debates was Ricardo. In his great work, *On the Principles of Political Economy and Taxation* (1817), he set out '[t]o determine the laws which regulate' the distribution of income

---

[74]   G. W. F. Hegel (1821), *Elements of the Philosophy of Right* (Cambridge, 1991), §182 Addition, p. 220.
[75]   Smith, *Wealth*, I. ii, pp. 26–7.

among the classes. To achieve this aim, he sought to devise a 'measure of value' which would not be affected by changes in this distribution. In doing so, he became the first rigorously to formulate what would later be known as the labour theory of value: '*The value of a commodity, or the quantity of any other commodity for which it will exchange, depends on the relative quantity of labour which is necessary for its production.*'[76]

Smith had tended to see the natural price of a commodity as a sort of composite of profit, rent, and wages. According to Ricardo, however, the natural price was independent of changes in these forms of income, since it depended simply on the labour necessary to produce it. The different class incomes represented a division of value created antecedently in production. Since therefore a rise in, say, labourers' wages would not lead to a commensurate increase in the price of their product, the income of at least one other class – landowners or capitalists – would have to fall. Ricardo indeed suggested that profits and wages were inversely related, so that if wages rose the rate of profit would fall. Class conflict was thus built into the basic economic mechanisms of civil society.

Ricardo, through his friend James Mill, was closely associated politically with Bentham and the Philosophical Radicals, who in their programmes for political reform targeted especially the privileges of the landed aristocracy in the British state and society. But his economic analysis had considerably more subversive implications at a time when the new working class created by the Industrial Revolution was beginning to engage in political and social agitation.

Like most nineteenth-century economists, Ricardo accepted Malthus's theory of population. This did not simply imply what came to be known as 'the iron law of wages' – the tendency for population to outstrip food production would keep wages from rising above a bare minimum of physical subsistence. Diminishing returns in agriculture further implied that the cost of producing a given quantity of food would tend to rise, and so consequently would the wage required to buy even the subsistence minimum, thereby causing profits to fall. 'The natural tendency of profits is to fall', Ricardo concluded; 'for, in the progress of society and wealth, the additional quantity of food required is obtained by the sacrifice of more and more labour.'[77]

Ricardo believed that the operation of this 'natural tendency' could be slowed down by technological innovations which increased the productivity of labour. Generally committed though he was to Smith's conception of the market as a self-equilibrating system (thus he defended Say's law, according to which supply and demand necessarily come into balance, against Malthus's criticisms), he nevertheless came up with specific arguments which cast doubt on whether this system actually maximized human welfare. Thus in the third edition of the *Principles*, published in 1821, he added a chapter 'On Machinery' which

---

[76]   D. Ricardo, *Works and Correspondence* (10 vols, Cambridge, 1951–2), I, pp. 5, 11.
[77]   Ibid., I, p. 120.

suggested that, under certain conditions, the introduction of machines would reduce employment, and that therefore 'the substitution of machinery for human labour, is often very injurious to the interests of the class of labourers'.[78] Coming at a time when groups of workers known as Luddites were sabotaging machines on the grounds that they destroyed jobs, this argument was political dynamite. His follower J. R. McCulloch protested furiously to Ricardo: 'If your reasoning . . . be well founded, the laws against the Luddites are a disgrace to the Statute book.'[79]

Perhaps not entirely coincidentally, Ricardo's successors retreated from some of his most distinctive themes: the labour theory of value, in particular, was soon dropped, becoming instead the property of socialist publicists who used it to prove that profits were an unjust deduction from labour. His chief influence on subsequent mainstream economists was to set new standards of rigorous analysis based on theoretical abstraction. But his work raised questions which would not go away, both about the future prospects for civil society and about its conflictual social basis. These questions would become a large part of the agenda for later social theorists.

[78] Ibid., I, p. 388.
[79] Ibid., VIII, pp. 384–5.

2

Hegel

2.1 Reconciling modernity

The Enlightenment, as even as brief and selective a survey as that offered in the previous chapter should indicate, did not constitute a simple and homogeneous body of doctrine. The thought developed by the eighteenth-century *philosophes* was complex, internally riven, riddled by tensions. This condition was not simply a consequence of the fact that individual thinkers took differing positions on various issues, though of course they did. Much more important was the fact that there were often strains internal to these positions. The reservations many leading figures of the Scottish Enlightenment expressed about the development of commercial society, even though they had played a decisive role in formulating an articulated theory of this as the latest progressive stage of world history, are a case in point. Caricatural readings of the Enlightenment as a simple-minded 'grand narrative' of infinite progress simply represent an obstacle to its understanding.

The *philosophes*, I suggested, sought to offer an account of the modern age which did not appeal to classical antiquity for models and justifications, but rather sought to legitimize it by means of the very forms of rationality which represented its claim to mark a distinct phase in European history. These forms were, of course, the kind of reasoning embodied in the seventeenth-century revolution in physics and the Enlightenment's own attempt to extend it to the understanding of society. But, as we saw in §1.5 above, this attempt produced a series of tensions and doubts internal to Enlightenment thought itself.

The resulting sense of confusion and uncertainty was more than merely philosophical. The eighteenth century concluded in the Great French Revolution (1789–94) and a series of wars which pitted France, first under Revolutionary regimes and then under Napoleon's ultimately imperial dictatorship, against the other Great Powers. The liberal historian Augustin Thierry wrote in 1827: 'There is not one amongst us children of the nineteenth century who does not know more on the score of rebellion and conquests, of the dismemberment of empires, of the fall of monarchies, of popular revolution and the consequent reactions than did Velly or Mably, or even Voltaire himself [all Enlightenment historians].'[1]

While attempts to treat these upheavals as a straightforward consequence of the Enlightenment might be simplistic, the revolutionary slogan of 'Liberty, Equality, and Fraternity' was only intelligible against the background of the *philosophes*' writings. 'C'est la faute de Rousseau' – it's Rousseau's fault – Napoleon himself said of the Revolution.[2] Whether the Jacobin Terror (1792–4) and the Napoleonic regime and its wars had discredited the ideals of the eighteenth century was one of the main themes of the debates which unfolded in Restoration France (see §3.1 below).

The significance of Hegel in this context is twofold.[3] In the first place, as Jürgen Habermas has argued, 'Hegel was the first to raise to the level of a philosophical problem the process of detaching modernity from the suggestion of norms lying outside of itself in the past.'[4] Hegel's transformation of the concept of civil society as he found it in the writings of the Scottish Enlightenment, which I mentioned in §1.5 above, is illustrative of his general philosophical approach. He sees himself as articulating the principles implicit in the development of European thought before him, and forming them into a coherent, intellectually compelling, theoretical whole.

Perhaps his greatest work, *The Phenomenology of Spirit* (1807), is an enormously rich and complex rational reconstruction of the entire prior movement of European thought from the Greeks onwards. It concludes in a condition which Hegel calls 'absolute knowing', or 'Spirit that knows itself as Spirit'.[5] This development represents the culmination of 'the culture of modern times, the thought of modern Philosophy', where 'the universal principle by means of which everything in the world is regulated, is the thought that proceeds from itself.'[6] Modernity is inaugurated by the Protestant Reformation of the sixteenth century, whose 'essence' is: 'Man is in his very nature destined to be free.'[7]

Thus part (although only part, as we shall see in §2.2 below) of what Hegel means by 'absolute knowing' has to do with the idea that, as Terry Pinkard puts it, modernity is '*self-grounding*': absolute knowing is 'the set of practices through which the modern community thinks about itself without attempting to posit

---

[1] Quoted in D. Johnson, *Guizot* (London, 1963), p. 325.

[2] Quoted in K. Löwith, *From Hegel to Nietzsche* (London, 1965), p. 238.

[3] Georg Wilhelm Friedrich Hegel (1770–1831): born and raised in Stuttgart; studied at Tübingen Theological Seminary, 1788–93; private tutor, 1793–1800; taught at the University of Jena, 1801–6; editor of *Bamberger Zeitung*, 1807–8; headmaster of the Nürnberg *Gymnasium*, 1808–16; Professor of Philosophy at the University of Heidelberg, 1816–18; Professor of Philosophy at the University of Berlin, 1818–31; died in a cholera epidemic.

[4] J. Habermas, *The Philosophical Discourse of Modernity* (Cambridge, 1987), p. 16.

[5] G. W. F. Hegel (1807), *The Phenomenology of Spirit* (Oxford, 1977), §798, p. 485.

[6] G. W. F. Hegel (1833–6), *Lectures on the History of Philosophy* (3 vols, London, 1963), III, p. 217.

[7] G. W. F. Hegel (1837), *Lectures on the Philosophy of History* (New York, 1956), p. 417.

any metaphysical "other" or set of "natural constraints" that would underwrite these practices'.[8] In other words, the development of European thought culminates, according to Hegel, in a form of consciousness which involves the explicit recognition that modernity is characterized by the attempt to justify itself from its own intellectual resources without any attempt to appeal to anything outside itself.

The trouble with this attempt is that, as we have seen, it issued in all sorts of tensions and uncertainties. The second respect in which Hegel is so important here is that he does not flinch from the conflicts internal to Enlightenment thought (or indeed thought generally) but positively welcomes and embraces them. 'Contradiction,' he says, 'both in actuality and in thinking reflection, is considered an accident, a kind of abnormality or paroxysm of sickness which will soon pass away.' But in fact 'Contradiction is at the root of all movement and life, and it is only in so far as it contains a Contradiction that anything moves and has impulse and activity.'[9] Such assertions are expressions of Hegel's peculiar philosophical method, the dialectic, which I consider in the following section. At present what matters is that, for Hegel, the self-understanding of modernity involves fully articulating its internal conflicts so that their nature can be properly assessed, and that the insights they offer can help achieve their ultimate reconciliation in the state of consciousness he calls 'absolute knowing'.

Hegel's ability to conceptualize the contradictions of modernity was at least to some extent a reflection of his own experience. Like many young European intellectuals of his day, Hegel, along with his two close friends and fellow students, the poet Hölderlin and the philosopher Schelling, had initially rallied enthusiastically to the French Revolution. They hoped it would sweep away the Germany of petty principalities against whose intellectual and political backwardness they chafed. Hegel's early writings of the 1790s counterpose the *ancien régime*, and in particular the 'positivity' of established Christianity, acceptance of whose teachings is enforced by the authority of the state, to, on the one hand, the city-states of ancient Greece and Rome, where 'in public as well as in private and domestic life, every individual is a free man, one who lived by his own laws', and, on the other hand, Christ himself, whom Hegel depicts as a Kantian figure, the teacher of universal moral laws 'based on the essence of reason alone and not on phenomena in the external world which for reason are mere accidents'.[10] This conflict between 'positivity' and the universal dictates of reason would overturn the old order: 'From the Kantian system and its highest completion I expect a revolution in Germany', Hegel told Schelling in 1795.[11]

---

[8] T. Pinkard, *Hegel's Phenomenology* (Cambridge, 1994), pp. 188, 262.

[9] G. W. F. Hegel (1812–16), *The Science of Logic* (2 vols, London, 1966), II, p. 67.

[10] G. W. F. Hegel, *Early Theological Writings* (Chicago, 1948), pp. 154, 79.

[11] 16 Apr. 1795, in G. W. F. Hegel, *The Letters*, ed. C. Butler and C. Seiler (Bloomington, 1984), p. 35.

Subsequent experience – in particular, the Jacobin Terror and the defeat of various movements for political reform in Germany – disillusioned Hegel. One consequence was to encourage him to become increasingly critical of the Enlightenment, and in particular of what he came to think of as its essentially abstract conception of reason. In one of the most striking sections of the *Phenomenology*, 'Absolute Freedom and Terror', Hegel argues that the Enlightenment culminates in the conception of an absolutely undifferentiated and unconditional universal freedom. Under the Jacobins, this absolute freedom, in the shape of Rousseau's general will, claims its right to rule society.

Rather than give itself substance by creating a differentiated set of social and political institutions, the general will seeks to rule directly. In doing so, it encounters as 'the greatest antithesis to universal freedom ... the freedom and individuality of actual self-consciousness itself'. By refusing itself 'the reality of an organic articulation', absolute freedom 'divides itself into extremes equally abstract, into a simple, inflexible cold universality, and into the discrete, absolute hard rigidity and self-willed atomism of actual self-consciousness'. This opposition is resolved through the Terror, where the resistance of private wills to the general will (or rather to the political faction which rules in its name) is overcome by the guillotine: 'The sole work and deed of universal freedom is therefore *death*, a death too which has no inner significance or filling, for what is negated is the empty point of the absolutely free self. It is thus the coldest and meanest of all deaths, with no more significance than cutting off a head of cabbage or swallowing a mouthful of water.'[12]

This critique of Jacobinism did not represent Hegel's rejection of the principles of the French Revolution. He came to think of Napoleon as the agent of these principles, famously describing him as 'this world soul ... astride a horse' when he saw the emperor riding through Jena, where he had just defeated the Prussian army (Hegel claimed to have completed the *Phenomenology* 'in the middle of the night before the battle of Jena').[13] His correspondence is full of sardonic comments about the European reaction which followed Napoleon's fall in 1814–15.

Yet, while his sympathies remained with the Revolution, Hegel became increasingly firmly committed to the belief that the decisive force behind the extraordinary political events through which he lived lay in philosophical reflection. Thus he wrote in 1808: 'I am daily ever more convinced that theoretical work accomplishes more in the world than practical work. Once the realm of representation [*Vorstellung*] is revolutionized, actuality [*Wirklichkeit*] will not hold out.'[14] Philosophy, he claimed much later in life, is 'the true theodicy', which uncovers the thread of reason running through all the world's

---

12   Hegel, *Phenomenology*, §590, pp. 359–60.
13   Letter to Niethammer, 13 Oct. 1806, in Hegel, *Letters*, p. 114.
14   Letter to Niethammer, 28 Oct. 1808, ibid, p. 179.

trouble and confusion. Indeed, '[t]he history of Philosophy is a revelation of what has been the aim of spirit throughout its history; it is the world's history in its innermost signification.'[15]

What philosophy revealed in the realm of politics was most fully outlined in the *Philosophy of Right* (1821). Here Hegel sought to distinguish his views sharply from the views of the contemporary Romantic movement, strongly associated in Germany with the early manifestations of nationalism, which sought to found political allegiance on the emotional enthusiasm of the people for the state (he often made biting comments about 'dumb Teutonism [*Deutschdumm*]').[16] The state for Hegel is '*an inherently rational entity*'. But 'this refined structure' cannot be understood on the basis of the abstract conception of reason characteristic of the Enlightenment in general and of Kantian philosophy in particular: 'since philosophy is *exploration of the rational*, it is for that very reason the *comprehension of the present and the actual*, not the setting up of a *world beyond* which exists God knows where – or rather, of which we can very well say that we know where it exists, namely in the errors of a one-sided and empty ratiocination.'[17]

It is in this context that Hegel makes the notorious claim: 'What is rational is actual; and what is actual is rational.'[18] This remark has been used by his critics to claim that the *Philosophy of Right* is merely a philosophical defence of the Prussian absolute monarchy whose servant, as a university professor, Hegel after all was (indeed, he claimed as much in a fawning letter presenting the book to a Prussian minister). But such views are unsustainable. For Hegel actuality (*Wirklichkeit*) is the unity of the outward appearance of things and their inner essence: the confused ways in which the world presents itself are there integrated into a rational structure. It follows that not everything that exists is actual: 'even Experience . . . has sense enough to distinguish the mere appearance, which is transient and meaningless, from what in itself really deserves the name of actual'. 'What is actual is rational' is therefore more or less a tautology. On the other hand, 'what is rational is actual' challenges the belief, which Hegel attributes chiefly to Kant, that 'Ideas and ideals are something far too excellent to have actuality, or something too impotent to procure it for themselves.'[19]

Reason for Hegel is not a set of principles inherently separate from the world which may at best act as a means of critically orienting ourselves. It is actively at work in the very organization of the social world. Hegel seeks to demonstrate this in the course of the *Philosophy of Right*. He takes his cue from the opposition, central to Rousseau's political philosophy and taken over by Kant,

[15] Hegel, *History of Philosophy*, III, p. 547.
[16] Letter to Paulus, 9 Oct. 1814, in Hegel, *Letters*, p. 312.
[17] G. W. F. Hegel (1821), *Elements of the Philosophy of Right* (Cambridge, 1991), pp. 21, 16, 20.
[18] Ibid., p. 20.
[19] G. W. F. Hegel (1817), *Hegel's Logic* (Oxford, 1975), §6, pp. 8–9.

between the general will and the private (or particular) will. The general will is, as Hegel's critique of the Jacobins had shown, inherently abstract. Its realm is that of Abstract Right, of the formal legal principles first systematically developed in ancient Rome. Here the subject is a person, the bearer of certain rights, for example, to own property and to make contracts. His freedom derives from these rights, and is dependent on the external arrangements of persons and things to which their exercise by him and others gives rise. It is for this reason that Abstract Right is inadequate as the basis of a state, at least in the modern world: it does not give expression to the freedom of the particular individual subject.

Where this subject becomes self-conscious, we enter the sphere of Morality, the realm of the particular will, and of Kant's critical philosophy. Here the right and the good depend on the self-conscious choice of the individual subject to adopt them – paradigmatically in the form of the Kantian categorical imperative, that is, of moral laws adopted as universally binding. 'This subjectivity, as abstract self-determination and pure certainty of itself alone, *evaporates* into itself all *determinate* aspects of right, duty, and existence.'[20] Everything now depends on whether its intentions are good or not, on whether the particular will embraces the universal moral law. There is nothing to prevent it choosing evil. This can take indirect forms, for example the dissimulation of evil intentions characteristic of hypocrisy, or the kind of casuistry practised by the Jesuits ('the end justifies the means'). Or the arbitrariness of individual choice may lead us to take refuge in irony, and the denial that there are any objective grounds on which to determine the right and the good. In any case, the self-assertion of individual subjectivity is unable to provide the universal with secure foundations.

These considerations do not lead Hegel to despair of reason, and perhaps to embrace relativism, denying that there is any fact of the matter about the social world. Rather, he seeks to achieve a reconciliation of particular and universal, of subjective and objective. The possibility of this reconciliation depends critically on recognizing that the individual subject does not exist in isolation (Hegel is contemptuously dismissive of the idea of a state of nature), but derives its existence from, and can only flourish in, a concrete, historically specific social context rooted not in abstract principles, but in custom and tradition. The name Hegel gives to this context is Ethical Life (*Sittlichkeit*). His model of Ethical Life is provided by the city-states of the ancient world. Here citizens derived their social existence, not from a set of abstract, timeless moral principles, but through participating in definite institutions which specified the roles from which individuals derived their identities, laid down the duties expected of them, and promoted the virtues on which the welfare of both the state and its members depended.

The mature Hegel came to the conclusion that the kind of immersion of the

---

[20]   Hegel, *Philosophy of Right*, §138, p. 166.

individual in public life characteristic of the classical *polis* was inconsistent with the assertion of individual subjectivity characteristic of modern freedom. He nevertheless believed that a form of Ethical Life capable of providing this freedom with its appropriate social setting was taking shape. This Ethical Life has three moments. The first, the family, has a natural basis and function, but, at least in modern society, it is the outcome of the free choice of two individuals to bind themselves into a new person. Family relationships cannot, however, serve as the basis of social life in general, since each family dissolves as the children attain adulthood and maturity and the parents die. 'The family disintegrates', therefore, '. . . into a *plurality* of families whose relation to one another is in general that of self-sufficient concrete persons and consequently of an external kind.'[21]

This plurality of self-sufficient persons constitutes the second moment of Ethical Life, civil society. Hegel derives his conception of civil society from the writings of the British political economists (see §1.5 above). It includes 'the system of needs' – the market economy proper, and the forms of public regulation which arise directly from these economic relationships – the legal system, the police (a term which Hegel uses broadly, following common eighteenth-century practice, to refer to all state activities concerned to secure public welfare and domestic stability), and the corporations (updated versions of the medieval guilds through which specific socio-economic groups govern their internal affairs).

On their own, however, these relationships cannot generate a stable social order. 'When the activity of civil society is unrestricted, it is occupied internally with *expanding its population and industry*.' As a result, 'the *accumulation of wealth* increases . . . But on the other hand, the *specialization* and *limitation* of particular work also increase, as do likewise the dependence and want of the class which is tied to such work; this in turn leads to an inability to feel and enjoy the wider freedoms, and particularly the spiritual advantages, of civil society.' Further, '[t]he inner dialectic of society drives it – or in the first instance *this specific society* – to go beyond its own confines and look for consumers, and hence the means it requires for subsistence, in other nations which lack those means of which it has a surplus or which generally lag behind it in creativity, etc.' This process leads to the development of international trade, with all its 'fluidity, danger, and destruction', and to the establishment of colonies for the surplus population of civil society.[22]

Thus, while acknowledging his debt to Smith, Ricardo, and other classical economists, Hegel does not follow them in conceiving modern commercial society as a self-equilibrating system which, by means of an 'invisible hand', integrates the diverse projects of individual agents in a manner that maximizes

---

[21]   Ibid., §181, p. 219.
[22]   Ibid., §243, pp. 266, 267–8; §247, p. 268.

the general welfare. On the contrary, unrestrained civil society generates a series of systemic dysfunctions – growing divisions between rich and poor, a shortage of markets, and a tendency towards external expansion which is both liberating and destabilizing. It is against this background that Hegel argues that the state – the third moment of Ethical Life – is necessary, in part, to contain and harmonize the conflicts of civil society. One can find plenty of precedents for Hegel's reasoning here – the early modern Cameralist school of German economists had, for example, argued that the proper functioning of markets depended on state regulation. But Hegel is the first major post-Enlightenment thinker, in the aftermath of the French Revolution, and as the Industrial Revolution began to make itself felt, to challenge classical political economy's conception of a self-regulating market. It is not wholly absurd to see his arguments here as an anticipation of Keynes's critique of *laissez faire* a hundred years later.

Hegel's conception of the state, however, goes well beyond these considerations. The state is for him the highest form of social reason, 'the Idea made manifest on earth'.[23] As 'the actuality of the ethical Idea' it has 'its immediate existence in *custom* and its mediate existence in the *self-consciousness* of the individual, in the individual's knowledge and activity, just as self-consciousness, by virtue of its disposition, has its *substantial freedom* in the state as its essence, its end, and the product of its activity'.[24] The thought, then, is that the state integrates the self-interested individuals of civil society into a political community by means of social institutions which allow them to realize their freedom. It does so by means of a differentiated and internally articulated political structure of the kind that the Jacobins refused to construct in their headlong pursuit of absolute freedom. In particular, the modern state combines a constitutional monarch, the executive power which he heads but which consists primarily of a permanent bureaucracy, and a legislature through which civil society gains political representation.

It is the detail of Hegel's analysis here which has made him most vulnerable to charges of serving as an apologist for Prussian absolutism – he employs fairly specious arguments in support of the hereditary principle, and defends the kind of corporate representation of social groups characteristic of the Estates which was one of early modern Germany's legacies to the nineteenth century. But even here we find him responding to what he sees as distinctively modern problems. He thinks that corporations can help to overcome the isolation of the individual in civil society, and allow the better-off to help the poor in a way that does not humiliate the latter. Similarly, the bureaucracy, as 'the *universal* estate – or more precisely, the estate which devotes itself to the *service of the government*', has 'the universal . . . as the end of its activity'.[25] Here

---

[23]   G. W. F. Hegel, *Lectures on the Philosophy of World History: Introduction* (Cambridge, 1975), p. 95.
[24]   Hegel, *Philosophy of Right*, §257, p. 275.
[25]   Ibid., §303, p. 343.

we see adumbrated themes which would later be developed by Durkheim and by Weber – respectively, the restoration of corporations to overcome the dysfunctions of industrial society, and bureaucracy as a decisive distinguishing feature of the modern state. However unsatisfactory Hegel's arguments and solutions may be, they represent an attempt to conceptualize a form of state capable of harmoniously reconciling the contradictions of modernity.

2.2 The labour of the negative

Hegel's account of Ethical Life offers an illustration of how he believes reason is at work in the world. Two apparently starkly counterposed moments develop in succession. The first, the family, is based upon the affective relations between husband and wife and between parents and children; the second, civil society, is constituted by the purely external and instrumental relationships between competing agents on the market. Each of these moments is presented as inherently limited and flawed. The state, however, reconciles them. It is a genuine political community: its members interact not simply for what they can get out of each other, but because they participate in the common 'substance' of the state – to put it in more contemporary terms, membership of the state is constitutive of their identity. At the same time, the state has a differentiated structure which allows the various interests of civil society political expression: these interests, and the individuals whose economic relationships produce these interests, are not simply submerged in the state.

The rational structure of Ethical Life thus has three stages. In the first two, apparently sharply opposed moments are counterposed; in the third, they are reconciled. (Incidentally, contrary to legend, Hegel does *not* call these three stages respectively 'thesis', 'antithesis', and 'synthesis'.) This triple structure, Hegel believes, is present everywhere: comprehending it is a prerequisite of gaining a proper understanding of the world. This comprehension depends crucially on grasping the positive and productive role of contradiction. Thus in the *Phenomenology* and the *Philosophy of History* Hegel analyses a succession of, respectively, forms of consciousness and political systems, each of which is undermined by tensions inherent in it. Contradiction is thus the moving principle of history.

In seeking to justify this conception of contradiction, Hegel directs considerable criticism towards what he calls the Understanding, which 'sticks to fixity of characters and their distinctness from one another: every such limited abstract it treats as having a subsistence and being of its own'. Understanding is that mode of thought which is most fully developed in the Enlightenment and above all in the philosophy of Kant. Hegel acknowledges its positive function, since he is strongly hostile to any doctrine (for example, German Romanticism and Schelling's idealism) which reduces knowledge to a vague intuition of the oneness of things: 'apart from Understanding there is no fixity or accuracy in the region of theory or of practice'.[26] The Understanding, which we see at work in the physical sciences, plays an essential role in distinguishing between things and identifying the causal regularities by which they are governed. But, at the same time, it treats the distinctions it makes as absolute. As a result it is inherently abstract. Just as Rousseau's general will necessarily found itself in conflict with the particular wills of the citizens, so the scientific laws of the Understanding function as abstractions, unable to comprehend and to integrate all the concrete variety of the world that falls under them.

The limitations of the Understanding are overcome only by the Dialectic, thought as 'negative reason', where 'these finite characterizations or formulae supersede themselves, and pass into their opposites'.[27] Here Hegel challenges what is generally seen as the most basic law of logic, both ancient and modern, the law of non-contradiction. Formally expressed as $\sim(p.\sim p)$, this law forbids the affirmation of a proposition and its negation. We cannot, in other words, simultaneously say that it is raining and that it is not raining. A proof dating back to the Middle Ages shows that a contradictory sentence implies every other sentence. So to affirm a contradiction is to say everything, and therefore – since the point of speaking is to say something definite – to say nothing.

Hegel believes that this reasoning is fundamentally mistaken. Contradictions do not vaporize content – they actually produce it:

> The one and only thing for *securing scientific progress* . . . is knowledge of the logical precept that Negation is just as much Affirmation as Negation, or that what is self-contradictory resolves itself not into nullity, into abstract Nothingness, but essentially only into the negation of its *particular* content, that such negation is not an all-embracing Negation, but is *the negation of a definite somewhat* which abolishes itself, and this is a definite negation, and that thus the result contains that from which it results . . . Since what results, the negation, is a *definite* negation, it has a *content*. It is a new concept, but a higher richer concept than that which preceded it; for it has been enriched by the negation or opposite of the preceding concept, and thus contains it, but contains also more than it, and is the unity of it and its concept.[28]

Negation thus draws out what was implicit but unarticulated in the starting-point. It is, for example, inherent in the concept of the family that, though its internal unity derives from the love its members feel towards one another, its relationship towards those outside it will be an instrumental one governed by whatever use they are to family members. Civil society therefore is the negation of the family, since it is based on self-interested rather than affectionate

26 *Hegel's Logic*, §80, p. 113; §80 *Zusatz*, p. 81.
27 Ibid., §79, p. 113; §81, p. 115.
28 Hegel, *Science of Logic*, I, pp. 64–5.

relations, but it represents a truth implicit in the nature of the family. So negation is a process of *differentiation* in which the starting-point is enriched and
complicated. But it is not the end of the story. Thought comprises a third stage,
after Understanding and Dialectic, the 'Speculative stage, or stage of Positive
Reason, [which] apprehends the unity of the terms (propositions) in their opposition – the affirmative, which is involved in their disintegration and in their
transition'.[29]

The third stage of the process thus re-establishes the unity of the counterposed
moments. This unity was present from the start. But the starting-point, the first
moment of each dialectical movement, is only an immediate – that is, an unconscious and undifferentiated – unity, just as the family is bound together by
the strong but narrowly focused and unreflecting emotion of love. Negation is
necessary to draw out the content implicit in this unity. But it is only what
Hegel calls first negation: it brings hitherto implicit content to the surface, but
in the form of an opposition between separate and conflicting elements, just as
civil society is ruled by the atomistic competition of self-interested individuals.
The third stage of the process overcomes this opposition; it is second negation
or, as Hegel sometimes puts it, the negation of the negation. Unity is restored,
but it is a unity enriched and made self-conscious by the experience of contradiction, just as the state is, like the family, a community, but one which offers
proper scope for the individuality and self-assertion of its members. Hegel
often seeks to bring out the character of the negation of the negation by appealing to the German word *aufheben*, which means both to cancel and
to preserve. The final stage of every dialectical movement does not merely
transcend the two previous moments: it incorporates their content with a new,
self-conscious unity.

It is important to understand that Hegel regards this dialectic (understood
broadly so as to incorporate both what he regards as the properly Dialectical
and the culminating Speculative stages of thought) as more than a formal method
which can be used to understand various aspects of the world: 'the method is
not an extraneous form', he says, 'but the soul and notion of the content'.[30]
Here we return to the issue, touched on in the previous section, of Hegel's
idealism, of his belief that thought rules the world. This in turn raises the question of the development of German philosophy after Kant.

Kant argued that the world of everyday experience and modern science
depended on the activities of a transcendental subject (§1.5 above). He also
insisted that we were forced to presuppose the existence of this subject (or
'transcendental unity of apperception'), but that, beyond that, we could say
nothing about it. Subsequent German idealists found, on the contrary, much to
say about the transcendental subject. Schelling in particular took the crucial

---

[29]   *Hegel's Logic*, §82, p. 119.
[30]   Ibid., §243, p. 296.

move of treating it as essentially supra-individual, and equating it with God. This was not, however, the God of traditional Christian theology, a distinct (though mysterious) person who creates and rules the world, but who remains beyond it. Schelling's God was the Absolute, identical with its creation, with nature (including its highest development, finite human minds) – less a personal creator than the implicit principle that moves the world. There thus emerges absolute idealism, which treats the world as the expression of this impersonal God.

Hegel followed Schelling along this road, affirming, for example, that 'the Absolute itself is the identity of identity and non-identity; being opposed and being one are both together in it'.[31] The Absolute thus incorporates everything. If it is, as Pinkard puts it, 'self-grounding', it is so partly because there is nothing outside it. But Hegel became increasingly uncomfortable with the idea of the Absolute as some kind of undifferentiated whole knowable only through a vague intuition of the oneness of things. In the *Phenomenology* he takes aim at Schelling's version of absolute idealism: 'To put this single insight, that in the Absolute everything is the same, against the full body of articulated cognition . . . to palm off the Absolute as the night in which, as they say, all cows are black – this is cognition reduced to vacuity.'[32]

Hegel's critique of the Enlightenment did not imply its total rejection. The identity of the Absolute and the world had to be rationally demonstrated, not simply affirmed or celebrated in vapid effusions of emotion. This rational demonstration, further, depends on a proper understanding of the nature of subjectivity, for 'everything turns on grasping and expressing the True, not only as *Substance*, but equally as *Subject*'. This claim reflects Hegel's understanding of modernity as the phase of world history where subjectivity comes into its own (see §2.1 above). But it also involves, more profoundly, a particular account of the structure of the subject:

> the living Substance is being which is in truth *Subject*, or, what is the same, is in truth actual only in so far as it is the movement of positing itself, or is the mediation of its self-othering with itself. This Substance is, as Subject, pure, *simple negativity*, and it is for this very reason the bifurcation of the simple; it is the doubling which sets up opposition, and then again the negation of this indifferent diversity and of its antithesis. Only this *self-restoring* sameness, or this reflection in otherness within itself – not an *original* or *immediate* unity as such – is the True. It is the process of its own becoming, the circle that presupposes its end as its goal, having its end also as its goal, having its end also as its beginning; and only by being worked out to its end, is it actual.[33]

---

[31]   G. W. F. Hegel (1801), *The Difference between Fichte's and Schelling's System of Philosophy* (Albany, NY, 1977), p. 156.
[32]   Hegel, *Phenomenology*, §16, p. 9.
[33]   Ibid., §§17–18, p. 10.

Packed into this dense and obscure passage is the essence of Hegel's philosophy. He conceives the subject (to borrow a formulation of Marx's) as a relation, not a thing. The subject is not a discrete focus of consciousness, as Western philosophy since Descartes had conceived it. Rather, '[i]t is the process of its own becoming.' But this process has a structure which is that of the dialectic outlined above. The subject is 'the doubling which sets up opposition, and then again the negation of this indifferent diversity and of its antithesis'. It breaks down the first '*original* or *immediate* unity', counterposing the self to an other which it conceives as quite distinct from this. But then this opposition is cancelled in the 'self-restoring sameness' that is the negation of the negation.

Not only does subjectivity have a dialectical structure – the dialectic is inherently a dialectic of subjectivity. The movement of internal differentiation and restoration of an enriched unity which Hegel analyses in his logical writings is the process through which consciousness becomes aware of itself as Spirit, that is, becomes 'conscious of itself as its own world, and of the world as itself'. Consciousness starts off in a mute and undifferentiated unity with nature. First negation breaks up this unity. It is a process of alienation: nature is now set up as an other separate from and opposed to the conscious self. The Speculative moment comes when consciousness now recognizes nature as *its* other, and thereby recognizes their inner unity. The immensely complicated transitions of the *Phenomenology* ultimately display this structure. The final moment of 'absolute knowing' is the point at which Spirit looks back at the entire preceding process and comprehends it as nothing other than its own self-development, the movement which allowed it to attain its present pinnacle from which the structure of reality is transparent to reason. Therefore, '[o]f the Absolute it must be said that it is essentially a *result*, that only in the *end* is it what it truly is.'[34] Philosophical knowledge is thus necessarily retrospective: as Hegel famously put it, 'the owl of Minerva begins its flight only with the onset of dusk'.[35]

Such is the power and richness of Hegel's thought that many of the best commentators on his work are strongly tempted to find ways of toning down his absolute idealism. Thus Robert Pippin suggests that Hegel's project involves 'a kind of expansion of the Kantian idea of a transcendental subject, Kant's formal way of considering "what any subject" must think in representing an object'.[36] How, then, does Hegel go beyond Kant? Terry Pinkard thinks that in the *Phenomenology* 'we . . . move away from a picture of ourselves *representing* the world to an understanding of ourselves as *participants* in various historically determinate social practices'.[37]

Now it is undoubtedly true that Hegel seeks to undermine the conception, dominant since Descartes, of the subject as an isolated centre of consciousness.

[34] Ibid., §438, p. 263; §20, p. 11.
[35] Hegel, *Philosophy of Right*, p. 23.
[36] R. Pippin, *Modernism as a Philosophical Problem* (Oxford, 1991), p. 67.
[37] Pinkard, *Hegel's Phenomenology*, p. 44.

In one of the most celebrated sections of the *Phenomenology*, the so-called Dialectic of Master and Slave, he analyses the desire for recognition, that is, the desire of each self-consciousness to be acknowledged as an autonomous subject by another subject: 'Self-consciousness exists in and for itself when, and by the fact that, it so exists for another; that is, it exists only in being acknowledged.'[38] Subjectivity is thus inseparable from inter-subjectivity: the self only exists as socially situated, as a member of a historically specific community of self-conscious human agents.

Hegel's conception of Absolute Spirit is, however, more than a socialized version of Kant's transcendental subject. Such an interpretation is hard to square with statements such as Hegel's affirmation that the content of Logic '*shows forth God as he is in his eternal essence before the creation of Nature and of a Finite Spirit*'.[39] Logic for Hegel is thus also ontology, revealing the structures of the world, and indeed theology, since those structures are of Absolute Spirit coming to self-consciousness. These apparently extravagant claims cannot be separated from Hegel's critique of Kant. Hegel unremittingly condemns the critical philosophy for its formalism, its conception of the categories of the understanding as subjective forms imposed on and external to the content provided for them by sense-experience. This separation of form and content leaves the conception of an objectivity independent of the human understanding as unknowable things-in-themselves, 'the *caput mortuum*, the dead abstraction of the "other", the empty undetermined Beyond'.[40] But: 'it appears that, on the contrary, Content has itself Form, indeed it is only through Form that it has Soul and subsistence, and that it is Form itself which changes only into the show of a Content, and also into the show of a something external to this show'.[41]

Thus Hegel overcomes the formalism of Kant's philosophy not simply by seeking to demonstrate the unity of form and content, but by advancing a conception of philosophical method in which form generates its own content: 'it is Form itself which changes only into the show of a Content, and also into the show of a something external to this show'. This show is the movement of the dialectic, in which Spirit comes to self-consciousness by positing a world alien from it and then coming to recognize that world as itself. Thus the negation of the negation in which the dialectic concludes is 'the innermost and most objective moment of Life and Spirit, by virtue of which a subject is personal and free'.[42]

Further, this dialectic of (absolute) subjectivity has a circular structure. Hegel says that Logic is 'a circle which returns upon itself, for mediation bends back its end into its beginning'.[43] The dialectical movement is a process of self-

---

[38]   Hegel, *Phenomenology*, §178, p. 111.
[39]   Hegel, *Science of Logic*, I, p. 60.
[40]   Hegel, *History of Philosophy*, III, p. 472.
[41]   Hegel, *Science of Logic*, I, p. 47.
[42]   Ibid., II, p. 478
[43]   Ibid., II, p. 484.

enrichment. The original unity of its starting-point is broken down and differentiated, but this serves only as, ultimately, a confirmation of that starting-point. At the conclusion of the process, in the negation of the negation, that unity is restored, but as a higher, more developed unity, one that has been rendered self-conscious by discovering that it contains determinate contents of which it was unaware at the beginning.

The form of reasoning that Hegel employs is thus teleological in that it conceives the dialectic as moving towards a predetermined end (*telos* is the Greek word for goal). The peculiarity of this end is that it is not a purpose which a conscious subject (even God conceived as a person distinct from his creation) has selected and arranged things so that it can be achieved. The goal of the dialectic is an objective purpose, implicit in the process from the beginning. The dialectical process itself is nothing but the attainment of that goal, which consists in Absolute Spirit's coming to self-consciousness, which takes the form of 'absolute knowing', of the retrospective survey of the entire process as the way in which that moment of rational self-transparency has been achieved.

The teleological character of Hegel's thought is most clearly evident in his philosophy of history. 'World history is the progress of the consciousness of freedom', he claims, a process which culminates in the modern European nation-state. Informing this progress is a deeper meaning: 'World history is the expression of the divine and absolute process of the spirit in its highest forms, of the progression whereby it discovers its own nature and becomes conscious of itself.' The succession of political forms which reaches its climax in modernity must thus be understood as specific contributions to the self-realization of Absolute Spirit. Indeed, the conflicts of men moved by particular interests and passions are merely the instruments of 'the universal Idea', which 'keeps itself in the background, untouched and unharmed, and sends forth the particular interests to fight and wear themselves out in its stead. It is what we may call the *cunning of reason* that it sets the passions to work in its service, so that the agents by which it gives itself existence must pay the penalty and suffer the loss.'[44]

This is as much a providential view of history as that developed by Christian thinkers such as Augustine and Bossuet (see §3.3 below). Self-interested human actions serve a hidden purpose of which those performing them are quite unaware. The difference between Hegel's version and the orthodox Christian one is that in his philosophy of history the purpose human actors unknowingly serve is not the plan formulated for mankind by a personal God; rather, it is implicit in the structure of the historical process itself, and comes to consciousness in the modern age, as philosophy finally grasps the meaning of this process.

[44] Hegel, *Philosophy of World History: Introduction*, pp. 54, 65, 89.

2.3   The debate over modernity

Hegel's philosophy is the most powerful single attempt to demonstrate that modernity contains within itself the intellectual resources rationally to justify its break with the past. In doing so it seeks also to show, according to the same standards of rational justification, that the modern state is in principle capable of providing the kind of political community that can hold together the conflicts characteristic of commercial societies. The result is one of the great philosophical enterprises of Western thought.

Yet, as Habermas points out, 'as absolute knowledge, reason assumes a form so overwhelming that it not only solves the initial problem of a self-reassurance of modernity, but solves it *too well*'.[45] For example, if by the time of the French Revolution we have reached the stage where it is philosophically possible to comprehend the meaning of the historical process, what happens now? Many commentators believe that Hegel regarded his own age as marking the End of History: once the conditions for 'absolute knowing' were established, everything subsequent could only be an afterthought. The evidence that Hegel seriously entertained the idea of an End of History is at best ambiguous, but the problem posed by the concept is at least arguably a consequence of his overall conception of the dialectic.

A more fundamental difficulty is posed by Hegel's absolute idealism. As we saw in §2.2 above, he conceives the dialectic as a self-justifying process whose conclusion is implicit in its starting-point, and whose course involves thought generating its own content from itself. Stated so baldly, this is an almost megalomaniac hyper-rationalism, in which thought by virtue of its rational structure produces the world. Many later thinkers have been influenced by Hegel, but they have usually tried to water down his absolute idealism, or, as in the case of his greatest follower, Marx, explicitly rejected it.

One might pose the problem in the form of a dilemma. We can, on the one hand, take what Hegel actually says seriously. In this case, we have a philosophical system which, if valid, does succeed in demonstrating the rationality of modernity and, as a consequence, in identifying the solution to its social and political problems. But who would seriously defend the claim that the Hegelian system is valid? We can, on the other hand, try and preserve whatever we regard as what Marx called the 'rational kernel within the mystical shell' of Hegel's philosophy by trying to play down his speculative hyper-rationalism.[46]

Pinkard, for example, writes: 'The *Phenomenology* offers a dialectical-historical narrative of how the European community has come to take what it does as authoritative and definitive for itself.'[47] This narrative is '*dialectical-*

45   Habermas, *Philosophical Discourse*, p. 42.
46   Marx, *Capital* (3 vols, Harmondsworth, 1976–81), I, p. 103.
47   Pinkard, *Hegel's Phenomenology*, p. 13.

historical' since it shows one form of consciousness is replaced by another because of tensions internal to the first form. This is a much weaker meaning of 'dialectical' than what Hegel himself would have accepted, since it does not entail that the conclusion of the process consists in the definitive rational understanding of that process.

It is not clear how different this reading of the *Phenomenology* is from that offered by the postmodernist philosopher Richard Rorty, who writes: 'What Hegel describes as the process of spirit gradually becoming self-conscious of its intrinsic nature is better described as the process of European linguistic practices changing at a faster and faster pace.'[48] The self-realization of Spirit then becomes a succession of what Rorty calls 'redescriptions', none of which can be shown to be rationally superior (in the sense of offering us a better insight into the nature of reality) to any other. Such an interpretation of Hegel sacrifices his embarrassingly ambitious conception of the dialectic, but at a high price: modernity's claim to be able to demonstrate its superiority over the past ceases to be rationally defensible.

Habermas suggests that, despite these difficulties, 'Hegel inaugurated the discourse of modernity. He introduced the theme – the self-critical reassurance of modernity.' He thereby set the terms for subsequent debate, in which '[t]he relation of history to reason remains constitutive'. The basic positions towards modernity were staked out during the debates among German philosophers which followed Hegel's death in 1831, in particular as a result of the attempt of the Young (or Left) Hegelians to dissociate his concept of dialectical reason from the Absolute, and to transform it into an instrument for criticizing the existing political order (see also §4.1 below). In these debates, three basic stances towards modernity were taken:

> *Left Hegelian* critique, turned toward the practical and aroused for revolution, aimed at mobilizing the historically accumulated potential of reason (awaiting release) against its mutilation, against the one-sided rationalization of the bourgeois world. The *Right Hegelians* followed Hegel in the conviction that the substance of state and religion would compensate for the restlessness of bourgeois society, as soon as the subjectivity of the revolutionary consciousness that incited restlessness yielded to objective insight into the rationality of the status quo . . . Finally, *Nietzsche* wanted to unmask the dramaturgy of the entire stage-piece in which both – revolutionary hope and the reaction to it – enter on the scene. He removed the dialectical thorn from the critique of a reason centred on the subject and shrivelled into purposive rationality; and he related to reason as a whole the way the Young Hegelians did to its sublimations: Reason is *nothing else* than power, than the will to power, which it so radiantly conceals.[49]

---

[48]   Rorty, *Contingency, Irony, and Solidarity* (Cambridge, 1989), p. 7.
[49]   Habermas, *Philosophical Discourse*, pp. 50, 392 n. 4.

This description of the three basic positions taken up towards modernity after Hegel provides a useful framework for considering the subsequent development of social theory, provided we are willing to interpret the positions a bit more broadly than Habermas does. The first stance towards modernity is represented above all by Marx, the greatest of the Young Hegelians. He rejected Hegel's absolute idealism, but kept his concept of history as a dialectical process motored by the contradictions inherent in specific social formations. Civil society, or rather bourgeois society (the same phrase, *bürgerliche Gesellschaft*, covers both concepts in German), is not the End of History, but simply a historically transitory social form whose claims to realize individual freedom are belied by its roots in capitalist exploitation. The Enlightenment aspiration to create an authentically rational society requires a further social revolution.

The second position is best seen as embracing all those who accept modern bourgeois society as it takes shape in the wake of Hobsbawm's 'dual revolution' as the closest we can hope to get to a rationally ordered social world. Modern liberalism is a prime exemplar of this kind of stance, though its most sophisticated exponents, such as Tocqueville and Mill, show a complex awareness of the tensions and dangers of modernity (see §3.2 below). The same awareness is also displayed by Durkheim and Weber, who both make clear their emphatic belief that the hope of a social revolution that will radically improve on actually existing modernity is the merest illusion. Later sociologists operate within the same framework, though sometimes (as in the work of Parsons: see §10.2 below), the kind of critical charge that is found, say, in Tocqueville or in Weber is defused.

Finally, Nietzsche stakes out a third position – the radical rejection of modernity (see §5.3 below). His attack overlaps with that of the reactionary opponents of the Enlightenment and the French Revolution discussed below in chapter 3, but goes much further. In particular, he develops a root-and-branch critique of the kind of scientific rationality which the *philosophes* took to be the source of the modern age's legitimacy. All forms of reason, he argues, are simply particular expressions of the will to power that is the fundamental tendency in both the physical and the social worlds. Nietzsche's critique of Western reason is a fundamental point of reference both for Weber and for Heidegger (see §9.2 below); his influence is evident also in contemporary theorists associated with postmodernism, most notably Foucault (see §11.3 below).

In a sense, Habermas suggests, 'we remain contemporaries of the Young Hegelians'.[50] Yet if the fundamental positions towards modernity were staked out between the 1830s and the 1880s, they have been greatly enriched, and sometimes clarified, by the subsequent development of social theory. Or so I hope to show in the rest of this book.

[50]   Ibid., p. 53.

3

Liberals and Reactionaries

3.1 Post-Revolutionary debates

France after the fall of Napoleon, under first the restored Bourbon monarchy (1815–30) and then the Orleanist regime of Louis Philippe (1830–48), experienced a period of extraordinarily rich and wide-ranging intellectual and cultural debate. In part, this was a consequence of the fact that, as Johan Heilbron puts it, 'around the year 1800, Paris was the centre of the scientific world'.[1] A series of reforms made during the last years of the *ancien régime* and under the Revolution and the Napoleonic Empire transformed the status of scientific teaching and research in France. Thus French researchers made a decisive contribution to the formation of the new science of biology at the beginning of the nineteenth century.

At the same time, however, that the physical sciences acquired a new salience in French culture, they came under direct challenge. Romantic writers such as Chateaubriand attacked the primacy of scientific reason, championing instead the emotions and intuition. The philosophers of the Enlightenment had attached great importance to the senses and the passions, but they had not usually counterposed them to reason. In doing so, Romanticism tended also to treat art and literature as a privileged source of experiences denied to a merely scientific understanding. The slogan *l'art pour l'art* – art for art's sake – was probably coined by Benjamin Constant in 1804.[2] In the hands of Baudelaire and Flaubert in the 1840s and 1850s the idea became a systematic ideology of Aestheticism which treated art as a distinct practice detached from the social world and liberated from any attempt to require writers and painters to respect prevailing religious and political beliefs or to produce work that was socially useful or even, by conventional standards, beautiful.

The resulting debates concerned more than merely aesthetic or philosophical issues. At stake was the historical and political meaning of the French Revolution.

---

[1] J. Heilbron, *The Rise of Social Theory* (Cambridge, 1995), p. 132.

[2] Ibid., p. 157.

Chateaubriand and some other early French Romantics were aristocrats who had been driven into exile by the Revolution. Their critique of scientific rationality was associated with a nostalgia for what the arch-survivor Talleyrand called the *douceur de vivre* – the sweetness of life – under the old regime. Often this attitude took the form of a straightforward political rejection of the Revolution, most rigorously expressed in Maistre's claim that '[t]here is a satanic quality to the French Revolution that distinguishes it from everything that we have ever seen or anything that we are likely to see.'[3] After 1820 the royalist 'ultras' who dominated French ministries seemed determined to turn back the clock to before 1789.

The Revolution did not, however, come under attack merely from the right. The years after 1815 made the impact of the 'dual revolution' increasingly clear. Following Britain's example, other parts of north-western Europe, notably in France and what in 1830 became Belgium, were being transformed by the spread of factories capable of mass-producing commodities. It became increasingly clear that a new form of social polarization, between the wage-labourers working in these factories and their employers, had emerged. By the end of the 1830s Chartism, the first mass political movement based on the new industrial working class, was spreading through Britain's manufacturing areas and threatening the stability of Europe's leading power.

As early as 1813 these developments led Francis Jeffrey, editor of the great Whig journal the *Edinburgh Review*, to question the optimistic view of the development of commercial society offered by Adam Smith and his followers:

> The effect then which is produced on the lower orders of society, by that increase of industry and refinement, and that multiplication of conveniences which are commonly looked upon as the surest tests of increasing prosperity, is to convert the peasants into manufacturers, and the manufacturers into paupers; while the chances of their ever emerging from this condition become constantly less, the more complete and mature the system is which originally produced it.[4]

The development of industrial capitalism offered a different angle on the question of the French Revolution's political legacy. The slogans of 1789 were liberty, equality, and fraternity. But while the Revolution had swept away the old feudal privileges and hierarchies, and institutionalized legal equality, profound class divisions remained, and were indeed being widened thanks to the Industrial Revolution. The first socialist thinkers – most notably Charles Fourier and the Comte de Saint-Simon – emerged in France under the Empire and the Restoration. They were fiercely critical of the Revolution, which they saw as a

---

[3] J. de Maistre (1797), *Considerations on France* (Cambridge, 1994), p. 41. Joseph, comte de Maistre (1753–1821): of Savoyard background, though his writings had their main impact in France; served the House of Savoy as a diplomat, notably as ambassador to St Petersburg, 1803–17; his most celebrated work is *The Saint-Petersburg Dialogues* (1821).

[4] Quoted in D. Winch, 'The System of the North', in S. Collini et al., *That Noble Science of Politics* (Cambridge, 1983), p. 55.

largely destructive event ('Saint-Simon's great teacher was M. de Maistre', Flaubert declared[5]), and of the unjustified class privileges which had survived it. Saint-Simon saw society divided between *industriels* – those who produced society's wealth, including not merely workers and other producers but also a growing number of scientists and other experts – and *oisifs* – the idle parasites who lived off them. Fourier denounced the competitive egoism encouraged by existing 'Civilization'; he advocated the formation of co-operative communities (or *phalanstères*) whose example would gradually lead humankind into the new social condition of 'Harmony'.

The intellectual climate of post-Revolutionary France was furthermore one in which the upheavals of the previous generation had inculcated a vivid sense of both the complexity of social structures and the transformations they had recently undergone. This sense was expressed with extraordinary sociological insight in the novels of Balzac, one of whose main themes is the subversion of aristocratic values and traditions by the unrestrained pursuit of self-interest, typically in the form of money-making. In seeking to construct a 'physiology' of the human types specific to the new commercial order, Balzac portrays society as a distinctive kind of objectivity. As one of his characters declares: 'Yes, Society is another kind of Nature!'[6]

Liberalism as a distinctive political current crystallized in Restoration France against the background of the assault on the heritage of 1789 from both right and left. Its representatives, who came from a mainly Protestant background, sought to dissociate the Revolution from the Jacobin Terror. Thus Constant, as we have seen (§1.5 above), distinguished the 'modern liberty' of the individual from the classical republican conception of collective liberty defended by Rousseau and Robespierre. The liberals defended as the authentic legacy of the Revolution the individual freedoms and the parliamentary institutions which they regarded as the distinctive strengths of the British system of government and which had been grudgingly and partially conceded by the restored Bourbon monarchy in the Constitutional Charter of 1814.

The threat posed to liberal constitutionalism by the 'ultra' ministries of the 1820s provoked what Larry Siedentop calls the 'Great Debate', in which a group of liberal intellectuals known as the *doctrinaires* sought to respond to their reactionary opponents. Siedentop writes: 'Liberals had to demonstrate that what the ultras proposed was not only unjust but impossible – that even if ultras could temporarily command political power, long-standing social and economic changes in France made their aristocratic programme of hardly more than antiquarian interest.'[7]

The required historical analysis of long-term socio-economic processes was

[5]   Quoted in P. Bourdieu, *The Rules of Art* (Cambridge, 1996), p. 81.
[6]   H. de Balzac, *A Harlot High and Low* (Harmondsworth, 1970), p. 152.
[7]   L. Siedentop, *Tocqueville* (Oxford, 1994), ch. 2 (quotation from p. 22).

provided by one of the leading *doctrinaires*, Guizot, in a series of celebrated lectures between 1827 and 1830.[8] Guizot was influenced by the 'spiritualist' critique of eighteenth-century empiricism developed by philosophers such as Maine de Biran and Victor Cousin, who argued that knowledge came not only from the effect of external bodies on senses such as sight and touch, but also from man's 'internal sense', which provided thought with content, notably by way of introspection. He therefore identified two mechanisms of historical change, 'social' and 'moral' development. The first involves 'the extension, the greatest activity, the best organization of the social relations: on the one hand, an increasing production of the means of giving strength and happiness to society; on the other a more equitable distribution, among individuals, of the strength and happiness produced'. The second, by contrast, consists in 'the development of the individual, internal life, the development of man himself, of his faculties, his sentiments, his ideas'.[9]

Having thus distinguished between changes in the 'internal' and 'external' condition of man, Guizot proceeds in fact to concentrate on the latter, on 'the history of external events, of the visible and social world'. The centrepiece of the detailed analyses he offers of social institutions and processes is a description of the struggle through which the burghers, or town-dwellers, began to win local political liberties from the feudal lords in twelfth-century France. 'The formation of a great social class, the bourgeoisie, was the necessary result of the local enfranchisement of the burghers.' The rise of the bourgeoisie in turn produces

> the contest of the classes, a contest which constitutes the fact itself, and which fills modern history. Modern Europe was born from the struggle of the various classes of society. Elsewhere . . . this struggle led to very different results: in Asia, for example, one class completely triumphed, and the government of castes succeeded to that of classes, and society sank into immobility. Thank God, none of this has happened in Europe. None of the classes has been able to conquer or subdue the others; the struggle, instead of being a principle of immobility, has been a cause of progress; the relations of the principal classes among themselves, the necessity under which they found themselves of combating and yielding by turns; the variety of their interests and passions, the desire to conquer without the power to satisfy it; from all this has arisen perhaps the most energetic and fertile principle of the development of European civilization.[10]

This class struggle (depicted in terms which seem to have influenced Marx in the opening lines of the *Communist Manifesto*) is thus responsible for what is

---

[8]   François-Pierre-Guillaume Guizot (1787–1874): born in Nîmes, grandson of a Protestant pastor; his father guillotined in April 1794; Professor of Modern History at the Sorbonne, 1812–30; held a series of official posts, 1814–20; the leading politician of the Orleanist monarchy after the 1830 Revolution; Minister of Education, 1832–7; Prime Minister 1840–8; brought down by the 1848 Revolution; devoted his lengthy retirement to historical writing.

[9]   F.-P.-G. Guizot (1828), *History of Civilization in Europe* (London, 1997), pp. 16–18.

[10]   Ibid., pp. 23, 129, 130.

for Guizot the most distinctive feature of European civilization, its pluralism – 'varied, confused, stormy; all forms, all principles of social organization co-exist therein; powers spiritual and temporal; elements theocratic, monarchic, aristocratic, democratic; all orders, all social arrangements mingle and press upon one another. There are infinite degrees of liberty, wealth, and influence.'[11] This confused diversity, reflecting the inability of any one class to conquer all the others, is the source of Europe's dynamism and creative energy. The peculiar virtue of representative government, Guizot believes, is that, as demonstrated by British political experience, it permits the articulation and reconciliation of diverse and conflicting interests.

Guizot's *History of Civilization in Europe* is an example of what one of the last representatives of the Scottish Enlightenment, Dugald Stewart, called 'theoretical history'. Like the Scottish *philosophes* and Hegel before him, Guizot was able to integrate theoretical enquiry and historical narrative into a single coherent discourse. But nineteenth-century intellectuals found this synthesis increasingly hard to sustain. Another debate of the 1820s, this time among British advocates of parliamentary reform, illustrates this difficulty. This pitted Whigs against Radicals. The Whigs defended the existing British constitution as a system of 'mixed government', judiciously combining the three classical political forms of monarchy, aristocracy, and democracy; they favoured an extension of the vote, but only of the most limited kind (as was actually implemented by the Great Reform Act of 1832). The Radicals advocated a much more thoroughgoing assault on 'Old Corruption', the whole system of patronage which fuelled the Hanoverian state. In 1817 Bentham and his followers rallied to the Radical programme of universal male suffrage, annual parliaments, and the secret ballot.

James Mill's *Essay on Government* (1820) sought to justify this programme. Its premises were provided by two of the leading doctrines of Bentham's utilitarianism, namely that 'the lot of every human being is determined by his pains and his pleasures', and that 'the concern of Government . . . is to increase to the utmost the pleasures, and diminish to the utmost the pains, which men derive from one another'. Mill agrees with Hobbes that the fact that humans are guided by their individual interest in their own pleasures and pains makes government necessary. But the same fact also implies that any form of government which vests power in any group narrower than the people themselves, as both monarchy and aristocracy do, will lead to the exploitation by the rulers of the ruled. Mill dismisses the Whig doctrine of the mixed constitution and the connected idea (defended also by Guizot) of parliamentary government as the representation of interests as liable to produce merely 'a motley Aristocracy'. Only democratic government, based upon the regular election of representatives by universal male suffrage, could secure the greatest happiness of the greatest number.[12]

---

[11] Ibid., pp. 29–30.
[12] J. Lively and J. Rees, eds, *Utilitarian Logic and Politics* (Oxford, 1978), pp. 55–6, 86.

This deductive proof of the necessity of democracy was subjected to the most devastating attack by Macaulay in a series of sparkling essays in the *Edinburgh Review*, which also effortlessly parried counter-thrusts made by the Philosophical Radicals.[13] Macaulay makes much of Mill's inconsistencies – for example, his opposition to female suffrage – while at the same time making clear the reason why Whigs like him objected to the political conclusions drawn from the premisses of the *Essay on Government*: 'How is it possible for any person who holds the doctrines of Mr Mill to doubt that the rich in a democracy such as that he recommends, would be pillaged as unmercifully as under a Turkish Pacha?' But Macaulay's objection to Mill's political theory is methodological as well as political. He denounces his opponent's attempt, which he compares to the methods of the medieval schoolmen, to arrive at political generalizations by means of deductions from a few abstract truths. To this he counterposes, as the basis of 'that noble Science of Politics', 'the method of Induction', which generalizes from carefully established facts.[14]

The contrast between Mill's method, abstract and deductive, and Macaulay's, historical and inductive, is all the more striking since the former's great *History of British India* is, as John Burrow puts it, 'not only the last, it is also the most elaborate and detailed example of Scottish conjectural history'.[15] The Scottish Enlightenment had combined a general conception of human nature with a theory of history in which society passed through a succession of 'modes of subsistence' (see §1.4 above). Mill managed to hold the two together in his *History* by declaring: 'Exactly in proportion as *Utility* is the object of every pursuit may we regard a nation as civilized.'[16] In other words, societies were to be identified as more or less progressive historically to the extent that they realized Bentham's greatest happiness principle: pre-colonial India, according to Mill, turned out very badly when measured by this bench-mark, thus justifying British rule. But the tension between abstract social science and concrete historical enquiry became increasingly hard to manage.

In part this was because history was now becoming identified with the critique of the Enlightenment and the Revolution. Burke was among the very first to make this move.[17] In his *Reflections on the Revolution in France* (1790), he portrayed social and political institutions as the product of slow, unconscious,

13   Thomas Babington Macaulay (1800–59): Whig Member of Parliament, 1830–4, 1839–47, 1852–7; member of the Supreme Council of India 1834–8; also held junior ministerial posts; given a barony in 1857; a supremely accomplished essayist, but chiefly remembered for his *History of England from the Accession of James the Second* (1848–61).

14   Lively and Rees, eds, *Utilitarian Logic and Politics*, pp. 120, 128.

15   J. W. Burrow, *Evolution and Society* (Cambridge, 1966), p. 48.

16   J. Mill, *The History of British India*, ed. W. Thomas (Chicago, 1975), p. 224.

17   Edmund Burke (1729–97): Irish politician and writer; author of *Philosophical Enquiry into the Origin of Our Ideas of the Sublime and the Beautiful* (1757); member of the British Parliament, 1766–94; a critic of British misrule in America, India, and Ireland, and a defender of the old regime in Europe.

organic growth embodied in tradition and established practice: to attempt to tamper with this complex and delicate fabric on the basis of a preconceived programme of radical reform, as the French Revolution did from the very beginning, was to invite disaster. Savigny, the founder of the German Historical School of Law, took this thought further when he opposed reformers' attempts, starting with the post-Revolutionary Code Napoléon, to found the entire legal system anew. Denouncing the Enlightenment's 'blind rage for improvement', and announcing the emergence of a new 'historical spirit', Savigny argues that 'the indissoluble organic connection of generations and ages' means there can be no escaping the influence of legal tradition. This, however, 'will be injurious to us so long as we ignorantly submit to it; but beneficial if we oppose to it a vivid creative energy – obtain the mastery of it by a thorough grounding in history, and thus appropriate to ourselves the whole intellectual wealth of preceding generations'.[18]

Thus for Savigny the study of history does not serve to trace modern society's progress by comparison with its predecessors; rather, it is a way of appropriating the accumulated wisdom of a particular nation expressed in its law, which, bearing 'an organic connection . . . with the being and character of the people', evolves according to an 'inward necessity'.[19] This privileging of tradition dovetailed with the Romantics' nostalgia for the past. The nineteenth-century cult of the Middle Ages, increasingly seen not, as the Enlightenment tended to, as a benighted age of barbarism and superstition, but as a harmoniously integrated society in which every individual was allocated a meaningful role, must be seen against this background.

Indeed, treating the past as a source of values and models to be used in assessing the present could serve as the basis of a critique of industrial capitalism. Lukacs coined the phrase 'Romantic anti-capitalism' to refer to this tendency of modern Western thought. Michael Löwy and Robert Sayre define 'Romantic anti-capitalism' as *'opposition to capitalism in the name of pre-capitalist values'*. This is a protean ideological current, which could take 'restitutionist' or conservative forms, seeking respectively to restore some version of feudal society or to preserve the status quo, but which could also articulate revolutionary impulses by using some ancient model as the inspiration for creating a more egalitarian society, as in the case of the more radical of the English Romantics (Byron and Shelley) and of Fourier's Utopian socialism.[20] In any of its forms,

---

[18]   F. K. von Savigny (1814), *Of the Vocation of Our Age for Legislation and Jurisprudence* (New York, 1975), pp. 20, 22, 132–3. Friedrich Karl von Savigny (1779–1861): born in Frankfurt am Main; studied at Marburg, Jena, Leipzig, and Halle universities; appointed Professor of Roman Law at the new University of Berlin, 1810; *Grosskanzler*, i.e. head of the Prussian juridical system, 1842–8.

[19]   Ibid., p. 27.

[20]   M. Löwy and R. Sayre, 'Figures of Romantic Anti-Capitalism', *New German Critique*, 32 (1984), *passim* (quotation from p. 46).

Romantic anti-capitalism challenged modernity's claim to be self-legitimating, and judged it wanting by the measure of an idealized past.

The polarization between history and theory was also encouraged by tendencies towards the professionalization of academic life. The early nineteenth century saw the emergence of modern historiography as an empirical discipline based in the universities. The injunction of one of its founders, Leopold von Ranke, to show the past 'wie es eigenlich gewesen' – as it actually happened – was an attempt to liberate historical enquiry from its classical role of providing practical guidance and to distance it from philosophies of history such as Hegel's. In fact, the new historiography was never as theoretically innocent as it claimed – Ranke, for example, conceived modern Europe as an organic unity of competing nations each endowed with its own unique character whose conflicts were regulated by the mechanism of the balance of power, and the rest of the world as barbarous or decadent. Nevertheless, the insistence in particular that professional historians should base their studies on archival research helped make the old Scottish style of 'conjectural history' seem obsolete.

Economics also evolved into a professional academic discipline, especially after the 'marginalist revolution' of the 1870s, which finally disposed of the remnants of Ricardo's labour theory of value. Smith had conceived political economy in broad terms, as 'a *branch* of the science of a statesman or legislator'.[21] The *Wealth of Nations* contains as much history as it does abstract analysis. But, by the late nineteenth century, the dominant definition of the subject, especially as given by British and Austrian economists, conceived economics as a formal and deductive science based on certain abstract propositions about human nature (arrived at, in fact, with the help of Bentham's utilitarianism). This move, which was strongly contested by the German school of historical economists, who preferred a much more inductive and descriptive approach, had already been justified by James's son John Stuart Mill in his 1836 essay 'On the Definition of Political Economy'. [22]

Here he calls economics 'an *abstract* science' and compares it to geometry:

> What is commonly understood by the term 'Political Economy' is not the science of speculative politics, but a branch of that science. It does not treat of the whole of man's nature as modified by the social state, nor of the whole conduct of man in society. It is concerned with him solely as a being who desires to possess wealth, and who is capable of judging the comparative efficacy of the means for obtaining it. It predicts only such of the phenomena of the social state as takes place in

[21]   Quoted in D. Winch, 'Higher Maxims', in Collini et al., *Noble Science*, p. 65.

[22]   John Stuart Mill (1806–73): his intensive education by his father and Bentham drove him to a nervous breakdown, described in his *Autobiography*; like his father he worked at the East India Company; assistant examiner, 1828–56; examiner, 1856–8; the first leading liberal to champion the emancipation of women.

consequence of the pursuit of wealth. It makes abstraction of every other human passion or motive; except those which may be regarded as perpetually antagonizing principles to the desire of wealth, namely, aversion to labour, and desire of the present enjoyment of costly indulgences.[23]

Before Marx, Comte was the major figure who sought to resist this process of scientific fragmentation and to seek to preserve social theory and historical enquiry as an integrated intellectual project.[24] His basic framework was provided by a philosophy of history recognizably derived from that of Turgot and Condorcet. Comte claimed to have discovered 'a great fundamental law, to which the mind is subjected to by an invariable necessity', namely that 'every branch of knowledge passes in succession through three different theoretical states: the theological or fictitious state, the metaphysical or abstract state, and the scientific or positive state'. In the theological stage, phenomena are explained by imagining fictitious beings – gods and the like; the metaphysical stage replaces these with more abstract but still imaginary entities such as essences and causes.

> Finally, in the positive state, the human mind, recognizing the impossibility of obtaining absolute truth, gives up the search after the origin and hidden causes of the universe and a knowledge of the final causes of phenomena. It endeavours now only to discover, by a well-combined use of reasoning and observation, the actual laws of phenomena – that is to say, their invariable relations of succession and likeness.[25]

Comte is thus the founder of positivism, broadly understood as the idea that the modern sciences constitute the only valid form of human knowledge. More interestingly, as Heilbron points out, he was 'the first to develop a *historical* and *differential theory of science*'.[26] Comte conceives his 'positive philosophy' as 'the observation of the rational methods that actually direct our various scientific researches'. He therefore proceeds to a detailed classification of the sciences, whose development he conceives as a process of progressive differentiation. The sciences constitute a definite order – what he calls an 'encyclopaedic series' – starting with the most abstract and complex, and proceeding

---

[23] *The Collected Works of John Stuart Mill*, IV (London, 1967), pp. 325, 323.

[24] Auguste Comte (1798–1857): expelled from the École Polytechnique in 1816 for political activity; worked as Saint-Simon's secretary before seeking to formulate his own theoretical system; the *Course of Positive Philosophy* (1830–42) (in which he coined the term 'sociology') originated as lectures delivered to an audience which included many of the leading French scientists of the day; suffered from mental illness in his later years; the *System of Positive Polity* (1851–4) sought to construct a 'Religion of Humanity'.

[25] A. Comte, *Cours de philosophie positive* (2 vols, Paris, 1975), I, pp. 21, 21–2; *Introduction to Positive Philosophy* (Indianapolis, 1970), pp. 1, 2.

[26] Heilbron, *Rise*, p. 200.

according to the greater specificity and complexity of each successive discipline: thus 'the six fundamental sciences' are mathematics, astronomy, physics, chemistry, physiology, and 'social physics', or sociology.[27]

Comte's conception of the sciences in general and of 'social physics' was deeply influenced by the formation of modern biology in the early years of the nineteenth century. Cuvier and other researchers sought to characterize the distinctiveness of living organisms by means of the concept of organization: every organism was a self-regulating system oriented on certain basic functions such as feeding, breathing, and reproduction. Comte closely analysed this conceptual revolution and sought to translate it into the study of the social world.

Following Condorcet, he sees the fundamental cause of historical change as lying in 'the general and necessary progress of the human spirit': the law of the three stages thus provides the basis of 'the science of social development'. This 'idea of the continuous progress, or rather of the gradual development of humanity' distinguishes sociology from biology. But in the study of 'social statics', the laws of coexistence of social phenomena, the biological concept of consensus, that is, of 'the fundamental solidarity of all the possible aspects of the social organism', plays a critical role. Indeed, 'the real notions of order and progress must, in social physics, be as strictly indivisible as in biology are those of organization and of life, from which indeed in the eyes of science they derive'. The 'revolutionary crisis of modern societies' arises from the way in which, since 1789, order and progress have been counterposed, so that 'all the great efforts in favour of order have been guided by a retrograde spirit, and the principal efforts for progress by radically anarchical doctrines'.[28] The positive philosophy may thus help to overcome this crisis by removing 'the actual confusion of men's minds' caused by 'the simultaneous employment of three radically incompatible philosophies – the theological, the metaphysical, and the positive'.[29]

This first encounter between biology and social theory in Comte's writings was to be of great moment. By explicitly formulating the concept of social evolution and associating it with the processes of growing complexity that contemporary biological scientists were seeking to conceptualize, Comte exerted a powerful influence on later theorists, notably Spencer (see §5.2 below) and Durkheim. But his own substantive social theory – and in particular his prediction that consensus would be re-established through the vesting of moral and intellectual authority in a 'Spiritual Power' modelled on the Catholic Church – caused even admirers such as the younger Mill to quail.[30] Those seeking a deeper understanding of modernity after the Revolution would have to look elsewhere.

[27]   Comte, *Cours*, I, pp. 41, 64; *Introduction*, pp. 20, 66–7 (translation modified).
[28]   Comte, *Cours*, II, pp. 101, 112, 123, 16; S. Andreski, ed., *The Essential Comte* (London, 1974), pp. 137, 138, 162, 150, 127 (translation modified).
[29]   Comte, *Cours*, I, p. 38; *Introduction*, p. 29.
[30]   J. S. Mill (1865), *Auguste Comte and Positivism* (Ann Arbor, 1961).

3.2 Agonistic liberalism: Tocqueville and Mill

No one more clearly expressed the dilemmas of the post-Revolutionary epoch than John Stuart Mill. He sought to remain faithful to Bentham's and his father's utilitarianism, and indeed was the major British thinker most receptive to Comte's positivism; at the same time, however, he showed a painful awareness of the Romantic critique of the soulless scientific rationality of modern Europe. His economic writings helped to lay the basis of modern economics as the abstract deductive science of self-regulating markets. But, in the penultimate book of his *Principles of Political Economy* (1848), he predicted that the tendency of the rate of profit to fall which Ricardo had attributed to the law of diminishing returns (see §1.5 above) would reach a 'minimum' where investment and output would no longer increase. Mill thought this 'stationary state' might in certain circumstances represent an improvement on the present, and further anticipated that 'the relation of masters and workpeople will be gradually superseded by partnership' in the form of either 'associations of the labourer with the capitalist' or 'association of the labourers among themselves'.[31]

The ambivalences endemic to Mill's thought are an example of what John Gray has felicitously called '*agonistic liberalism*', by which he means 'a stoical and tragic liberalism of unavoidable conflict and irreparable loss among inherently rivalrous values'.[32] Regarding modernity as the highest possible social expression of human rationality – what Habermas calls the 'Right Hegelian' position on modernity (see §2.3 above) – does not imply that one is necessarily blind to the costs and tensions involved in achieving and maintaining this form of society. Weber is the later social theorist who most fully embodies this complex view. But the most interesting representative of agonistic liberalism in the post-Revolutionary period is undoubtedly Tocqueville.[33]

Tocqueville's roots in the Norman nobility might have turned him against the French Revolution. Indeed, his great-grandfather Malesherbes, previously a prominent critic of the *ancien régime*, perished on the guillotine for serving as Louis XVI's defence lawyer when the latter was tried before the Revolutionary Convention; only Robespierre's fall saved Tocqueville's parents from a similar fate. Nevertheless, early on he identified himself with the liberal defenders of

---

[31] *The Collected Works of John Stuart Mill*, III (London, 1965), p. 769.

[32] J. Gray, *Isaiah Berlin* (London, 1995), p. 1. Gray coins the phrase to refer more or less exclusively to Berlin's version of liberalism (though he does recognize Weber as a precursor: ibid., p. 58). But the expression seems to admit wider application, particularly since Gray's claims for Berlin's originality are somewhat overstated.

[33] Alexis-Charles-Henri Clérel, comte de Tocqueville (1805–59): born into the old Norman nobility; trained as a lawyer and employed briefly as a magistrate; toured the United States and Canada, 1831–2; parliamentary deputy, 1839–48; member of the National Assembly, 1848–51; Minister of Foreign Affairs, 1849; retired from politics after Louis-Napoleon Bonaparte's 1851 *coup d'état*.

the Revolution under the Restoration, writing later: 'I have broken with part of my family, with beloved attachments and precious memories, to embrace the cause and ideas of '89.'[34] Confronted with Gobineau's theory of racial inequality (see §3.3 below), he expostulated: 'Do you not see inherent in your doctrine all the evils engendered by permanent inequality – pride, violence, scorn of fellow men, tyranny and abjection in all their forms?'[35]

Nevertheless, Tocqueville's aristocratic background may have allowed him to consider the problematic condition of contemporary society with a greater detachment than, say, the troubled Mill. The intellectual framework of his writings is, in many respects, an eighteenth-century one reflecting particularly the influence of Montesquieu. He systematically contrasts aristocracy and democracy, but relates this less to political institutions in the first instance than to the entire complex of ideological and social conditions associated with these different forms of government. In doing so he was following the example of Guizot and the other *doctrinaires* during the 'Great Debate' of the 1820s (see §3.1 above). As Larry Siedentop puts it,

> Restoration liberals called the emergent society 'democratic', whereas eighteenth-century Scots had called it 'commercial'. The difference is revealing. The Scottish usage made the 'mode of subsistence' perhaps the crucial factor in social change, whereas French liberals emphasized the different beliefs or norms which helped to constitute aristocratic and democratic societies – the former marked by inequality of rights and conditions, the latter by equality of rights and conditions.[36]

Tocqueville also took one of his leading themes from the *doctrinaires*. They feared that the bureaucratic and centralized state developed under the absolute monarchy, further strengthened by the Revolution and the Empire, and inherited by the Restoration regime represented a fundamental threat to individual freedom. In 1822 their leader, Royer-Collard, warned that greater social equality was producing an 'atomized society' (*société en poussière*) vulnerable to bureaucratic despotism.[37] This concern informs Tocqueville's writings. His last major work, *The Ancien Régime and the Revolution* (1856), left unfinished at his death, charts the development of centralization under the Bourbon monarchy, and seeks to demonstrate how it fragmented French society, and encouraged the kind of abstract and irresponsible intellectual speculation which reached its apogee in the Jacobin regime.

The problem of centralization also forms the starting-point of Tocqueville's

---

[34]   Letter to Corne, 13 Nov. 1845, quoted in A. Jardin, *Tocqueville* (New York, 1988), p. 396.
[35]   Letter to Gobineau, 17 Nov. 1853, in J. A. de Gobineau, *Selected Political Writings*, ed. M. D. Biddiss (London, 1970), p. 178.
[36]   Siedentop, *Tocqueville*, p. 27.
[37]   Ibid., p. 26.

main contribution to social theory, in the two volumes of *Democracy in America* (1835, 1840). Since, 'sooner or later, we shall arrive, like the Americans, at an almost complete equality of condition', the point of studying the United States is to acquire a better sense of the direction in which Europe is moving. Tocqueville is struck by the Americans' success in organizing a republican form of government on a continental scale, and at the same time sustaining a high degree of decentralization, reflected not simply in the federal constitution, but especially in the vitality of New England township meetings. He nevertheless discovers a new version of the old danger in the shape of 'the tyranny of the majority' expressed both in the operation of political institutions and the power of public opinion:

> The authority of a king is physical and controls the actions of men without subduing their will. But the majority possesses a power that is physical and moral at the same time, which acts upon the will as much as upon the actions and represses not only all contest, but all controversy.
>
> I know of no country in which there is so little independence of mind and real freedom of discussion as in America.[38]

Tocqueville's diagnosis of the threat to individual freedom represented by the tyranny of the majority, particularly in the shape of public opinion, heavily influenced Mill in his best-known work, *On Liberty* (1859). Characteristically he there seeks to square the circle by reconciling a right of individual self-development with utilitarianism's concern with the greatest happiness of the greatest number, appealing to 'utility in the largest sense, grounded in the permanent interests of man as a progressive being'. Meanwhile, Mill warns that Europe is 'decidedly advancing towards the Chinese ideal of making all people alike'.[39] This fear that the West was declining into a static Oriental despotism obsessed many nineteenth-century liberals. Tocqueville himself saw such a condition as a consequence of centralization: 'China appears to me to present the most perfect instance of that species of well-being which a highly centralized administration may furnish to its subjects. Travellers assure us that the Chinese have tranquillity without happiness, industry without improvement, stability without strength, and public order without public morality.'[40]

Mill's reflections on the problem take the form of a contribution to normative political theory – that is, he seeks to characterize in abstract terms the nature of individual freedom and to identify the limits of legitimate state interference in that freedom. Tocqueville offers, by contrast, particularly in the second volume of *Democracy in America* (1840), a socio-historical analysis of the circumstances productive of threats to modern liberty. There, in the

---

[38] A. de Tocqueville, *Democracy in America* (2 vols, New York, n.d.), I, pp. 14, 273.
[39] J. S. Mill, *On Liberty* (Harmondsworth, 1974), pp. 70, 138.
[40] Tocqueville, *Democracy*, I, p. 94 n. 49.

tradition of early modern French *moralistes* and of Montesquieu (see §1.3 above), he concentrates less on exploring the political and social structures, and more on examining the *moeurs* – the beliefs and customs – characteristic of democratic societies.

Tocqueville depicts a form of life governed primarily by the attainment of individual well-being. This helps to explain the peculiar dynamism and restlessness of democratic societies, as each individual seeks to maximize his material gratifications. It also accounts for a certain 'softening' of manners, and for the replacement of patriarchal authority within the family by relations based on affection and intimacy. But this transformation of the family highlights one of the critical consequences of equality of condition, a powerful tendency towards the privatization of social life: 'Democracy loosens social ties but tightens natural ones; it brings kindred more closely together, while it throws citizens more apart.'[41]

Democratic societies are permeated with individualism. Tocqueville is careful to distinguish this quality from the universal and instinctually based defect of selfishness, or excessive self-love (*egoïsme*). Individualism is a modern phenomenon 'of democratic origin'; it consists in 'a mature and calm feeling, which disposes each member of the community to sever himself from the mass of fellows and to draw apart with his family and friends, so that after he has thus formed a little circle of his own, he willingly leaves society at large to itself'. Its effect is in particular to undermine the individual citizen's incentive to take part in public life. 'Selfishness blights the germ of all virtue; individualism, at first, only saps the virtues of public life; but at the same time it attacks and destroys all the others and is at length absorbed in downright selfishness.'[42]

The absorption of individuals in their private affairs which equality of condition encourages facilitates the destruction of political freedom. Thus equality and despotism 'perniciously complete and assist each other. Equality places men side by side, unconnected by any common ties; despotism raises barriers to keep them asunder; the former predisposes them not to consider their fellow creatures, the latter makes general indifference a sort of public virtue.' Indeed, Tocqueville fears a distinctively modern form of despotism combining 'the principle of centralization and that of popular sovereignty', 'an immense and tutelary power, which takes it upon itself alone to satisfy their [i.e. the citizens'] gratifications and to watch over their fate', an 'absolute, minute, regular, provident, and mild' power that keeps men 'in perpetual childhood'.[43]

It is no part of Tocqueville's argument that this new form of benevolent despotism is an inevitable consequence of equality of condition. On the contrary, he claims that '[t]he Americans have combated by free institutions the

[41]   Ibid., II, p. 208.
[42]   Ibid., II, p. 104.
[43]   Ibid., II, pp. 109, 336–7.

tendency of equality to keep men asunder and they have subdued it.' He lays particular stress on the role of civil and political associations in American life, since 'associations ought, in democratic nations, to stand in lieu of those powerful private individuals whom equality of condition has swept away'.[44] They may thus, like Montesquieu's 'intermediary powers' stand between the naked individual and a potentially over-mighty state.

But Tocqueville conceives of the role of 'free institutions' as more than the negative one of imposing limits on central power. Just as individualism saps public institutions by undermining civic participation, so the remedy lies in encouraging citizens to play an active role in political life: hence Tocqueville's interest in the direct democracy of the New England town meeting. As Roger C. Boesche points out, '[t]his insistence on widespread democratic participation as an essential component to the word *freedom* . . . sets him apart from almost all his nineteenth-century liberal counterparts.'[45]

In Mill and the *doctrinaires* we can see take shape what Judith Sklar memorably called the 'liberalism of fear', whose 'overriding concern is to secure the political conditions that are necessary for the exercise of personal freedom'.[46] From this perspective, public life can easily be represented as a threat, something to be warded off in order to preserve the private zone of individual freedom. In conceiving the public sphere more positively, and citizenship as active participation in political affairs, Tocqueville harks back to the classical republican tradition of Machiavelli and Rousseau.

The overall effect of Tocqueville's analysis is, however, greatly to increase the sense of modernity as inherently conflicted. Thus he characterizes the long-term consequences of the 'democratic revolution' on men in the following terms: 'They had sought to be free in order to make themselves equal; but, in proportion as equality was more established with the aid of freedom, freedom itself was thereby rendered more difficult of attainment.'[47] This presented the political problems of modern times as much more deep-seated than a liberal of a slightly earlier generation such as Constant had suggested. For Constant the French Revolution had gone off the rails by seeking to achieve an ancient collective freedom inapproriate to modern commercial societies (see §1.5 above). Tocqueville, by contrast, argued that there was an endemic conflict between the two prime modern values of equality of condition and individual freedom. So, of the ideals of the French Revolution, liberty and equality were eternally at odds with one another, while fraternity had dissolved into the endless pursuit of private gratification endemic in democratic societies.

---

[44] Ibid., II, pp. 110, 117.

[45] R. C. Boesche, 'The Strange Liberalism of Alexis de Tocqueville', *History of Political Thought*, 2 (1981), p. 518.

[46] J. N. Sklar, 'The Liberalism of Fear', in N. L. Rosenblum, ed., *Liberalism and the Moral Life* (Cambridge, Mass, 1989), p. 21.

[47] Tocqueville, *Democracy*, II, p. 333.

This diagnosis has helped to constitute the problem-situation of modern social theory. Tocqueville's analysis of the privatizing tendencies of modern democracy evidently has contemporary resonances. It has been deployed in order to provide the social underpinnings of one of the more interesting accounts of postmodernity.[48] And his exploration of the causes and consequences of political centralization is plainly an important contribution to the discourse on modern bureaucracy most fully developed by Weber. Tocqueville's dissection of democratic society does, however, suffer from an obvious weakness which is perhaps closely related to the preoccupations with *moeurs* and with public life that are the source of the insights it offers. As noted above, in drawing on Montesquieu and the earlier *moraliste* tradition, he effectively sidesteps the analysis of commercial society developed by the Scottish Enlightenment.

This precludes him from considering, as Hegel had already begun to do (see §2.1), the extent to which the problems of modernity were related to the distinctive economic mechanisms and class antagonisms of what Marx would soon call capitalist society. It is not that Tocqueville ignores economic matters. He notes the Americans' absorption in 'a kind of virtuous materialism' as they pursue their private pleasures amidst the bustle and instability of commercial life. He also argues, in what is in effect a side-glance at the effects of the Industrial Revolution in Britain, that the division of labour is subordinating workers to their masters, and producing thereby a 'manufacturing aristocracy' that is 'one of the harshest that ever existed in the world' (though, because the manufacturers lack a sense of collective identity, 'one of the most confined and the least dangerous').[49] But Tocqueville shows little of the understanding displayed in their different ways by Smith, Hegel, Ricardo, and the younger Mill that modern life is bound up with a new form of economic system with its own peculiar dynamics and conflicts. His writings, for all the insights they offer, resonate as much with early modern political thought as they do with the work of later theorists for whom the existence of capitalism has become a fundamental reference-point.

3.3 Providence and race: Maistre and Gobineau

Less surprisingly perhaps, the same quality of being situated as it were midway between older ways of thinking and the theoretical revolution represented by the Enlightenment is displayed by the most resolute opponents of the French Revolution. Maistre is a particularly interesting example of this stance. His political writings repeatedly affirm that human affairs are governed by divine Providence: 'Nothing happens by chance in this world, and even in a secondary

[48]   G. Lipovetsky, *L'Ère du vide* (Paris, 1983).
[49]   Tocqueville, *Democracy*, II, 141, 170.

sense, there is no disorder, for disorder is commanded by a sovereign hand that submits it to a rule and forces it to contribute to a good.'[50]

The immediate source of this providential view of history is undoubtedly the great seventeenth-century Catholic divine Bossuet.[51] In his *Discourse on Universal History* (1681) Bossuet argues that the successive epochs of world history (which he conceives largely in biblical terms as the ages of Adam, Noah, Abraham, and so on) are permeated by God's secret plan.

> This is why all those who govern feel themselves subjected to a greater power. They achieve more or less than they intended, and their plans never lack unexpected effects. Neither are they masters of the dispositions which past centuries have made in affairs, nor can they predict the course which the future will take, far from being able to force it. He alone holds all in his hands, who knows the name of everything that is and that is not yet, who presides over all times, and anticipates all discussions.[52]

Bossuet's hold on nineteenth-century French intellectuals is indicated by the fact that even Comte praised 'the great Bossuet' for conceiving 'universal history' as 'one homogeneous series'.[53] Maistre employs Bossuet's framework in order to analyse contemporary events, but he paints a much darker picture than Louis XIV's court preacher did at the apogee of Bourbon absolutism. The French Revolution, as we have seen, Maistre declares to be 'radically *bad*'. But its evil is merely one instance of that which permeates the whole of creation. He spurns the 'modern philosophy that tells us *all is good*': 'in a very real sense, *all is evil*, since nothing is in its place'. Indeed, the king of Dahomey was right to say that 'God made the world for war', as is shown by 'the long series of massacres that has soiled every page of history. One sees war raging without interruption, like a continued fever marked by terrifying paroxysms.'[54]

From this perspective, imbued with a pervasive sense of original sin, '[m]an is evil, horribly evil.' Social order is maintained only through the regular application of violence. Thus the executioner is 'the horror and the bond of human association. Remove this incomprehensible agent from the world, and at that very moment order gives way to chaos, thrones topple and society disappears.' For '[e]vil exists on the earth and acts constantly, and by a necessary consequence it must be continually repressed by punishment.'[55]

What, then, is the meaning of the French Revolution according to Maistre? It

50   Maistre, *Considerations*, p. 9.
51   Jacques Bénigne Bossuet (1627–1704): Bishop of Condom, 1669–81; Bishop of Meaux, 1681–1704; tutor of the Dauphin (for whom he wrote the *Discourse*); most celebrated for his sermons; even Voltaire admired his prose style.
52   *Oeuvres complètes de Bossuet* (19 vols, Besançon, 1840), IX, p. 262.
53   Comte, *Cours*, II, p. 237; *Essential Comte*, p. 200.
54   Maistre, *Considerations*, pp. 41, 31, 23, 24.
55   J. Lively, ed., *The Works of Joseph de Maistre* (London, 1965), pp. 200, 192–3.

is impossible for the republican regime to sustain itself indefinitely (Maistre wrote the *Considerations on France* in 1796, not long after Robespierre's fall), for 'nothing is new, and a large republic is impossible, since there has never been a large republic'. Moreover, since 'every imaginable institution is founded on a religious concept', a form of government which blasphemously claims to base itself on human reason alone is doomed from the start. The suffering caused by the Terror and the Revolutionary Wars are God's punishment for the impious arrogance evinced by this claim: 'in our epoch, coming down to our level, Providence punishes like a human tribunal'.[56]

But God condescends to use even the 'vilest instruments' for his own larger purposes: 'this monstrous power, drunk with power and success, the most frightful phenomenon that has ever been seen and the like of which will never be seen again, was both a horrible chastisement for the French and the sole means of saving France'. The triumph of the counter-revolution over the republic would have meant France's eclipse in the European state system. The Jacobins, with their centralizing ruthlessness and revolutionary *élan*, were the means through which this outcome was prevented, and France's leading position was preserved for God's plan. Thus: 'When we think about it, we can see that once the revolutionary movement was established, only Jacobinism could have saved France and the monarchy.'[57]

In a brilliant essay on Maistre, Isaiah Berlin argues that his 'deeply pessimistic vision is the heart of the totalitarianisms, of both left and right, of our terrible century'.[58] Yet, in conceptual terms at least, there is very little that is new in Maistre. His view of a world ruled by evil, war, and bloodshed, though expressed in particularly forceful terms, derives from orthodox Augustinian Christianity's claim that the Fall of Man introduced a radical fault into God's creation. Maistre's political theory proper combines a bizarre revival of the medieval doctrine that the pope is the source of all secular authority with the traditional claims of classical thought. Thus, as we have seen, he rules out the possibility of the French republic surviving because 'nature and history together', or rather ancient and early modern philosophers and historians, 'prove that a large indivisible republic is an impossibility'. What distinguishes Maistre is the extremity of his political language – itself a reaction to both the novelty and (to him) the moral scandal the Revolution represented, and the lucid realism he often displays in his analyses. Thus he argues that revolutions have their laws, which will, in time, favour the restoration of the monarchy. He notes, for example, the emergence of an 'aristocracy of office' in Revolutionary France that will, as in Cromwellian England, help produce the desire for political stability necessary to revive the monarchy.[59]

[56] Maistre, *Considerations*, pp. 33, 41, 14.
[57] Ibid., pp. 8, 16.
[58] I. Berlin, *The Crooked Timber of Humanity* (London, 1991), p. 127.
[59] Maistre, *Considerations*, pp. 32, 90.

An undeniably new note is, however, sounded by Gobineau.[60] His *Essay on the Inequality of the Human Races* (1853–5) takes aim at two of the basic assumptions of the Enlightenment. First, Gobineau denies the idea of historical progress. He does not believe, for example, that the moderns have achieved any real intellectual or political improvement on ancient Greece and Rome. His concern is with 'the fall of civilizations', 'the most striking, and at the same time, the most obscure, of all the phenomena of history'. The decline of civilization is, moreover, inevitable: 'every assemblage of men, however ingenious the network of social relations that protect it, acquires on the very day of its birth, hidden among the elements of its life, the seed of its inevitable death'.[61]

Why are civilizations doomed to collapse? Gobineau's answer to this question represents his second challenge to the Enlightenment. As the title of the essay declares, he rejects the idea of human equality which was axiomatic for the *philosophes*, however much this assumption might be qualified by, for example, the racism we saw Hume and Jefferson display towards blacks (§1.5 above). Gobineau declares: 'The irreconcilable antagonism between different races and cultures is clearly established by history, and such innate repulsion must imply unlikeness and inequality.' His classification of humankind reduces them to variants of three fundamental races – in descending order of intellectual and physical powers and even of beauty, the 'white', the 'yellow', and the 'black'. 'The great human civilizations are but ten in number and all of them have been produced upon the initiative of the white race', and in particular of the Aryans originating in central Asia who are the source of all that is vigorous and creative in the European racial stock.[62]

Yet decline and death are, as we have seen, built into every civilization from the start. The fundamental cause is the tendency for different races to mix. Civilizations are typically founded by the colonization or conquest of an inferior 'female' race by a superior 'male' one. The master-race usually has fewer members than the groups over whom it rules. Conquerors and conquered inevitably intermarry: initially this racial mixing invigorates the civilization, but, over time, it progressively drains away the original vitality of the masters. The civilization accordingly degenerates: 'The word *degenerate*, when applied to a people, means . . . that the people has no longer the same intrinsic value as it ought to have, because it has no longer the same blood in its veins, continual adulterations having gradually affected the quality of that blood.' The outcome can be seen in the confusion of races and cultures that demoralized and

---

[60] Joseph Arthur de Gobineau (1816–82): born to a bourgeois family in Bordeaux, though he assumed the title of comte in 1855; trained as an Orientalist; after working as a journalist, Tocqueville's secretary when the latter was Foreign Minister in 1849; thereafter served as a diplomat till 1877.

[61] Gobineau, *Selected Political Writings*, pp. 42, 43.

[62] Ibid., pp. 133, 142.

ultimately destroyed imperial Rome. Modern Europe is returning to this 'state' of '*romanity*' as the Aryan stock is adulterated through admixture with 'degenerate' races.[63]

Gobineau's racial theory was merely the most systematic articulation of a widespread ideological reorientation which occurred in mid-nineteenth-century Europe. The Western colonization of the rest of the world encouraged some European intellectuals to treat racial difference as the fundamental category by means of which to understand the social world. Robert Knox, the Edinburgh anatomist who employed the grave-robbers Burke and Hare, expressed essentially the same view as Gobineau's when he declared in *The Races of Man* (1850): 'race is everything; literature, science, art – in a word, civilization, depends on it'.[64]

The development of particular forms of knowledge could be mobilized in support of this construction of race. Thus William Jones's suggestion at the end of the eighteenth century that the classical Hindu language of Sanskrit was the common ancestor of a distinctive family of Indo-European languages was reinterpreted in racial terms, so that linguistic affinities became signs of the existence of a common Aryan race. Maine's anthropological writings, immensely influential on Victorian thought, were informed by the assumption that '[c]ivilization is nothing but a name for the old order of the Aryan world, dissolved but perpetually reconstituting itself under a vast variety of solvent influences.'[65]

Gobineau's elaboration of such beliefs into a philosophy of history effected a fateful fusion of biology and social theory. One can detect in his writings the obsessions with degeneration and miscegenation which permeate subsequent racist literature, including *Mein Kampf*. It would, however, be a mistake to overstate the modernity of Gobineau's thought. The concept of biological evolution, whose complex intermingling with racist ideology I consider in chapter 5, is quite absent from it. The *Essay* antedates Darwin's *Origin of Species*, which was published in 1859. Despite his own ambivalence towards Christianity, Gobineau in his account of the sources of racial difference accepts the biblical figure for the age of the earth of between 6,000 and 7,000 years.

The fact that different human groups can successfully interbreed leads him reluctantly to reject the idea of polygenesis – the simultaneous creation of several distinct human races – which had fascinated the Enlightenment. But, if the human species began as one, it soon broke apart into races whose differences are 'absolutely fixed, hereditary, and *permanent*'. These differences 'were fixed in the earliest epoch of our terrestrial life . . . that immediately after the crea-

---

[63]   Ibid., pp. 59, 153.
[64]   Quoted in Burrow, *Evolution*, p. 130.
[65]   Quoted in ibid., p. 161. Sir Henry Maine (1822–88): occupied chairs in law at Oxford and the Inns of Court, and then, after serving as Legal Member of the Council of India, 1862–9, at Oxford again and Cambridge; most celebrated work: *Ancient Law* (1861).

tion, when the earth was still shaken by its recent catastrophes and without any defence against the fearful effects of their last death-throes'. The races formed in this terrible geological shaking up are set onto permanently different paths: 'their primordial unity cannot and does not have the slightest influence on their destinies'.[66]

This quasi-theological conception of history informs Gobineau's account of the future as well as that of the origins of humankind. History reveals no dynamic principle – say, what Darwin would soon call natural selection (see §5.1 below) – merely the constant patterns arising from conquest and racial intermixture: 'transcending any transitory or voluntary action of either an individual or a nation, these fundamental determining factors in life operate with imperturbable independence and impassiveness'. Their inevitable outcome will be the disappearance of the human species. The ultimate achievement of the great Aryan peoples has been to create a single world-civilization, thereby fulfilling 'the supreme goal of all history', for 'the ultimate aim of the toil and suffering, the pleasures and triumphs of humanity is to attain, one day, supreme unity'. But the attainment of this unity implies the racial confusion and degeneration which destroyed Rome, now on a global scale, and hence the disappearance of the white race. Racial weakness will bring in its wake population decline, and eventually the 'final obliteration' of humanity in another 6,000 or 7,000 years' time.[67]

So Gobineau, like Maistre, sees the hidden hand of Providence at work in history. His version of this philosophy of history culminates in the fatalism with which Tocqueville taxed him in their correspondence. Gobineau claimed that his theory depicted humankind's fate beyond good and evil: 'I am not telling people "You are acquitted" or "You are condemned". I am saying "You are dying."'[68] Fascist ideology would take his view of history as race war, and his obsession with biological degeneration, and marry them to the idea of a decisive assertion of collective will. In this form, Gobineau's pessimism would help incubate horrors beyond the imagination of even the darkest nineteenth-century thinkers.

---

[66] Gobineau, *Selected Political Writings*, pp. 103, 106–7, 167.
[67] Ibid., pp. 163, 171–2, 174.
[68] Letter to Tocqueville, 20 Mar. 1856, ibid., p. 181.

4

Marx

4.1 The adventures of the dialectic

Hegel's response to the profound tensions which the aftermath of the French Revolution had exposed in European society was to interpret them as specific instances of a much larger pattern. World history was essentially a process of constant transformation driven by the contradictions internal to and constitutive of successive social and political forms. Yet at the same time as thus dramatically generalizing from the experience of his own generation, caught up as it was in the whirl of the 'dual revolution', Hegel sought to freeze the dialectical process, to treat it as a circular movement which simply developed what was implicit in its starting-point and whose conclusion consisted in the reconciliation of all conflicts within the self-transparency of Absolute Spirit. The effect was to undercut the awareness of tension and instability expressed in his claim that 'Contradiction is the root of all movement and life'. Dialectical reason can then seem like an almost Buddhist quietism, the contemplation of the eternal pattern of things well captured in these lines of T. S. Eliot (himself a student of the late Victorian British Hegelians): 'Only by the form, the pattern, I Can words or music reach I The stillness, as a Chinese jar still I Moves perpetually in its stillness.'[1]

Quite aside from the philosophical difficulties involved in Hegel's absolute idealism, his description of his philosophy of history as 'a theodicy' which 'should enable us to comprehend all the ills of the world, including the existence of evil, so that the thinking spirit may be reconciled with the negative aspects of existence' seemed to imply the kind of complacent acceptance of suffering and oppression that Voltaire had attacked in *Candide*.[2] It was

---

[1] T. S. Eliot, 'Burnt Norton', in *Collected Poems 1909–1962* (London, 1963), p. 194.
[2] G. W. F. Hegel, *Lectures on the Philosophy of World History: Introduction* (Cambridge, 1975), pp. 42–3.

precisely against this stance that the great Russian critic of the 1830s and 1840s, Vissarion Belinsky, rebelled:

> I thank you most humbly, Eger Fedorovich [i.e. Hegel], I acknowledge your philo-
> sophical prowess, but with all due respect to your philosophical cap and gown, I
> have the honour to inform you that if I should succeed in climbing to the highest
> rung of the ladder of progress, even then I would ask you to render me an account
> of all the victims of life and history, of all victims of chance, superstition, the
> Inquisition, Philip II, and so forth. Otherwise I should hurl myself head first from
> that very top rung.[3]

But what if one were to liberate Hegel's dialectic from his absolute idealism, and to abandon his essentially theological attempt to justify 'the existence of evil'? Then one could truly say, in the words of Belinsky's contemporary Aleksandr Herzen: 'The philosophy of Hegel is the algebra of revolution.'[4] This was the step that Marx took.[5] He was by no means the first to have the idea of setting Hegel on his feet, as Engels famously put it – that is, of secularizing the Hegelian dialectic.[6] Hegel's philosophy exercised a peculiar fascination for young radical intellectuals in the 1830s and 1840s. This was particularly so not simply, as we have seen, in Russia, but in Germany itself. In these countries the Holy Alliance – the absolute monarchies of Austria, Russia, and Prussia – sought after 1815 systematically to repress any signs of a revival of the radical-democratic impulses unleashed by the French Revolution. In this climate of repression and censorship, political criticism was displaced onto philosophical speculation. 'In politics the Germans *thought* what other nations did', Marx later wrote.[7] Hegel said much the same thing: 'We have commotion of every

---

[3]   Letter to Botkin, Mar. 1841, quoted in A. Walicki, *A History of Russian Thought from the Enlightenment to Marxism* (Stanford, 1979), p. 124.

[4]   A. Herzen, *My Past and Thoughts*, abr. edn, ed. D. Macdonald (Berkeley, 1982), p. 237.

[5]   Karl Heinrich Marx (1818–83): born in Trier to a secularized Jewish family; studied law and then philosophy at Bonn and Berlin universities; editor-in-chief of the *Rheinische Zeitung*, 1842–3; moved to Paris in 1843 and Brussels in 1845; leader of the Communist League, 1847–50; editor-in-chief of the *Neue Rheinische Zeitung*, 1848–9; after the defeat of the 1848 Revolution went into exile in London, where he spent the rest of his life, often in great poverty; founder and leader of the International Working Men's Association (the First International), 1864–72.

[6]   K. Marx and F. Engels, *Collected Works* (50 vols, London, 1975–   ), XXVI, p. 383; hereinaf-ter *CW*. Friedrich Engels (1820–95): born in Barmen to a family of Protestant mill-owners; worked in Manchester for the family firm Ermen and Engels, 1842–4, obtaining the material for *The Con-dition of the Working Class in England*; Marx's closest friend and collaborator from 1844 onwards; took part in armed struggles in Elberfeld and the Palatinate during the death-agony of the 1848 Revolution; worked at Ermen and Engels, 1850–69, providing the Marx family with indispensable financial support; edited the second and third volumes of *Capital* after Marx's death; during the last twenty-five years of his life, his home in London became one of the main centres of the British and international labour movement.

[7]   *CW* III, p. 181.

kind within us and around us, but through them all the German head quietly keeps its nightcap on and silently carries on its operations beneath it.'[8]

By the 1840s 'the German head' was thinking revolution. The group of young German intellectuals known as the Young Hegelians emerged at the beginning of this decade. They had in common the aim of emancipating the Hegelian dialectic from the Absolute, but differed over precisely what this implied. Bruno Bauer, for example, argued that Absolute Spirit was merely a metaphor for human self-consciousness. He thereby replaced Hegel's absolute idealism with a version of subjective idealism, according to which history was a succession of forms of consciousness. Feuerbach by contrast developed a much more original critique of Hegel based on a version of the naturalistic materialism which became increasingly influential in German intellectual culture around the middle of the nineteenth century.[9]

Feurbach's main tools in this critique were the concepts – taken over by Marx – of inversion and alienation. He argued that the different forms of religion, reaching their climax in Christianity, involved the transposition of distinctively human powers onto alien and fictional entities. This was a process of inversion: the 'subject' – man, the active and creative factor in history – was reduced to the status of a 'predicate', that is, of a dependent attribute, the creation of a being – God – that was in fact the product of the human imagination. It was also a process of alienation: man lost his essential powers to a being which he conceived as fundamentally other than him. Hegel's absolute idealism was a rarefied and abstract version of this same process, in which everything physical and human is reduced to means for the self-realization of an impersonal God, the Absolute, that was just as imaginary as the more naïve versions worshipped in conventional religions. What was required, Feuerbach argued, was an inversion of this inversion. Man must recognize himself as the real subject of the process, thereby resuming control over the capacities he had ascribed to God and the Absolute, and recognizing these latter entities for the fictions they were.

Though Feuerbach rightly saw himself as a critic of Hegel, his arguments remained in many ways within a Hegelian framework. Hegel also conceived the dialectical process as one of alienation, in which Spirit loses itself in Nature, which it counterposes to itself as an other, only to rediscover later the essential identity of subject and object, self and other. Moreover, the emancipation Feuerbach seeks from the hold of religion and idealism is an intellectual one. For all his philosophical differences with Bauer, he too conceived history as a succession of forms of consciousness; both argued that political liberation from Prussian absolutism depended on a process of enlightenment. In particu-

[8]   G. W. F. Hegel, *Lectures on the History of Philosophy* (3 vols, London, 1963), III, p. 426.

[9]   Ludwig Andreas Feuerbach (1804–72): his most important work, *The Essence of Christianity* (1841), was translated into English by the novelist George Eliot; declared: 'Der Mensch ist was er isst' – Man is what he eats.

lar, the Young Hegelians tended to see the critique of religion as the precondition of any broader political challenge to the established order in Germany. In this they recapitulated the French Enlightenment's conception of history as (in Condorcet's words) 'the progress of the human mind', and its view of orthodox Christianity as the main underpinning of the *ancien régime*. The German head had thus not yet shed its nightcap.

Marx in his first political writings in the early 1840s displays both his growing discomfort with this broad approach and an attempt to use some of Feuerbach's main categories to develop a more materialistic analysis of society. Thus in the *Contribution to a Critique of Hegel's Philosophy of Right* (1843), he persistently taxes Hegel with inverting subject and predicate by treating political institutions as expressions of the Absolute Idea. Marx concedes that '[i]t shows Hegel's profundity that he feels the separation of civil from political society as a *contradiction*.' Rather, however, than the state reconciling the conflicts of civil society, '[t]he atomism into which civil society plunges in its *political act* follows necessarily from the fact that the community, the communal being in which the individual exists, is civil society separated from the state, or that the *political state* is an abstraction from it.' The modern state is indeed like God in Feuerbach's critique of Christianity – an alienated projection of the communal social life which only exists in the impoverished form of a civil society riddled with competition and instability. Fortunately, however, civil society is beginning to transcend this alienated condition by demanding political expression in the form of universal male suffrage: '*Electoral reform* within the *abstract political state* is therefore the demand for its *dissolution*, but also for the *dissolution of civil society*.'[10]

Marx thus identifies Feurbachian inversion – the restoration of the real subject to its proper place – with the most radical political demand of the day, and thus (not only in his argument but also in the minds of Europe's ruling classes) with social revolution. Plainly, pursuing this analysis required taking a closer look at the structure of civil society. Like Hegel before him, Marx closely studied the classical political economists. These researches helped to prompt an important shift away from Feuerbach. As a first approximation to characterizing the extent of the latter's break with Hegel, one might say that he replaced the Absolute with Man as the subject of the dialectic. But what is Man? Feuerbach rejected the more straightforward forms of individualism: 'The essence of man is contained only in the community, in *the unity of man with man*.'[11]

To underline both the primacy of the communal over the individual, and humanity's growing awareness of this truth, Feuerbach often tended to use the expression 'species-being' (*Gattungswesen*) to refer to human nature. His account of species-being was, however, fraught with difficulties. Thus a central

[10]   *CW* III, pp. 75, 79, 121.
[11]   L. Feuerbach, *Manifestes philosophiques*, ed. L. Althusser (Paris, 1973), p. 198.

aspect of the human essence that had been concealed by Christianity and idealist philosophy was, Feuerbach argued, man's unity with nature. Man's awareness of this, and more particularly of his neediness, his dependence on nature,
derived more from his senses and emotions than his reason (there is a Romantic
strain in Feuerbach's philosophy). As this summary suggests, Feuerbach conceives man's relationship to nature as essentially passive: one of his key concepts, sensibility (*Sinnlichkeit*), was used by Kant to designate the receptive
faculty through which sense-impressions are taken in by human consciousness.
Thus conceived, species-being is abstract and indeterminate, offering little access to the rich historical development which Hegel had so successfully achieved.
It was therefore highly vulnerable to Max Stirner's attack in *The Ego and its
Own* (1844) on the concept of 'Man' as simply the latest in a series of abstract
'spooks' – God, the State, the Absolute – which merely served to suppress the
irreducible reality of the individual subject.

Marx makes extensive use of the concept of species-being in the first major
work to reflect his reading of classical political economy, the *Economic and
Philosophic Manuscripts of 1844*, but he gives it a radically different content.
Human beings' relationship to nature is indeed fundamental, but it is an active
relationship defined by the productive activities through which they transform
their physical and social environment. This stance implies a more positive appraisal of Hegel's philosophy than Feuerbach's: 'Hegel's standpoint is that of
modern political economy. He grasps *labour* as the *essence* of man.' The trouble is that 'the only labour which Hegel recognizes is *abstractly mental
labour*'.[12] It is necessary instead to understand labour naturalistically, as
the co-operative activities undertaken by human beings in order to produce
the use-values required to meet their needs.

Once this step is taken, one's view of history is transformed. Marx, in the
Manuscripts at any rate, still treats it as a process of alienation, but what is
alienated now is not the Idea or Man, but social labour. Modern bourgeois society is the very acme of alienation, since it rests on the worker's loss of control
over his labour and his subordination to the capitalist. '*Private property* is thus
the product, the result, the necessary consequence of *alienated labour*.' Indeed,
'[p]olitical economy has merely formulated the laws of estranged labour.' It
follows from this diagnosis that alienation cannot be cured by any mere intellectual enlightenment. Ending the alienation of labour requires social – or more
precisely socialist – revolution: 'the emancipation of society from private property is expressed in the *political* form of the *emancipation of the workers*.'[13]

Marx's transformation of Hegel and Feuerbach made a break with the Young
Hegelians inevitable, a move consummated in *The German Ideology* (1845–7).
This work is at once the first outline of what would become known as the mate-

---

[12]   *CW* III, p. 333.
[13]   *CW* III, pp. 279, 280.

rialist conception of history and an unrelenting polemic against the idealism of the Young Hegelians. Before going on to consider Marx's historical materialism in the following section, it is worth pausing briefly to reflect on the novel view of the relationship between beliefs and representations, on the one hand, and social relations and institutions, on the other, which these writings of the 1840s began to develop.

The idea that thoughts were to be considered not solely in terms of their truth-content, but also with respect to the social role they might perform was very far from new. The more radical *philosophes* had attacked orthodox Christianity as a body of myths which helped to sustain an unjust social order. Thus Holbach argues that 'despotism is the work of superstition'. Superstition itself is an essentially intellectual fault: 'Man is superstitious only because he is fearful; he is fearful only because he is ignorant.' Rulers and priests conspire to keep men ignorant: 'The majority of sovereigns are afraid to enlighten men; accomplices of the priesthood, they ally themselves with it to smother reason and to persecute all those who have the courage to announce it.' The solution is therefore to encourage rational thinking, for '*[a]s soon as man dares to think, the empire of the priest is destroyed.*'[14]

Man's intellectual underdevelopment and self-interested manipulation thus combine to preserve social oppression. Against the background of such beliefs the stress laid by both the Enlightenment and the Young Hegelians on the theoretical exposure of religious myth as the precondition of political liberation becomes intelligible. Already in Feuerbach, however, we see a shift. He argues that the various forms of religious alienation cannot be understood as mere error. They represent a necessary stage in the development of human consciousness: in particular, the most advanced state of alienation in Christianity is a precondition of man's arriving at consciousness of himself as a species.

Marx takes this analysis, which evidently reflects Hegel's influence, a step further. In a famous passage of his 1843 Introduction to *A Contribution to the Critique of Hegel's Philosophy of Right*, he writes: '*Religious* distress is at the same time the *expression* of real distress and also the *protest* against real distress. Religion is the sigh of the oppressed creature, the heart of a heartless world, just as it is the spirit of spiritless conditions. It is the *opium* of the people.' Usually only the final sentence is quoted, but, set in the context of the entire passage, it figures in an argument that religion cannot be understood primarily as a set of false beliefs, or even as the work of manipulative priests and kings. Religious faith is a reflection of real needs in a distorted social world, the displacement of the aspiration to a better life onto a world beyond. Consequently, '[t]he demand to give up illusions about the existing state of affairs is the *demand to give up a state of affairs which needs illusions.*'[15] Religious

---

[14]   Baron d'Holbach, *Textes choisis* (Paris, 1957), I, pp. 137, 143, 123, 142.
[15]   *CW* III, pp. 175, 176.

illusions will thus survive any purely intellectual refutation so long as the social conditions which produced them continue to exist. Present here is the kernel of Marx's theory of ideology – that is, of his attempt to show that the widespread acceptance of certain beliefs has social causes which arise from the contradictions of class society. What, then, are these contradictions?

4.2   History and capitalism

Marx wrote in 1852:

> I do not claim to have discovered either the existence of classes in modern society or the struggle between them. Long before me, bourgeois historians had described the historical development of this struggle between the classes, as had bourgeois economists their economic anatomy. My own contribution was 1. to show that the *existence of classes* is merely bound up with *certain historical phases in the development of production*; 2. that the class struggle necessarily leads to the *dictatorship of the proletariat*; 3. that this dictatorship itself constitutes no more than a transition to the *abolition of all classes* and to a *classless society*.[16]

The Scottish Enlightenment made possible the exploration of the 'economic anatomy' of the classes by developing a conception of history as a succession of 'modes of subsistence' (see §1.4 above). Marx took over this conception of history: thus *The German Ideology* follows *The Wealth of Nations* in treating the development of the division of labour as the motor of historical progress. Marx, however, elaborates a considerably more complex set of concepts than those used by Smith or Millar. The master-concept of his theory of history is that of the mode of production. Though this expression has several uses in Marx's writings, its most important is to specify a number of basic economic types of society. Thus he refers to the ancient (or slave), the Asiatic, the feudal, and the capitalist modes of production. Each of these constitutes a distinctive socio-economic system with its own 'laws of motion'.

The Scots' 'modes of subsistence' were characterized by the form of technology on which they were based – hunting, pasturage, agriculture, and manufacture. As the list just given indicates, Marx's modes of production are distinguished, in the first instance, by the social relations they involve. Each mode is in fact a complex, internally differentiated entity. It combines a given level of development of the productive forces with a specific set of production relations (or, as Marx sometimes puts it, social relations of production). The productive forces consist, in the first instance, in the basic elements of production – human labour-power and the material means of production it employs.

---

[16]   Letter to Weydemeyer, 5 Mar. 1852, *CW* XXXIX, pp. 62, 65.

Their use represents the productive powers of the society in question, measured by the productivity of labour.

The level of development of the productive forces reflects at any given time the particular technology human beings use in order to meet their needs. This technology presupposes knowledge of nature which is applied in production. The operation of this technology, further, typically involves a particular form of social co-operation among the direct producers, what Marx in *Capital* calls the 'labour-process'. Changes to the labour-process, resulting from the discovery of new techniques, or from improvements in the social organization of production, allow increases in the productivity of labour – in other words, the development of the productive forces.

This account of the productive forces reflects Marx's view of human beings as inventive social producers. Social co-operation is an essential feature of human existence. He contemptuously dismisses what he calls the 'Robinsonades' of bourgeois thought, which seek to develop a theory of society by starting from man alone in the state of nature, as if he were Robinson Crusoe on his desert island: 'Production by an isolated individual outside society . . . is as much an absurdity as is the development of language without human beings living *together* and talking to each other.'[17] Human beings at the same time, however, have a flexibility and a capacity to monitor self-consciously their thoughts and actions that is denied other animal species. They are therefore able to innovate, to come up with new ways of producing, thanks to which the productive forces develop.

Marx calls the labour-process 'the universal condition for the metabolic interaction between man and nature, the everlasting nature-imposed condition of human existence'. As we saw in the previous section, he envisages the relationship between humanity and its natural environment as a dynamic one. Improvements in the productive forces allow human beings to gain greater control over their physical context. But the labour-process represents only one aspect of social production:

> The taste of the porridge does not tell us who grew the oats, and the process we
> have presented does not reveal the conditions under which it takes place, whether
> it is taking place under the slave-owner's brutal lash or the anxious eye of the
> capitalist, whether Cincinnatus undertakes it tilling his couple of acres, or a sav-
> age, when he lays low a wild beast with a stone.[18]

To answer these questions it is necessary to consider the relations of production. These consist fundamentally in the social relations of effective control over the productive forces: 'Whatever the social form of production, workers and means of production always remain its factors . . . For any production to

[17] K. Marx, *Grundrisse* (Harmondsworth, 1973), p. 84.
[18] K. Marx, *Capital* (3 vols, Harmondsworth, 1976–81), I, pp. 290–1.

take place they must be connected. The particular form and mode in which this connection is effected is what distinguishes the different economic epochs of the social structure.'[19] The nature of this 'connection' between labour-power and the means of production depends crucially on who controls them. Where they are controlled by the direct producers themselves, either collectively (as under primitive or advanced communism) or individually (as in certain egalitarian peasant societies), the scope for class differentiation is extremely limited. Classes and the conflicts between them arise where a minority controls the productive forces.

Exploitation provides the link between minority control and class antagonism. It occurs wherever a group has consolidated a sufficient degree of control over the productive forces to compel the direct producers to labour not simply to meet their own needs, and those of their dependants, but also to support this dominant group. Exploitation thus consists in the appropriation of surplus labour – that is labour over and above the necessary labour required to support the direct producers – by the minority controlling the productive forces. The result is the division of society between exploiters and exploited. It is this necessarily antagonistic relationship which is the basis of class division. As Geoffrey de Ste Croix puts it, 'class . . . is essentially the way in which exploitation is reflected in a social structure'.[20] Modes of production are thus to be differentiated, not according to the form of technology which they use, but in terms of the kind of exploitation on which they rest: 'What distinguishes the different economic formations of society . . . is the form in which this surplus-labour is in each case extorted from the immediate producer, the worker.'[21]

The resulting conception of the social structure is succinctly summarized in this famous passage:

> The specific form in which unpaid surplus-labour is pumped out of the direct producers determines the relationship of domination and servitude, as this grows directly out of production itself and reacts back on it in turn as a determinant. On this is based the entire configuration of the economic community arising from the actual relations of production, and hence also its specific political form. It is in each case the direct relationship of the owners of the conditions of production – a relationship whose particular form naturally corresponds to a certain level of development of the type and manner of labour, and hence to its social productive power – in which we find the innermost secret, the hidden basis of the entire social structure, and hence also the political form of the relationship of sovereignty and dependence, in short, the specific form of the state in each case.[22]

[19] Ibid., II, p. 120.
[20] G. E. M. de Ste Croix, *The Class Struggle in the Ancient Greek World* (London, 1981), p. 51.
[21] Marx, *Capital*, I, p. 325.
[22] Ibid., III, p. 927.

Marx develops and elaborates the complex set of distinctions which constitutes his theory of modes of production in the course of writing the vast body of manuscripts devoted to the study of one particular mode – capitalism – and culminating in the three volumes of *Capital* (1867, 1885, and 1894). Here his starting-point is provided by classical political economy, and in particular by Ricardo, who does indeed portray the class structure of modern society as an antagonistic one, since landlords, capitalists, and workers can each only increase their respective shares of the net product by reducing those of the others (see §1.5 above). But neither Ricardo nor any other classical economist distinguishes between the forces and the relations of production. They are therefore led to assume in particular that any complex productive process must necessarily be organized through investment by a private enterpreneur who claims compensation in the form of profit.

Marx introduces the concept of production relations in *The Poverty of Philosophy* (1847) in order to distinguish capital, conceived as a historically specific social relationship, from the means of production (machinery and the like) which it uses. The effect of confusing technology and social relations, as the political economists do, is to eternize bourgeois society by presenting its specific features as necessary prerequisites of production:

> When the economists say that present-day relations – the relations of bourgeois production – are natural, they imply that these are the relations in which wealth is created and productive forces developed in conformity with the laws of nature. These relations therefore are themselves natural laws independent of the influence of time. They are eternal laws which must always govern society. Thus there has been history, but there is no longer any.[23]

Necessarily, therefore, Marx's stance towards classical political economy is a critical one – he both appropriates and transforms its leading theories by approaching them from within a very different framework. Thus he takes over Ricardo's labour theory of value, but makes it the basis of his account of capitalist exploitation. Capitalism is what Marx calls a system of generalized commodity production – in other words, the products of labour typically take the form of commodities which are bought and sold on the market. Their market prices tend to gravitate around their values – that is, the socially necessary labour time required to produce them. But labour-power itself is a commodity. In other words, capitalist relations of production presuppose the separation of the direct producers from the means of production – the often brutal process of dispossessing peasants of their land that Marx describes in the English case in part 8 of *Capital*, volume I.

The expropriation of the peasantry gives rise to the peculiarly ambiguous freedom of the worker under capitalism: he is 'free in the double sense that as a

[23] *CW* VI, p. 174.

free individual he can dispose of his labour-power as his own commodity, and that, on the other hand, he has no other commodity for sale . . . he is free of all the objects needed for the realization of his labour-power'.[24] The relationship between worker and capitalist on the labour market is similarly ambiguous. In formal, legal terms, they are equal, since the worker is not a slave or a serf subject to the direct physical power of his or her prospective employer. But in real terms, those of the relations of production, they are unequal, since the worker must sell his or her labour-power in order to live while the capitalist controls the means of production which the worker lacks. The result of their market exchange is thus a bargain on unequal terms, as a result of which the worker is exploited.

Marx's account of this process depends critically on the distinction between labour and labour-power. Labour-power is a commodity like any other, and it therefore has a value that consists in the value of those goods and services which the worker must purchase in order to live and that is represented by the wage he or she is paid. The *use* of this labour-power consists in the activity of labour. Labour, according to the labour theory of value, is the source of the value of commodities. Now the worker typically creates more value in a working day than the value of his or her labour-power. Four hours may be taken up with necessary labour, which creates value equal to that of the consumer goods the daily wage can purchase; the other four hours, of surplus labour, create *surplus value* for the capitalist, value for which he has advanced no corresponding value. The profits of capital consist in this surplus value, representing the worker's unpaid surplus labour, and thus, Marx claims, are nothing but the fruits of exploitation.

This argument posits a systematic discrepancy between how things appear and how they really are in capitalist society. The surface consists in 'the sphere of circulation or commodity-exchange', of market transactions such as those between capitalist and worker. These apparently consist in exchanges between free and equal commodity-owners, 'a very Eden of the innate rights of man . . . the exclusive realm of Freedom, Equality, Property and Bentham'. Beneath the surface, however, once we enter 'the hidden abode of production', we discover that the worker is exploited. An understanding of the underlying structure of the capitalist economy is, however, impeded by the very operation of that economy. The fact that the products of human labour circulate on the market gives rise to what Marx calls 'the fetishism of the commodity': 'the definite social relation between men themselves . . . assumes here, for them, the fantastic form of a relation between things'.[25]

Since the social relationship between producers is mediated by the exchange of their products, the market economy comes to be seen as an autonomous

[24]   Marx, *Capital*, I, pp. 272–3.
[25]   Ibid., I, pp. 279–80, 165.

process governed by natural laws beyond human control. The extreme version of this fetishism is what Marx calls the 'trinity formula' developed by post-Ricardian economists, according to which the three 'factors of production' – land, labour, and capital – each derives an income (respectively, rent, wages, and interest) by virtue of its contribution to the productive process. This theory, which completely effaces the distinction between the forces and relations of production,

> completes the mystification of the capitalist mode of production, the reification of social relations, the immediate coalescence of the material relations of production with their historical and social specificity: the bewitched, distorted, topsy-turvy world haunted by Monsieur le Capital and Madame la Terre, who are at the same time social characters and things.[26]

What commodity fetishism thus occults is not simply the contradiction between capital and labour. Marx in fact identifies two fundamental conflicts constitutive of the capitalist mode of production. The first consists in the exploitation of wage-labour; the second arises from the competitive accumulation of capital and is responsible for the regular economic crises to which bourgeois society is liable. This mode of production is distinguished from earlier forms of class society by, among other things, the fact that the prime objective of exploitation is not the consumption of the exploiters themselves. The bulk of the surplus value extracted from the working class is reinvested in the expansion and improvement of production.

This process, the accumulation of capital, had already been highlighted by Smith and other political economists. Marx's account of its causes is not fundamentally different from theirs, but it sets them in a broader historical context, and his assessment of its consequences does part company from theirs. The bourgeoisie, he argues, is a class divided among competing, mutually antagonistic, capitals: 'Capital exists and can only exist as many capitals.'[27] Individual capitalists compete with each other in order to gain for themselves the largest possible share of the surplus value they have collectively extracted from the working class: 'The capitalists, like hostile brothers, divide among themselves the loot of other people's labour.'[28]

It is this process of competition which is responsible for the accumulation of capital. Marx rejects any cultural or psychological explanation for the priority the capitalist gives to accumulation: 'in so far as he is capital personified, his motivating force is ... but the acquisition and augmentation of exchange-values ... As such, he shares with the miser an absolute drive towards self-enrichment. But what appears in the miser as the mania of an individual is

---

[26] Ibid., III, p. 969 (translation modified).
[27] Marx, *Grundrisse*, p. 414.
[28] K. Marx, *Theories of Surplus-Value* (3 vols, Moscow, 1963–72), II, p. 29.

in the capitalist the effect of a social mechanism in which he is merely a cog.'[29] An individual firm which fails to match its rivals' investment in productivity-enhancing innovations will find itself undercut and driven out of business. This is the 'social mechanism' that promotes capitalism's tendency to expand the productive forces. The peculiar dynamism and instability of bourgeois society arise from this tendency:

> The bourgeoisie cannot exist without constantly revolutionizing the instruments of production, and thereby the relations of production, and with them the whole relations of society . . . Constant revolutionizing of production, uninterrupted disturbance of all social conditions, everlasting uncertainty and agitation distinguish the bourgeois epoch from all earlier ones. All fixed, fast-frozen relations, with their train of ancient and venerable prejudices and opinions, are swept away, all new-formed ones become antiquated before they can ossify. All that is solid melts into air, all that is holy is profaned, and man is at last compelled to face with sober senses, his real conditions of life, and his relations with his kind.[30]

These celebrated lines from the *Communist Manifesto*, written shortly before the 1848 revolutions, explain the 'everlasting uncertainty and agitation' of modern times as a consequence of the particular motivations which capitalist production relations encourage in economic actors. But, if this condition is thus historically situated, its termination is also announced. Capitalism is not the end of history, merely a transitory form of social production. The very tendency towards capital accumulation that is the source of its dynamism also reveals its inherent limits.

In the third volume of *Capital*, Marx discusses the tendency of the rate of profit to fall which Ricardo had already postulated (see §1.5 above). Ricardo based his explanation of this tendency on Malthus's law of population: diminishing returns in agriculture would make it more expensive to produce food and thereby cause wages to rise and profits to fall. Henryk Grossman describes this theory as 'pseudo-dynamics, as the dynamic factor is not inherent in the economic process itself, but is rather a natural force which influences the economic process from the outside'.[31] Marx, by contrast, treats the tendency of the rate of profit to fall as a consequence of the intrinsic character of capitalism as a socio-economic system.

Central to his account is the suggestion that capital accumulation will progressively change the structure of production itself. To conceptualize this structure Marx distinguishes between variable capital, which is invested in employing labour-power, and constant capital, the value of machinery, raw materials, and

---

[29]   Marx, *Capital*, I, p. 739.
[30]   *CW* VI, p. 487.
[31]   H. Grossmann, 'Marx, Classical Political Economy and the Problem of Dynamics', II, *Capital and Class*, 3 (1977), p. 67.

other means of production (the rationale for these names is that only variable capital is responsible for the self-expansion of capital, since labour is the source of surplus value). The investment imposed on capitals by competition tends to be labour-saving – in other words, it increases the productivity of labour by allowing fewer workers to produce a given output with the help of more machinery. The ratio of constant to variable capital – what Marx calls the organic composition of capital – therefore rises. A given investment is therefore liable to consist in a larger proportion of capital invested in the means of production and a smaller proportion invested in labour-power than in the immediate past. But only labour-power creates value and surplus value. If the total investment grows relative to the variable capital invested in labour-power, then the rate of profit – the return the capitalist makes on this total investment – must fall.

An obvious objection to this theory is that it is surely irrational for capitalists to undertake investments which lead to a fall in the rate of profit. Marx's explanation appears to lack what are sometimes called 'microfoundations' – in other words, it gives no account of the motivations which would lead capitalists to produce this result. In fact, Marx does provide such an account. He suggests that innovations are initiated by some individual capitalist who undertakes a productivity-enhancing investment because it will lower his costs of production below the average for his sector. The innovator is thereby able to reap extra profits and to undercut his rivals. They in turn must copy his innovation if they are to stay in business. Once they do so, average costs in the sector fall to the level established by the innovator. His special advantage disappears, but, as a result of this round of innovation, the organic composition of capital has risen, and so the overall rate of profit falls. A series of individually rational decisions produces a globally irrational result. Smith had pointed to the way in which individual actions combine to produce unintended consequences (see §1.3 above): here, however, there is no 'invisible hand' to ensure that these consequences maximize the general welfare.

Two other features of Marx's theory of what he calls 'the law of the tendency of the rate of profit to fall' are worth noting. First, whereas Ricardo explains falling profits by falling productivity (specifically in the agricultural sector), for Marx they are a consequence of *rising* productivity. The growth of means of production relative to labour-power represents the increased productivity of labour: each worker operates a larger quantity of machinery and processes more raw materials in order to produce a greater number of goods. Yet the expression in value terms of this development of the productive forces is the rising organic composition of capital and hence a fall in the rate of profit: 'The progressive tendency for the general rate of profit to fall is thus simply *the expression, peculiar to the capitalist mode of production*, of the progressive development of the social productivity of labour.'[32]

---

[32] Marx, *Capital*, III, p. 319.

Secondly, Marx only posits a *tendency* of the rate of profit to fall rather than an absolute trend. He argues that there are 'counteracting influences at work, checking and cancelling the effect of the general law, and giving it simply the character of a tendency'. Indeed: 'the same causes which produce a fall in the general rate of profit provoke counter-effects that inhibit this fall, delay it and in part even paralyse it'. Marx discusses various such 'counteracting factors', though perhaps the most interesting of these – recurrent economic crises – is not formally listed as one. 'Crises are never more than momentary and violent solutions of the existing contradictions,' he argues, 'violent eruptions that re-establish the disturbed balance for the time being.' Crises occur when the fall in the rate of profit makes new investment irrational. Output and employment fall, and firms go bankrupt. This process represents the destruction of capital, since assets decline in value and may even be physically scrapped. The effect is to reduce the overall amount of capital in the economy. But the falling rate of profit originated in the fact that total investments had risen relative to the source of surplus value, namely labour-power. The destruction of capital during a recession, by reducing the size of these investments, will tend to restore the rate of profit to a level where economic expansion can be resumed:

> The periodical devaluation of the existing capital, which is a means, immanent to the capitalist mode of production, for delaying the fall in the profit rate and accelerating the accumulation of capital-value, disturbs the given conditions within which the process of circulation and reproduction-process of capital take place, and is therefore accompanied by sudden stoppages and crises in the production process. [33]

Economic crises are thus 'immanent' to the capitalist mode of production as both a consequence of, and a means of temporarily overcoming, the tendency of the rate of profit to fall. Yet the fact that stable economic growth can only be restored for a while by such disruptive means is a sign of the inherent limits of bourgeois society: 'The *true barrier* of capitalist production is *capital itself.*'[34] The business cycle of boom and slump which Marx was the first systematically to analyse arises from the extreme tensions caused by the subordination of the development of the productive forces to the priorities of competitive accumulation.

4.3   Class struggle and revolution

The conflict which Marx discerned between the forces and relations of production in capitalist society was, he believed, merely one instance of a larger pattern. Successive modes of production have each experienced a systemic crisis deriving from this same conflict:

[33]   Ibid., III, pp. 339, 345, 347, 358.
[34]   Ibid., III, p. 358.

At a certain stage of development, the material productive forces of society come into conflict with the existing relations of production or – this merely expresses the same thing in legal terms – with the property relations within the framework of which they have operated hitherto. From forms of development these relations turn into their fetters. Then begins an epoch of social revolution.[35]

Each mode of production thus experiences, broadly speaking, two phases – the first in which the relations of production stimulate the development of the forces of production, the second in which they become limits to further economic growth. A peculiarity of the capitalist mode of production is that both these phases are to some degree integrated in the trade cycle, growth and stagnation succeeding each other during the course of each individual cycle. How, then, do these structural contradictions, the result of tendencies inherent in every mode of production, bring about social revolution, and thus the establishment of new production relations permitting the further development of the productive forces?

It is here that the class struggle assumes particular importance. Marx and Engels gave their most precise formulation of its role in 1879, near the end of the former's life: 'For almost 40 years we have emphasized that the class struggle is the immediate motive force of history and, in particular, that the class struggle between bourgeoisie and proletariat is the great lever of modern social revolution.'[36] To call the class struggle 'the *immediate* motive force of history' suggests that there is a more fundamental one behind it. Marx in fact posits two mechanisms of historical change – the tendency for structural contradictions to develop between the forces and relations of production, and the class struggle arising from the division of society between exploiters and exploited. The latter is a chronic feature of every class society – 'an uninterrupted, now hidden, now open fight', in the words of the *Manifesto* – but it becomes more intense when a systemic crisis develops, ushering in 'an epoch of social revolution'.[37]

Do such periods of acute class struggle inevitably produce social revolution itself? Numerous commentators have been quick to claim that Marx believed that they do, and accordingly to ascribe to him a fatalistic or deterministic conception of history. There are certainly passages in his writings which support such an interpretation. Thus, after describing the expropriation of the small producers during the phase of the 'primitive accumulation' of capital, Marx declares: 'But capitalist production begets, with the inexorability of a natural process, its own negation. This is the negation of the negation' in which the capitalist expropriators are themselves expropriated.[38] Here we see the influence on him of the teleological philosophy of history developed by Hegel and

[35] K. Marx, *A Contribution to the Critique of Political Economy* (London, 1971), p. 21.
[36] *CW* XXIV, p. 269.
[37] *CW* VI, p. 482.
[38] Marx, *Capital*, I, p. 929.

inherited by Feuerbach, according to which alienation is a necessary phase of development in order to achieve the full, enriched self-consciousness that is the goal of the dialectical process (see §§2.2 and 4.1 above).

Yet much of Marx's thinking is hard to reconcile with such a historical tele-ology. 'Men make history,' he famously wrote, 'but they do not make it just as they please; they do not make it under circumstances chosen by themselves, but under circumstances directly encountered, given and transmitted from the past.'[39] Human action is constrained, this passage suggests; it is subject in particular to the structural limits constituted by the forces and relations of production, but it is not determined in such a way as to make what happens the inevitable conse-quence of these limits. In the even more celebrated opening lines of the *Mani-festo*, Marx says that the class struggle in the past 'each time ended, either in the revolutionary reconstitution of society at large, or in the common ruin of the contending classes'. This suggests that the systemic crisis of a mode of produc-tion poses alternatives rather than determining outcomes. But the same chapter concludes with the prediction that the 'fall [of the bourgeoisie] and the victory of the proletariat are equally inevitable'.[40]

Two poles can thus be detected in Marx's thought, each resting on one of the mechanisms of historical change he posits – the tendency for the productive forces to develop, on the one hand, with the implications of inevitable progress this can be made to carry, and the class struggle, on the other, full of contingen-cies and uncertainties. Later Marxists would gravitate towards one of these poles – for example, Kautsky towards the first and a more fatalist version of historical materialism (see §5.2 below), Lukács towards the second and a theory of class subjectivity (see §9.1 below).

Marx's account of socialist revolution certainly inclines in the latter direc-tion. His theory of the tendency of the rate of profit to fall does not imply that capitalism is liable to break down simply because of its economic contradic-tions (some later Marxists did seek to develop a theory of capitalist collapse, most notably Rosa Luxemburg in *The Accumulation of Capital* [1913], but such attempts were always fiercely contested by other Marxist economists). Marx's own expectations for the downfall of capitalism depended crucially on the de-velopment of the working class into a self-conscious political subject capable of taking control of society. Socialist revolution is indeed necessarily a process of *self*-emancipation: 'The emancipation of the working class must be achieved by the working class itself.'[41]

In thus making working-class self-emancipation the key to social transfor-mation Marx was going against the mainstream of contemporary radical thought. The Utopian socialists certainly thought of the emerging industrial proletariat

---

[39]   *CW* XI, p. 103.
[40]   *CW* VI, pp. 482, 496.
[41]   *CW* XXIV, p. 269.

as the chief victim of bourgeois society. But, precisely because of its sufferings and deprivations, the working class was thought to be incapable of undertaking independent political action. Social change would come about as a result of the action of an enlightened elite, whether this was identified with progressively-minded businessmen, as it was by Fourier who hoped to persuade them to finance his phalansteries, or with the kind of revolutionary conspiracies to which Auguste Blanqui and other early French communists devoted their political activity.

Marx believed that neither gradual reform nor insurrectionary putsches could fundamentally transform society. He also rejected the idea that the working class was too corrupted and distorted by its material situation to carry out a revolution as 'bound to divide society into two parts, one of which is superior to society'.[42] His opposition to what he regarded as elitist conceptions of social change did not mean that Marx denied the existence of obstacles to revolution. On the contrary, his theory of ideology, first developed with respect to religion (see §4.1 above), asserted that social mechanisms caused the widespread acceptance of beliefs supportive of the existing order. Thus:

> The ideas of the ruling class are in every epoch the ruling ideas: i.e., the ruling class which is the ruling *material* force of society is at the same time its ruling *intellectual* force. The class which has the means of material production at its disposal, consequently also controls the means of mental production, so that the ideas of those who lack the means of mental production are on the whole subject to it.[43]

This passage from *The German Ideology* asserts what is sometimes called the 'dominant ideology thesis': the social power of the exploiting class allows it to impose its ideas on society generally. This theory bears at least a family resemblance to the Enlightenment critique of organized religion as a conspiracy of priests and rulers: both seem to view the masses as passive receptacles for the 'ruling ideas'. The theory of commodity fetishism developed in *Capital* (see §4.2 above) posits a different mechanism which does not presume on mass passivity. The daily workings of the market economy encourage individuals to see it as an autonomous process governed by natural laws. This perception is not simply an error: 'To the producers . . . the social relations between their private labours appear as *what they are*, i.e. they do not appear as direct social relations between persons in their work, but rather as material relations between persons and social relations between things.'[44] The social relations between producers are mediated by the exchange of their products on the market: it is this real feature of a commodity economy which facilitates the perception of capitalism as a natural phenomenon outside human control.

[42] *CW* V, p. 7.
[43] *CW* V, p. 59.
[44] Marx, *Capital*, I, p. 166 (emphasis added).

The class struggle represents the main counter-force to such pressures to accept the existing order. Marx sees this as arising in the first instance from the economic conflict within the process of production over the distribution of the net product between wages and profits. Contrary to legend, he does not accept the Malthusian 'iron law of wages', according to which workers' incomes tend towards a bare minimum of physical subsistence (see §1.5 above). On the contrary, the share of profits (and hence of wages) may be set anywhere within the limits set by this physical minimum and the net value created by the workers: 'The fixation of its actual degree is only settled by the continuous struggle between capital and labour . . . The matter resolves itself into a question of the respective powers of the combatants.'[45]

This analysis leads Marx (going once more against the socialist orthodoxy of his day) to view trade unions positively, since the better organized workers are, the better they will fare in the struggle over distribution. Trade unions can, however, only combat the effects of capitalist exploitation rather than abolish it altogether; the capitalists' control over investment, and their consequent power to increase the rate of unemployment and thereby to undermine workers' bargaining position, gives them the ultimate advantage in purely distributional conflicts. The most important function of trade unions for Marx is their role in increasing workers' self-confidence and strengthening their organization. The experience of class struggle, even over relatively narrow economic issues, helps the workers to transform themselves from mere victims of exploitation into self-conscious subjects increasingly willing to take on the task of social transformation. The latter process must thus be understood as the 'coincidence of changing of circumstances and of human activity or self-change'.[46]

The trajectory of the working-class movement would be from economic issues concerning either individual employers or groups of them to political ones involving confrontation with the state (Marx was here to some degree generalizing from the experience of the early British workers' movement as it developed from early attempts to form trade unions to the Chartist demands for manhood suffrage in the 1840s). Already in his early writings Marx had criticized the limited character of the 'political emancipation' achieved by the French Revolution: 'The so-called *rights of man* . . . are nothing but the rights of a *member of civil society*, i.e. the rights of egoistic man, of man separated from other men and from the community.' A fuller 'human emancipation' was necessary to overcome the separation of the state from civil society.[47]

Once he had formulated his materialist conception of history, Marx came to see the kind of state produced by 'political emancipation', the modern liberal parliamentary state, as, like indeed all states, a means of class domination. The

[45] *CW* XX, p. 146.
[46] *CW* V, p. 4.
[47] *CW* III, pp. 162, 168.

exploiting class might exercise its political domination indirectly – neither in Napoleon III's Second Empire (1851–70) nor in post-Reform Britain, Marx believed, did industrial capital directly exercise political power, even though the state still promoted its interests, but universally '[p]olitical power . . . is merely the organized power of one class for oppressing another'.[48]

This theory of the state explains his further belief that the 'dictatorship of the proletariat' was a necessary prerequisite for the achievement of communism. In overthrowing capitalism, the workers would have to forge their own state in order to overwhelm bourgeois resistance and lay the basis of the future society. Marx's view of what this state would be like became more definite as a result of the Paris Commune of 1871, when the city's lower classes briefly took control. He described the Commune as 'the political form at last discovered under which to work out the economic emancipation of labour'. The features of the Commune which he stressed were those which broke down the distinction between the state apparatus and the mass of the population and extended popular participation in government – the abolition of the standing army and the police, their replacement by a popular militia, the election subject to the right of immediate recall of judges and other public officials, and the reduction of their salaries to the average wage. Indeed, the Commune 'was a Revolution against the *State* itself, this supernaturalist abortion of society, a resumption by the people for the people, of its own social life'.[49]

Already in the early 1840s Marx had focused his criticism on the modern state as an abstraction alienated from an atomized civil society and proposed its dissolution along with that of civil society itself (see §4.1 above). This theme continues to inform his later political writings, where it is not only integrated into his mature theory of history, but also reinforced by a ferocious critique of the bureaucratic nature of the modern state. Thus Marx, in a manner strikingly similar to Tocqueville's, traces the development of the French state, 'with its enormous bureaucratic and military organization, with its extensive and artificial state machinery, with a host of officials numbering half a million, besides an army of another half a million, this appalling parasitic body', and argues that 'all revolutions perfected this machine instead of breaking it. The parties that contended in turn for domination regarded possession of this huge state edifice as the principal spoils of the victor.'[50]

Socialist revolution, then, effects the destruction of this bureaucratic and military apparatus, and replaces it with political institutions through which the working class directly participates in the process of government. This conception of revolution indicates that Marx does not equate socialism with the expansion of state power, say, through the nationalization of the means of production.

[48] *CW* VI, p. 505.
[49] *CW* XXII, pp. 334, 486.
[50] *CW* XI, pp. 185–6.

On the contrary: 'Freedom consists in converting the state from an organ super-imposed upon society to one completely subordinate to it.'[51] Furthermore, Marx's view of socialism as self-emancipation seems to bear a family resemblance to the classical republican conception of liberty as the property of a collective agent (see §1.5 above). Transformed and rendered self-confident through the experience of the class struggle, the workers under the dictatorship of the proletariat cease to be subjects and become citizens in the real sense of the word, collectively exercising self-mastery through their active participation in, and direction of, the political process. In this version, however, Rousseau's problem of overcoming the conflict between the private and the general will is apparently avoided, since it is the workers' *class* interest that leads them to undertake 'universal emancipation'. Marx thus conceives the proletariat as the 'universal class' which Hegel had thought the bureaucracy to be.

Even this universal emancipation is, however, merely a prelude to the attainment of a developed communist society. Deeply critical of the Utopian socialists' attempts to anticipate the course of history by developing detailed accounts of post-capitalist society, Marx says very little about communism. In one of his last important texts, the *Critique of the Gotha Programme* (1875), he suggests that distribution in the 'higher phase of communist society' will be regulated by the principle 'From each according to his abilities, to each according to his needs.' Operating on this basis presupposes certain conditions only gradually achieved after the overthrow of capitalism, notably the transcendence of 'the enslaving subordination of the individual to the division of labour, and thereby also of the antithesis between mental and physical labour', labour's becoming 'not only a means of life but life's prime want', and the further growth of the productive forces 'with the all-round development of the individual'.[52]

This passage shows Marx attempting to give a historically realistic account of the conditions on which a communist society would depend (how successfully is, of course, another matter). It also presupposes the view of human nature he had developed in his early writings, notably the *Economic and Philosophic Manuscripts*, where labour is affirmed as 'the essence of man' (see §4.1 above). A society where labour is 'life's prime want' is one where human beings are able to fulfil themselves as inventive social producers. It is because, on this view, well-being consists in self-realization through creative activity that the members of communist society can be persuaded to accept a distributional principle which abjures material incentives and allocates on the basis of need. Furthermore, since human beings fulfil themselves actively, socialist revolution marks, not the end of history, but the end of the 'prehistory of human society':[53] history – the refashioning of the world by social labour – will con-

---

[51]   *CW* XXIV, p. 94.
[52]   *CW* XXIV, p. 87.
[53]   Marx, *Contribution*, p. 22.

tinue after classes have been abolished. Marx's vision of communism is thus closely connected with the theory of human nature that continues to inform his mature writings.

Marx continues to command our attention not simply because of his enormous influence. His social theory is comparable only to Hegel's in the complex and integrated analysis it offers of modernity within a broader interpretation of history. Weber is perhaps the only modern social thinker whose writings match Marx's scope and depth (indeed, their historical range is much greater), but his is a much tenser, more ambivalent theory, always, as it were, on the verge of breaking into fragments. But thus comparing Marx with Hegel serves to highlight the reasons why so many express profound scepticism about him. For, in constructing a 'grand narrative' that claims in principle to comprehend the entire course of history, is he not liable to a materialist reductionism as disabling as Hegel's idealist reductionism? Most of the numerous detailed criticisms of individual aspects of Marx's thought (though not all – the issue of the internal consistency of his economic theory has provoked extensive debate) – for example, his supposed neglect of national and ethnic conflicts, and his apparent failure to anticipate capitalism's capacity to renew itself – as well as the assessment of the historical fate of his doctrine after the Russian Revolution, turn ultimately on this fundamental question. How well the tradition he founded has been able to deal with this challenge may emerge in the rest of this book.

5

Life and Power

5.1 Evolution before and after Darwin

Marx's is the most important instance of the class of evolutionary social theories. It involves, in other words, a theory of history which (1) distinguishes between kinds of society (on the basis of the forces and relations of production that prevail in them); (2) specifies the mechanisms which cause one kind of society to change into another (contradictions between the forces and relations, and class struggle); and (3) claims that these changes cumulatively represent the increase of a specific property (the development of the productive forces). Earlier versions of such theories of history had, of course, been developed during the Enlightenment (see §1.4 above). Around the middle of the nineteenth century, however, a variant of evolutionary social theory became increasingly influential which treated the pattern of development of human history as merely a specific case of the process of evolution at work in the living world generally.

This development is, of course, closely associated with Darwin's theory of evolution by natural selection.[1] Yet the idea of an evolutionary conception of both nature and society had been formulated before his *Origin of Species* was published in 1859. Spencer wrote in an essay which appeared two years earlier:

> It is settled beyond dispute that organic progress consists in a change from the homogenous to the heterogeneous.

---

[1] Charles Robert Darwin (1809–82): born into the English upper middle class; studied at Edinburgh and Cambridge universities; abandoned the idea of taking the cloth for scientific studies; took part in HMS *Beagle*'s scientific survey, 1831–6; formulated the theory of natural selection in 1838, but only published it in 1859 after A. R. Wallace developed a version of the same idea; intellectually daring but personally timid – the prospect of confrontation sent him to bed with stomach troubles.

Now, we propose in the first place to show, that this law of organic progress is the law of all progress. Whether it be in the development of the Earth, in the development of Life upon its surface, in the development of Society, of Government, of Manufactures, of Commerce, of Language, Literature, Science, Art, this same evolution from the simple to the complex, through successive differentiations. From the earliest traceable cosmical changes down to the latest results of civilization, we shall find that the transformation of the homogenous into the heterogeneous, is that in which progress essentially consists.[2]

Darwin thus cannot be seen as the parent of such views. The scientific model offered by Sir Charles Lyell in his *Principles of Geology* (1830) – the reconstruction of the historical past on the basis of inferences from uniform laws of nature – exerted a powerful influence on Victorian social scientists. One of the main problems which their theories were constructed to address was that of the evidence of 'primitive' societies provided by archaeological evidence and, more importantly, by the experience of colonial administration in Europe's Asian and African empires. The concept of a progressive evolutionary sequence allowed practitioners of the new discipline of anthropology (or ethology) both to affirm the continuity of human social forms and to differentiate between 'barbarous' and 'civilized' societies, with, of course, modern Western civilization constituting the chief instance of the latter. Thus the outcome of the comparisons conducted by Maine in *Ancient Law* (1861) is that 'the movement of the progressive societies has hitherto been a movement *from Status to Contract*', from feudal and Asiatic hierarchy to modern bourgeois individualism.[3]

Inasmuch as evolutionists such as Spencer drew on evolutionary biology, it tended to be the version developed by Lamarck.[4] In his *Philosophie zoologique* (1809), Lamarck advanced the idea of 'transformism': the existing world of living organisms is the result of the gradual modifications their ancestors underwent over the course of time. These transformations constitute a directional process, a movement from the simple to the complex, that represents at the same time the progressive perfection of the living world: increased complexity is a sign of greater perfection. This process is driven by two forces, a kind of inner drive that 'ceaselessly tends to make organization more complex', and the adaptations which organisms make to cope better with their environment. Lamarck believed that organisms were so plastic that the action on them of their environment would directly cause adaptive modifications in them; he

[2]   H. Spencer, *Essays: Scientific, Political, and Speculative* (3 vols, London, 1891), I, p. 10. Herbert Spencer (1820–93): the largely self-educated author of a voluminous body of philosophical, scientific, sociological, and political writings.

[3]   H. S. Maine, *Ancient Law*, ed. F. Pollock (London, 1907), p. 174.

[4]   Jean Baptiste Pierre Antoine de Monet, Chevalier de Lamarck (1744–1829): natural historian; helped establish the National Museum of Natural History in Paris in 1794.

further argued that these adaptations would be passed on to the organisms' descendants: 'the generation between the individuals in question preserves the acquired modifications'.[5]

Lamarck's theory of evolution is thus teleological, since the process of gradual modification is governed by the goal of perfection, even if nature is no longer conceived as the creation of a divine artificer. François Jacob writes:

> According to Lamarck, finality does not involve a primary intention, a decision to produce a living world and gradually guide its development. It is made up of short-term finalities, so to speak, each centred on the well-being of an organism that is to be produced later, since adaptive intention always *precedes* realization. In the end, the plan followed by nature is aimed at providing the world with always more complex, more perfect and better adapted organisms.[6]

One can understand why such a theory should appeal to those eager to present their own society as the pinnacle of the entire evolutionary process; we shall see how this conception of change as a process of progressive differentiation exerted a powerful influence on social theorists, commencing with Spencer (§5.2 below). It is, however, crucial to understand that Darwin's theory of evolution is radically at odds with this conception. In the *Origin of Species*, he sought to establish two fundamental points. First, he offered evidence of the *fact* of evolution – of 'descent by modification'. In other words, existing species of plants and organisms are not 'special creations', as Christian orthodoxy still asserted, products of divine design, but are the descendants of earlier species. But Darwin's real originality lay in the explanation he offered for evolution – natural selection: 'I am convinced that Natural Selection has been the main but not exclusive means of modification.'[7]

Darwin indeed calls his book 'one long argument' for natural selection. This argument is based on the following premises. In the first place, 'many more individuals of each species are born than can possibly survive . . . consequently, there is a frequently recurring struggle for existence'. Secondly, individual organisms vary, usually in small, but sometimes in significant ways. Thirdly, Darwin affirmed 'the strong principle of inheritance': organisms are able to pass on variations to their offspring. He confessed to not understanding the mechanisms through which this happened: 'Our ignorance of the laws of variation is profound.'[8] (According to the 'Modern Synthesis' established in twentieth-century biology, inheritance operates through the genes – strings of DNA molecules which govern the manufacture of proteins – passed on by parents to their offspring.) Finally, organisms exhibit differential fitness: relative

[5]   Quoted in F. Jacob, *The Logic of Living Systems* (London, 1974), pp. 147–8, 149.
[6]   Ibid., p. 150.
[7]   C. Darwin, *The Orgin of Species by Means of Natural Selection* (Harmondsworth, 1968), p. 69.
[8]   Ibid., pp. 435, 68, 202.

to a given environment, some variations will allow organisms to reproduce better than others.

From these premises, Darwin drew the following conclusion:

> Owing to this struggle for life, any variation, however slight and from whatever cause proceeding, if it be in any degree profitable to an individual of any species, in its infinitely complex relations to any other organic beings and to external nature, will tend to the preservation of that individual, and will generally be inherited by its offspring. The offspring, also, will thus have a better chance of surviving, for, of the many individuals which are periodically born, but a small number can survive. I have called this principle, by which each slight variation, if useful, is preserved, by the term Natural Selection.[9]

The theory of natural selection offers an explanation of evolution that is, as Elliott Sober puts it, 'selectional' rather than 'developmental'.[10] Historical materialism is an example of a developmental theory: according to Marx, societies change as a result of the contradictions internal to them. But, for Darwin, evolution occurs not because individuals develop, but because they *vary*. More specifically, the fact that some of these variations adapt the organisms bearing them better to their environment and that these organisms are able to pass on these variations to their descendants changes the composition of the population of organisms over time – these descendants, other things being equal, come to represent a larger proportion of the population.

But, further, as Jacob puts it, '[v]ariation occurs randomly, that is, without any relation between cause and result.'[11] This does not mean that adaptive variations are simply accidents lacking any causal explanation. On the contrary, Darwin was strongly influenced by Lyell's 'uniformitarian' assumption that the same causal laws operate universally. The crucial point is that the causes of variations have nothing to do with their potentially adaptive consequences. Evolution is thus a blind process, driven not as Lamarck claimed by an implicit force driving towards greater perfection, but by the interaction between independently varying organisms and their environment. All the diversity of life is thus to be understood primarily as the consequence of 'this very slow, intermittent action of natural selection'.[12]

In formulating the theory of natural selection Darwin was influenced by his extensive reading of Scottish political economy. Sober points to the analogy between Smith's 'invisible hand' (see §1.3 above) and the idea that 'the struggle for existence favours individual adaptive characteristics and thereby increases the level of adaptedness in the population'.[13] Darwin himself says the concept

---

[9] Ibid., p. 115.
[10] E. Sober, *The Nature of Selection* (Chicago, 1993), pp. 147ff.
[11] Jacob, *Logic*, p. 174.
[12] Darwin, *Origin*, p. 153.
[13] Sober, *Nature*, p. 189.

of the 'Struggle for Existence' is 'the doctrine of Malthus applied with mani-
fold force to the whole animal and vegetable kingdoms'. But he is careful to
qualify this statement: 'I use the term Struggle for Existence in a large and
metaphorical sense'.[14]

For one thing, success in this struggle does not consist in killing off rivals (as
is suggested by such lurid pictures of evolution as are invoked by Tennyson's
image of 'Nature, red in tooth and claw'), but in survival and, above all, in
reproductive success. For another the struggle need not be with other organisms; it can be with the environment: 'there must in every case be a struggle for
existence, either one individual with another of the same species, or with the
individuals of distinct species, *or with the physical conditions of life*'.[15] The use
Darwin makes of Malthus is thus a complex one: while the latter uses his theory
that population rises faster than food production in an attempt to demonstrate
that society cannot move beyond a condition of inequality, Darwin treats natural selection as a creative force that is responsible for the immense diversity of
the living world.

A further difference with Lamarck is that Darwin is reluctant to depict the
evolutionary process as one of increasing perfection culminating in the human
species. When initially formulating the concept of natural selection in 1837 he
wrote: 'It is absurd to talk of one animal being higher than another. *We* consider
those, where intellectual faculties are most developed, as highest. – A bee doubtless would [use] . . . instincts' as a criterion.[16] Elsewhere he wrote: 'Never use
the words higher and lower.'[17] In the *Origin* itself he does sometimes violate
this injunction. But at the same time he insists: 'I believe . . . in no law of necessary development.'[18] As Sober puts it,

> Darwin thought of organisms as being modified by their *local* environments; his
> theory of natural selection gives no role to the Lamarckian idea . . . that evolution is
> driven by some central force that tends in all populations to produce a single sort of
> progressive change. Natural selection predicts a bush rather than a ladder. Oppor-
> tunistic populations evolve in the various directions that environments fortuitously
> make available; they do not unfold in accordance with some internal dynamic.[19]

It is therefore necessary to distinguish an evolutionary theory, either of
nature or of history, from evolution*ism*. In the domain of social theory, as
Erik Olin Wright puts it, the latter involves the idea that 'societies inexorably
develop towards some end-state of increasing adaptation to environmental
or material conditions'. By contrast, he suggests,

[14]   Darwin, *Origin*, pp. 116–17.
[15]   Ibid., p. 117 (emphasis added).
[16]   Quoted in A. Desmond and J. Moore, *Darwin* (London, 1992), pp. 232.
[17]   Quoted in J. W. Burrow, introduction to Darwin, *Origin*, p. 33.
[18]   Darwin, *Origin*, p. 348.
[19]   Sober, *Nature*, p. 172.

For a theory of society to be evolutionary three conditions must hold:

(1) The theory involves a typology of social forms which *potentially* has some kind of directionality to it . . .

(2) It is possible to order these forms in such a way that the probability of staying at the same level of the typology is greater that the probability of regressing.

(3) In this ordered typology, there is a positive probability of moving from a given level of the typology to the next higher level.[20]

Thus understood, an evolutionary theory merely implies that 'there is some process, however weak and sporadic, which imparts a directionality to movements from one form to another', but 'there is no claim that societies have needs or teleologically driven tendencies towards achieving some final state'.[21] Darwin and indeed Marx are largely free of evolutionism in this latter, teleological sense. But, of course, there may be a considerable difference between the actual content of a theory and the version in which it comes to be widely accepted and propagated. The enormous impact of Darwin's theory of evolution by natural selection in late nineteenth-century Europe and America undoubtedly helped to entrench an evolutionist view of the world. More specifically, it was used to justify both Western domination of the rest of the world and the prevalence of *laissez-faire* capitalism in Western societies themselves.

Spencer coined the phrase 'the survival of the fittest', which Darwin subsequently adopted.[22] This slogan appeared to legitimize existing social hierarchies as the outcome of natural selection. Thus the Yale social scientist William Graham Sumner wrote in 1883: 'The millionaires are a product of natural selection, acting on the whole body of men to pick out those who can meet the requirement of certain work to be done . . . They get high wages and live in luxury, but the bargain is a good one for society.'[23] Here Smith's 'invisible hand' and Darwin's struggle for existence are brought together in the ideological synthesis that has come to be known as Social Darwinism.

Racist theorizing was already well established before the appearance of the *Origin*, as we saw in §3.3 above. Nevertheless, as Richard Hofstadter puts it, '[a]lthough Darwinism was not the primary source of the belligerent ideology and dogmatic racism of the late nineteenth century, it did become a new instrument in the hands of the theorists of race and struggle.'[24] In Britain and the United States this kind of thinking tended to take the form of 'Anglo-Saxonism': as practised by E. A. Freeman, for example, the comparative study of political institutions revealed the primacy even among Aryans of the 'Anglo-Saxon

[20] E. O. Wright, 'Giddens's Critique of Marx', *New Left Review*, 138 (1983), p. 26.

[21] Ibid.

[22] H. Spencer (1864), *The Principles of Biology* (2 vols, London, 1898), I, pp. 530–1.

[23] Quoted in R. Hofstadter, *Social Darwinism in American Thought* (Boston, 1955), p. 58.

[24] Ibid., p. 172.

race', distinguished by its (somewhat contradictory) capacity for both self-government and the imperial stewardship of 'lesser' races.

As rivalries among the Great Powers began to intensify towards the turn of the century, this cocktail of race theory and vulgarized Darwinism took on a more anxious and belligerent tone. Thus the Revd Josiah Strong predicted in 1885 that, as the land filled up,

> Then will the world enter upon a new stage of its history – the *final competition of races for which the Anglo-Saxon is being schooled*. If I do not read it amiss, this powerful race will move down upon Mexico, down upon Central and South America, out upon the islands upon the sea, over upon Africa and beyond. And can anyone doubt that the result of this competition of races will be the 'survival of the fittest'?[25]

In fact, however, the reception of Darwin's thought cannot be reduced to such racist and *laissez-faire* appropriations. Marx's very positive response to the *Origin* is well known: 'Darwin's book is very important and serves me as a natural-scientific basis for the class struggle in history . . . Despite all deficiencies, not only is the death-blow dealt for the first time here to "teleology" in the natural sciences, but its rational basis is empirically explained.'[26] Engels cited the theory of evolution as one case of the emergence of a more historical conception of nature in the physical sciences of the day. The parallels he detected between Darwin and Marx encouraged him to formulate the idea of certain universal dialectical laws at work in both the physical and the social worlds. But Engels nevertheless insisted that evolution by natural selection involved a distinctly different causal pattern from that present in human history. This difference arose crucially from human beings' ability consciously to monitor and control their actions, and therefore to make their history a far less blind process than that of other species:

> Darwin did not know what a bitter satire he wrote on mankind, and especially on his countrymen, when he showed that free competition, the struggle for existence, which the economists celebrate as the highest historical achievement, is the normal state of the *animal kingdom*. Only conscious organization of social production, in which production and distribution are carried on in a planned way, can lift mankind above the rest of the animal world as regards the social aspect, in the same way that production in general has done this for mankind in the specifically biological aspect.[27]

The same complexity of response is to be found at the more popular level. Thus in Germany, Darwin's main impact was to help encourage the development

---

[25] Quoted ibid., p. 179.
[26] Letter to Lassalle, 16 Jan. 1861, in Marx and Engels, *Selected Correspondence* (Moscow, 1965), p. 123.
[27] F. Engels, *Dialectics of Nature* (Moscow, 1972), p. 35.

of a very widely read literature by authors such as Ernst Haeckel and Wilhelm Bölsche devoted to the popularization of evolutionary biology. This grew out of earlier traditions, notably the fairly reductive scientific materialism developed by Ludwig Büchner, Carl Vogt, and Jakob Moleschott in the 1850s – although it often also took over Romantic conceptions of the mystical unity of nature, as in Bölsche's 'erotic monism'. The political bent of this popular Darwinism was liberal-progressive and anti-clerical. In the repressive climate in which Bismarck introduced the Anti-Socialist Laws at the end of the 1870s, Darwinism was treated with hostility in conservative circles: the ultra-reactionary *Kreuzzeitung* even blamed the attempts on the life of Kaiser Wilhelm I which provided the pretexts for these laws on the 'ape theory'. Meanwhile, according to Alfred Kelly, at a time when state persecution did not prevent the rapid development of the Social Democratic Party (SPD), '[w]ith the exception of Bebel's *Women and Socialism*, popular Darwinism dominated worker nonfiction reading.'[28]

Popular Darwinism of this kind did not necessarily challenge the racist assumptions which had become deeply embedded in Western culture by this time. 'No woolly haired nation has ever had an important history', Haeckel declared.[29] But the most critical step towards a genuinely malign fusion of biology and social theory came at the beginning of the twentieth century with the increasing acceptance of August Weismann's theory that inheritance depended on the transmission of an immortal 'germ-plasm' from parents to offspring. This, together within the rediscovery of Gregor Mendel's researches into the mechanism of heredity, laid the basis for modern genetics. Its short-term impact, however, was to help encourage the belief that social phenomena were to be understood in terms of the biological conditions underlying them.

Francis Galton had invented eugenics in 1865. Based on the assumption that individual abilities were inherited, it sought to study how selective breeding could serve to increase the quality of the human race. Galton wrote:

> If a twentieth part of the costs and pains were spent in measures for the improvement of the human race that is spent on the improvement of the breed of horses and cattle, what a galaxy of genius might we not create! We might introduce prophets and high priests of civilization into the world as surely as we can propagate idiots by mating *crétins*. Men and women of the present day are, to those we might hope to bring into existence, what the pariah dogs of the streets of an Eastern town are to our own highly-bred varieties.[30]

The eugenicist movement took strength from the development of gene theory. William E. Kellicott summed up its basic doctrine in 1911: 'the Eugenicist

---

[28]   A. Kelly, *The Descent of Darwin* (Chapel Hill, 1981), p. 128.
[29]   Quoted ibid., p. 117.
[30]   F. Galton (1865), 'Hereditary Talent and Character', in R. Jacoby and N. Glauberman, eds, *The Bell Curve Debate* (New York, 1995), pp. 394–5.

believes that no other single factor in determining social conditions and practices approaches in importance that of racial structural integrity and character'.[31] Eugenics was thus a form of biological determinism – that is, it asserted (1) that social structures are caused by, and therefore must be explained in terms of, biological structures, and (2) that 'race', conceived as a set of fixed characteristics transmitted by inheritance, is the most important of the biological structures on which social structures are based. The obvious implication was that the main way to improve society was to encourage the racially 'superior' to mate with each other, and to discourage 'inferior' types from breeding at all. The list of crimes which this structure of beliefs has legitimized during the twentieth century is a long one, ranging from the compulsory sterilization of the 'unfit' (twelve American states passed sterilization laws between 1907 and 1915) to the Nazis' attempts to 'cleanse' Europe of the Jews, the Roma and Sinti, and other supposedly biologically 'inferior' types. It continues still to exert its influence through the persistently advocated theory that social inequalities reflect innate differences in intelligence.

This very widespread attempt to construct social problems in terms defined by biology has deeper roots than can be accounted for on the basis of the influence of any theory. Thus the increasing tendency of late Victorian reformers to treat poverty and social unrest in the East End of London as a problem of racial 'degeneration' to be addressed through a programme of 'national hygiene' reflected growing anxieties about domestic class conflict and foreign competition.[32] To appreciate, against this background, the diverse ways in which evolutionary biology was appropriated and integrated into social theory let us consider the differences – and the similarities – between two authors strongly identified with, respectively, liberalism and socialism.

5.2   Two evolutionists: Spencer and Kautsky

(1) *Individualist sociology: Spencer.* Spencer's sociology represents perhaps the most systematic attempt to restate social theory in terms derived from evolutionary biology. As we have already seen, even before Darwin published his theory Spencer had declared 'the law of organic progress' to be 'the law of all progress'. He further conceived 'organic progress' in Lamarckian terms, defending as 'the *only* law of organic modifications of which we have any evidence' the proposition that 'acquired peculiarities resulting from the adaptation of constitution to conditions, are transmissible to offspring', and never entirely abandoning this view after the *Origin* appeared.[33]

---

[31]   Quoted in Hofstadter, *Social Darwinism*, p. 163.

[32]   G. Stedman Jones, *Outcast London* (Harmondsworth, 1984), chs 16–18.

[33]   H. Spencer, *Essays*, I, p. 91; compare (1886) 'The Factors of Organic Evolution', ibid., I, pp. 389–466.

Spencer's substantive social theory thus reflects the belief that '[a] Society is an Organism.'[34] Conceiving society in these terms is an old conservative standby, used (as Shakespeare does in the opening scene of *Coriolanus*) both to assert the mutual interdependence of the different classes, and to remind the lower orders of their subordinate place in the state. However, it would misrepresent Spencer to portray his position as primarily a defence of the status quo. As John Burrow puts it, 'generally speaking his approach to *contemporary* institutions is that of an impatient *laissez-faire* radical'.[35] Spencer's political impatience leads him to interlard even his theoretical writings with vigorous criticisms of the rigidity of Victorian Britain, of, for example, its cult of royalty, hypocritical Christian morality, and brutal colonial policies.[36]

How then does he square this liberal individualism with an evolutionary conception of society? Competition, conceived as a fundamental tendency at work everywhere in nature, plays a crucial role in providing the necessary connection. 'As carried on throughout the animate world at large, the struggle for existence has been an indispensable means to evolution . . . Without universal conflict there would have been no development of the active powers.' Furthermore: 'the struggle for existence between societies has been instrumental to their evolution'.[37]

Driven by the competition among individuals, species, and societies, evolution consists in a process of progressive differentiation, that is, in the development of a more complex and internally articulated organization leading to increased efficiency: 'These differences of function and consequent differences of structure, at first feebly marked, slight in degree and few in kind, become, as organization progresses, definite and numerous; and in proportion as they do this the requirements are better met.'[38] The division of labour, first discovered by economists, also operates in the living world as 'the "physiological division of labour"' . . . Scarcely can I emphasize enough the truth that in respect of this fundamental trait, a social organism and an individual are entirely alike.'[39]

The progressive differentiation of social organisms leads, over time, to a tendency for one form of co-operation to be replaced by another. 'There is a spontaneous co-operation which grows up without thought during the pursuit of private ends; and there is co-operation which, consciously devised, implies distinct recognition of public ends.' The paradigm case of the first kind of co-operation is a market economy where specialized producers co-operate by exchanging goods and services without any need for conscious regulation to achieve

[34]   H. Spencer (1882), *The Principles of Sociology* (3 vols, London, 1893), I, title of pt. II, ch. II, pp. 437–50.
[35]   J. Burrow, *Evolution and Society* (Cambridge, 1966), p. 227.
[36]   H. Spencer (1872–3), *The Study of Sociology* (London, 1894), pp. 136–41.
[37]   Spencer, *Principles of Sociology*, III, pp. 240–1.
[38]   Spencer, *Study*, p. 327.
[39]   Spencer, *Principles of Sociology*, I, p. 440.

this result. In the case of the second kind, 'compulsory co-operation', 'individual wills are constrained, first by the joint wills of the entire group, and afterwards more definitely by the will of a regulative agency which the group evolves'.[40]

Spencer calls societies where this form of co-operation prevails 'militant', and those based on 'spontaneous co-operation' 'industrial'. The former tend to organizational rigidity; in them, individuals tend to be ranked according to inherited status. 'Under the industrial *régime*', by contrast, 'the citizen's individuality, instead of being sacrificed by the society, has to be defended by the society. Defence of the individual becomes the society's essential duty.'[41] The two types of society have historically existed in various combinations. In the earlier stages of social evolution, compulsory co-operation was necessary to produce any form of stable order. The more complex society becomes, however, the more impossible it becomes to co-ordinate increasingly specialized activities on the basis of coercion: 'in the social organism as it advances to a high structure, there develops an extensive and complex trading system'.[42]

Consequently, societies where the militant type prevails are becoming obsolescent. This involves a change in the form taken by the struggle for existence – namely from war to economic competition, as Spencer explains in a passage in which he demonstrates his willingness to sacrifice the 'unfit' at the altar of progress:

> Severe and bloody as the process [i.e. war] is, the extirpation of inferior races and inferior individuals, leaves a balance of benefit to mankind during phases of progress in which the moral development is low, and there are no quick sympathies to be seared by the infliction of pain and death. But high societies, composed of members fitted to closer co-operation, cannot carry out destructive activities without injurious reactive effects on the moral natures of their members. After this stage has been reached, the purifying process, continuing still an important one [*sic*], has to be effected by industrial war – by a competition between societies during which the best, physically, emotionally, and intellectually, spread most, and leave the least capable to disappear gradually, from failing to leave a sufficiently numerous posterity.[43]

This historical sociology issues in a somewhat ambivalent attitude on Spencer's part towards his own day. On the one hand, he argues that, in competition among industrial societies, those where the remnants of the militant type are relatively strong will find themselves at a disadvantage: 'So that by survival of

---

[40] Ibid., III, pp. 245, 247.
[41] Ibid., III, p. 607.
[42] Spencer, *Study*, p. 330.
[43] Ibid., p. 195.

the fittest must be produced a social type in which individual claims, considered as sacred, are trenched on by the State no further than is requisite to pay the cost of maintaining them, or rather, of arbitrating among them.'[44]

On the other hand, Spencer was well aware that the trend in nineteenth-century Europe was away from, rather than towards, such a minimal state. He rails against the 'power-worship [that] idealizes the State', and 'sways in common all orders of politicians, from the old-world Tory to the Red Republican'. He moreover recognizes that the strengthening of state power was driven less by the survival of the old absolute monarchies than by what he regards as misguided efforts at social reform which, by keeping the 'unfit' alive, simply weaken society: 'if the inferior are helped to increase, by shielding them from that mortality which their inferiority would naturally entail, the effect is to produce, generation after generation, a greater inferiority'.[45]

There therefore seems to be no automatic tendency for the industrial type to prevail over the militant. Indeed, the latter springs up in new guises. Thus socialism 'involves in another form the principle of compulsory co-operation'. Industrial societies which are foolish enough to adopt any kind of 'communistic distribution' will find themselves at a competitive disadvantage, since in them 'the superior' are not allowed to keep 'the entire proceeds of their labour', some of which is diverted 'for the benefit of the inferior and their offspring'.[46] But, beyond gesturing towards the power of received tradition, Spencer offers very little in the way of an explanation of why such misguided faith in various kinds of compulsory co-operation should persist. Despite his effort to formulate an evolutionary social theory, he remains strongly wedded to an Enlightenment rationalism which treats what it identifies as erroneous beliefs as the products of ignorance and prejudice.

(2) *Evolutionary socialism: Kautsky.* If Spencer was a champion of extreme *laissez faire*, Kautsky was the leading theoretician of the SPD, and, given the centrality of German social democracy to the Second International (1889–1914), of the world socialist movement as well.[47] Where Spencer saw the evolutionary process culminating in an individualist social order, Kautsky conceived human history as a movement from one form of communism, that prevailing in 'primitive' societies, to a far more advanced form resting on the development of the productive forces under capitalism. Drawing on the rapidly developing anthropological research of the late nineteenth century, Kautsky estimated that

---

[44] Spencer, *Principles of Sociology*, III, p. 607.

[45] Spencer, *Study*, pp. 156, 168–9, 339.

[46] Spencer, *Principles of Sociology*, III, pp. 604, 610.

[47] Karl Johann Kautsky (1854–1938): born in Prague to a theatrical family, and raised in Vienna, but spent most of his life in Germany; editor of *Die Neue Zeit*, the SPD weekly, 1883–1917; author of numerous books and pamphlets, and editor of various of Marx's works, notably *Theories of Surplus-Value*.

'primitive communism' had lasted 800,000 years, class society a mere 10,000–15,000 years: 'Measured solely according to its temporal duration, it is then not classless society, but rather society divided into classes that presents itself to us as the exception, a mere episode in the history of human society.'[48]

Yet, despite this radically different perspective on the course of history, there are certain important points of convergence between Kautsky and Spencer. The former's original intellectual formation was Darwinist rather than Marxist. He read *The Descent of Man* before the *Communist Manifesto*, and later contrasted his background to that of Marx and Engels: 'They started out with *Hegel*; I started out with *Darwin*. The latter occupied my thoughts earlier than Marx, the development of organisms earlier than the economy, the struggle for existence of species and races earlier than the class struggle.' Indeed, like Spencer, Kautsky preferred Lamarck's theory that 'the acquisition and hereditary transmission of new characteristics through the influence of new conditions' is the main evolutionary force, to Darwin's theory of evolution by natural selection.[49]

This 'materialist neo-Lamarckism', as Kautsky called it, did not in fact issue in anything resembling the Social Darwinism discussed in §5.1 above.[50] He specifically rejected the idea that society is an organism, argued that the pattern of human history could not be reduced to that of biological evolution, denied that the members of 'primitive' societies were intellectually inferior to their counterparts in 'advanced' societies, and criticized the racist and nationalist theories increasingly influential among German scholars. Yet Kautsky's historical materialism has a decidedly more fatalist cast than that of Marx and Engels. Criticizing Engels for being too ready to adopt Hegel's teleology, he reinterpreted the historical dialectic in Lamarckian terms as an interaction between organism and environment in which it is the latter that plays the active role in the relationship. Thus: 'It is the environment that poses the problem that the mind has to solve.'[51]

In response to problems posed by the environment, human beings develop 'artificial organs' – tools and other means of production. This creates a new kind of environment for humankind, a social environment which in turn generates problems whose solution requires the development of new technologies and forms of organization. Where the artificial organs are unequally distributed, class exploitation arises. Unlike Engels, whose explanation of the development of classes in *The Origin of the Family, Private Property and the State* (1884) concentrated on a endogenous process of differentiation within individual societies, Kautsky claimed that class divisions were the product of the

[48]   K. Kautsky (1927), *The Materialist Conception of History*, abbr. edn, ed. J. H. Kautsky (New Haven, 1988), p. 250.
[49]   Ibid., pp. 7, 46–7.
[50]   Quoted in J. H. Kautsky, introduction to Kautsky, *Materialist Conception*, p. xxxiii.
[51]   Ibid., p. 34.

conquest of one society by another. He envisaged a pattern rather like that which Ibn Khaldûn depicted in medieval Islam (see §1.1 above), where nomadic herdsmen conquered sedentary agriculturalists: conqueror and conquered then evolved into exploiter and exploited.

This emphasis on the salience of inter-state competition in the creation of class antagonisms is associated with a hostility to militarism reminiscent of Spencer's contrast between militant and industrial societies. Marx had called force 'the midwife of every old society which is pregant with a new one'.[52] Kautsky by contrast declared that 'war has proved to be a terrible obstacle to technological and economic advancement', and predicted that 'the movement in the direction of eternal peace through world commerce must finally become irresistible, all the more so as at the same time technological development is intensifying the devastations of every war to the level of diabolical insanity'.[53]

Kautsky was prone to regard historical forces as 'irresistible'. He saw the development of class society as an organic process culminating in the replacement of capitalism by socialism. Expounding the SPD's Erfurt programme in 1892, he declared: 'The capitalist social system has run its course. Its dissolution is now only a question of time. Irresistible economic forces lead with the certainty of doom to the shipwreck of capitalist production. The substitution of a new social order for the existing one is no longer desirable, it is inevitable.'[54] Kautsky did not believe that socialism could be achieved independently of human action; rather, historical necessity would operate through the agency of class conflict. Thus: 'Socialism is inevitable because the class struggle and the victory of the proletariat is inevitable.'[55]

This did not mean that Kautsky thought history should be forced by precipitate action. He famously called the SPD 'a revolutionary party, but not a party that makes revolutions'.[56] Though he opposed his old friend Eduard Bernstein's attempt in the great 'revisionist' controversy at the turn of the century to turn the SPD into a openly reformist party, Kautsky also backed the party leadership in resisting the pressures of Rosa Luxemburg and the radical left for a campaign of mass strikes to democratize the German imperial state. Socialism was gradually being prepared for within the bowels of capitalism, Kautsky believed. In particular, modern liberal democracy provided the necessary framework for the government of any complex industrial society, socialist as well as capitalist: 'democracy also makes it possible to wrest this whole immense state apparatus with its irresistible power out of the hands of the great exploiters that still hold it today and thus to turn the apparatus of domination into an apparatus of

---

[52] K. Marx, *Capital* (3 vols, Harmondsworth, 1976–81), I, p. 916.
[53] Kautsky, *Materialist Conception*, pp. 77, 79.
[54] K. Kautsky (1892), *The Class Struggle* (New York, 1971), p. 117.
[55] K. Kautsky (1906), *Ethics and the Materialist Conception of History* (Chicago, 1918), p. 206.
[56] K. Kautsky (1909), *The Road to Power* (Atlantic Highlands, NJ, 1996), p. 34.

emancipation'. Liberal democracy allowed the working class to take power peacefully by means of the ballot box, and convert 'the preceding *class state*' into a '*workers' state* or *social-welfare state*'.[57]

From this perspective, developments after 1914 represented an aberration. Consistent with his view of the destructive character of military conflict, Kautsky argued that the First World War was economically irrational. Capitalism was evolving through mergers and cartels to a phase of 'ultra-imperialism' where national economic differences would be progressively overcome. The imperial rivalries and arms races which lay behind the outbreak of war in August 1914 represented a stage of history that was receding into the past: 'the capitalist economy is seriously threatened by these disputes. Every far-sighted capitalist today must call on his fellows: capitalists of all countries, unite!'[58] While opposing the war, Kautsky ferociously condemned the Russian Revolution of October 1917. The attempt to carry through a socialist revolution in an economically backward country was doomed to failure, and could only result in a particularly brutal capitalist dictatorship. Bolshevism, in undertaking this project, represented a voluntarist regression from Marxism, a disastrous assertion of will in defiance of material circumstances.

During the brief period of stability Europe enjoyed in the 1920s Kautsky expressed the hope that '[t]he excitement caused by the World War is beginning to subside. The economic abnormalities resulting from it are beginning to give way once again to normal economic conditions in which the force of economic laws is again manifesting itself.' In these circumstances, the labour movement could resume its project of winning power by parliamentary means, since '*[t]he more the capitalist mode of production flourishes, the better the prospects of the socialist regime that takes the place of the capitalist one.*' Amidst economic prosperity and social reform, the League of Nations' efforts to resolve international conflicts peacefully stood a good chance of succeeding. Mussolini's attempt to upset the apple-cart was unlikely to be copied elsewhere. A fascist coup in Germany would require a million-strong mass movement: 'In an industrialized country, it is impossible to get hold of such a large number of scoundrels in the prime of life for capitalist purposes.'[59]

These expectations were of course soon overturned, first by the outbreak of the Great Depression in 1929 and then by the National Socialist seizure of power in Germany in 1933. These events had tragic consequences for Kautsky and his immediate family. Kautsky himself died in October 1938 in Amsterdam, where he had fled after the Nazi *Anschluss* in Austria earlier that year. His son Benedikt spent seven years in the concentration camps, and his wife Luise died in

---

[57] Kautsky, *Materialist Conception*, pp. 387, 450.
[58] K. Kautsky (1914), 'Imperialism', in J. Riddell, ed., *Lenin's Struggle for a Revolutionary International* (New York, 1984), p. 180.
[59] Kautsky, *Materialist Conception*, pp. lxix, 439, 449, 394.

Auschwitz. 'Abnormality' had become the norm, throwing into question the optimistic cast of Kautsky's version of historical materialism.

5.3 Nature as the will to power: Nietzsche

Spencer and Kautsky represent two highly influential attempts to treat the course of human history as a succession of social forms whose structure and development are best understood on the basis of a general theory of biological evolution. Their belief that history understood in these terms was moving in the right direction (even if their views of this direction were strikingly different) reflects the self-confident bourgeois society of late nineteenth-century Europe. As this society entered what Eric Hobsbawm has called the 'Age of Extremes' ushered in by the outbreak of the First World War, so the faith in historical progress expressed by Spencer and Kautsky became increasingly hard to sustain. The case of Kautsky is especially striking since he survived Europe's descent into the abyss by nearly a quarter of a century, but never abandoned the world-view he had developed in the 1870s and 1880s.

Evolutionist optimism in fact came under challenge well before 1914. This attack was never more forcefully expressed than by Nietzsche.[60] His thought is particularly interesting because it dramatizes one of the main tensions in modern social theory – that between a naturalism that treats humankind as continuous with nature and an anti-naturalism which insists on what sets human beings apart from other species. Social Darwinism and biological racism are repellent instances of naturalism; Weber is the most important champion of anti-naturalism; Marxism, even in its Kautskyan version, seeks to span the two positions. Nietzsche develops a critique of modernity that is peculiar in the way in which it combines naturalism and anti-naturalism. The human subject is naturalized, reduced to an incoherent cluster of biological drives, while nature is subjectivized, since all aspects of the physical as well as the social world are expressions of the will to power.

It is necessary, then, in the first place to register the virulence of Nietzsche's critique of modernity. His contempt for European bourgeois society is comprehensive. The various ideological catch-words of his day – progress, evolution, democracy, nationalism, socialism – are all dismissed as the merest shibboleths. The pursuit of the ideas of the French Revolution – Liberty, Equality, Fraternity – has produced the universal mediocrity which Nietzsche sums up in the image of the Last Man:

---

[60] Friedrich Nietzsche (1844–1900): son of a Prussian Lutheran pastor; Professor of Classical Philology at the University of Basle, 1868–79; the decade after his retirement from this post marked an extraordinarily concentrated burst of creativity; in 1889 suffered a mental breakdown from which he never recovered; during his last years his sister Elizabeth Förster-Nietzsche turned him, quite contrary to the main thrust of his writings, into a prophet of German nationalism.

The earth has become small, and upon it hops the Last Man, who makes everything small. His race is as inexterminable as the flea; the Last Man lives longest.

'We have discovered happiness,' say the Last Men and blink . . .

Nobody grows rich and poor any more: both are too much of a burden. Who still
wants to rule? Who obey? Both are too much of a burden.

No herdsman and one herd. Everyone wants the same thing, everyone is the same:
whoever thinks otherwise goes voluntarily into the madhouse.[61]

The obverse of this attack on the levelling and homogenizing tendencies
allegedly endemic to modern Europe is, predictably enough, a positive evalu-
ation of aristocratic society:

Every elevation of the type 'man' has hitherto been the work of an aristocratic
society – and so it will always be: a society which believes in a long scale of
orders of rank and differences of worth between man and man and needs slavery
in some sense or another. Without the *pathos of distance* such as develops from
the incarnate differences of classes, from the ruling caste's looking out and down
on subjects and instruments and from its equally constant exercise of obedience
and command, its holding down and holding at a distance, that other, more
mysterious pathos could not have developed either, that longing for an ever-
increasing widening of distance within the soul itself, the formation of ever-higher,
rarer, more remote, tenser, more comprehensive states, in short precisely the elevation of the type 'man', the continual 'self-overcoming of man'.[62]

Up to a point, this aristocratic critique of modernity is familiar enough. Romantic anti-capitalist denunciations of the present in the name of an idealized
past were common in post-Revolutionary Europe; Nietzsche's polemics often
recall those of Maistre, written in prose as vivid and savage as his (see ch. 3
above). But the passage just cited strikes a different note as well. The significance of aristocratic societies lies in their contribution to the 'self-overcoming
of man'. Nietzsche is uninterested in, indeed contemptuously spurns, the elevation of humanity collectively as an ethical or political goal, but he is very
interested in the elevation of particular individuals: 'the *goal of humanity* cannot lie in its end but only *in its highest exemplars*'.[63] These exceptional individuals are set apart from 'those who have nothing else to do but drag the past
a few steps further through time and who never live in the present – that is to
say, the many, the great majority. We, however, *want to become those we are –*
human beings who are new, unique, incomparable, who give themselves laws,
who create themselves.'[64]

---

[61]   F. Nietzsche (1883–5), *Thus Spoke Zarathustra* (Harmondsworth, 1969), I. 5, p. 46 (translation
modified).

[62]   F. Nietzsche (1886), *Beyond Good and Evil* (Harmondsworth, 1973), §257, p. 173.

[63]   F. Nietzsche (1873–6), *Untimely Meditations* (Cambridge, 1983), p. 111.

[64]   F. Nietzsche (1882), *The Gay Science* (New York, 1974), §335, p. 266.

Self-mastery, which Rousseau and Kant, Tocqueville and Marx, in their different ways saw as potentially the property of all men at least, can now be achieved only by a handful of individuals. Moreover, giving a law to oneself (Rousseau's definition of freedom: see §1.5 above) is now a matter of self-creation. What Nietzsche says here can only be understood in the light of the earlier development of German classical idealism. One of the strongest tendencies of this philosophical tradition was to treat aesthetic experience as a privileged mode of access to reality, capable of offering insights denied to rational, discursive knowledge. Hegel strongly resisted this tendency (art is the lowest form of Absolute Spirit, subordinated to religion and philosophy), but others – Schelling and Schopenhauer, for example – gave powerful expression to it. Alexander Nehemas has drawn attention to what he calls 'Nietzsche's aestheticism, his essential reliance on artistic models for understanding the world and life and for evaluating people and actions'.[65] As this makes clear, Nietzsche does not privilege aesthetic experience on the basis of the doctrine of art for art's sake, as a kind of flight from the world. On the contrary, we must see '[t]he world as a work of art that gives birth to itself.'[66] The process of self-creation which some individual humans are able to achieve is thus merely an instance of the cosmic process of 'self-overcoming' that is the world itself.

Artistic creation as Nietzsche sees it is not the discovery of harmonious structures immanent in the world portrayed by classical criticism. Rather, like Modern art, it is a dissonant, discordant process whose products are tense with the conflicts from which they arose. These conflicts are, in the first instance, those constitutive of human history. In *On the Genealogy of Morals* (1887), Nietzsche dismisses attempts to treat morality in either Kantian or utilitarian terms as, respectively, an autonomous system of abstract laws, or actions whose consequences maximize the general welfare. In doing so, he challenges any attempt to discern in history a unified pattern, whether that pattern is derived from Hegelian teleology or from the more conventional evolutionary schemes discussed in the previous section. 'Genealogy', as Foucault puts it, '. . . seeks to re-establish the various systems of subjection: not the anticipatory power of meaning, but the hazardous play of dominations.'[67] This implies a sociology of moral belief. As Hans Barth observes of Nietzsche's later writings, '[t]he traditional morals he subjects to criticism are treated more and more as the expression of certain classes.'[68]

In particular, Nietzsche argues that valuations of good and bad emerge in aristocratic societies where they permit the ruling class to affirm itself and its way of life. Morality in its Christian and modern understandings, which have in

---

[65] A. Nehemas, *Nietzsche: Life as Literature* (Cambridge, Mass., 1988), p. 39.

[66] F. Nietzsche (1906), *The Will to Power* (New York, 1968), §797, p. 419.

[67] M. Foucault, 'Nietzsche, Genealogy, History', in P. Rabinow, ed., *The Foucault Reader* (Harmondsworth, 1986), p. 83.

[68] H. Barth, *Truth and Ideology* (Berkeley, 1976), p. 160.

common the idea that the self should deny itself in the interests of others, originates in the revolt of the lower orders against their masters, a particularly subtle
kind of revolt which takes the form, not of open rebellion, but of inverting the
values of the noble morality:

> The slave revolt in morality begins when *ressentiment* itself becomes creative
> and gives birth to values: the *ressentiment* of natures that are denied the true
> reaction, that of deeds, and compensate themselves with an imaginary revenge,
> while every noble morality develops from a triumphant affirmation of self, slave
> morality from the outset says No to what is 'outside', what is 'different', what is
> 'not itself'; and this *No* is its creative deed.[69]

The apogee of this 'slave morality' is reached in Christianity, which systematically devalues life in the name of a world beyond. The triumph of Christianity represents the subjection of the values of the master to those of the slave in
the shape of a systematic negation of this world, a process which reaches its
climax in the levelling mediocrity of post-Revolutionary Europe, a 'nihilism'
in which everything is devalued. Nietzsche proclaims the struggle of *'Dionysus
versus the crucified'*.[70] The Greek god Dionysus stands for the affirmation of
life, Christ for its negation. Nietzsche seeks a 'revaluation of all values': in
other words, he wishes – rather like Feuerbach and Marx in their struggle with
Hegel – to invert the inversion accomplished by slave morality, and reinstate a
system of valuation in which select individuals can once again affirm themselves and life. But in doing so he takes aim not merely at Christianity, but goes
further back, into the history of Greek philosophy: it is Socrates and his pupil
Plato who are responsible for transforming the world of experience into mere
'appearance' to which is counterposed an inaccessible 'truth' or 'reality' beyond the bounds of the senses. 'My philosophy is an *inverted Platonism*,'
Nietzsche wrote in 1870–1, 'the farther removed from true being the purer, the
finer, the better it is. Living in semblance as goal.'[71]

But what is this life, this 'semblance' which Nietzsche champions? German
Romanticism gave rise to a philosophy of nature (*Naturphilosophie*) which
conceived a kind of inner impulse running through the whole of the physical
world, inorganic and organic alike, and reaching its highest expression in human subjectivity which represented the whole of nature in microcosm. Nietzsche
also conceives nature as a totality, but its process is in no sense a directional
one, or oriented towards a goal: events arise from no inner necessity, but occur
rather in the realm of accident – they are 'fragments and limbs and dreadful
chances'.[72] This does not mean that they have no discernible structure. But the

---

[69]   F. Nietzsche, *On the Genealogy of Morals and Ecce Homo* (New York, 1969), p. 36.
[70]   Ibid., p. 335.
[71]   Quoted in M. Heidegger, *Nietzsche* (4 vols, San Francisco, 1991), I, p. 154.
[72]   Nietzsche, *Zarathustra*, II. 20, p. 160.

pattern Nietzsche sees in nature generally is the same as that revealed in the *Genealogy of Morals* – the endless struggle for domination among competing centres of power: '*This world is the will to power and nothing else besides! And you yourselves are also this will to power and nothing else besides!*'[73]

Such assertions appear to represent the most fantastic anthropomorphism – the megalomaniac projection of the patterns of intentional human action onto nature as a whole. Indeed, Heidegger ascribes to Nietzsche '*a metaphysics of the absolute subjectivity of the will to power*', though not an idealist metaphysics, since here 'subjectivity is absolute as subjectivity of the body; that is, of drives and affects'.[74] Yet the will to power is nothing like the will as it has traditionally been conceived, that is, as the faculty of a subject which consciously sets itself goals and seeks to achieve them. Nietzsche indeed denies the individual human subject any coherence or unity: 'our body is only a social structure composed of many souls . . . *L'effet, c'est moi.*'[75] As for the will to power, it is 'not a being, not a becoming, but a *pathos* – the most elemental fact from which a becoming and effecting first emerge'.[76] As Richard Schacht comments, '*pathos*' here means 'a fundamental disposition or tendency'. Thus, ' "will to power" for Nietzsche is simply the basic tendency of all forces and configurations of forces to extend their influence and dominate others'.[77]

Nature in its entirety – the human world as well as the interactions of physical bodies and the development of living organisms – is thus the continuous process of transformation arising from the endless struggle among a multiplicity of rival centres of power. The natural kinds and physical laws scientists 'discover' represent at best the ephemeral outcome of these conflicts; Darwin's theory of evolution by natural selection is an inadequate approximation to the reality of the eternal struggle, not to survive and reproduce, but to dominate. Reality is therefore inherently plural: it has no single essence, no inner purpose from which all else flows. It is also inherently ambiguous. The world is constituted by a set of shifting relations of force. It follows that, depending on one's position within these relations, the interpretation that one puts on the world is likely to be different. Indeed, there is '[n]o limit to the way in which the world can be interpreted.'[78]

One of the longest-standing themes in Nietzsche's writings concerns the relativity of knowledge to the interests of those concerned. Thus he declares: 'Truth is the kind of error without which a certain species could not live. The value for *life* is ultimately decisive.'[79] It is on this basis that, for example, he

[73] Nietzsche, *Will to Power*, §1067, p. 550.
[74] Heidegger, *Nietzsche*, IV, p. 147.
[75] Nietzsche, *Beyond Good and Evil*, §19, p. 20. 'I am the effect' – a pun on Louis XIV's declaration 'L'état c'est moi' – 'I am the state'.
[76] Nietzsche, *Will to Power*, §635, p. 229.
[77] R. Schacht, *Nietzsche* (London, 1983), pp. 207, 220.
[78] Nietzsche, *Will to Power*, §600, p. 326.
[79] Ibid., §493, p. 272.

counterposes to what he regards as the suffocating historical self-conscious-ness of nineteenth-century Europe ' "the unhistorical" . . . the art and power of *forgetting* and of enclosing oneself within a bounded *horizon*'.[80] Historical in-terpretation, indeed interpretation generally, is necessarily selective – it omits as well as includes; this selection is relative to the interests, not of 'life' in the abstract, but of the particular form of life, the particular centre of power from whose perspective the interpretation is made. Nietzsche's 'perspectivism' leads him to the denial of the possibility of objective truth, and thereby to all the difficulties in which any form of scepticism necessarily entangles itself. He nevertheless comes to see it as one of the main implications of his doctrine of the will to power. Thus he writes of 'the necessary perspectivism by virtue of which every centre of force – and not only man – construes all the rest of the world from its own viewpoint, i.e., measures, feels, forms, according to its own force'.[81]

This process of construing and valuing the world from a specific perspective is in many respects the decisive feature of the will to power. To see the latter as a drive to dominate in primarily socio-political terms is to misunderstand Nietzsche. As Schacht puts it, ' "power" for Nietzsche is fundamentally a mat-ter of transformation, involving the imposition of some new pattern of ordering relations upon forces not previously subject to them'.[82] This process of form-giving is essentially aesthetic. Art achieves greatness, Nietzsche argues, in 'the grand style': 'This style has in common with great passion, that it disdains to please; that it forgets to persuade; that it commands; that it *wills* – To become master of the chaos one is; to compel one's chaos to become form: to become logical, simple, unambiguous, mathematics, *law* – that is the grand ambition here.'[83] This is what 'becoming what one is' means – mastering oneself by turning one's life into a work of art, shaping the chaos which not simply each individual but the entire world is into a formed whole. Nietzsche saw his own life as precisely such a process which, through the revaluation of all values that it sought to effect, would help make possible the 'overman' (*Übermensch*), the higher type of humanity in which such creative self-mastery is consummated.

Heidegger therefore seeks to distance Nietzsche from any form of biological determinism: '*Nietzsche thinks the "biological", the essence of what is alive, in the direction of commanding and poetizing, of the perspectival and the hor-izontal: in the direction of freedom.* He does *not* think the biological . . . bio-logically at all.'[84] This is something of an overstatement. Nietzsche does not see the formation of the 'highest exemplars' of humanity as a purely cultural

---

[80] Nietzsche, *Untimely Meditations*, p. 120.
[81] Nietzsche, *Will to Power*, §636, p. 339.
[82] Schacht, *Nietzsche*, p. 229.
[83] Nietzsche, *Will to Power*, §842, p. 444.
[84] Heidegger, *Nietzsche*, III, p. 122.

process achieved through education, experience, and debate. On the contrary, he seems to envisage something comparable to what Darwin calls the 'artificial selection' of species of domestic animals, in which particular human types are cultivated through 'breeding', so that the characteristics which 'higher' men have acquired through their self-formation are transmitted, in the Lamarckian fashion so pervasive in nineteenth-century evolutionary thinking, to their descendants.

This tension between the biological and cultural is one of the many running through Nietzsche's thought. The doctrine of his whose interpretation is most disputed is that of the eternal recurrence of the same, the 'absymal thought' that everything eternally repeats itself.[85] This idea represents the extreme limit to which Nietzsche takes his rejection of all interpretations of reality which treat it as moving in a definite direction, whether or not this direction is understood in teleological terms as movement towards a goal. His formulations of the eternal recurrence of the same in his published writings are expressed in highly metaphorical terms. It is quite unclear whether or not Nietzsche intends us to take the idea literally – though he does in his notebooks present it as a cosmological theory about the fundamental tendencies of the universe – or rather as a kind of ultimate test of one's willingness to affirm life even if everything recurs eternally, rather than give way to the temptation to sink into fatalist pessimism.

Commentators also disagree over the idea's consistency with the doctrine of the will to power. The latter presents the world in the aspect of 'becoming', as a process of continual transformation; yet if everything recurs, this movement is ultimately enfolded within an endlessly repeated cycle. As Nietzsche himself puts it, '[t]hat *everything recurs* is the closest *approximation of a world of becoming to a world of being.*'[86] The stasis of being thus apparently triumphs over restless becoming. For this reason, the Nazi philosopher Alfred Bäumler argued that the will to power represented the essence of Nietzsche's thought, and that, inasmuch as the eternal recurrence was incompatible with it, it should be played down; Heidegger strongly contested this position.

These tensions and ambiguities help to explain why Nietzsche's intellectual heritage is so diverse. The Nazis took from him chiefly the idea of the will to power, which they understood as the drive of nations and exceptional individuals to dominate, and married it to a vulgar Darwinian conception of life as eternal struggle, and to biological racism, to produce an ideology bearing very little resemblance to Nietzsche's own philosophy. Weber, and more recently post-structuralists such as Foucault, took over his view of history as the interplay of forms of domination, and his perspectivism, building these into their own theories. And the later Heidegger, after his involvement in National

---

[85]　Nietzsche, *Zarathustra*, III. 2. 2, pp. 178–9.
[86]　Nietzsche, *Will to Power*, §617, p. 330.

Socialism, took what he regarded as Nietzsche's ultimately unsuccessful attempt to escape the subjectivism of modernity as one of the starting-points of his meditations on how Europe had gone wrong.

These conflicting interpretations do not in any way diminish – indeed they are symptomatic of – Nietzsche's significance. The force of his rejection of modernity lies in its not being undertaken in the name of an idealized past. Nietzsche replaced the vista of historical progress evoked by the Enlightenment and evolutionists such as Spencer and Kautsky with the grim panorama of an endless struggle for domination, and at the same time he offered the artistic life – or life as a work of art – as the best way of responding to this situation. In doing so, he posed questions which continue to press on us.

6

Durkheim

6.1 Social evolution and scientific objectivity

Evolutionary social theory came in the mid-nineteenth century, as we saw in the previous chapter, to conceptualize society as an organism to be analysed in terms analogous to those used by evolutionary biology. But one potential implication of this way of thinking about society could draw it away from the attempt to place social phenomena within an evolutionary schema. A key development involved in the constitution of the life sciences at the end of the eighteenth century was the attempt to analyse organisms in terms of their *function*. Living bodies were conceived, in other words, as organized systems composed of interdependent parts, each of which played a specific role in securing certain states essential to the system's continued existence. The employment of this kind of functional analysis in social theory implied analysing specific processes and institutions from the standpoint of their contribution to the overall well-being of the society in question. To the extent that functional analysis comes to predominate in the study of society the issue of where a society belongs in an evolutionary sequence of types of social formation – along with, indeed, the broader question of the historical emergence and trajectory of the society – tends to recede into the background.

Social theorists have always employed functional analysis: classical political economy traces the way in which the interactions of self-interested actors contribute, via the 'invisible hand', to a state of market equilibrium which maximizes the general welfare; Marx's concept of structural contradiction is a tool for identifying *dys*functions – the tendencies intrinsic to particular modes of production which come to impede their effective operation. But a strain of social theory focusing primarily on the analysis of functions only emerges at the end of the nineteenth century. Durkheim played the main part in its creation.[1]

---

[1] Émile Durkheim (1859–1917): like Marx of Jewish, indeed rabbinic, origins; studied at the École Normale Supérieure in Paris, 1879–82; studied in Germany, 1885–6; *chargé de cours* in social science and pedagogy at the Faculty of Letters, Bordeaux, 1887–1902; *chargé de cours* in the science of education at the Sorbonne, 1902–17.

It is important not to see this shift as a purely methodological replacement of one type of analysis by another. More than any other social theorist of the first rank, Durkheim sought to constitute sociology as a distinct and autonomous science with its own theoretical protocols and professional infrastructure. Göran Therborn has suggested that 'the central sociological contribution to a scientific discourse on society . . . *has essentially consisted in the discovery and study of the ideological community* – i.e. community of values and norms – *in human aggregates of various types and sizes*', and that formulating this concept of the 'ideological community' necessitated a 'sociological critique of political economy' in whose formulation Durkheim played a decisive role.[2]

Certainly the condition of Western society at the end of the nineteenth century seemed to signal the limits of *laissez faire*. Evolutionists such as Spencer and Maine had depicted a progression from status to contract, from militant to industrial society – in other words, the course of history was moving towards the kind of exclusively market-based social order which the theoretical models of Smith, Ricardo, and later marginalist economists postulated. But, as Spencer was painfully aware (see §5.2 above), as the nineteenth century drew to a close, the trend was in the opposite direction, towards greater state regulation of and intervention in economic and social life.

This re-emergence of what came to be called 'collectivism' was, in part, a consequence of political developments. By the late nineteenth century industrial capitalism had broken out of its original, mainly British, base and was coming to predominate throughout western Europe and North America.This brought in its wake the emergence of increasingly powerful and assertive working-class movements. The concomitant (and, to a large degree, consequent) extension of the suffrage obliged liberal and conservative politicians to offer social reforms in order to defuse the threat of these movements and to win workers' votes: Bismarck's introduction of social insurance in an unsuccessful attempt to undermine German Social Democracy is a classic instance of this process.

The increased state regulation of Western societies which these reforms promoted also facilitated the development of empirical social enquiry. Public bureaucracies and private philanthropists gathered growing bodies of data about different aspects of social life. Increasingly organized numerically, this material was sought and employed in order to provide information about the social 'problems' which state policy increasingly sought to identify and redress. But it also made possible both the pursuit of specific studies and the formulation of empirical generalizations by social scientists. One major nineteenth-century intellectual achievement was the development of the discipline of statistics, and in particular the refinement by Adolphe Quételet of the concept of a statistical law as a property of a population which can only be under-

---

2 G. Therborn, *Science, Class and Society* (London, 1976), pp. 224, 247.

stood in probabilistic terms. Previously scientists had tended to conceive natural laws as operating deterministically, so that the behaviour of every event falling under them could, in principle, be predicted by them; statistical laws, by contrast, made claims only about the relative frequency with which events would conform to their predictions.

The first statistical laws to be formulated were often generalizations from data gathered by bureaucrats and reformers concerned to identify the social problems generated by industrial capitalism. Ian Hacking writes: 'Many of the first law-like regularities were first perceived in connection with deviancy: suicide, crime, madness, disease.' Indeed, he suggests that

> statistical laws do apply to classes. It is laws about 'them', about the other, that are to be determined, to be analysed, and to be the basis for legislation. The classes in question are not abstract entities but rather social realities. Inevitably it is the labouring or criminal or colonial classes that are the chief objects to be changed, for their own good.[3]

The development of statistical techniques and the results of their application provided the means to transform sociology from the philosophy of history it had remained in Comte's and Spencer's hands into a form of empirical enquiry. Moreover, the constitution of sociology as an established academic discipline took place in a context where *laissez faire* was widely perceived to have failed both intellectually and practically. Durkheim insists on the inability of unrestrained economic individualism to provide the prerequisites of a stable social order: 'It is therefore extremely important that economic life should be regulated, should have its morals raised, so that the conflicts that disturb it have an end and further, that individuals should cease to live their lives in a moral vacuum where the life-blood drains away even from individual morality.'[4]

This stress on the necessity of moral regulation implies, as Therborn argues, a critical stance towards political economy. Durkheim praises 'the economists . . . for having first pointed out the spontaneous character of social life, showing that constraint can only cause it to deviate from its natural course and that normally it arises not from arrangements imposed from without, but from its own free internal nature'. They have nevertheless failed to see that 'liberty itself is the product of regulation'. Therefore, he declares in his first major work, *The Division of Labour* (1893), his aim is 'to constitute the science of morality', that is, 'to treat the facts of moral life according to the methods of the positive sciences'.[5]

This ambition suggests the continuity between Durkheimian sociology and the *moraliste* tradition of early modern and Enlightenment French thought –

---

[3]   I. Hacking, *The Taming of Chance* (Cambridge, 1990), pp. 3, 120.

[4]   E. Durkheim, *Professional Ethics and Civic Morals* (London, 1957), p. 12.

[5]   E. Durkheim, *The Division of Labour* (Houndmills, 1984), pp. 320, xv.

the study of human conduct in its relationship to social institutions and customs (see ch. 1 above). But in Durkheim's case this concern with 'moral life' thus understood springs from his preoccupation with the dislocations and antagonisms of what he tends to call (following Saint-Simon and Spencer) industrial society. Thus he argues that *anomie*, or the absence of moral regulation, is responsible for

> the continually recurring conflicts and disorders of every kind of which the economic world affords so sorry a spectacle. For, since nothing restrains the forces present from reacting together, or prescribes limits to them that they are obliged to respect, they tend to grow beyond all bounds, each clashing with the other, each warding off and weakening the other . . . Men's passions are stayed only by a moral presence they respect. If all authority of this kind is lacking, it is the law of the strongest that rules, and a state of warfare, either latent or acute, is necessarily endemic.[6]

This conception of moral regulation as a means of preventing, or at least controlling, social conflict suggests a theory with a conservative cast. Indeed, Durkheim himself wrote that 'the object of sociology as a whole is to determine the conditions for the conservation of societies'.[7] He was not, however, a thinker of the political right. Anthony Giddens has suggested that '[i]t makes some sense to see both Weber and Durkheim as attempting to reconstruct liberalism in the context of a critique of Marxism on the one side, and of conservative thought, on the other.'[8] Or, in the terms formulated by Habermas (see §2.3 above), Durkheim and Weber seek to defend modernity (albeit critically) against those, such as Nietzsche, who reject it, and those, such as Marx, who seek to revolutionize it.

Durkheim strongly identified with the liberal parliamentary institutions of the French Third Republic (1871–1940). When these institutions were challenged by the monarchist and militarist right during the Dreyfus Affair in the 1890s, Durkheim was one of the first defenders of Dreyfus (a Jewish army officer falsely accused of espionage), and an active participant in the republican, anti-clerical Ligue des Droits de l'Homme. He may have owed his appointment to the Sorbonne to his Dreyfusard sympathies. According to Georges Friedmann, subsequent to the Affair, 'Durkheimian sociology established itself, alongside secular morality, in the official teaching of the Third Republic, through the various grades of teaching, and in particular through the *écoles normales* [teachers' colleges].'[9] In his effort to develop sociology in France

---

[6]   Ibid., pp. xxxii–xxxiii.

[7]   Undated letter to Bouglé, quoted in S. Lukes, *Émile Durkheim* (Harmondsworth, 1975), p. 139.

[8]   A. Giddens, 'Weber and Durkheim: Coincidence and Divergence', in W. J. Mommsen and J. Osterhammel, eds, *Max Weber and his Contemporaries* (London, 1987), p. 188.

[9]   Quoted in Lukes, *Durkheim*, p. 376.

into an institutionalized discipline, Durkheim founded in 1896 the journal *L'Année sociologique*, and gathered around him, first in Bordeaux and then in Paris, an influential group of pupils and collaborators.

Durkheim's political outlook will be considered in more detail alongside his substantive social theory in the following section. But it is worth first noting the extent to which his work, at least initially, was a development of themes explored by earlier evolutionary social theorists. *The Division of Labour*, though quite distinctive in conceptualizing society as essentially a moral reality, reverberates with echoes of Comte and Spencer. Both understood social evolution as a process of progressive differentiation; Spencer treated the development of the division of labour as the principal mechanism on which this process depended (see §§3.1 and 5.2 above). But how would not a society fragmented into specialized individuals be liable to disintegration? Comte's argument that the re-establishment of consensus would restore the basis of a stable social order seemed to threaten the suppression of the individual freedom characteristic of modernity; Spencer, by contrast, believed that this freedom could be secured only by uninhibited *laissez faire*, a state of affairs which, as we have seen, Durkheim regarded as the main source of *anomie* and social conflict.

Durkheim posed the problem thus:

> How does it come about that the individual, whilst becoming more autonomous, depends more closely on society? How can he become at the same time more of an individual and yet more linked to society? For it is indisputable that these two movements, however contradictory they appear to be, are carried out in tandem. Such is the nature of the problem. It has seemed that what resolved this apparent antinomy was the transformation of social solidarity that arises from the ever-increasing division of labour.[10]

Durkheim counterposes two types of solidarity. The first, mechanical solidarity, is characteristic of what he calls 'segmented societies'. Here each constituent part of society is identical to every other – social functions are, in other words, relatively undifferentiated. Social solidarity depends in these circumstances on 'beliefs and sentiments common to all members of the group'. Organic solidarity, by contrast, arises where the division of labour has developed, so that individuals are allocated to different social roles. Here 'the society to which we are solidly joined is a system of different and special functions united by definite relationships'.[11] It is in this context that Durkheim introduces one of his best-known concepts, that of the collective consciousness (*conscience collective*):

> Two consciousnesses exist within us: the one comprises only states that are personal to each of us, characteristic of us as individuals, while the other comprises states that are common to the whole of society. The former represents only our

---

[10] Durkheim, *Division*, p. xxx.
[11] Ibid., p. 83.

individual personality, which it constitutes; the latter represents the collective type, and consequently the society without which it would not exist. When it is an element of the latter determining our behaviour, we do not act with an eye to our own personal interest, but are pursuing collective ends.[12]

Mechanical and organic solidarity are distinguished by the extent to which the collective consciousness prevails over the individual in them. 'Solidarity that derives from similarities is at its *maximum* when the collective consciousness completely envelops our total consciousness, coinciding with it at every point. At that moment our individuality is zero.' Where organic solidarity prevails, however, 'each one of us has a sphere that is peculiarly our own, and consequently a personality'. The role of the collective consciousness diminishes, taking the form of 'modes of thinking and feeling of a very general, indeterminate nature, which leave room for an increasing multitude of individual acts of dissent'. As organic solidarity becomes the main form of social integration, '[i]t is the division of labour that is increasingly fulfilling the role that once fell to the common consciousness. This is mainly what holds together social entities in the higher type of society.'[13]

The distinction between mechanical and organic solidarity is one of a series of binary contrasts by means of which social theorists have sought to conceptualize the difference between modern societies and their predecessors. Maine's distinction between status and contract, and Spencer's between militant and industrial societies are instances of this kind of contrast (see ch. 5 above), as is that drawn by Tönnies between *Gemeinschaft* (community) and *Gesellschaft* (association).[14]

Tönnies regarded the transition from one kind of society to another as essentially a process of loss: individuals in pre-modern *Gemeinschaft* were bound into the social whole by a series of primarily affective connections; social relationships in modern *Gesellschaft* are cold and egoistic, based on individuals' rational calculations of their interests. Thus 'Gemeinschaft should be understood as a living organism, Gesellschaft as a mechanical aggregate and artifact.' *Gemeinschaft* has its roots in rural life, and above all in the *Heimat* (home country) constituted by the ties of tradition and kinship which are found on land long settled and worked by the same peasant community. *Gesellschaft*, whose structure was best portrayed by Hobbes and Marx, is urban and cosmopolitan; its principal agent is the merchant, the eternal outsider. Its triumph 'means the doom of culture'.[15] Tönnies lived to see the victory of National Socialism, which

[12]   Ibid., p. 61.
[13]   Ibid., pp. 84, 85, 122, 123.
[14]   Ferdinand Tönnies (1855–1936): born in Schleswig-Holstein; studied at Strassbourg, Jena, Bonn, Leipzig, and Tübingen universities; took his *Habilitation* (qualifying him as a university teacher), on Hobbes, at Berlin University in 1881; worked for the Prussian Statistical Bureau; Professor of Economics and Statistics at Kiel University, 1913–16; president of the German Sociological Society, 1909–33.
[15]   F. Tönnies, *Community and Association* (London, 1974), pp. 39, 270.

he opposed. He nevertheless helped to formulate the version of Romantic anti-capitalism frequently drawn on by the German nationalist right when attacking modernity (see §9.2 below).

Durkheim, by contrast, is closer to Maine and Spencer in thinking that the development of organic solidarity constitutes progress over its predecessor: 'Here, then, the individuality of the whole grows at the same time as that of the parts. Society becomes more effective in moving in concert, at the same time as each of its elements has more movements that are peculiarly its own.' But Durkheim disagrees with both Spencer and Tönnies in so far as they treat the division of labour as a utilitarian arrangement among self-interested individuals, and thus fail to see that 'co-operation has its intrinsic morality'.[16]

The Division of Labour thus offers an evolutionary theory; indeed Durkheim, like Comte and Spencer, conceives social evolution as a process of differentiation in which progressively more complex types replace their simpler predecessors. Yet he denies that 'the different types of society are set out in gradations according to the same ascending linear series'. Employing an image used by Darwin to characterize the direction of biological evolution, Durkheim argues that 'if it were possible to draw up the complete genealogical table of social types, it would have rather the shape of a bushy tree, doubtless with a single trunk, but with diverging branches'. He further denies that progress along a particular branch – say, that from mechanical to organic solidarity – represents an increase in the sum of human happiness: 'there is no connection between the variations in happiness and the progress in the division of labour'.[17] Finally, Durkheim criticizes 'the former philosophy of history', of which he regards even Comte as an example, for its teleological modes of thinking, in which 'the social environment has been perceived as a means whereby progress has been realized, and not the cause which determines it'.[18]

Seeking to distinguish Durkheim's theory of social evolution from that of his predecessors, Steven Lukes denies that, as commentators such as Talcott Parsons have claimed, the explanation of social change in *The Division of Labour* is 'biologistic'.[19] Lukes's interpretation relies chiefly on the fact that this explanation, generalized in *The Rules of Sociological Method* (1895), isolates two factors as chiefly responsible for the development of the division of labour. 'These are: firstly, the number of social units or, as we have also termed it, the "volume" of the society; and secondly, the degree of concentration of the mass of people, or what we have called the "dynamic density".'[20]

Roughly speaking, the idea is that the more tightly packed together greater

---

[16]   Durkheim, *Division*, pp. 85, 168.
[17]   Ibid., p. 100 n. 17.
[18]   E. Durkheim, *The Rules of Sociological Method and Selected Texts on Sociology and its Method*, ed. S. Lukes, London (1982), pp. 140, 143.
[19]   Lukes, *Durkheim*, pp. 167–8.
[20]   Durkheim, *Rules*, p. 136.

numbers of people are, the more intense competition among them for scarce resources will be; social actors are likely to react to this state of affairs by seeking to maximize their relative advantages through greater specialization, thereby promoting a more developed division of labour. Thus Durkheim denies Spencer's claim that environmental differences are a sufficient condition of functional specialization: 'If labour becomes increasingly divided as societies become more voluminous and concentrated, it is not because the external circumstances are more varied, it is because the struggle for survival becomes more strenuous.'[21]

Whatever we think of this Darwinian version of Smith's 'invisible hand' as an explanation of the division of labour, Lukes is right to say that the causes it identifies are exclusively social ones. This does not, however, settle the question of whether or not there are biologistic strains in Durkheim's thought. Thus consider these remarks of Spencer's on the relationship between biology and sociology:

> There are two distinct but equally important ways in which these sciences are connected. In the first place, all social actions being determined by the actions of individuals, and all actions of individuals being vital actions that conform to the laws of life at large, rational interpretation of social actions implies knowledge of the laws of life. In the second place, a society as a whole, considered apart from its living units, presents phenomena of growth, structure, and function analogous to those of growth, structure, and function in an animal; and these last are useful keys to the first.[22]

Spencer thus proposes two connections between biology: first, societies are reducible to the individuals composing them, which in turn must be understood as organisms; second, social processes operate in ways analogical to those in the living world. Durkheim emphatically denies the first claim. In the *Rules* he famously defends the autonomy of sociology on the basis that 'social facts must be treated as things'. Durkheim's evolving conception of social facts will be considered more closely in the following section. What is relevant for present purposes is that he denies that social facts are reducible to individuals and their properties. Thus: 'society is not the mere sum of individuals, but the system formed by their association represents a specific reality which has its own characteristics'.[23]

This position was crucial to Durkheim's project of constituting sociology as a science distinct from economics. The development of marginalist economics towards the end of the nineteenth century involved the explicit formulation of what has come to be known as methodological individualism, the doctrine that

---

[21]   Durkheim, *Division*, p. 208.
[22]   H. Spencer, *The Study of Sociology* (London, 1894), p. 326.
[23]   Durkheim, *Rules*, pp. 35, 129.

social structures are the unintended consequences of individual actions. Thus the Austrian economist Carl Menger, a leader of the marginalist revolution, highlighted those 'social phenomena [which] come about as the unintended result of individual efforts (pursuing *individual interests*) without a *common will* directed towards their establishment', and argued that 'human *individuals* and their *efforts*' are 'the final elements of our analysis' in 'the exact social sciences', the equivalent of forces and atoms in physics.[24]

Methodological individualism is, in effect, a generalization of the conception of explanation which became entrenched in economics as a result of the marginalist revolution, in which the optimization of the general welfare is an unintended consequence of the self-interested choices of individual market actors. Although Durkheim was, as we saw above, willing in specific cases to employ this type of explanation, he sympathized with the marginalists' opponents, the German Historical School, for whom the economy was an evolving social organism rather than the aggregate of individual actions (see §7.1 below). Further, if the reduction claim made by Spencer and Menger went through, then the space for Durkheim's autonomous 'science of morality' would vanish. Hence his insistence on the autonomy of social facts: thus he argues that the existence of 'collective tendencies' as 'things, forces *sui generis* which dominate the consciousness of single individuals . . . is brilliantly shown by the statistics of suicide', which do not change from year to year.[25] More generally: *'The determining cause of a social fact must be sought among antecedent social facts and not among the states of the individual consciousness.'*[26]

But if Durkheim's opposition to methodological individualism absolves him of the charge of direct biological reductionism, the situation is much less clear when it comes to the second connection Spencer posits between biology and sociology, which consists in their conceptualizing processes analogously. Durkheim systematically contrasts the normal and the pathological. Thus he argues that '[i]f normally the division of labour produces social solidarity, it can happen, however, that it has entirely different or even opposite results.' These 'pathological' or 'deviant' forms include the effects of economic crises and of bankruptcies, which are 'so many partial breaks in organic solidarity', conflict between labour and capital, and scientific specialization. 'In all these cases, if the division of labour does not produce solidarity, it is because the relationships between the organs are not regulated; it is because they are in a state of *anomie*.'[27]

Durkheim says that a social fact is normal when it corresponds to 'the average type' in a historical given society, 'the hypothetical being which might be constituted by assembling in one entity, as a kind of individual abstraction, the

[24] C. Menger (1883), *Problems of Economics and Sociology* (Urbana, 1963), pp. 133, 142 n.1.
[25] E. Durkheim (1897), *Suicide* (London, 1989), p. 307.
[26] Durkheim, *Rules*, p. 134.
[27] Durkheim, *Division*, pp. 291, 292, 304.

most frequently occurring characteristics of the species in their most frequent forms'. He conceives normality thus understood in broad terms, so that, for example, 'crime is a phenomenon of normal sociology', since it is inevitable that individuals will not always conform to the collective consciousness. Never theless, '[t]he principal purpose of any science of life, whether individual or social, is in the end to define and explain the normal state and to distinguish it from the abnormal.'[28]

There is therefore an important respect in which Durkheim conceives society as an organism, capable of experiencing both health and illness. It is, indeed, by seeking to identify the normal condition of a specific society that sociology can offer moral and political guidance as well as describe and explain:

> if what is desirable is declared to be what is healthy, and if the state of health is something definite, inherent in things . . . [t]here is no longer need to pursue des- perately an end which recedes as we move forward; we need only to work stead- ily to maintain the normal state, to re-establish it if it is disturbed, and to rediscover the conditions of normality if they happen to change . . . His role [i.e. that of the statesman] . . . is that of the doctor: he forestalls the outbreak of sickness by main- taining good hygiene, or when it breaks down, seeks to cure it.[29]

This medical conception of sociology reflects a widespread assumption in the nineteenth-century life sciences. Thus, when Durkheim writes that 'the study of deviant forms will allow us to determine better the conditions for the exist- ence of the normal state', he echoes the great physiologist Claude Bernard, who declared: 'Every disease has a corresponding normal function of which it is only the disturbed, exaggerated, diminished or obliterated expression.'[30] Claims of this nature implied, first, that the mechanisms at work in normal and path- ological states are identical, and, secondly, that the distinction between the two conditions is an objective one, as Durkheim puts it, 'inherent in things'.

But the second of these implications at least is very hard to defend. As Georges Canguilhem puts it, '[t]o define the abnormal as too much or too little is to recognize the normative character of the so-called normal state. The normal or physiological state is no longer simply a disposition which can be revealed and explained as a fact, but a manifestation of an attachment to some value.' In his great study of nineteenth-century medical thought, Canguilhem demonstrates the difficulty of finding an objective criterion by means of which to distinguish the normal and the pathological. Defining the normal statistically, in terms of the average, for example, as Quételet and Durkheim do (though in different ways), faces the problem that, by definition, many individual cases will deviate

---

28 Durkheim, *Rules*, pp. 91–2, 106 n. 10, 104.
29 Ibid., p. 104.
30 Durkheim, *Division*, p. 291; Bernard, quoted in G. Canguilhem, *The Normal and the Patho- logical* (New York, 1991), p. 68.

from the average. But how far must a case deviate from the average before it becomes abnormal? Canguilhem concludes:

> To set a norm [*normer*], to normalize, is to impose a requirement on an existence, a given whose variety, disparity, with regard to the requirement, present themselves as a hostile, even more than an unknown, indeterminant. It is, in fact, a polemical concept which negatively qualifies the sector of the given which does not enter into its extension while it depends on it for its comprehension.[31]

The difficulty of drawing a non-arbitrary dividing-line between the normal and the pathological is brought out by Durkheim's discussion of crime. He declares that 'to make crime a social illness would be to concede that sickness is not something accidental, but on the contrary derives in certain cases from the fundamental constitution of the living creature'.[32] Crime cannot be a pathological condition because it is so universally present in society: so persistent an abnormality would imply that society itself is inherently defective. Thus Durkheim's employment of the distinction between the normal and the pathological is not merely indicative of the presence of biological forms of reasoning in his writings; it demonstrates the extent of his attachment to social stability.

In his conception of sociology (though not in his substantive social theory), Durkheim remained in many ways a loyal follower of Comte. Comte, like Durkheim, argued that sociology is an autonomous science whose object is irreducible to the results of individual action. Like Durkheim also, he nevertheless regarded sociology and biology as closely related, and indeed played an important part in developing the theory of the normal and the pathological. None of this is to diminish the significance of Durkheim's work, or to ignore the respects in which it differs from, or goes beyond, Comte. Yet while, as we shall see, Weber strongly resists the tug of evolutionary social theory, Durkheim's thought in certain crucial ways rests upon and creatively develops its assumptions.

6.2   Society as a moral reality

Durkheim in *The Division of Labour* characterizes the process of social differentiation as consisting in, among other things, the progressive liberation of the individual personality from the collective consciousness. While this conception of social evolution thus contrasts the relative weight of the collective consciousness in two types of social solidarity, it does not rely chiefly on beliefs and representations in order to explain the movement from one to the other. On the contrary, the main causes of social differentation are, as we have seen, what

[31]   Canguilhem, *Normal*, pp. 56–7, 239.
[32]   Durkheim, *Rules*, p. 98.

Durkheim calls the volume and density of society. He even writes: 'Everything occurs mechanically. A break in the equilibrium of the social mass gives rise to conflicts that can only be resolved by a more developed form of the division of labour; this is the driving force for progress.'[33] Indeed, Lewis Coser suggests that 'in *The Division of Labour* he is largely a structural analyst not as far removed from Marx as certain commentators have sometimes been inclined to think'.[34]

Yet, subsequent to this work, Durkheim increasingly comes to conceptualize society as a moral entity constituted by collective representations which are no less mental states for being irreducible to the properties of individual consciousness. The extent of this shift may be registered in a review he wrote in 1897 of Antonio Labriola's *Essays on the Materialist Conception of History*. Here, while agreeing with Marxists that 'social life must be explained not by the conception of it formed by those who participate in it, but by the profound causes which escape their consciousness', Durkheim nevertheless argues that 'the economic factor' given explanatory primacy in historical materialism 'is secondary and derived':

> Not only is the Marxist hypothesis unproven, but it is contrary to facts which appear established. Sociologists and historians tend increasingly to come together in their common affirmation that religion is the most primitive of all social phenomena . . . But we know of no means of reducing religion to economics, nor of any attempt really at effecting this reduction.[35]

Relative to this shift, *The Rules of Sociological Method* is generally seen by commentators as a transitional work which, in seeking to make explicit the approach employed in *The Division of Labour*, also in certain respects points towards Durkheim's later view that 'religion is the most primitive of all social phenomena'. Thus in the *Rules* he offers the following definition of social facts: '*A social fact is a way of acting, whether or not fixed, capable of exerting over the individual an external constraint.*' As instances of social facts, he includes both 'collective representations' and 'social facts of an "anatomical" or morphological nature'. The latter include 'the number and nature of the elementary parts of society, the way in which they are articulated, the degree of coalescence they have attained, the distribution of the population over the earth's surface, the extent and nature of the network of communications, the design of dwellings, etc.' – all the factors, in other words, which Durkheim had cited when seeking to explain the development of the division of labour.[36]

Yet when Durkheim comes to defend his conception of social facts against

---

[33]   Durkheim, *Division*, p. 212.
[34]   L. Coser, introduction, ibid., p. xviii.
[35]   Durkheim, *Rules*, pp. 171, 174, 173.
[36]   Ibid., pp. 59, 57.

neo-Kantian philosophers who accused him of a kind of metaphysical collectivism, he tends in effect to equate these facts with collective representations.
Thus in 'Individual and Collective Representations' (1898), he writes:

> While one might perhaps contest the statement that all social facts without excep-
> tion impose themselves from without upon the individual, the doubt does not
> seem possible as regards religious beliefs and practices, the rules of morality and
> the innumerable precepts of law – that is to say, all the most characteristic mani-
> festations of collective life. All are expressly obligatory, and this obligation is the
> proof that these ways of acting and thinking are not the work of the individual but
> come from a moral power above him, that which the mystic calls God or which
> can be more scientifically conceived.[37]

Thus, having made exteriority and constraint necessary conditions of the
existence of social facts, Durkheim reached a position where he could only
confidently treat collective representations as meeting these conditions. He further argued that these representations are 'partially autonomous realities' that
develop independently of their 'substratum' in the 'morphological' facts that
had preoccupied him in *The Division of Labour*:

> They [collective representations] have the power to attract and repel each other
> and to form amongst themselves various syntheses which are determined by their
> natural affinities and not by the condition of their matrix. As a consequence, the
> new representations born of these syntheses have the same nature; they are im-
> mediately caused by other collective representations and not by this or that
> characteristic of the social structure.[38]

Durkheim therefore affirms: 'Collective psychology is sociology, quite simply.'[39] His mature sociology is thus what David Lockwood calls 'normative
functionalism', that is, '[t]he idea that society is a moral and ultimately a religious entity whose intrinsic feature is a set of commonly held values and beliefs.'[40] One can appreciate how serious a problem the 'pathological forms' of
the division of labour constitute for this perspective: economic crises and class
conflict in particular represent at best the partial effectiveness, at worst the breakdown, of any unifying moral consensus.

Durkheim's most famous monograph, *Suicide* (1897), displays a similar preoccupation with the consequences of moral regulation – and of its absence.
Consistent with his general method, he insists that suicide has social rather than
individual causes which may be ascertained through the analysis of statistical
regularities. This analysis demonstrates, he claims, that, in modern societies at

[37]   E. Durkheim, *Sociology and Philosophy*, ed. C. Bouglé (London, 1953), p. 25.
[38]   Ibid., p. 31.
[39]   Ibid., p. 34 n. 1.
[40]   D. Lockwood, *Solidarity and Schism* (Oxford, 1992), pp. 7–8.

any rate, 'suicide varies inversely with the degree of integration of the social groups of which the individual forms a part'. Durkheim proceeds to isolate two pairs of contrasting types of suicide – egoistic/altruistic and anomic/fatalistic. Egoistic suicide is a consequence of individualism; it arises from the despair caused by 'the relaxation of social bonds, a sort of collective asthenia, or social malaise'. But, '[i]f . . . excessive individuation leads to suicide, insufficient individuation has the same effects.' Altruistic suicide 'is surely very common among primitive peoples', where people kill themselves out of a sense of social obligation – for example, where they have, through age or illness, become a burden on society, or when their superiors die.[41]

Anomic suicide is the direct consequence of the weakness of moral regulation in modern society. *Anomie* – 'de-regulation' – is most evident in the ups and downs of the business cycle, which are directly related to rises in the suicide rate; indeed it is 'in a chronic state' in trade and industry generally:

> There the state of crisis and *anomie* is constant and, so to speak, normal. From top to bottom of the ladder, greed is aroused without knowing where to find its ultimate foothold. Nothing can calm it, since its goal is far beyond all it can attain. Reality seems valueless by comparison with the dreams of fevered imaginations; reality is therefore abandoned, but so too is possibility abandoned when it in turn becomes reality. A thirst arises for novelties, unfamiliar pleasures, nameless sensations, all of which lose their savour once known. Henceforth one has no strength to endure the least reverse.[42]

If, '[i]n anomic suicide, society's influence is lacking in the basically individual passions, thus leaving them without a check-rein', its counterpart, fatalistic suicide, is a consequence of 'excessive regulation, that of persons with futures pitilessly blocked and passions violently choked by oppressive discipline', by 'excessive physical or moral despotism'. Yet Durkheim's primary concern is with those forms of suicide which arise from a lack of social constraint and moral regulation, not with their excess: he relegates fatalistic suicide to a footnote on the grounds that it is of 'little contemporary importance'.[43]

Durkheim's description of *anomie* recalls Marx's evocation of the 'everlasting uncertainty and agitation' of 'the bourgeois epoch' in the *Communist Manifesto*. But their explanations of this condition are very different. For Marx the constantly disturbed state of modernity is a consequence of the competitive accumulation of capital, and of the dynamic instability it brings in its train. Durkheim's diagnosis of *anomie*, by contrast, recalls long-standing themes of Western thought – in particular, Plato's argument that both a healthy self and a properly governed city require reason to direct and control our sensual desires

---

[41] Durkheim, *Suicide*, pp. 209, 214, 217, 219.
[42] Ibid., pp. 253, 254, 256 (translation modified).
[43] Ibid., pp. 258, 276 n. 25.

and passions. It is because these appetites have escaped regulation that modernity is out of joint.

How, then, is this condition to be remedied? The answer is implicit in the diagnosis: through the establishment of an appropriate kind of moral regulation. This requires, Durkheim believes, a series of institutional reforms. In *Suicide* and the preface to the second edition of *The Division of Labour* (1902), he advocates the restoration of a modernized version of the medieval guilds, what he calls 'the occupational group or corporation', arguing that 'the corporation has everything needed to give the individual a setting to draw him out of his moral isolation; and faced with the actual inadequacy of the other groups, it alone can fulfil this indispensable office'.[44] Durkheim argues that such corporations, operating on a national scale, should undertake 'functions of mutual assistance', '[m]any educational activities', and 'a certain type of artistic activity'.[45]

This remedy might seem to smack of a conservative nostalgia for the Middle Ages. Yet Durkheim rejects any attempt 'to revive traditions and practices that no longer correspond to present-day social conditions' and argues that 'to find ways of harmonious co-operation between those organs that still clash discordantly together' requires 'diminishing those external inequalities that are the source of all our ills'. This would involve, at the very least, establishing equality of opportunity by eliminating all competitive advantages that derive from hereditary privilege. But, though sympathetic to the more moderate wing of French socialism represented by Jean Jaurès, Durkheim argues that 'the progress of the division of labour implies . . . an ever-increasing inequality', because of differences in natural talents and the necessity of hierarchical organization to secure efficient performance.[46] He does not believe that collective ownership of modern industrial technology would end the present 'state of anarchy . . . for, let me repeat, this state of anarchy comes about not from this machinery being in these hands and not in those, but because the activity deriving from it is not regulated'.[47]

Nor, on their own, would national corporations overcome *anomie*. Indeed, by powerfully articulating the interests of specific occupational groups, they might promote further social disintegration. 'The only means of averting this collective particularism and all it involves for the individual, is to have a special agency with the duty of representing the overall collectivity . . . vis-à-vis these individual collectivities.' This duty is performed by the state. Unlike Marx and Weber, Durkheim does not conceive the state as primarily a coercive institution. A properly functioning state is a necessary condition of the realization of the individual. More particularly, 'the State is a special organ whose

---

[44]   Ibid., pp. 378–9.
[45]   Durkheim, *Division*, p. liii.
[46]   Ibid., pp. 339–40, 314.
[47]   Durkheim, *Professional Ethics*, p. 31.

responsibility it is to work out certain representations which hold good for the collectivity'. Its 'whole life . . . consists not in exterior action, in making changes, but in deliberation; that is in representations . . . Strictly speaking, the State is the very organ of social thought.'[48]

The state is thus the highest expression of the collective consciousness. Furthermore, as collective representations become more clearly articulated, they become the objects of conscious reflection, and of criticism and debate. Democracy is the institutional expression of this process. Its development is a response to the needs of complex, rapidly changing modern societies:

> When things go on happening in the same way, habit will suffice for conduct, but when circumstances are changing continually, habit, on the contrary, must not be in sovereign control. Reflection alone makes possible the discovery of new and effectual practices, for it is only by reflection that the future can be anticipated. That is why deliberative assemblies are becoming ever more widely accepted as an institution. They are the means by which societies can give considered thought to themselves, and therefore they become the instrument of the almost continuous changes that present-day conditions of collective existence demand.[49]

The development of democratic institutions also reflects, Durkheim concedes, the modern demand for individual freedom. But this freedom does not 'consist in rebelling against nature – such a revolt being futile and fruitless, whether attempted against the forces of the material world or those of the social world. To be autonomous means, for the human being, to understand the necessities he has to bow to and accept them with a full knowledge of the facts.'[50] This essentially Stoic conception of freedom as the recognition of necessity is one of a number of respects in which Durkheim's political theory recalls that of Hegel (see §2.1 above). Hegel after all advocated a revival of corporations as a means of helping to overcome the conflicts and instability of civil society; he also conceived the modern state (admittedly without the structures of representative democracy which Durkheim regarded as indispensable mechanisms of collective reflection and deliberation) as the embodiment of the interests of society as a whole.

There are other echoes in Durkheim's political theory. Tocqueville had also believed that a combination of democratic public life and vital private associations was necessary to reconcile the individual and society (§3.2 above). Rousseau, like Durkheim, sought to find institutional means to channel and control individuals' private desires so that they were subordinated to the common interest (the general will). One such means was education, on which Durkheim also laid great stress. Thus he wrote of the teacher: 'Just as the priest

48   Ibid., pp. 62, 50, 51.
49   Ibid., p. 90.
50   Ibid., p. 91.

is the interpreter of God, so he . . . is the interpreter of the great moral ideas of his time and country.'[51]

The importance he ascribed to education helps to explain the intellectual prominence Durkheim gained in the Third Republic. The politically dominant Radicals, fiercely anti-clerical but socially conservative, relied on the system of lay, public, elementary schools as the key conduit for instilling republican values in the mass of the population: Durkheim provided a social-theoretical justification for this strategy. Georges Sorel, then a Marxist, accurately described him in 1895 as the theorist of the 'new ideas of conservative democracy, establishing more justice in economic relations, favouring the intellectual and moral development of the people, encouraging industry to develop in more scientific directions', and supporting 'the intervention of the State'.[52]

6.3   Meaning and belief

Durkheim's conception of society as 'ultimately a religious entity' (as Lockwood puts it) reaches its apogee in his last major work, *The Elementary Forms of the Religious Life* (1912). This study of the religious beliefs and practices of 'primitive' societies, drawing heavily on case-studies of Australian aboriginal bands, reflects Durkheim's growing preoccupation with the evidence which anthropological research provided about the nature and sources of social order. Though his thought continued to display evolutionist assumptions – as Lukes points out, '[h]e simply took it as axiomatic that there is an identity between (cultural and structural) simplicity and evolutionary priority' – this shift in focus implied that the problematic Durkheim had inherited from Comte and Spencer of placing individual societies within an evolutionary sequence of progressive differentiation no longer occupied the foreground of his thinking.[53] In this sense, the *Elementary Forms* is one of the harbingers of the reaction against evolutionary theories of all kinds which reaches its climax in structuralism and post-structuralism (see ch. 11 below).

Rather than seek to offer a necessarily inadequate summary of an extraordinarily rich and complex work, I shall simply isolate four key themes of the *Elementary Forms*. First, Durkheim criticizes the rationalistic conception of religion which informs the writings of the mainly British anthropologists on whose researches he drew. Thus for F. W. Tylor and other theorists of animism, who see supernatural beings as projections of human mental states, 'religious beliefs are so many hallucinatory representations, without any objective foundation whatsoever'. Durkheim rejects such interpretations, which have their

---

[51]   Quoted in Lukes, *Durkheim*, p. 116.
[52]   Quoted ibid., p. 320.
[53]   Ibid., p. 456.

origins in the Enlightenment view of religion as 'a vast error imagined by the priests':

> It is undeniably true that errors have been able to perpetuate themselves in history; but, except under a union of very exceptional circumstances, they can never perpetuate themselves unless they were *true practically*, that is to say, unless, without giving us a theoretically exact idea of the things with which they deal, they express well enough the manner in which they affect us, either for good or for bad.[54]

The 'practical truth' of religious beliefs lies not in their formal correspondence with the world but in the needs they answer. The mistake made by the Enlightenment and its successors among students of 'primitive' religion arises in part from their treating religious belief as a matter of the transactions between human beings and their natural environment. Once the problem is defined in these terms, it is easy enough to demonstrate the inadequacy of most religious representations from the standpoint of the modern physical sciences. But, Durkheim suggests, '[l]et us suppose that religion responds to quite another need than that of adapting ourselves to sensible objects: then it will not risk being weakened by the fact that it does not satisfy, or only badly satisfies this need.'[55]

The need which religion fulfils is *social*. This brings us to our second theme, Durkheim's theory of religion proper:

> The power thus [i.e. through religion] imposed on his [i.e. the individual's] respect and become the object of his adoration is society, of which the gods were only the hypostatic form. Religion is in a word the system of symbols by means of which society becomes conscious of itself; it is the characteristic way of thinking of collective existence.[56]

Society is therefore 'ultimately a religious entity' because what is venerated in religion is society itself. 'One must choose between God and society', Durkheim says, but he declares himself 'quite indifferent to this choice, since I see in the Divinity only society transfigured and expressed symbolically'.[57] He famously defines religion in terms of the polarity between sacred and profane:

> the real characteristic of all religious phenomena is that they always suppose a bipartite division of the whole universe, known and knowable, into two classes which embrace all that exists, but which radically exclude each other. Sacred things are those which the interdictions protect and isolate; profane things, those to which these interdictions are applied.[58]

---

[54]   E. Durkheim (1912), *The Elementary Forms of the Religious Life* (New York, 1965), pp. 86, 87, 98–9.

[55]   Ibid., p. 102.

[56]   Durkheim, *Suicide*, p. 312.

[57]   Durkheim, *Sociology and Philosophy*, p. 52 (translation modified).

[58]   Durkheim, *Elementary Forms*, p. 56.

Nevertheless, as Lukes points out, 'Durkheim's dichotomy between the sacred and the profane . . . derives from and is explained by the basic, and multiple, dichotomy between the social and the individual' that is at the heart of his thought.[59] Thus he argues that the Australian aborigines' classification of natural kinds, including the totemic objects attached to particular clans to which interdictions apply, mirrors the internal structure of their societies, and in particular their sub-division into clans, marriage-classes, and moieties (or phatries). Thus *'the classification of things reproduces the classification of men'*, so that 'if totemism is, in one aspect, the grouping of men into clans according to natural objects (the associated totemic species), it is also, inversely, a grouping of natural objects in accordance with social groups'.[60]

From this perspective, Durkheim argues, '[r]eligion ceases to be an inexplicable hallucination and takes a foothold in reality. In fact, we can say that the believer is not deceived when he believes in the existence of a moral power upon which he depends and from which he receives all that is best in himself: this power exists, it is society.' This theory amounts to a functional explanation of religion as 'the system of ideas with which individuals represent to themselves the society of which they are members, and the obscure but initimate relations which they have with it'.[61] Like any functional account of a social practice, Durkheim's theory must specify the mechanisms through which this practice performs the role he claims for it. We may consider his analysis of religious ritual, our third theme, as an attempt to meet this requirement.

Durkheim argues that cults play a 'preponderating role . . . in all religions . . . This is because society cannot make its influence felt unless it is in action, and it is not in action unless the individuals who compose it are assembled together and act in common.' Religious rituals serve to bring the members of society together in a shared reaffirmation of their collective identity. Thus 'the effect of the cult is to recreate periodically a moral being on which we depend as it depends on us', namely society. But the effect of the ceremonies involved in the cult is not simply intellectual or spiritual; they act on the collective sentiments of those gathered there. Through their common actions, the assembled participants in the rituals achieve an emotional high pitch, a condition of 'collective effervescence'.[62]

'When emotions have this vivacity,' Durkheim argues, 'they may well be painful, but they are not depressing; on the contrary, they denote a state of effervescence which implies a mobilization of all our active forces and even a supply of external energies.' These states of effervescence thus involve a release of surplus energy which finds expression 'in supplementary and

[59]   Lukes, *Durkheim*, p. 26; compare pp. 20–1.
[60]   E. Durkheim and M. Mauss (1903), *Primitive Classification* (London, 1963), pp. 11, 17–18.
[61]   Durkheim, *Elementary Forms*, p. 257.
[62]   Ibid., pp. 465, 389, 405.

superfluous works of luxury, that is to say, works of art', and in the 'exuberant movements' performed, less for well-defined cultic purposes than because of the pleasure they give, by participants in rituals. But this 'recreational' dimension of the cult is subordinate to its predominant function: to send the members of society back to their mundane, profane lives with a renewed sense of their shared identity:

> For a society to become conscious of itself and maintain at the necessary degree of intensity the sentiments which it thus attains, it must assemble and concentrate itself. Now this concentration brings about an exaltation of the mental life which takes form in a group of ideal conceptions where is portrayed the new life just awakened; they correspond to this new set of psychical forces which we have at our disposition for the daily tasks of existence. A society can neither create itself nor recreate itself without at the same time creating an ideal.[63]

Durkheim's analysis of these states of 'collective effervescence' is one of his most striking ideas. It would seem to admit of application to social practices other than religious rituals – for example, to collective movements whose aim is not to reaffirm, but rather to reform or even to revolutionize society. But of more immediate relevance is an important implication of this analysis: if the continued existence of a society depends on its renewal through collective acts whose emotional dynamic requires the postulation of an 'ideal', then not simply is society the real object of cultic veneration, but all societies necessarily have a religious dimension. Indeed, Durkheim says that 'there is something eternal in religion: it is the cult and the faith'.[64] This remark indicates the distance he has travelled from Enlightenment rationalism: he treats precisely those features of religious life which even those *philosophes* who were not atheists were inclined to dismiss as debased superstitious practices as indispensable requirements of any functioning society.

The same distance is also measured by the fourth theme from Durkheim's theory of religion, namely the sociology of knowledge it implies. He attaches great significance to the systems of categories characteristic of 'primitive' religions – for example, those embodied in the Australian totemic beliefs touched on briefly above. Durkheim's discussions of them in the *Elementary Forms* and in *Primitive Classification*, written jointly with his nephew Marcel Mauss, represent one of the starting-points of Lévi-Strauss's structural anthropology (see §11.2 below). As we have seen, Durkheim and Mauss claim to have discovered 'a close link, and not an accidental relation, between the [Australian] social system and this logical system' of totemic classification. But this is merely the starting-point of a much more ambitious thesis:

[63]   Ibid., pp. 453–4, 426, 470.
[64]   Ibid., p. 478.

Society was not simply a model which classificatory thought followed; it was its own divisions which served as divisions for the system of classification. The first logical categories were social categories, the first classes of things were classes of men into which these things were integrated. It was because men were grouped, and thought of themselves in the form of groups, that in their ideas they grouped other things, and in the beginning the two modes of grounding were merged to the point of being indistinguishable.[65]

Thus Durkheim argues that the various basic categories Western thought inherited from the Greeks – space, time, class, number, cause, personality, etc. – originated in these primitive classifications: 'they are a product of religious thought', and therefore are, like religious beliefs and concepts generally, 'essentially collective representations', displaying 'the mental states of the group'. Consequently, 'they should depend on the way in which this is founded and organized, upon its morphology, upon its religious, moral and economic institutions, etc.'[66]

Durkheim calls these fundamental categories 'the framework of the intelligence'. His general conception of their role reflects the influence of neo-Kantians like one of his teachers, the philosopher Émile Boutroux. But Kant regarded the categories of the understanding as the necessary condition of any possible experience. In assigning the categories a historical origin, Durkheim might appear to be weakening their force, or relativizing them to specific social conditions. This is not, however, his intention. Thus he writes:

If men did not agree upon these essential ideas at every moment, if they did not have the same conception of time, space, cause, number, etc., all contact between their minds would be impossible, and with that, all life together. Thus society could not abandon the categories to the free choice of the individual without abandoning itself. If it is to live there is not merely need of a satisfactory moral conformity, but also there is a minumum of logical conformity beyond which it cannot safely go. For this reason it uses all its authority upon its members to forestall such dissidence. Does a mind ostensibly free itself from these forms of thought? It is no longer considered a human mind in the full sense of the word and is treated accordingly . . . This seems to be the origin of the exceptional authority which is inherent in reason and which makes us accept its suggestions with confidence. It is the very authority of society, transferring itself to a certain manner of thought which is the indispensable condition of all common action.[67]

This rather alarming passage, in implying that those who do not accept the prevailing categories will be the object of social sanctions, calls to mind Canguilhem's suggestion that to normalize is to impose requirements on an

---

[65] Durkheim and Mauss, *Primitive Classification*, pp. 40–1, 82–3.
[66] Durkheim, *Elementary Forms*, pp. 22, 28.
[67] Ibid., pp. 22, 30 (translation modified).

often recalcitrant reality (see §6.1 above). It also implies that the compelling force which leads us to accept certain arguments as valid and certain sentences as true ultimately derives from the power of the collective consciousness to overwhelm the individual. Durkheim makes out this claim most fully in lectures he gave in 1913–14. Here he sought to respond to an attack mounted on the classical conception of truth as the correspondence of our representations to reality by William James and other American pragmatist philosophers. James argued that, instead of measuring our beliefs by what he claimed amounted to an unattainable ideal, we should appraise them in terms of their practical utility.

This critique necessarily represented a challenge to Durkheim, who had inherited from Comte, and indeed from the rationalist tradition stemming from Descartes, the conception of science as objective knowledge. He declares that '[o]ur whole French culture is basically an essentially rationalistic one ... A total negation of rationalism would thus constitute a danger, for it would overthrow our whole national culture.' Durkheim nevertheless brings to the patriotic task of defending rationalism a significant degree of sympathy with pragmatism. Not only has it awakened philosophy from its dogmatic slumber, but 'it has, in common with sociology, a sense of *life* and *action*. Both are children of the same era.'[68]

James plays this sense off against the traditional conception of truth, counterposing to what he regards as an abstract conception of reason the varying contexts of action from which beliefs derive their actual meaning. Sociology goes part of the way with pragmatism here, says Durkheim, since it too 'introduces a *relativism* which rests on the relation between the physical environment on the one hand and man on the other'. But, in the central role which sociology (at least as practised by Durkheim) gives to society and to collective representations lies the means of trumping James's attempt to demolish the concept of objective truth. Durkheim focuses on what he calls 'the more or less physical impossibility of not admitting the truth. When our mind perceives a true representation, we feel that we cannot but accept it as true. The true idea *imposes itself* on us.'[69]

Thus viewed, truth assumes a different aspect: 'The problem is not to know by what right we can say that a given proposition is true or false. What is accepted as true today may quite well be held to be false tomorrow. What is important is to know what has made men believe that a representation conforms to reality.' Durkheim seems ready to concede to the pragmatists that the sentences we hold true are at best warrantedly assertible – in other words, they are simply what, given our existing beliefs, we are entitled to assert, rather than representing the way the world actually is. His interest lies in identifying the

---

[68]   E. Durkheim (1955), *Pragmatism and Sociology*, ed. E. Cuvillier and J. B. Allcock (Cambridge, 1983), p. 1.
[69]   Ibid., pp. 69–70, 73.

force whereby what we hold true 'imposes itself on us'. The answer is, in the light of the foregoing discussion, a predictable one:

> In the life of the human race, it is the collectivity which maintains ideas and representations, and all collective representations are by virtue of their origin invested with a prestige which means that they have the power to *impose themselves*. They have a greater psychological energy than representations emanating from the individual. That is why they settle with such force in our consciousness. That is where the very strength of truth lies.[70]

So society makes sentences true. This hardly seems like a convincing answer to James and his co-thinkers. A contemporary pragmatist such as Richard Rorty might readily concede the point, but then proceed to subvert it by pointing out that society itself constantly changes. What is warrantedly assertible at one time is thus undermined by successive 'redescriptions' bound up with larger social changes. Truth then becomes a protean concept, its content constantly changing along with the society from which it derives its power of imposition; it is, moreover, hard to resist the suspicion that too rapid a series of redescriptions might weaken this power. The resulting climate of uncertainty and scepticism is indeed part of what Durkheim thinks is wrong with modernity – its *anomie*, or lack of moral regulation. His failure to recognize that his defence of rationalism is open to this kind of objection seems to reflect a tendency to hypostatize society into an eternal essence. As E. E. Evans-Pritchard put it, 'it was Durkheim not the savage who made society into a god'.[71]

This tendency is indeed the main source of the wider difficulties in his social theory. Durkheim's preoccupation with the way in which values and beliefs contribute to social stability has been enormously influential on twentieth-century social thought. Theorists from such different backgrounds as Parsons and Habermas bear his brand. But Durkheim's 'normative functionalism' suffers from an evident flaw. *Anomie*, as we have seen, is principally caused by economic instability and social conflict. Yet, as Lockwood observes, ' "class" and "economic life" are concepts in Durkheim's sociology which remain almost entirely unexplicated. They refer to forces whose disordering effects are always analysed by reference to the normative structure; they are themselves not conceived of as having a structure which is worthy of detailed consideration.'[72] Durkheim offers a theory of the sources of social order, but not one of the forces undermining it. From this there stems the peculiar pathos of his sociology: it provided no means of explaining the First World War, in which Durkheim's son and many of his pupils perished, nor the era of heightened conflict which that war ushered in. That task fell to others.

[70] Ibid., pp. 85–6.
[71] E. E. Evans-Pritchard, *Nuer Religion* (Oxford, 1956), p. 313.
[72] Lockwood, *Solidarity*, p. 78.

7

Weber

7.1 Prussian agriculture and the German state

Durkheim and Marx offer two starkly counterposed images of modernity: the first is so preoccupied with the dangers posed to the normative integration of society that he cannot offer an account of the processes he believes to be subversive of social stability; the second offers a comprehensive theory of the conflicts and uncertainties endemic to modern bourgeois society, yet predicts their resolution in a future communist society without (so many of his critics argue) providing the conception of the nature and ends of human action which would be required to justify this prediction. The particular interest of Weber lies in the fact that he develops a distinctive account of the historical significance of capitalism as part of a body of thought which displays as strong a sense of the inherently conflictual character of social reality as Hegel and Marx did, but combines this with an attempt to understand the role played by irreducibly different, and indeed antagonistic, values in governing human conduct.[1]

Misunderstandings surround most major social theorists: Weber is no exception to this rule. His fate has been to emerge, in the American-led reconstruction of sociology after the Second World War, as the patron saint of 'value-free' social science (see §10.2 below). Fortunately, he is a much more interesting thinker than this conventional portrait suggests. That Weber's points of reference were very different from those of the postwar orthodoxy which sought to envelop him is suggested by a remark he made a few weeks before his death in 1920:

[1] Max Weber (1864–1920): born in Erfurt, the son of a prominent National Liberal member of the Germain Reichstag and Prussian Landtag; studied law at the universities of Heidelberg, Berlin, and Göttingen; Professor of Economics at the University of Freiburg, 1894–6; moved to the University of Heidelberg to take over Karl Knies's chair in Political Science in 1896; suffered a severe mental breakdown in 1897, from which it took him several years to recover; resigned his chair in 1903 but sufficiently recovered to resume work; in 1904 took over, with Edgar Jaffé and Werner Sombart, the joint editorship of the *Archiv für Sozialwissenschaft und Sozialpolitik*; Professor of Economics at the University of Munich, 1919–20.

The honesty of a present-day scholar, and above all, a present-day philosopher, can be measured by his attitude to Nietzsche and Marx. Whoever does not admit that considerable parts of his own work could not have been carried out in the absence of the work of these two, only fools himself and others. The world in which we spiritually and intellectually live today is a world substantially shaped by Marx and Nietzsche.[2]

Yet, if Weber oriented himself with respect to Marx and Nietzsche, he nevertheless hewed his own path. Reconstructing the precise content of the theories which resulted is perhaps more difficult than it is in the case of other major social theorists. This is partly because, as Keith Tribe says, 'Weber's work is fragmentary not only in the sense that his efforts were spread over several fields, any one of which was usually the defining province of a scholar; much of his published work was radically incomplete, hastily written, unrevised, proofed at speed, after publication the manuscripts discarded.'[3] Moreover, Weber, particularly in his methodological writings, often expressed himself obscurely and elliptically. Recent scholarship helps to provide a better understanding of the sources and development of his thought, but offering an overview of the results is a particularly hazardous enterprise.

Weber seems to have regarded himself primarily as an economist. As late as 1918, he spoke of 'we political economists'.[4] In his 1895 inaugural lecture at Freiburg, Weber included himself among 'the disciples of the German Historical School'.[5] The Historical School represented the dominant version of economics studied in Germany during the nineteenth century. Its leading practitioners conceived economics as primarily a historical and descriptive science concerned with understanding society as a concrete, evolving whole. Thus Karl Knies wrote in 1853:

> If ... political economy genuinely bases itself on the real facts of people and state, if it seeks to solve the problems arising in people and state, then it should not detach its domain and task from that of life in its entirety, but must rather treat both as a living member of a living body ... Since political economy has to respect this context, and in its own concerns contributes to the solution of the moral-political problems of the whole, it is therefore enjoined to take its place with the *moral and political sciences*.[6]

Such a conception of political economy was plainly quite at odds with the version formulated by J. S. Mill, which became entrenched, especially in Britain and Austria, as a result of the 'marginalist revolution' of the 1870s (see §3.1

---

2 Quoted in W. Hennis, *Max Weber* (London, 1988), p. 162.
3 K. Tribe, translator's introduction, ibid., p. 10.
4 H. H. Gerth and C. Wright Mills, eds, *From Max Weber* (London, 1970), p. 129.
5 M. Weber, *Political Writings*, P. Lassman and R. Speirs ed. (Cambridge, 1994), p. 19.
6 Quoted in Hennis, *Max Weber*, p. 120.

above). Here economics was conceived as an abstract and deductive theory which artificially isolated one aspect of human behaviour for study. These conflicting conceptions of economics were at stake in the debate which developed in the 1880s known as the *Methodenstreit* – the battle over methods – pitting Austrian marginalists, led by Carl Menger, against German historical economists, headed by Gustav von Schmoller.

Weber was eventually to adopt a methodological position that was, as we shall see in the following section, in certain crucial respects closer to Menger than to Schmoller and Knies. Nevertheless, he sought, like the Historical School, to explore the wider social context of economic processes, and to relate them to the pursuit of moral and political objectives. This can be seen in his first writings to have a general impact, published between 1894 and 1897, and devoted to the state of Prussian agriculture. These were far from being works of disengaged scholarship, but instead resonated with the contemporary concerns of the German elite.

The German Reich, unified in 1871, was from its foundation the greatest military power in Europe. By the outbreak of war in 1914, it had also surpassed Britain and established itself as the second biggest industrial economy. Rapid industrialization transformed German society – in the rapidly expanding cities, an affluent bourgeoisie and an industrial proletariat both took shape. But the modernity Germany had achieved by the end of the nineteenth century was a complex and troubled one. The Reich's constitution provided for a parliament, the Reichstag, elected by universal male suffrage, but allowed such extensive powers to the emperor in his role as German head of state and king of Prussia that the predominantly Prussian civilian bureaucracy and military hierarchy were able largely to evade political accountability. The Junkers, as the landed nobility east of the Elbe were known, traditional base of the Prussian monarchy, benefited from a variety of state subsidies. Tariffs introduced by Bismarck in 1879 were widely seen as consummating a 'marriage of iron and rye', binding together the Junkers and the chiefs of increasingly cartellized heavy industries such as coal and steel. Weber himself described the outcome of this policy as 'the feudalization of bourgeois capital'.[7]

By the end of the nineteenth century, Germany was undoubtedly a highly successful modern capitalist state. But any claims on its behalf as a liberal polity were much more dubious. The National Liberals (of whom Weber's father was a leading member) represented the wing of Prussian liberalism which had abandoned their opposition to Bismarck's defence of absolute monarchy after he had, through a succession of diplomatic manoeuvres and victorious wars, secured German unification. They played an important part in developing the Reichstag into something approximating a genuine parliament, though its position in the state remained a subordinate one.

---

[7]   M. Weber (1897), 'Germany as an Industrial State', in K. Tribe, ed., *Reading Weber* (London, 1989), p. 215.

The presence of the Social Democratic Party (SPD), with a mass working-class base and a substantial bloc of deputies, both created pressure for democratic reforms and suggested to the German ruling class that surrendering to this pressure would be dangerous. Meanwhile, rivalries among the Great Powers became increasingly threatening as the nineteenth century drew to a close, chiefly because of the destabilizing consequences of Germany's emergence as a world power. On the Continent, Germany and Austria–Hungary faced France and Russia; moreover, Germany's decision in 1898 to build a battle fleet unleashed an arms race with Britain (which interpreted the move as a challenge to its naval and colonial supremacy) that helped drive Europe into the First World War.

In this context, the condition of Prussian agriculture – the economic base of a key section of the German ruling class – was more than a merely academic question. In 1891–2 the Verein für Sozialpolitik (German Social Policy Association) surveyed 4,000 landowners on the condition of rural labour east of the Elbe. The Verein had been set up in 1873. It reflected mainly the influence of Schmoller and other historical economists: it was critical of *Manchestertum*, or unrestrained free-market economics, and sought to devise state policies that would limit the attraction of the SPD for workers. Weber was asked to analyse the results of the survey on rural labour.

Weber's writings of the 1890s reflect both Marx's influence and the distance between the two men. Weber's researches into ancient economic history, which immediately preceded his study of Prussian agriculture, already showed an analytical interest in distinguishing between types of economic structure – 'natural' or barter economy (a concept he owed to the historical economist J. K. Rodbertus), the basis of feudalism; slave society, which permitted the limited development of commerce; and modern capitalism with its roots in free wage-labour. Weber's explanation of the decline of classical antiquity was essentially an economic one: 'It is clear, therefore, that the disintegration of the Roman Empire was the inevitable political consequence of a basic economic development: the gradual disappearance of commerce and the expansion of a barter economy.'[8]

It is a sound generalization that when any European intellectual considers the decline of Rome, he is usually wondering whether his own civilization will succumb to a similar fate. In the Freiburg Address Weber, speaking on behalf of his own, younger generation of German bourgeois, conjures up the threat of historical decadence: 'At our cradle stood the most frightful curse history can give any generation as a baptismal-gift: the hard fate of the political *epigone*.'[9] This preoccupation with decline is probably in part a response to Nietzsche's comprehensive critique of European nihilism. But it also arose from more urgent social and political concerns.

[8]   M. Weber, *The Agrarian Sociology of Ancient Civilizations* (London, 1976), p. 408.
[9]   Weber, *Political Writings*, p. 24.

Weber's writings on East Elbian agriculture are concerned to draw attention to changes in what he calls 'the labour-organization [*Arbeitsverfassung*] of the large landed properties'. This had been 'a form of communal economy, patriarchally ruled and directed', based on a legally subordinated workforce of peasant smallholders required to provide the landowner with their families' labour. The Junkers, however, in response to their political decline and under competitive pressure from 'the wealthy commercial bourgeoisie', were transforming themselves into 'entrepreneurs working according to *commercial* principles': 'world-wide conditions of production . . . now began to rule the enterprises'.[10] This implied a move towards the intensive cultivation of cashcrops such as sugar beet, and, as a consequence, the proletarianization of the rural workforce. The beet estates, in particular, were becoming increasingly reliant on low-paid and unskilled Polish seasonal labourers.

Weber's concern with the consequences of these developments is, in part, national and racial. Thus he warns of 'a Slavic invasion which could mean a cultural regression of major proportions'.[11] His writings on East Elbian agriculture contain odious racist remarks, for example, about 'Polish animals'.[12] But he is also concerned with the negative impact which the decline of the traditional Prussian estate may have on the German polity. For '[t]he East Elbian estates are not merely economic units, but local political *centres of domination* [*Herrschaftscentren*]. Based upon Prussian traditions, they provided the material basis for a stratum of the population accustomed to possessing both political authority within the state, and the political and military forces of state power.'[13] Their decline implies that the Junkers can no longer play a leading role in the state: 'the centre of gravity of the political intelligentsia is shifting irresistibly into the cities. *This* shift is the decisive *political* factor in the agrarian development of eastern Germany.'[14]

Four dimensions may be distinguished in the broader reflections which this analysis provokes in Weber. In the first place, the erosion of Junker power represents a crisis for the German state, since there is no other class capable of assuming the role of political leadership. Though he proclaims himself 'a member of the bourgeois [*bürgerlich*] classes' and identifies with 'their views and ideals', Weber denies that 'the German bourgeoisie has the maturity today to be the leading political class of the German nation'. This is a consequence of its lack of political education. It was not the bourgeoisie but Bismarck who unified Germany; his 'Caesarist' rule, moreover, denied it the opportunity to gain the

---

[10] M. Weber (1894), 'Developmental Tendencies in the Situation of East Elbian Rural Labourers', *Economy and Society*, 8 (1979), pp. 177, 179, 180.

[11] Ibid., p. 200.

[12] Quoted in K. Tribe, 'Prussian Agriculture – German Politics: Max Weber 1892–7', in Tribe, ed., *Reading Weber*, p. 114.

[13] Weber, 'Developmental Tendencies', p. 178.

[14] Weber, *Political Writings*, p. 23.

necessary experience in exercising political power. As for the working class, despite the organizational and electoral successes of the SPD, it lacks the dynamism or courage either to constitute a threat to the existing order or to reinvigorate it: the SPD leaders are 'infinitely more harmless than they think they are, for there is not a spark of that Catilinarian energy to *act* in them, nor the slightest trace of that mighty *nationalist* passion' shown by the Jacobins during the French Revolution.[15]

Implicit in this diagnosis is a second theme: there is no necessary correspondence between economic and political processes. Germany's industrial might is no guarantee that it will enjoy political leadership of the required quality. Thus Weber argues for the closure of Germany's eastern border with Poland and a policy of systematic land purchases and colonization by German peasants east of the Elbe in order to preserve the 'national' character of the region even though these measures will produce economically sub-optimal results: 'I do not believe that the colonization of the German East – initially at least – will lead to an improvement in agricultural technique . . . but I regard it as necessary and possible because the prevailing international relations of competition render the land of the German East valueless from the point of view of production for the world market.'[16] Where the national interest commands it, the state must be willing to override the dictates of economic rationality.

This did not mean that Weber advocated simply defying the logic of the market. He opposed proposals to make Germany an autarkic economy whose grain supply would be provided by a highly protected East Elbian agriculture. Higher tariffs would transform Germany into an internationally uncompetitive '*rentier* capitalism' and promote 'the proliferation of this *feudalization of bourgeois capital*' which under Bismarck had prevented the bourgeoisie from developing its political capacities. Moreover maximizing grain yields would require the further capitalization of East Elbian agriculture: the resulting increases in productivity would reduce the size of the rural workforce and thereby promote the very process of depopulation Weber was seeking to prevent. To prevent this outcome, Germany must buy an increasing proportion of its food supply abroad, and finance these imports by a corresponding growth in its export of manufactured goods. Weber acknowledges 'the enormous risk which the inevitable outward economic expansion of Germany places upon us', but regards it as 'unavoidable'.[17]

Thirdly, economic processes are not to be understood primarily as a means of welfare-maximization, but from a perspective of eternal struggle which smacks of both Nietzsche and Social Darwinism: 'Our successors will hold us answerable to history not primarily for the kind of economic organization we hand down

[15] Ibid., pp. 23, 25–6. Catiline was the leader of an unsuccessful insurrectionary conspiracy under the Roman Republic in the first century BC.
[16] Quoted in Tribe, 'Prussian Agriculture', p. 115.
[17] Weber, 'Germany', pp. 214, 216, 220.

to them, but for the amount of elbow-room we conquer and bequeath to them. In the final analysis, processes of economic development are *power* struggles too.'[18] Thus the risk involved in Germany's increased reliance on foreign trade is

> the same risk that all great trading industrial peoples of the past, all leading peoples in cultural development in the past at the time of their greatness have taken upon themselves, and it is my opinion that we are not pursuing a policy of national *comfort* but rather of *greatness*, hence we must take this burden upon our shoulders if we wish to have a national existence other than that of Switzerland, for example.[19]

Finally, economics is not a neutral science: 'As an explanatory and analytical science, political economy is *international*, but as soon as it makes *value-judgements* it is tied to the particular strain of mankind (*Menschentum*) we find within our own nature.' Accordingly, '[t]he science of political economy is a *political* science. It is a servant of . . . the enduring power-political interests of the nation', and 'the criterion of value of a German economic theorist, can therefore only be a German policy or criterion.'[20] Weber here echoes long-standing formulations of the German Historical School. Thus Friedrich List had accused Adam Smith of seeking 'to prove that "political" or *national* economy must be replaced by "cosmopolitical" or world-wide economy'.[21]

The strident nationalist tone of Weber's writings, however, strikes a new note. He dismisses what he calls the 'eudaimonism' of those economists who, influenced by Bentham, see the maximization of human welfare as the goal of their science: 'We do not have peace and human happiness to hand down to our successors, but rather the *eternal struggle* to preserve and raise the quality of our national species.'[22] Such statements seem a world away from the cosmopolitanism of the Enlightenment. Weber was by no means alone in relating his theoretical preoccupations to the construction of national interests. Durkheim, as we saw (§6.3 above), invoked sociology to defend French rationalism against American pragmatism; he also wrote anti-German pamphlets during the First World War.

Weber is, however, the major theorist whose thought most profoundly internalizes the world of Great Power rivalries that took shape at the end of the nineteenth century. An assertive German nationalism runs through all his writings. He responded to the outbreak of war in August 1914 with enthusiasm, offering his sister, who had just lost her husband in the battle of Tannenberg, the rather doubtful comfort: '*Whatever* the outcome, *this war is great and wonderful.*'[23] After Germany's defeat, and the incorporation of parts of her territory

---

[18]   Weber, *Political Writings*, p. 16.
[19]   Weber, 'Germany', p. 213.
[20]   Weber, *Political Writings*, pp. 15, 16.
[21]   Quoted in Hennis, *Max Weber*, p. 118.
[22]   Weber, *Political Writings*, p. 16.
[23]   Letter to Lili Schäffer, 18 Aug. 1914, quoted in W. J. Mommsen, *Max Weber and German Politics 1890–1920* (Chicago, 1984), pp. 190–1.

into newly independent states such as Poland and Czechoslovakia, Weber vigorously supported the armed resistance mounted in their areas by the Freikorps, groups of extreme right-wing ex-officers many of whom later joined the Nazis. He declared in December 1918: 'He who is not willing to employ revolutionary methods in regions where a German irredenta will emerge, and risk the scaffold and prison, will not deserve the name of nationalist in the future.'[24]

7.2 Science and the warring gods

Eternal conflict and struggle thus form one of the main elements of Weber's thought. Yet his writings of the 1890s could, at a pinch, be treated as the work of an especially talented historical economist strongly influenced by Social Darwinism. Thus he argues that 'it is not the alleged export policy, but rather the *increase in population* – whatever may be the economic organization of the earth – which will in future intensify the struggle for existence, the struggle of man against man'.[25] There is no evidence that Weber ever abandoned this essentially Malthusian prognosis. Nevertheless, his writings from 1903 onwards, after he had recovered from his mental breakdown, make it clear that Weber was strongly opposed to the attempt to assimilate physical and social processes characteristic of evolutionists such as Spencer (see ch. 5). Thus he rejected the idea of an evolutionary process of progressive differentiation implicit in 'the familiar value-free concept of the biologists: "higher" = "more differentiated", or more simply, "more complicated". As if the embryo and placenta, etc., were not the most complicated things known to biology.'[26]

In doing so, Weber was participating in a widespread trend in European thought at the start of the twentieth century. Anti-naturalism – the denial that human beings and the social world they created could be understood using the same methods and concepts as those of the physical sciences – represented a powerful reaction to the evolutionism and empiricism which had become entrenched in Western intellectual culture, particularly as a result of the impact of Darwin. This reaction took diverse, and often mutually incompatible, forms. The most important version of anti-naturalism in Germany was neo-Kantianism, represented by various schools which developed Kant's distinction between a realm of appearances governed by the laws of nature and a 'noumenal' realm in which the subject could give itself moral laws into an opposition between the worlds of external nature and human culture.

The 'human' or 'cultural' sciences (*Geisteswissenschaften*, an expression coined in the German translation of J. S. Mill's *System of Logic* to designate

---

[24] Quoted in ibid., pp. 312-13.
[25] Weber, 'Germany', p. 218.
[26] Letter to Rickert, 2 Nov. 1907, quoted in Hennis, *Max Weber*, p. 244 n. 25.

what he called the 'moral sciences'[27]) therefore required a different method from that of the physical sciences. For Wilhelm Dilthey, for example, this method is essentially interpretive, consisting in understanding: the empathetic identification of, for example, the historian with the subjects whose actions he seeks to reconstruct: 'The basis of the human studies [*Geisteswissenschaften*] is not conceptualization but total awareness of a mental state and its reconstruction based on empathy. Here life grasps life.'[28]

Weber was undoubtedly influenced by neo-Kantianism, particularly the variety developed by Heinrich Rickert. Like Rickert, he conceived cultures as systems of values irreducible to physical processes. But, as Wilhelm Hennis has pointed out, 'for Weber's generation, Nietzsche was the decisive intellectual experience'.[29] The Nietzsche on whom Weber drew was not the biologist of power he was frequently construed as being by his German readers, particularly as a result of the publication of his notebooks under the title *The Will to Power* in 1906. Weber dismissed what he called 'the *weakest* part of Nietzsche, the biological embellishments which are heaped around his thoroughly moralistic teaching'.[30]

Nietzsche is of importance for Weber for two reasons. First, he derives from Nietzsche a belief in the primacy of power in social life. Thus:

> Domination [*Herrschaft*] in the most general sense is one of the most important elements of social action . . . The structure of dominancy and its unfolding is of decisive importance in determining the form of social action and its orientation toward a 'goal'. Indeed, domination has played a decisive role particularly in the most important social structures of the past and present, viz., the manor on the one hand, and the large-scale capitalist enterprise on the other.[31]

Secondly, however, Nietzsche is important to Weber as a moralist. For Nietzsche, the will to power consists primarily in the creative process of imposing a new pattern, new values, on an inherently chaotic reality (see §5.3 above). While, as the passage just quoted indicates, Weber is interested in domination as a mundane, socio-political phenomenon, power-struggles are for him ultimately conflicts of value. He takes over Nietzsche's pluralism and perspectivism, and in particular his denial that there is any objective way of adjudicating between rival systems of values: 'the various value-spheres of the world stand in irreconcilable conflict with one another'.[32]

Weber makes this assertion in his famous 1918 lecture 'Science as a Voca-

---

27 H.-G. Gadamer, *Truth and Method* (London, 1975), pp. 5 and 500 n. 1.
28 W. Dilthey, *Selected Writings*, ed. H. P. Rickman (Cambridge, 1976), p. 181.
29 Hennis, *Max Weber*, p. 148.
30 Letter to Jaffé, 13 Sep. 1907, quoted in ibid., p. 150.
31 M. Weber (1922), *Economy and Society* , ed. G. Roth and C. Wittick (2 vols, Berkeley, 1978), II, p. 941.
32 Gerth and Mills, eds, *From Max Weber*, p. 147.

tion'. Here he presents value-pluralism as a consequence of a historical process. The 'disenchantment' of the world – in other words, the collapse of transcendent religious interpretations of reality (see §7.3 below) – has produced a state of affairs resembling that of classical antiquity, in which different gods – Aphrodite, Apollo, and the like – made competing, and equally valid, claims to veneration: 'Many old gods ascend from their graves; they are disenchanted and hence take the form of impersonal forces. They strive to gain power over our lives and again they resume their eternal struggle with one another.' Since we no longer believe in a single transcendent deity who is the source of all meaning, we are confronted with 'an unceasing struggle of these gods with one another. Or speaking directly, the ultimate possible attitudes toward life are irreconcilable and hence their struggle can never be brought to a final conclusion.'[33]

Where does value-pluralism leave the status of science itself? Values operate in scientific research at a number of different levels. In the first place, they govern the selection of those phenomena which are considered worthy of study in the first place:

> the significance of cultural events presupposes a *value-orientation* towards those events. The concept of culture is a *value-concept*. Empirical reality becomes 'culture' because and insofar as we relate it to value ideas. It includes those segments and only those segments of reality which have become significant to us because of this value-relevance. Only a small portion of existing concrete reality is coloured by our value-conditioned interest and it alone is significant to us. It is significant because it reveals relationships which are important to us due to their connection with our values. Only because and to the extent that this is the case is it worthwhile for us to know it in its individual features.[34]

We ascribe meaning to social events rather than finding it there: 'the *meaning* we ascribe to the phenomena – that is, the relations which we establish between these phenomena and "values" – is a logically incongruous and heterogeneous factor which cannot be deduced from the "constitutive" elements of the event in question'. Furthermore, ' "[m]eaningfully" interpretable human action ("action") is identifiable only by reference to "valuations" and "meanings".' Weber therefore agrees with Dilthey that the *Geisteswissenschaften* are interpretive sciences. Nevertheless, research in them, just as in the physical sciences, consists in discovering the causal relationships in which the events selected for their 'value-relevance' are involved. Furthermore, the knowledge gained through scientific research is logically independent of our evaluations: 'There is simply no bridge which can span the gap from the *exclusively*

---

[33] Ibid., pp. 149, 152.
[34] M. Weber, *The Methodology of the Social Sciences*, ed. E. A. Shils and H. A. Finch (New York, 1949), p. 76.

"empirical" analysis of given reality with the tools of causal explanation to the confirmation or refutation of the "validity" of our value-judgements.'[35]

Weber seems to think that these 'tools of causal explanation' are, in principle at least, capable of providing objective knowledge of the world: 'All scientific work presupposes that the rules of logic and method are valid; these are the general foundations of our orientation on the world and, at least for our special question, these presuppositions are the least problematic aspect of science.'[36] What is problematic is the value of science itself: 'The *objective* validity of all empirical knowledge rests exclusively upon the ordering of the given reality according to categories which are *subjective* in a specific sense, namely, in that the *presuppositions* of our knowledge are based on the presupposition of the *value* of those *truths* which empirical knowledge alone is able to give.'[37] But the validity of this presupposition, as that of all value-judgements, cannot itself be established by scientific means: 'It can only be *interpreted* with reference to its ultimate meaning, which we must reject or accept according to our ultimate position towards life.'[38]

The methods of scientific research may thus be objective, but they operate within an inherently subjective framework, since the objects of study, the purposes for which specific researches are pursued, and the overall cultural role of science itself all derive from value-ascriptions which are subject to no rational adjudication. The famous 'value-neutrality' of social science comes down to the requirement that scholars should sharply distinguish between the objective means they employ and the subjective goals they pursue. Weber was disgusted by the tendency of nationalist scholars such as the historian Heinrich von Treitschke to use their intellectual authority to legitimize their political views:

> One cannot demonstrate scientifically what the duty of an academic teacher is. One can only demand of the teacher that he have the intellectual integrity to see that it is one thing to state facts, to determine mathematical or logical relations or the internal structures of culture values, while it is another thing to answer questions of the *value* of culture and its individual contents and the question of how one should act in the cultural community and in political associations. These are quite heterogeneous problems. If he asks further why he should not deal with both types of problem in the lecture room, the answer is because the prophet and the demagogue do not belong on the academic platform.[39]

This rather tortuous attempt to square Nietzschean perspectivism with a conditional commitment to scientific rationality is closely related to Weber's

[35] M. Weber (1903–6), *Roscher and Knies* (New York, 1975), pp. 108, 185, 117.
[36] Gerth and Mills, eds, *From Max Weber*, p. 143.
[37] Weber, *Methodology*, p. 110.
[38] Gerth and Mills, eds, *From Max Weber*, p. 143.
[39] Ibid., p. 146.

efforts to establish the distinctive properties of the *Geisteswissenschaften*. Physics is an example of what Rickert called 'nomological science'. It employs, in other words, the form of explanation most fully analysed by Carl Hempel as the 'covering-law' model (*nomos* is the Greek word for law). Here events are explained by being deduced from a universal law of nature. This model is not relevant to the study of the social world: 'The logical ideal of such a [nomological] science would be a system of *formulae* of absolutely general validity . . . It is obvious that historical reality, including those "world-historical" events and phenomena which we find so significant, could never be deduced from these *formulae*.'[40]

The covering-law model of explanation cannot therefore capture the individuality of the historical processes which our value-judgements pick out as being of cultural significance. This argument suggests that the study of social phenomena must take the form of accounts of specific historical episodes. This would, however, rule out the possibility of any general social theory. But Weber does not take this course. Instead, he argues that, while seeking to discover social-scientific 'laws' is futile, another form of conceptualization plays an indispensable role in the study of the social world. This is the construction of ideal types which portray in heightened, indeed sometimes caricatured, form characteristic social relationships, and thereby serve to illuminate the workings of actual processes and institutions:

> The ideal typical concept will help to develop our skill in imputation in *research*: it is no 'hypothesis' but it offers guidance to the construction of hypotheses. It is not a *description* of reality but it aims to give unambiguous means of expression to such a description . . . An ideal type is formed by the one-sided *accentuation* of one or more points of view and by the synthesis of a great many diffuse, discrete, more or less present and occasionally absent *concrete individual* phenomena, which are arranged according to those one-sidedly emphasized viewpoints into a unified *analytical* construct (*Gedankenbild*). In its mental purity, this mental construct (*Gedankenbild*) cannot be found empirically anywhere in reality. It is a *utopia*. Historical research faces the task of determining in each individual case, the extent to which this ideal construct approximates to or diverges from reality.[41]

Ideal types play an important role in Weber's historical sociology. Thus he famously distinguishes between 'three pure types of legitimate domination' – rational-legal domination, 'resting on a belief in the legality of enacted rules', and finding its purest form in bureaucratic administration; traditional domination, 'resting on an established belief in the sanctity of immemorial traditions'; and charismatic domination, 'resting on devotion to the exceptional sanctity, heroism or exemplary character of an individual person, and of the normative

40   Weber, *Roscher and Knies*, p. 64.
41   Weber, *Methodology*, p. 90.

patterns revealed or ordained by him'.[42] These ideal types are often exemplified by historically variable concrete combinations: thus modern 'plebiscitary democracy' involves a form of charismatic authority grafted onto bureaucratic-legal structures of domination (see §7.4 below).

But the most important use to Weber of the concept of ideal types is that it allows him to situate his sociology with respect to marginalist economics. Durkheim, writing from a standpoint sympathetic to the German Historical School, conceived his sociology as a theory of collective representations irreducible to the self-interested actions of individual market actors (see §6.1 above). Weber, however, attacks the Historical School for its tendency to hypostatize abstract concepts, which he regards as 'a consequence of the bioanthropological aspects of the various influences which the atrophied remains of the great Hegelian ideas exercised upon the philosophy of history, language, and culture'.[43] A proper understanding of political economy requires resort to the concept of ideal types:

> Pure economic theory, in its analysis of past and present society, utilizes ideal-typical concepts exclusively. Economic theory makes certain assumptions which scarcely correspond completely with reality but which approximate it in various degrees and asks: how would men act under these assumed conditions, if their actions were entirely rational? It assumes the dominance of purely economic interests and precludes the operation of political or other non-economic considerations.[44]

This formulation is very similar to that used by Carl Menger during the *Methodenstreit* when he argues that 'exact economics' (as opposed to those aspects of the science devoted to historical research or policy-oriented research) studies 'the formations of social life . . . from the point of view of the free play of human self-interest uninfluenced by secondary considerations, by error, or ignorance'.[45] The marginalist revolution, crucially, involved a redefinition of the concept of value. The remnants of the Ricardo–Marx labour theory of value, according to which commodities are exchanged in proportion to the socially necessary labour-time required to produce them, were removed. Henceforth, value was understood subjectively and from the standpoint, not of production, but of consumption. A theory of the market economy was constructed starting from the preferences of the individual consumer, on the assumption that the consumer can arrange his or her preferences in an order representing the relative intensity of the wants they express, and acts rationally in the sense of choosing the means best suited to achieve the ends specified by these preferences.

42   Weber, *Economy and Society*, I, p. 215.
43   Weber, *Roscher and Knies*, p. 207.
44   Weber, *Methodology*, pp. 43–4.
45   C. Menger (1883), *Problems of Economics and Sociology* (Urbana, 1963), p. 88.

Consequently, as Lionel Robbins puts it, '[t]he phenomena of the exchange economy itself can only be explained by *going behind* such relationships and invoking those laws of choice which are best seen when contemplating the behaviour of the isolated individual.'[46]

Weber in effect makes the procedures of marginalist economics the paradigm case of social explanation. Sociology, he says, is 'a science concerning itself with the intepretive understanding of social explanation and thereby with a causal explanation of its course and consequences'. Interpretive understanding primarily involves identifying the subjective meaning of the action for the person performing it – the beliefs and desires from which it arose. 'Action in the sense of subjectively understandable orientation of behaviour exists only as the behaviour of one or more *individual* human beings.' This implies a commitment to methodological individualism, the doctrine that social phenomena are the unintended consequences of individual actions: 'When reference is made in a sociological context to a state, a nation, a corporation, a family, or an army corps, or to similar collectivities, what is meant is *only* a certain kind of development of actual or possible actions of individual persons.'[47] Thus, while Durkheim counterposed his science of 'social facts' to methodological individualism, 'Weber's interpretive sociology', as Göran Therborn points out, 'is a generalization of marginalist economics.'[48]

7.3   History and rationalization

Weber does not simply take marginalist economics as a model: he offers a historical account of the circumstances in which its assumptions come to seem valid. Not long before his death in 1920, he wrote:

> A product of modern European civilization, studying any problem of universal history, is bound to ask himself to what combination of circumstances should be attributed the fact that in Western civilization, and in Western civilization only, cultural phenomena have appeared which (as we like to think) lie in a line of development having *universal* significance and value.[49]

This 'line of development' consists in 'the specific and peculiar rationalism of Western culture', which is manifested in a variety of spheres – law, art, music, architecture, education, politics, and economic life.[50] This characteriza-

---

[46]   L. Robbins, *An Essay on the Nature and Significance of Economic Science* (London, 1932), p. 20.
[47]   Weber, *Economy and Society*, I, pp. 4, 13, 14.
[48]   G. Therborn, *Science, Class and Society* (London, 1976), p. 293.
[49]   M. Weber (1904–5), *The Protestant Ethic and the Spirit of Capitalism* (London, 1976), p. 13; the introduction published in the English translation (pp. 13–31) was in fact written for *Gesammelte Aufsätze zur Religionssoziologie* (1920), a collection of Weber's writings on the sociology of religion.
[50]   Ibid., p. 26.

tion of the historical trajectory of the West naturally poses the question of what Weber means here by 'rationalism'. He argues that action can be rational in one of two ways. It may be '*instrumentally rational* (*zweckrational*), that is, determined by expectations as to the behaviour of objects in the environment and of other human beings; these expectations were used as "conditions" or "means" for the attainment of the actor's own rationally calculated ends'. Alternatively, action may be '*value-rational* (*wertrational*); that is, determined by a conscious belief in the value for its own sake of some ethical, aesthetic, religious, or other form of behaviour, independently of the prospects of success'.[51]

Value-rationality is concerned with the ends of action, instrumental rationality with the means:

> Choice between alternative and conflicting ends and results may well be determined in a value-rational manner. In that case, action is instrumentally rational only in respect to the choice of means. On the other hand, the actor may, instead of deciding between alternative and conflicting ends in terms of a rational orientation to a system of values, simply take them as given subjective wants and arrange them on a scale of consciously assessed relative urgency. He may then orient his action to this scale in such a way that they are satisfied as far as possible in order of urgency, as formulated in the principle of 'marginal utility'.[52]

As this reference to 'marginal utility' suggests, the assumption made by neoclassical economists that actors optimize – that is, select the best means to realize their wants – is an important source of Weber's concept of instrumental rationality. 'Why the human animal attaches particular values . . . to particular things is a question we do not discuss', Lionel Robbins says.[53] The wants expressed in agents' preferences are simply taken as given. Instrumental rationality is therefore not concerned with choosing the ends of action: it pertains only to the selection of the means best suited to achieving these ends.

It is this form of rationality – instrumental rationality – which, Weber believes, comes increasingly to prevail in the different culture-spheres in the modern West. Thus what characterizes modern capitalism is 'the rationalistic organization of (formally) free labour'.[54] Similarly, bureaucracy – in other words, hierarchically organized systems of administration based on a clear division of labour and staffed by technically qualified officials who are paid a salary and appointed and promoted on the basis of merit – is, 'from a technical point of view, capable of attaining the highest degree of efficiency and is in this sense formally the most rational known means of exercising authority over human beings'. Indeed, '[t]he development of modern forms of organization in all fields

[51]   Weber, *Economy and Society*, I, pp. 24–5.
[52]   Ibid., I, p. 26.
[53]   Robbins, *Nature and Significance*, p. 86.
[54]   Weber, *Protestant Ethic*, p. 21.

is nothing less than identical with the development and continual spread of bureaucratic administration.'[55]

Weber's most famous work, *The Protestant Ethic and the Spirit of Capitalism* (1904–5), represents his first major study of this process of rationalization. Rather like Marx in his theory of capital accumulation (see §4.2 above), Weber identifies the spirit of capitalism with 'the earning of more and more money, combined with the strict avoidance of all spontaneous enjoyment of life . . . Man is dominated by the making of money, by acquisition as the ultimate purpose of life.'[56] Marx explains the priority given to the self-expansion of capital by the pressure of competition on individual firms. In speaking rather of the capitalist *spirit*, Weber is expressing his interest in 'acquisition as the ultimate purpose of life' as an ethic, as a way of organizing one's life, as *Lebensführung* – conduct of life.

Viewed in this light, the capitalist spirit is a form of asceticism, in that it requires us to subordinate our satisfactions in the pursuit of ever more wealth. It differs radically, however, from the best-known form of Western asceticism, that of the monasteries of medieval Catholicism, where the flesh was denied as part of an attempt to escape the world for the contemplation of the goodness of a transcendent God. The capitalist spirit is a form of what Weber calls 'inner-worldly asceticism': self-denial is part of a process through which we shape and control this world. As such it bears a resemblance to the Protestant concept of a 'calling' (*Beruf*), according to which '[t]he only way of living acceptably to God is not to surpass worldly morality in monastic asceticism but solely through the fulfilment of the obligations imposed upon the individual by his position in the world.'[57]

Weber argues that the origins of the capitalist spirit are to be found in the form of inner-wordly asceticism which developed from the Protestant Reformation of the sixteenth and seventeenth centuries. Calvinism, the most radical version of Reformed Christianity, accepted the dogma of predestination. This held that all humans were inherently sinful, but that, by virtue of divine grace and that alone, some had been chosen for salvation. Humankind was thus divided between the elect and the damned. How could the believer expect that he or she was among the first rather than the second group? By resolutely believing that one has been chosen, 'since lack of self-confidence is the result of insufficient faith, hence of imperfect grace . . . In order to attain that self-confidence intensely worldly activity is recommended as the most suitable means. It and it alone disperses religious doubts and gives the certainty of grace.'[58]

The Calvinist's self-assurance in being one of the elect found expression in the systematic effort to control both his or her own life and that of the

[55] Weber, *Economy and Society*, I, p. 223.
[56] Weber, *Protestant Ethic*, p. 53.
[57] Ibid., p. 80.
[58] Ibid., pp. 111–12.

surrounding natural world. The purpose of this effort was not, however, primarily the gratification of material needs, but rather to provide confirmation of salvation. Thus: 'The Reformation took rational Christian asceticism and its methodical habits out of the monasteries and placed them in the service of active life in the world.' In doing so, it provided 'the most powerful conceivable lever for the expansion' of the capitalist spirit: 'When the limitation of consumption is combined with this release of acquisitive activity, the inevitable practical result is obvious: accumulation of capital through ascetic compulsion to save.'[59]

The *Protestant Ethic* provoked an enormous, and far from resolved, historical debate about the relationship between the Reformation and the rise of modern capitalism. Our interest here is less in the validity of Weber's historical interpretation than in the light it casts on his broader social theory. One issue concerns how he situates his argument relative to Marxist accounts of the development of capitalism, which tend to deny religious ideologies an autonomous role in the process. Kautsky, for example, argues that 'the Puritan ethic arises out of the class struggle of the self-confident and defiant bourgeoisie, especially of the craftsman against the feudal nobility, hence out of an economic basis'.[60] In the final lines of his essay, Weber denies that he is offering an idealist theory of history in which capitalism is simply a consequence of the Reformation: 'it is, of course, not my aim to substitute for a one-sided materialistic an equally one-sided spiritualistic causal interpretation of culture and of history'.[61]

Weber is at his most elliptical when discussing the role played by economic forces in history. Thus he distinguishes between 'the so-called "materialistic conception of history"', which he says 'is to be rejected most emphatically', and 'the economic *interpretation* of history', which he advocates. The first depends on 'the antiquated notion that all cultural phenomena can be *deduced* as a product or function of the constellation of material interests'; the second involves 'the analysis of cultural and economic phenomena with special reference to their economic conditioning'.[62] The distinction is ultimately a consequence of Weber's epistemology. Reality is infinitely diverse; our theories simply pick out those aspects whose study is relevant to our values. A theory of history which, like Marx's, claims to have discovered the underlying structure of social reality, seeks to impose an inappropriate 'nomological' conception of scientific explanation on the infinite variety of cultural phenomena. Rather than seek a one-way causal chain linking the economic base to the ideologico-political superstructure, the *Geisteswissenschaften* must seek to capture the

[59] Ibid., pp. 235 n. 79, 172.
[60] K. Kautsky (1927), *The Materialist Conception of History*, abr. edn., ed. J. H. Kautsky (New Haven, 1988), p. 369.
[61] Weber, *Protestant Ethic*, p. 183.
[62] Weber, *Methodology*, p. 68.

historically variable interactions between different, relatively autonomous aspects of social life:

> For the forms of social action follow 'laws of their own' . . . and even apart from this fact, they may in a given case always be codetermined by other than economic causes. However, at some point economic conditions tend to be causally important, and often decisive, for almost all social groups, at least those which have major cultural significance; conversely, the economy is usually also influenced by the autonomous structures of social action within which it exists. No significant generalization can be made as to when and how this will occur. However, we can generalize about the degree of elective affinity between concrete structures of social action and concrete forms of economic organization; that means, we can state in general terms whether or not they further or impede or exclude one another – whether they are 'adequate' or 'inadequate' in relation to one another.[63]

The concept of 'elective affinity' (*Wahlverwandtschaft*) is one Weber's main tools of historical interpretation. Michael Löwy writes: 'For Weber it designates the kind of active relationship (based on a certain structural analogy) between two social or cultural configurations, leading to mutual attraction, mutual influence, and mutual reinforcement.'[64] Thus there is an elective affinity between the Protestant ethic and the capitalist spirit, both of which are forms of inner-wordly asceticism. Similarly, capitalism and bureaucracy, two types of instrumentally rational social organization, are bound together by an elective affinity for one another:

> On the one hand, capitalism in its modern stage of development requires the bureaucracy, though both have arisen from different historical sources. Conversely, capitalism is the most rational economic base for bureaucratic administration and enables it to develop in the most rational form, especially because, from a fiscal point of view, it supplies the necessary money resources.[65]

An elective affinity is a relationship of functional compatibility between two social forms; to posit the existence of such a relationship is therefore to make no claim about the causal primacy of one form over another. Weber thus regards social explanation as inherently pluralistic: while one form of social power may provide the focus of study in a particular case and relative to certain value-interests, in general none can claim explanatory priority over the others. This explanatory pluralism is reflected in his treatment of social stratification, where he distinguishes class, conceived primarily in terms of shared economic situation, particularly in the market, from status, that is, 'an effective claim to social esteem in terms of positive or negative privileges'. Thus: 'Classes are stratified

---

[63] Weber, *Economy and Society*, I, p. 341.
[64] M. Löwy, *On Changing the World* (Atlantic Highlands, NJ, 1993), p. 46.
[65] Weber, *Economy and Society*, I, p. 224.

according to their relations to the production and acquisition of goods; whereas status groups are stratified according to the principles of their *consumption* of goods as represented by special styles of life.'[66]

Weber treats class and status as potentially rival principles of social organization, arguing that 'the principle of status stratification', which forms the basis of caste societies, for example, is opposed to 'a distribution of power which is regulated exclusively by the market'. But both are specific instances of the unremitting struggle for power among rival groups. Thus, as Weber famously puts it, ' "[c]lasses", "status groups", and "parties" are phenomena of the distribution of power within a community.' One characteristic pattern of this struggle is the striving to create socially closed relationships: 'Usually one group of competitors takes some externally identifiable characteristic of another group of (actual or potential) – race, language, religion, local or social origin, descent, residence, etc. – as a pretext for attempting their exclusion . . . Such group action may provoke a corresponding reaction on the part of those against which it is directed.'[67] On this view, the sources of social division are diverse, and therefore do not admit of explanation on the basis of any single factor, whether material or ideal.

There is, however, one famous, but characteristically obscure, passage where Weber seems to assign historical primacy to ideologies: 'Not ideas, but material and ideal interests, directly govern men's conduct. Yet very frequently the "world images" that have been created by "ideas" have, like switchmen, determined the tracks along which action has been pushed by the dynamic of interest.'[68] He makes this remark in the introduction to a series of essays with the collective title *Die Wirtschaftsethik der Weltreligionen* (The Economic Ethics of the World Religions) – which were published between 1915 and 1919. Embracing detailed studies of Confucianism, Hinduism, Buddhism, and Judaism (one on Islam was planned but never written), these essays broadened out the analysis of rationalization which Weber had broached in the *Protestant Ethic* into what Friedrich Tenbruck calls 'a general inquiry into the role of rationality in history'.[69]

How does Weber view religion? He denies that 'the specific nature of a religion is a simple "function" of the social situation of the stratum which appears as its characteristic bearer'. In doing so he seems to have in mind less the Marxist theory of ideology, than Nietzsche's interpretation of Christianity as the product of lower-class *ressentiment*, of 'a slave revolt in morality' (see §5.3 above). Nevertheless, his interest in the great religions reflects a Nietzschean preoccupation (seen also in his definition of status in terms of lifestyle) with the

---

[66] Ibid., I, p. 305; II, p. 937.
[67] Ibid., II, pp. 936, 927; I, pp. 341–2.
[68] Gerth and Mills, eds, *From Max Weber*, p. 280.
[69] F. H. Tenbruck, 'The Problem of Thematic Unity in the Works of Max Weber', in Tribe, ed., *Reading Weber*, p. 59.

stylization of life, with the organization of one's appetites, dispositions, and capacities according to a particular set of values. The world religions represent 'different forms of "rationalization" of life-conduct (*Lebensführung*)'. More specifically, they constitute particular answers to what theologians call the problem of evil, that is, to the essentially metaphysical question of why so many suffer, in particular as a result of occupying an inferior social position, without apparently having done anything to merit this fate. At the core of every major religion is a 'theodicy of suffering' which offers 'an ethical interpretation of the "meaning" of the distribution of fortunes among men'.[70]

Weber believes that only three theodicies provide coherent answers to the problem of evil. Hinduism does so through the doctrine of karma, according to which every living being's present lot is a consequence of the good and evil it has committed not simply in its present but also in its past lives; the transmigration of souls, through which an individual soul may pass in successive lives through different kinds of existence – animal, vegetable, and mineral – as well as different social statuses, provides the mechanism through which rewards and punishments are allocated, a cycle from which the individual may escape through the pursuit of salvation by contemplation and the renunciation of wordly existence. Zoroastrianism posits a dualistic universe divided between two separate and opposed orders of being representing respectively the forces of light and dark, good and evil, spirit and matter: suffering is a consequence of the fact that good does not always triumph over evil in the eternal struggle between these two equal powers. Finally, the Christian doctrine of predestination, formulated by St Augustine and taken over by Calvinism, affirms the omnipotence of a single, transcendent God. Evil is a consequence of man's freely chosen rebellion against divine law, and suffering is its just punishment: the salvation for which we must hope arises from the inscrutable, and therefore from a human viewpoint apparently arbitrary, operation of God's grace.

Weber thus attaches great importance to the theoretical content of the various systems of religious beliefs: 'We are interested in . . . the influence of those psychological sanctions which, originating in religious belief and the practice of religion, gave a direction to practical conduct and held the individual to it. Now these sanctions were to a large extent derived from the peculiarities of the religious ideas behind them.'[71] The relative autonomy of these ideas, and their ability to act as 'switchmen', setting the direction in which the 'dynamic of interest' moves derives from the intrinsic logic they develop as particular solutions to the problem of suffering and injustice. Weber writes in the passage immediately preceding that in which he uses the metaphor of 'world images' as 'switchmen':

[70] Gerth and Mills, eds, *From Max Weber*, pp. 275, 269, 270.
[71] Weber, *Protestant Ethic*, pp. 97–8.

In the past, it was the work of intellectuals to sublimate the possession of sacred values into a belief in redemption. The conception of the idea of redemption, as such, is very old, if one understands by it a liberation from distress, hunger, drought, sickness, and ultimately suffering and death. Yet redemption attained a specific significance where it expressed a systematic and rationalized 'image of the world' and represented a stand in the face of the world. For the meaning as well as the intended and actual psychological quality of redemption has depended upon such a world image and such a stand.[72]

The dynamic of rationalization thus depends crucially on the work of intellectuals in developing religious ideologies into rationally articulated theoretical systems, and thereby drawing out the logical consequences of the particular theodicies they embody. This does not, however, mean that Weber treats the history of religions as essentially the autonomous development of different sets of beliefs. On the contrary, he argues that 'the nature of the desired sacred values has been strongly influenced by the nature of the external interest-situation and the corresponding way of life of the ruling strata and thus by the social stratification itself', though he characteristically goes on immediately to add that the influence goes the other way as well.[73]

More generally, Weber's sociology involves what Michael Mann calls '"organizational materialism": Ideologies are attempts to grapple with real social problems, but they are diffused through specific media of communication and *their* characteristics may transform ideological messages, so conferring ideological power autonomy.'[74] Or, to put it in another way, the relative autonomy of religious systems derives not simply from their intrinsic content but also from the power-dynamics of the organizations through which they are transmitted and preserved. Every form of authority – including religious authority – requires 'the existence and functioning of an administrative staff . . . For the habit of obedience cannot be maintained without organized activity directed to application and enforcement of the order.' But every administrative organization develops its own distinctive interests irreducible either to the forms of legitimate domination or to economic class-structures, so that 'historical reality involves a continuous, though for the most part latent, conflict between chiefs and their administrative staffs for appropriation and expropriation in relation to one another'.[75]

Thus one force promoting Western rationalization was the interest of the managers of competing European states in developing more efficient means for extracting resources from their subjects and thereby strengthening their military machines: the resulting organizational innovations, particularly under the

---

[72] Gerth and Mills, eds, *From Max Weber*, p. 280.
[73] Ibid., p. 287.
[74] M. Mann, *The Sources of Social Power*, II (Cambridge, 1993), p. 36.
[75] Weber, *Economy and Society*, I, p. 264.

absolute monarchies of the sixteenth and seventeenth centuries, helped lay the basis of modern bureaucracy. The interests of these proto-bureaucratic states in turn interwove with those of the emerging bourgeoisie in the cities of early modern Europe:

> This competitive struggle [among states] created the largest opportunities for modern western capitalism. The separate states had to compete for mobile capital, which dictated to them the conditions under which it would assist them to power. Out of this alliance of the state with capital, dictated by capital, arose the national citizenship class, the bourgeoisie in the modern sense of the word. Hence it is the closed national state which afforded to capitalism its chance for development.[76]

Weber's analysis of charisma is closely related to his sociology of religion. The paradigm case of the charismatic leader is the founder of a new religion – the teacher (Buddha), saviour (Christ), or prophet (Muhammed). Charismatic authority is sharply counterposed to traditional and legal domination. The latter's most typical forms, respectively patriarchalism, where obedience takes the form of personal loyalty to a ruler whose customary authority is modelled on that of a master over his household, and bureaucracy, 'are antagonistic in many respects, but they share *continuity* as one of their most important characteristics. In this sense, both are structures of everyday life'. Charismatic authority, by contrast, responds to 'needs . . . which *transcend* the sphere of everyday economic routine'. Its bearer represents the irruption of the exceptional into the everyday. His authority derives from the recognition that he is 'extraordinary and . . . endowed with supernatural, superhuman, or at least specifically exceptional powers'. Indeed:

> charisma in its most potent forms disrupts rational rule as well as tradition altogether and overturns all notions of sanctity. Instead of reverence for customs that are ancient and hence sacred, it enforces the inner subjection to the unprecedented and absolutely unique and therefore Divine. In this purely empirical and value-free sense charisma is indeed the specifically creative revolutionary force in history.[77]

History therefore displays according to Weber an alternation between rule-bound routine, whether the source of the rules is tradition or a system of bureaucratically administered laws, and short-lived bursts of creative transformation inspired by ideas which admit of no rational justification. Charismatic domination is necessarily unstable since it derives from the personal qualities of the founder, which cannot outlive him: 'Every charisma is on the road from a

---

[76] M. Weber (1923), *General Economic History* (New Brunswick, 1981), p. 337.
[77] Weber, *Economy and Society*, II, p. 1111, I, p. 241, II, p. 1117.

turbulently emotional life that knows no economic rationality to a slow death by suffocation under the weight of material interests; every hour of its existence brings it nearer to this end.' There thus develops 'the routinization of charisma' – the attempt to preserve the founder's authority by transforming it into a more everyday form of traditional or legal domination (or some combination of the two). This process springs from 'the desire to transform charisma from a unique, transitory gift of grace of extra-ordinary times and persons into a permanent possession of everyday life', but its effect is progressively to destroy the necessarily exceptional sources from which the charismatic claim to rule derived in the first place, while simultaneously permitting 'the appropriation of powers and of economic advantages by the followers or disciples'.[78]

Weber's account of this dialectic of routine and charisma is no doubt in part a generalization from the history of world religions – for example, the transformation of the egalitarian moral communities of early Christianity into the great worldly power of the Catholic Church. But it also reflects his sense of the sheer weight with which everyday routine bears down on brief outbursts of creative innovation. Although Weber presents charisma primarily as a break with tradition, he argues that *rational discipline* is 'the most irresistible force' in the 'waning of charisma'. Rationalization is thus the greatest threat to individual creativity: 'Discipline inexorably takes over ever larger areas as the satisfaction of political and economic needs is increasingly rationalized. This universal phenomenon more and more restricts the importance of charisma and of individually differentiated conduct.'[79]

As we have seen, Weber believes that the Calvinist doctrine of predestination played a crucial role in the most developed form of the rationalization process, in the modern West. The world is no longer seen as a complex of ascertainable meanings and purposes which it is possible to manipulate by means of the use of magic intended to secure the co-operation of individual deities or lesser spirits. Rather, it is the apparently meaningless product of the inscrutable will of a single, transcendent God. 'The great historic process in the development of religions, the elimination of magic from the world [*Entzauberung der Welt*] which had begun with the old Hebrew prophets and, in conjunction with Hellenistic scientific thought, had repudiated all magical means to salvation as superstition and sin, came here to its logical conclusion.'[80]

Disenchantment reaches its climax when the process of rationalization directs itself onto the central dogmas of religion itself – a stage only fully achieved in the modern West. 'The general result of the modern form of thoroughly rationalizing the conception of the world and of the way of life, theoretically and practically, in a purposive manner has been a shift into the realm of the

[78]   Ibid., II, pp. 1120, 1121; I, p. 249.
[79]   Ibid., II, pp. 1148–9, 1156.
[80]   Weber, *Protestant Ethic*, p. 105 (passage added in 1920 edition).

irrational.' Intellectuals' attempts to develop a coherent theoretical articulation of religious 'world-images' eventually expose the 'irrational presuppositions, which have been accepted as "given" and which have long been incorporated into such ways of life'. Religious experience then becomes the domain of the *ir*rational, of the search for mystical states of being as a kind of compensation for the thorough rationalization of the world by modern science, bureaucracy, and capitalism: 'The unity of the primitive image of the world, in which everything was concrete magic, has tended to split into rational cognition and mastery of nature, on the one hand, and into "mystic" experiences, on the other.'[81]

This denouement is arguably implicit in Weber's theory of rationality. Recall that he distinguishes between instrumental and value rationality (or, as he tends to put it when discussing economic processes, formal and substantive rationality). Instrumental rationality pertains to means, value-rationality to ends. But Weber does not believe it is possible rationally to justify the ultimate values on the basis of which the ends of action are chosen. Reason cannot adjudicate between the warring gods, the rival value-spheres. A great world religion can still this conflict by integrating the different possible ends of action into the particular theodicy it offers its followers. In doing so it makes possible a certain rationalization of life-conduct – the value-rational ordering of life according to the ethical scheme implied by the theodicy. But once reason focuses critically on the values central to this scheme, the irrational foundations of the religious 'world-image' are exposed – not because of the nature of the particular values in question, but because *all* values lack rational justification. And then we are left, as Weber describes the plight of us moderns in 'Science as a Vocation', torn between the warring gods.

Plainly this argument is only as strong as its premiss, the doctrine of value-pluralism, according to which there is no objective, rationally defensible criterion on the basis of which one can accept or reject evaluative judgements. If one denies this premiss – as, for example, Habermas does (see §11.4 below), then one's assessment of Weber's philosophy of history, for that is what his account of rationalization amounts to, is likely to be highly critical. Weber in any case believes that the role of the Protestant ethic and other religious rationalizations is over. The rationalization process now has an autonomous dynamic, driven by the forces of economic and political competition:

> The Puritan wanted to work in a calling; we are forced to do so. For when asceticism was carried out of the monastic cells into everyday life, and began to dominate worldly morality, it did its part in building the tremendous *cosmos* of the modern economic order. This order is now bound to the technical and economic conditions of machine production which today determine the lives of all the

---

[81]   Gerth and Mills, eds, *From Max Weber*, pp. 281, 282.

individuals who are born into this mechanism, not only those who are directly concerned with economic acquisition with irresistible force. Perhaps it will so determine them until the last ton of fossil coal is burnt. In [the Puritan divine Richard] Baxter's view the care for external goods should only lie on the shoulders of the 'saint like a light cloak, which can be thrown aside at any moment'. But fate decreed that the cloak should become an iron cage.[82]

7.4 Liberal imperialism and democratic politics

Wolfgang Mommsen, perhaps the most important student of Weber's politics, has commented on Weber's tendency to think in antinomical terms, adopting apparently starkly counterposed positions – notably liberalism and nationalism – and rendering the tension between them explicit by formulating each in extreme terms:

> positions which had originally co-existed in an unclear relationship started progressively to diverge until, finally, they took on an antinomical structure. The unconditionality of Weber's thinking, which the latter owed to Nietzsche, and the clear appreciation of the power character of all social relations, which he learned from Marx, led him finally to abandon the framework of classical liberal theory and to search for a new, more solid foundation for liberal postulates. This extreme radicalization of alternative positions, so typical of Weber's political thinking, reveals as it were the flaws and contradictions within the liberal system of values which appears when the latter is confronted with the conditions of advanced industrial societies.[83]

Wilhelm Hennis, another, equally distinguished, commentator, denies that Weber can be considered as a liberal: '[w]ithout some degree of success, some faith in the course of events, there is no Liberalism.' Weber is not a liberal thinker, nor a sociologist. He belongs rather to the tradition of classical political thought. Along with Machiavelli, Rousseau, and Tocqueville, he is concerned with 'the unfolding of the soul, an unfolding that appeared to be possible not on an individual basis, but rather communally, associatively, ultimately in the ancient sense of *politics*'. From this perspective, 'it would appear that Weber's real concern was with the historical genesis of "the rational *Lebensführung*" [conduct of life]'.[84]

Relating Weber in this way to the classical republican tradition is a valuable corrective to misleading treatments which turn him into the tutelary deity of postwar American sociology, and throws an important light on his theoretical concerns. But to make the belief that value-conflict can be overcome a defining

---

[82] Weber, *Protestant Ethic*, p. 181.
[83] W. J. Mommsen, *The Political and Social Theory of Max Weber* (Cambridge, 1989), p. 27.
[84] Hennis, *Max Weber*, pp. 174, 196, 27.

feature of liberalism, as Hennis does, is to give too one-sided an account of this tradition. Weber is arguably the most important representative of what John Gray calls 'agonistic liberalism': like Tocqueville and Mill before him (see §4.2 above), but far more systematically than they, he regards modernity as constituted by the irresoluble conflict between rival values.

Weber certainly brings to political debates a powerful sense of the historical specificity and the fragility of liberal institutions. Thus during the Russian Revolution of 1905 he warned Russian liberals not to rely on 'the "automatic" effect of *material* interests' to produce the reform of the tsarist autocracy they advocated. 'Modern "liberty" arose from a unique, never to be repeated set of circumstances', he argues: the expansion of the Atlantic economy, the distinctive structures of early modern capitalism, the scientific revolution, and the Protestant ethic combined to produce 'the particular "ethical" character and the cultural values of modern man'. The further development of capitalism is likely, however, to undermine rather than to reinforce these values:

> If it were *only* a question of the 'material' conditions and the complex of interests directly or indirectly 'created' by them, any sober observer would have to say that all *economic* indicators point in the direction of growing 'unfreedom'. It is absolutely ridiculous to attribute to the high capitalism which is today being imported into Russia and already exists in America – this 'inevitable' economic development – any elective affinity with democracy, let alone with liberty (in any sense of the word). The question should be: how can these things exist at all for any length of time under the domination of capitalism? In fact they are only possible where they are backed up by the determined *will* of a nation not to be ruled like a flock of sheep. We 'individualists' and supporters of 'democratic' institutions must swim 'against the tide' of material constellations.[85]

Weber's view of capitalism is in many ways very similar to Marx's. He does not see it, as Adam Smith and his *laissez-faire* successors did, as an economically efficient means of realizing individual freedom. It is, on the contrary, a system of domination. 'Capital accounting in its most rational shape thus presupposes the *battle of man with man*' in the shape of competition. 'Strict capital accounting is further associated with social phenomena of "shop discipline" and the appropriation of the means of production, and that means: with the existence of a "system of domination".'[86] Weber indeed endorses Marx's view of the ambiguous 'double freedom' of the worker: 'only when in consequence of the existence of workers who in the formal sense voluntarily, but actually under the compulsion of the whip of hunger, offer themselves, the cost of products may be unambiguously determined in advance.'[87]

[85]   M. Weber, *The Russian Revolutions*, ed. G. C. Wills and P. Baehr (Cambridge, 1995), pp. 108–9.

[86]   Weber, *Economy and Society*, I, pp. 93, 108.

[87]   Weber, *General Economic History*, p. 277.

The separation of the worker from the means of production which, according to Marx, makes capitalist exploitation possible is, however, one instance of a much broader process of bureaucratization. 'Everywhere we find the same thing: the means of operation within the factory, the state administration, the army and university departments are concentrated by means of a bureaucratically structured human apparatus in the hands of the person who has command over (*beherrscht*) this human apparatus.'[88] There is no alternative to bureaucratization in the modern world:

> The primary source of the superiority of bureaucratic administration lies in the role of technical knowledge which, through the development of modern technology and business methods in the production of goods, has become completely indispensable. In this respect, it makes no difference whether the economic system is organized on a capitalistic or a socialistic basis. [89]

Not only will the introduction of social ownership of the means of production not improve the situation. By eliminating the private entrepreneur, 'the only social type who has been able to maintain at least relative immunity from subjection to the control of rational bureaucratic knowledge', it will actually make matters worse.[90] Although 'high capitalism' involves a considerable centralization of economic power in the hands of cartels, corporations, and banks, it preserves a separation of private and public spheres and thus makes it possible to play off rival oligarchies against one another. Socialism would eliminate this room for manoeuvre:

> The embarrassing thing would be that, whereas the political and private-economic bureaucracies (of syndicates, banks, and giant concerns) exist alongside one another at present, as separate entities, so that economic power can still be curbed by political power, the two bureaucracies would then be a single body with identical interests and could no longer be supervised or controlled.[91]

'There is a paradox here', Mommsen points out.[92] Weber believes that the dynamic of capitalism is driving us into the 'iron cage' of bureaucracy; but at the same time he argues that by preserving, as far as possible, the market competition that is a main element in this dynamic, we can stave off the inevitable. Thus he writes that 'the much reviled "anarchy" of production and the equally reviled "subjectivism" . . . *alone* can take the individual out of the broad mass and throw him back on himself '.[93] As long as it is preserved, capitalism retains a degree of dynamism and openness to individual self-assertion.

---

[88]   Weber, *Political Writings*, p. 281.
[89]   Weber, *Economy and Society*, I, p. 223.
[90]   Ibid., I, p. 225.
[91]   Weber, *Political Writings*, p. 286.
[92]   Mommsen, *Political and Social Theory*, p. 39.
[93]   Weber, *Russian Revolutions*, p. 110.

Weber nevertheless insists that the effort to preserve liberal values and institutions '"against the tide" of material constellations' must be based on a realistic recognition that 'the future belongs to bureaucratization'.[94] The only coherent
alternative to this standpoint is a religious rejection of the world on the basis of
consciously chosen values, of which Weber regarded Tolstoy's pacifistic rural
socialism and some forms of anarchism as contemporary examples. He presents
this choice most starkly in a letter to Robert Michels, when the latter was a kind
of Marxist syndicalist:

> There are *two* possibilities. Either: (1) 'my kingdom is not of this world' (Tolstoy,
> *or a thoroughly thought-out* syndicalism . . .) . . . *Or*: (2) Culture – (i.e., *object-*
> *ive*, a culture expressed in *technical*, etc., 'achievements') *affirmation as adapt-*
> *ation* to the sociological condition of *all* 'technology', whether it be economic,
> political or whatever . . . In the case of (2), all talk of 'revolution' is farce, every
> thought of abolishing the 'domination of man by man' by any kind of 'socialist'
> social system or the *most* elaborated form of 'democracy' a *utopia* . . . Whoever
> wishes to live as a 'modern man' even in the sense that he has his daily paper and
> railways and trams – he *renounces* all those ideals which vaguely appeal to *you*
> as soon as he leaves the basis of revolutionism *for its own sake, without* any
> 'objective', without an 'objective' being thinkable.[95]

Any attempt to adapt to existing reality, and to calculate instrumentally, seeking to adjust means and ends, necessarily imprisons us in the 'iron cage'. To
escape it, we must unconditionally reject the world. The alternatives Weber
poses here form a major theme of his writings on the sociology of religion, and
are most fully developed in the famous contrast he draws in his 1919 lecture
'Politics as a Vocation' between the ethics of 'responsibility' and those of
'principled conviction':

> there is a profound opposition between acting by the maxim of the ethic of con-
> viction (putting it in religious terms: 'The Christian does what is right and places
> the outcome in God's hands'), and acting by the maxim of the ethic of respons-
> ibility, which means that one must answer for the (foreseeable) *consequences* of
> one's actions.[96]

Action based on the ethic of conviction is value-rational: everything is subordinated to the pursuit of certain ultimate values. But agents thus motivated must
confront the problem of the means used to achieve the ends defined by these
values. Revolutionary socialists, for example, are willing to use violence to
remove capitalism. 'Anyone who makes a pact with the means of violence –
and any politician does this – is at the mercy of specific consequences.' Revol-

---

[94] Weber, *Economy and Society*, II, p. 1401.
[95] Letter of 4 Aug. 1908, quoted in Hennis, *Max Weber*, p. 246 n. 45 (translation modified).
[96] Weber, *Political Writings*, pp. 359–60.

utionary action requires the development of a movement whose followers will be governed by the material interests that promote the routinization of charisma: 'the emotionalism of revolution is then followed by a return to traditional, *everyday existence*' which negates the objectives for which the movement was founded in the first place.[97] The only coherent form of the ethics of conviction therefore involves abstaining from all violent means, and therefore renouncing this world altogether. Those who wish to engage in political life must adopt the ethics of responsibility, and, using the tool of instrumental rationality that binds them to bureaucracy, carefully weigh the consequences of their actions.

Socialist revolution therefore has no place in a world increasingly dominated by bureaucracy: 'Such an apparatus makes "revolutions", in the sense of the forceful creation of entirely new formations of authority, more and more impossible – technically, because of its control over the modern means of communication (telegraph etc.) and also because of its increasingly rationalized inner structure.'[98] Weber wrote these lines before the First World War, but the actual occurrence of 'impossible' revolutions in Russia in 1917 and in Germany itself in 1918 did not alter this assessment. He dismissed the Bolshevik regime as 'a military dictatorship, not it is true of generals, but of corporals'.[99] He called the German Revolution 'a bloody carnival that does not deserve the honourable name of a revolution', and declared of the leaders of the extreme-left Spartacists: '[Karl] Liebknecht belongs in the madhouse and Rosa Luxemburg in the zoo.'[100] (Shortly after Weber made the latter remarks in January 1919 Luxemburg and Liebknecht were murdered by the Freikorps.)

Weber nevertheless saw the fall of the imperial regime in November 1918 as an important opportunity to reform the German state. In the years before the November Revolution he had developed a systematic critique of what he described as the system of 'personal rule' in the Reich. The remnants of absolute monarchy behind a façade of 'pseudo-constitutionalism' permitted both Kaiser Wilhelm II himself and the civil and military bureaucracy to evade political responsibility for a series of blunders in foreign policy culminating in the outbreak of war in 1914. The origins of this set-up could be traced to the timidity of the German bourgeoisie at the time of unification, and its readiness to subordinate itself to Bismarck's 'Caesarism' (see §7.1 above); among its effects was Germany's defeat and the collapse of the monarchy in 1918.

Weber's advocacy of initially relatively limited constitutional reforms therefore sprang less from any discrepancy between the Wilhelmine regime and abstract norms of democratic legitimacy than from his belief that existing political structures prevented Germany from effectively pursuing its interests as a world power. During the war he advocated what Mommsen describes as the 'liberal

[97]   Ibid., pp. 364, 365.
[98]   Weber, *Economy and Society*, II, p. 989.
[99]   Weber, *Political Writings*, p. 299.
[100] Quoted in Mommsen, *Weber and German Politics*, pp. 296, 305.

imperialist' policy of expansion into eastern and central Europe, where Poland, the Ukraine, and the Baltic states would gain political independence subject to German hegemony within 'a middle European tariff and economic union'. [101] The successful assertion of German interests depended, however, on the establishment of responsible parliamentary government:

> There are only two choices: either the mass of citizens is left without rights in a bureaucratic 'authoritarian' state which has only the appearance of parliamentary rule, and in which the citizens are 'administered' like a herd of cattle; or the citizens are integrated into the state as 'co-rulers'. A *nation of masters* (*Herrenvolk*) – and only such a nation can and may engage in 'world politics' – has no choice in this matter.[102]

The concept of *Herrenvolk* now has Nazi resonances, but for Weber the term seems to have had, at least in part, the classical republican connotation of a people whose free political institutions allow them to enjoy collective autonomy within the international state system (though where this would leave small nations in a German-dominated Mitteleuropa is another matter). Nevertheless, his advocacy of a form of democratic government for Germany after the fall of the monarchy does not spring from the belief that this would allow the people to govern. On the contrary, Weber's view of politics is resolutely elitist. The modern state is not even potentially a political community but is necessarily based on domination and coercion – 'an institutional association of rule (*Herrschaftsverband*) which has successfully established the monopoly of physical violence as a means of rule within a territory'.[103] 'Political action is always determined by the "principle of small numbers"', he writes, 'that means, the superior political manoeuvrability of small leading groups. In mass states, this caesarist element is ineradicable.'[104]

Nevertheless, rule by 'small leading groups' of democratic politicians is one important way of fending off the complete triumph of bureaucratization. The experience of bureaucratic administration is a poor training for the inherently volatile and creative process of formulating, winning support for, and implementing policies. '"To be above parties" – in truth, to remain outside the realm of struggle for power – is the official's role, while this struggle for personal power, and the resulting personal responsibility, is the lifeblood of the politician as well as of the entrepreneur.' One reason for the failure of the German Reich's foreign policy before and during the First World War was that political decision-making was largely in the hands of bureaucrats lacking the skill or inclination to take initiatives and run risks. 'The essence of politics', by

---

[101] Ibid., pp. 205ff.
[102] Weber, *Political Writings*, p. 129.
[103] Ibid., p. 316.
[104] Weber, *Economy and Society*, II, p. 1414.

contrast, '. . . is *struggle*, the recruitment of allies and of a *voluntary* following.' Therefore '[p]oliticians must be the countervailing force against bureaucratic domination', both by making the executive accountable for its decisions,
and by providing the creative qualities required for effective leadership of a
Great Power.[105]

This political critique of bureaucracy implies the contrast, central to Weber's
historical sociology, between the routines common to traditional and bureaucratic modes of domination, and charisma as the revolutionary and creative
irruption of the exceptional into the everyday (see §7.3 above). Democracy is
indeed a rationalized form of charismatic domination. In the case of the great
religious movements, the followers' recognition of the leader arises from the
latter's charismatic qualities: 'But, when the charismatic organization undergoes progressive rationalization, it is readily possible that, instead of recognition being treated as a consequence of legitimacy, it is treated as the basis of
legitimacy: *democratic legitimacy*.'[106]

Democratic charisma does not, however, derive solely from the recognition
of the electorate. The competition of politicians to gain election to parliament,
and once there to secure advancement, acts as a mechanism for the selection
of those individuals exercising creative political leadership. With the development of modern mass politics, involving the competition of bureaucratic party
machines using the press and other media to win the support of an electorate
increasingly coextensive with the adult population, the ultimate test of political leadership becomes the capacity to win popular support:

> Active political democratization means that the political leader is no longer pro-
> claimed as a candidate because he has proved himself in a circle of *honoratiores*
> [notables], then becoming a leader because of his parliamentary accomplishments,
> but that he gains the trust and the faith of the masses in him and his power with
> the means of mass demagogy. In substance, this means a shift towards a *caesarist*
> mode of selection. Indeed, every democracy tends in this direction. After all, the
> specifically caesarist technique is the plebiscite. It is not an ordinary vote or elec-
> tion, but a profession of faith in the calling of him who demands these acclamations.[107]

Weber seems to have modelled his conception of the 'democratic Caesarist'
political leader on the great Victorian Liberal Gladstone and his famous campaigns in support of an enlightened foreign policy and Irish Home Rule.
Gladstone is hardly the most alarming of political figures, but the theory of
'plebiscitary leader democracy' (*Führer-Demokratie*) Weber developed in
post-revolutionary Germany makes the 'Caesarist politician' a largely unaccountable figure: 'Plebiscitary democracy – the most important type of

[105]   Ibid., II, pp. 1404, 1414, 1417.
[106]   Ibid., I, pp. 266–7.
[107]   Ibid., II, p. 1451.

Führer-Demokratie – is a variant of charismatic authority, which hides behind a legitimacy that is *formally* derived from the will of the governed.'[108] The formal character of popular ratification suggests that 'plebiscitary democracy' will contain as large an element of personal rule as the quasi-absolutist monarchy of which Weber became such an unremitting critic. Indeed, in the debates on the constitution of the Weimar Republic which replaced the imperial regime, Weber advocated the establishment of a popularly elected president independent of parliament and enjoying many of the emperor's powers. In the event, a more limited version of this proposal was adopted, though even under this arrangement President Paul von Hindenburg used his emergency powers to undermine parliamentary institutions after 1930 and to enable the Nazis to suppress their political opponents.

Weber's authentic commitment to liberal values would no doubt have led him fiercely to oppose Hitler's rise to power had he lived to see it. But his conception of 'plebiscitary democracy', by according the initiative to a charismatic leader and giving the people a purely passive role, held strong attractions for the anti-parliamentary right. Outlining his views in May 1919 to General Erich Ludendorff, Weber said: 'In a democracy the people choose a leader whom they trust. Then the chosen man says, "Now shut your mouths and obey me. The people and the parties are no longer free to interfere in the leader's business."' Ludendorff, who had exercised quasi-dictatorial powers in the last years of the Great War, and who was to take part in Hitler's abortive Bavarian putsch in October 1923, commented: 'I could like such a democracy.'[109]

Weber's reduction of the role of democratic procedures to the formal ratification of the leader's initiatives was exploited by the most brilliant representative of the authoritarian right under Weimar, the legal theorist Carl Schmitt. Dismissing parliamentary institutions as a mere shell, Schmitt relocated sovereignty in the president, whose capacity to intervene and to resolve crisis situations constituted the fount of all legitimate authority (see §9.2 below). As Mommsen puts it, 'Schmitt's theory of the plebiscitary authority of the Reich president . . . is a one-sided but conceptually consistent extension of Weber's own programme.'[110]

The theory of 'plebiscitary democracy' displays the polarity that runs through Weber's thought between the formal, instrumental rationality of bureaucratized capitalism and the substantively irrational interventions – in this case provided by the charismatic leader – through which values are creatively transformed. Herbert Marcuse sardonically commented: 'It is difficult not to think here of Hegel's *Philosophy of Right* where the state of civil society, the rational state, culminates in the "accidental" monarch who is determined only by the contingency of birth.'[111] But it is, of course, Nietzsche who is the most direct

[108]   Ibid., II, p. 268.
[109]   Quoted in M. Weber, *Max Weber* (New York, 1975), p. 653.
[110]   Mommsen, *Weber and German Politics*, pp. 382–3.
[111]   H. Marcuse, *Negations* (Harmondsworth, 1972), p. 221.

philosophical influence here: the 'democratic Caesarist' leader bears a suspicious resemblance to the 'overman' who fashions himself into a coherent whole by the destruction of old values and the invention of new ones.

Weber's political theory certainly displays what Mommsen calls the 'antinomical structure' of his thought – its tendency, in other words, to seek to combine sharply formulated and apparently antithetical positions. With the exception of Hegel and Marx, Weber, more than any thinker discussed in this book, seems to hold all the tensions of modernity in a conflicted unity. But these tensions constantly threaten to become polarities that rip his thought apart.

Consider, for example, the contrast between the disdain he evinces for what Lyotard would call 'grand narratives' – the attempts by the Enlightenment, Hegel, and Marx to offer interpretations of the whole of human development – and the fact that his theory of rationalization amounts to a philosophy of world history; or the closely related tension between the privileging of historical contingency implicit in his account of the *Geisteswissenschaften*, and the repeated declarations that humanity's imprisonment in the 'iron cage' of bureaucratized capitalism is 'inevitable'. Then again, capitalism is both one of the main levers of rationalization, but its preservation will prevent the complete triumph of bureaucracy. Finally, Weber's theory of rationality is relentlessly paradoxical. Instrumental rationality conquers the world through the means of bureaucracy and the scientific knowledge it applies. But the value of this knowledge cannot be justified, and a thoroughly rationalized world will sink into a torpor as stagnant as the most traditional form of patriarchalism unless it is shaken up by bursts of irrational charismatic creativity.

No wonder then that Weber's writings could provide a starting-point both for the root-and-branch critique of capitalism developed by Lukács and the Frankfurt School and for the functionalist sociology of Talcott Parsons. His thought is enormously rich and suggestive, but it gives the impression of being so riven by irreconcilable conflicts that, as soon as any pressure is applied, it shatters into a thousand fragments. The ambiguity of Weber's intellectual heritage is a consequence of the contradictions that define his most basic concepts.

8

The Illusions of Progress

8.1 The strange death of liberal Europe

The struggle that runs through Weber's thought over the theoretical and practical role of reason is symptomatic of a much larger shift in Western intellectual culture around the start of the twentieth century. Those forms of rationality, particularly associated with the modern physical sciences, which the Enlightenment had seen as a liberating force, were now subjected to widespread questioning. Their ability to provide an adequate account of the world, and in particular of the sources of human motivation, was fiercely disputed; equally, the process of historical development from which modern societies heavily dependent on the systematic practical application of scientific knowledge had emerged became the object of close critical scrutiny.

The anti-naturalist reaction to the evolutionist, naturalistic materialism which had apparently triumphed in the mid-Victorian era was one symptom of this shift (see §7.2 above), though the general trend among German neo-Kantians and American pragmatists was less to deny any validity to the methods of the natural sciences than to offer a different interpretation of their nature, and to restrict their domain of application. More explicitly irrationalist philosophies were also available – for example, in the reception of Nietzsche's writings, and in the doctrines of vitalist philosophers such as Henri Bergson, for whom life was a dynamic force underlying and overwhelming the flimsy structures erected by human reason.

A similar revaluation of factors lying outside the domain of scientific rationality was visible in sociology. Whatever their differences, Durkheim and Weber broke radically with the Enlightenment critique of religion as a cynical fraud perpetrated on the guillible masses by priests and rulers: religious beliefs were to be considered from the standpoint of their functional role, whether that was seen as lying in their contribution to the normative integration of society, or in the solution they offered to the universal human experience of suffering and injustice. The Italian economist and sociologist Vilfredo Pareto argued that human actions largely originate in 'non-logical' motivations that represent the 'residues' – all that is excluded from the instrumental rationality which, according to marginalist economics, governs the behaviour of market actors. The British Fabian political scientist Graham Wallas similarly proposed to study the workings of liberal polities on the assumption that human beings are moved largely by irrational forces.

This intellectual shift was related to larger social and political developments. Commenting on the first major modern anti-Semitic movement, Karl Lueger's Christian Social Party, which took control of Vienna in 1897, Joachim Fest writes: 'The mass party Lueger formed with the aid of emotional slogans was living proof that anxiety was – as happiness had been a century before – a new idea in Europe, powerful enough even to bridge class interests.'[1] The emergence of radical racist nationalism as a popular force (Hitler was a great admirer of Lueger) was one symptom that liberal values and institutions were coming under increasing pressure. In 1934 the historian George Dangerfield published a famous book called *The Strange Death of Liberal England* in which he argued that the great reforming Liberal administration of 1905–15 was already being seriously challenged by movements willing to use extra-parliamentary, indeed violent, methods – militant trade unionists, feminist suffragettes, and Irish Republicans and Unionists – even before it was swept away by the Great War. Norman Stone argues that 'what Dangerfield said of Great Britain can be applied, almost without qualification, to the countries of the continent. Before the First World War, parliamentary government was in crisis everywhere.'[2]

The anxieties fuelling the mass movements of the left and the right which by 1914 were emerging to threaten the survival of liberal political institutions reflected the transformation Europe had undergone in the previous generation. Industrialization meant that a growing proportion of the population were wage-earners living in a relatively small number of large towns and cities. Urbanization combined with the great agricultural depression of the late nineteenth century in turn eroded traditional mechanisms of social control, and undermined what had been predominantly agrarian ruling classes, as Weber observed in the case of Prussia (see §7.1 above). The two most advanced industrial economies, the United States and Germany, were pioneering forms of organization based on large corporations often closely linked to investment banks and allied to each other in cartels. The emergence of what its chief analyst, the Austrian Marxist economist Rudolf Hilferding, called 'organized capitalism' seemed to sound the

---

[1]   J. C. Fest, *Hitler* (Harmondsworth, 1977), p. 43.
[2]   N. Stone, *Europe Transformed 1878–1919* (London, 1983), p. 10.

death-knell of both *laissez-faire* economics and liberal politics. The spread of suffrage in the late nineteenth century enouraged the development of bureaucratic party machines – the German Social Democratic Party was one of the first examples – organized to mobilize the votes of a mass electorate.

The widespread sense of dislocation produced by these developments found its most powerful expression in the artistic revolution occurring roughly between 1890 and 1930. Modernism, as it is usually known, represented a radicalization of the Aestheticism often championed by nineteenth-century French writers. 'Art for art's sake' was the slogan of those who sought in aesthetic experience a refuge from a debased and mediocre social world: for Baudelaire, for example, the aristocratic values which no longer had a place in bourgeois society could be transmuted into those of an art which held the vulgarity of everyday life in contempt even when it provided the 'pure' artist with his raw material.

The variety of movements now included under the label 'Modernism' – for example, Art Nouveau, *Jugendstil*, Cubism, Expressionism – take the further step of increasingly making the work of art itself their subject, so that art becomes reflexive, concerned primarily to explore the processes through which the art-work is constructed. This process of self-exploration often leads Modernist artists to capture in their works the new rhythms of the industrialized, massified, urban world in which they now lived, but in doing so they often evoked chiefly the disintegration of the subject, the individual self's dispersal amid the fragments of an atomized social world. The oblique relationship which a Modernist work of art characteristically took up towards its object is well expressed in this rather baffled description of the style of Henry James's later novels by his brother, the philosopher William James:

> yours being to avoid naming it straight by dint of breathing and sighing all round and round it, to arouse in the mind of the reader who may have had a similar perception already (Heaven help him if he hasn't!) the illusion of a solid object, made . . . wholly out of impalpable materials, air, and the prismatic interferences of light, ingeniously focused by mirrors on empty space. But you do it, that's the queerness! And the complication of innuendo and associative reference on the enormous scale to which you give way to it does so *build out* the matter for the reader that the result is to solidify, by the sheer bulk of the process, the like perception from which *he* has to start![3]

One other feature of the exceptionally intellectually and artistically creative period at the turn of the century is that it marked the moment when Jews gained grudging admission to elite 'society'. The general secularization of European society was reflected in the elimination of most surviving forms of legal

---

[3]   Letter to Henry James, 4 May 1907, in *The Selected Letters of William James*, ed. E. Hardwick (New York, 1993), p. 233.

discrimination. At the same time a small minority of Jews came to occupy positions of considerable economic power, though nowhere, with the exception of the Austro-Hungarian Empire, where they dominated high finance and industry, did they have the primacy of which anti-Semites accused them.

The development of racial anti-Semitism as a mass political force signified by Lueger's capture of Vienna and, more or less simultaneously, the Dreyfus Affair in France indicates how contested Jewish advancement was; the immigration into western Europe and North America of Jewish peasants fleeing poverty and pogroms in the tsarist empire provided racist demagogues with a ready-made outlet for the anxieties of the age. But, for whatever reason, the liberal, secularized Jewish middle class which was the chief beneficiary of emancipation provided the age with many of its most gifted intellectuals, among them Durkheim, Freud, Lukács, Simmel, and Wittgenstein. Perhaps among the benefits of an all too precarious advancement was a privileged insight into the world to which they had suddenly gained admission.

8.2   Objectivity and estrangement: Simmel

Richard Hamann, in a pioneering study of Modernism (which he called 'Impressionism', using the term much more broadly than is usual), wrote in 1907 that 'impressionism as a style goes along with a centralizing tendency, a developed money economy, the domination of capitalism and the commercial and financial strata who provide its distinctive tone. Modern impressionism as art and life is totally at home in metropolitan centres – Berlin, Vienna, Paris, London.' Hamann described Simmel's *The Philosophy of Money* (1900) as 'a completely impressionistic philosophy'.[4]

Simmel's writings represent an exceptionally interesting theoretical response to the developments described in the previous section. His thought does indeed seem to have gained much of its momentum from living in the capital of the new German industrial and military superpower. 'Berlin's development from a city to a metropolis in the years around and after the turn of the century coincides with my own strongest and most extensive development', he told his son.[5] David Blackbourn describes Berlin in these years as 'metropolis, world city and epitome of the modern spirit: it had a vigorous café culture, abundant theatres, journals and publishers, alongside dealers, galleries, and private patrons of avant-garde art, especially among the wealthy Jewish bourgeoisie'.[6]

---

[4]   Quoted in D. Frisby, *Fragments of Modernity* (Cambridge, 1985), p. 85. Georg Simmel (1858–1918): born in Berlin, son of a Jewish businessman; took his doctorate on Kant at the University of Berlin, 1881; repeatedly passed over for chairs at the universities of Berlin and Heidelberg; a private income allowed him to pursue his career as a scholar; finally appointed to a chair at the University of Strassberg, 1914.

[5]   Quoted ibid., p. 69.

[6]   D. Blackbourn, *The Long Nineteenth Century* (London, 1997), p. 387.

In *The Philosophy of Money* and the closely related essay 'The Metropolis and Mental Life' (1902–3), Simmel seeks to understand the new form of social existence represented by Berlin and cities like it, from a perspective that is less in any conventional sense sociological than distinctively philosophical. One contemporary reviewer wrote that 'behind Simmel's whole work there stands not the ethical but the aesthetic ideal'.[7] Nietzsche's attempt to rethink the role of values in human life so that they did not purport to express universal moral laws or the order of the universe, but rather guided the aesthetic shaping of individual life according to certain ideals (see §5.3), had an enormous impact on German intellectuals of Simmel's generation. One of Simmel's most influential works was *Schopenhauer and Nietzsche* (1907), and he was attracted by the circle around the poet Stefan George, who made a cult of 'Holy Art'. Why did a philosopher with these interests concern himself with that most mundane and vulgar of social phenomena, money?

The answer is that money symbolizes the essential structure of reality itself: 'The philosophical significance of money is that it represents within the practical world the most certain image and the clearest embodiment of the formula of all being, according to which things receive their meaning through each other, and have their being determined by their mutual relations.' Value – which Simmel seems to treat as simultaneously an economic, an ethical, and an aesthetic concept – runs parallel to reality (or being) itself. It is 'never a "quality" of the objects, but a judgement upon them which remains inherent in the subject'. In that sense Simmel's theory of value, like that of marginalist economics but unlike Marx's labour theory of value (which he explicitly rejects), is a subjective one.[8]

But if value originates in the rankings we impose on things in the world, it finds expression in a set of objective relationships among them. We value desirable objects that we cannot immediately enjoy, but which it is in some way difficult to obtain and thus are at a distance from us. On the market we exchange something desirable for something we desire yet more. But exchange has a significance that transcends its function of need-satisfaction. Through their market relationships things acquire an objectivity arising from the distance they thereby gain from individual subjects and their needs. Moreover, exchange is 'the economic-historical realization of the relativity of things'. Truth, Simmel argues, is 'a relative concept like weight'. It is not a quality that inheres in objects which we can see or touch or taste. Rather, the truth of any sentence depends on that of others on which we rely when deducing or empirically corroborating it. But the totality of the sentences we hold true serves primarily practical ends: it 'has validity only in relation to specific physio-psychological

---

[7]   Quoted in D. Frisby, introduction to G. Simmel, *The Philosophy of Money* (London, 1978), p. 12.
[8]   Ibid., pp. 128–9, 63.

organizations, their conditions of life and the furthering of their activity'. Therefore, 'relativity is not a qualification of an otherwise independent notion of
truth but is the essential feature of truth'.[9]

So far, so Nietzschean. But the particular twist that Simmel gives to this
pragmatist conception of truth is to establish a parallelism between theoretical
knowledge and economic exchange: 'Relativity is the mode in which representations become truth, just as it is the mode in which objects of demand become
values.' What Smith and Marx called the exchange-value of a commodity is
necessarily relative, since it consists in the quantities of other objects for which
it can be exchanged. Hence the significance of money:

> If the economic value of objects is constituted by their mutual relationship of
> exchangeability, then money is the autonomous expression of this relationship.
> Money is the representative of abstract value. From the economic relationship,
> i.e. the exchangeability of objects, the fact of this relationship is extracted and
> acquires, in contrast to those objects, a conceptual existence bound to a visible
> symbol.[10]

Money is thus the relativity that constitutes economic value – and indeed the
world itself – made autonomous and objective. Moreover: 'This relativity, in
turn, increasingly dominates the other qualities of the objects that evolve as
money, until these objects are nothing more than embodied relativity.' This is
reflected in the tendency (never fully realized) for money's function as symbol
and facilitator of universal exchange to supplant whatever specific qualities the
money-commodity (say, gold) may have. It therefore helps to promote a growing preoccupation with the abstract and the relative rather than the concrete and
the material: 'money is involved in the general development which in every
domain of life and in every sense strives to dissolve substance into free-floating
processes'.[11]

This tendency towards abstraction also contributed to the development of the
modern sciences: 'Money economy and the dominance of the intellect are intrinsically connected.'[12] At the same time, money's universality, its detachment
from immediate social contexts, meant that in the past it was the strangers, the
excluded, for example, persecuted religious minorities, who specialized in its
use (Simmel, who was denied academic advancement because he was a Jew,
was especially sensitive to the precarious position of outsiders).

Money is thus the universal means through which humans achieve their purposes, 'the purest form of the tool'. It can thereby play a liberating role by
enhancing individual independence. When social relationships are universally

---

[9]   Ibid., pp. 101, 106, 108, 116.
[10] Ibid., pp. 116, 120.
[11] Ibid., pp. 127, 168.
[12] *The Sociology of Georg Simmel*, ed. K. H. Wolff (New York, 1950), p. 411.

mediated by the purchase and sale of goods and services in exchange for money, we are no longer personally dependent on others. 'Thus the city-dweller is no longer dependent on any of them as particular individuals but only upon their objective services which have a money value and may therefore be carried out by any interchangeable person.' But at the same time, the relativization of everything which the omnipresence of money induces means that objects and persons are no longer valued for their intrinsic qualities. It promotes a universal social fragmentation, and 'the reduction of qualitative determinations to quantitative ones', so that 'everything that is specifically, individually, and qualitatively determined' is interpreted as 'the more or less, the bigger or smaller, the wider or narrower, the more or less frequent of those colourless elements and awarenesses that are only accessible to numerical determination'.[13]

Two characteristic stances struck by the inhabitants of the great metropoleis are in fact responses to 'the height of the money culture'. Cynicism, 'the disparagement of all old values', and 'the blasé attitude', 'indifference to [the]. . . specific qualities' of things, arise from the 'mutual de-individualization and levelling' produced by the universal permeation of social relationships by money. As part of the same process, 'the conceivable elements of action become objectively and subjectively calculable rational relationships and in so doing progressively eliminate the emotional reactions and decisions which only attach themselves to the turning points of life, to the final purposes'.[14] This contrast is analogous to that drawn by Weber between instrumentally rational action, which selects the most effective means for achieving a given end, and value-rational action, where a life is ordered according to certain consciously adopted ends (see §7.3 above).

For Simmel the problem presents itself as 'the divergence of the subjective and the objective factor' in culture, and its cause lies in the division of labour, which 'separates the working person from the work produced and endows the product with objective independence'. Subjectivity and objectivity, emotion and reason, quality and quantity, substance and form, are sharply counterposed: 'the objective spirit of things exists in unblemished perfection, but yet lacks the values of the personality that cannot be dissolved in objectivities'. This social world drained of meaning encourages the search for sensation and variety which is one of the main responses to metropolitan life. It also underlies the taste for the indirect and the incomplete characteristic of Modernism (and evoked above by James),

> the present vividly felt charm of the fragment, the mere allusion, the aphorism, the undeveloped artistic style. All these forms, familiar to all the arts, place us at a distance from the substance of things; they speak to us 'as from afar'; reality is touched not with direct confidence but with fingertips that are immediately

13   Simmel, *Philosophy of Money*, pp. 210, 300–2, 277, 278.
14   Ibid., pp. 255, 256, 393, 431.

withdrawn. The most extreme refinement of our literary style avoids the direct characterization of objects; it only touches a remote corner of them with the word, and grasps not the things but the veil that envelops them.[15]

The characteristic indirection of Modern art is a correlate of the same features present in money itself: 'supplied with all the unique qualities of being able to transcend distances, of concentrating power and of penetrating everywhere – qualities that are the result of its *distance* from all that is specific and one-sided – money enters service of the specific wants or forms of life'. The peculiar abstraction of modern life – its domination by social relationships based on calculations of individual advantage – is a consequence of the abstraction of money itself, of its distance from concrete situations and needs, which in turn reflects the fact that reality itself is relativity, having no absolutely secure foundations on which to rest:

> Money, as an institution of the historical world, symbolizes the behaviour of objects and establishes a special relationship between itself and them. The more the life of society becomes dominated by monetary relationships, the more the relativistic character of existence finds its expression in conscious life, since money is nothing other than a special form of the embodied relativity of economic goods that signifies their value.[16]

Simmel thus offers an extraordinary philosophical interpretation of modern capitalism which historically situates the kind of Modernist art, with which he strongly identifies, as an expression of the prevalence of money as a kind of quintessence of the relativity of things themselves. As such, it naturally invites a comparison with Marx's *Capital*, one of the themes of whose third volume is the development of the financial system into an autonomous process operating independently of production. One contemporary reviewer commented: 'some passages of *The Philosophy of Money* read like a translation of Marx's economic discussions into the language of psychology'.[17]

Simmel himself described his method as an attempt 'to construct a new story beneath historical materialism such that the explanatory value of the incorporation of economic life into the causes of intellectual life is preserved, while these economic forces are recognized as the result of more profound valuations and currents of psychological or even metaphysical pre-conditions'.[18] He envisaged a kind of infinite regress in which his metaphysical grounding of the economic base would then be subject to a fresh materialist interpretation, under which a new philosophical storey would be built, and so on *ad infinitum*.

---

[15] Ibid., pp. 453, 457, 467, 474.
[16] Ibid., pp. 496, 512.
[17] Quoted in Frisby, introduction to Simmel, *Philosophy of Money*, p. 11.
[18] Ibid., p. 56.

One obvious difference between Simmel and Marx is that the latter conceives the autonomization of money in the shape of money-capital, which seeks interest from loans to productive capitalists employing wage-labour, as systematically misleading about the reality of capitalist relations of production: money-capital appears to have the ability to expand itself when in fact interest is part of the surplus value extracted from workers in production. Thus:

> In interest-bearing capital, the capital-relationship reaches its most superficial and fetishized form . . . The result of the overall reproduction process appears as a property devolving on a thing in itself . . . In interest-bearing capital, therefore, this automatic fetish is elaborated into its pure form, self-valorizing value, money breeding money, and in this form it no longer bears any marks of its origin.[19]

For Simmel, however, there is no dislocation between appearance and reality: the relativization of all human qualities achieved by money reveals the relativity constitutive of the world itself. For all the historical knowledge he deploys in his account of the development of money, this process, and the objectivized, alienated world to which it gives rise, seem to be a realization of a tendency inherent in things. 'Modernity is then itself an eternal present', as David Frisby puts it.[20]

8.3   The self dissected: Freud

In their different ways both Simmel and Weber offer extremely subtle and suggestive analyses of what they regard as the peculiarly ambivalent and problematic character of modernity. In doing so, they relativize scientific reason, situating it historically and identifying what seem to them to be its limits. There is, however, one aspect of the Enlightenment heritage which they largely take for granted, namely the subject itself. The self as it is conceptualized by Descartes is, as Charles Taylor puts it, 'self-defining': directly aware of its own mental states, it provides, through this self-certainty, the basis on which all knowledge of the world is constructed.[21] German classical idealism from Kant to Hegel brought out the difficulties involved in this presupposition, but, rather than abandon it, transformed the subject into the transcendental condition of all experience, or even into the Absolute, source of all the content of the world (see §1.5 and ch. 2 above).

Nietzsche had already questioned the autonomy and coherence of the subject, but the decisive step of cracking open the self and exposing the forces

---

[19]   K. Marx, *Capital* (3 vols, Harmondsworth, 1976–81), III, pp. 515–16.
[20]   Frisby, *Fragments*, p. 108.
[21]   C. Taylor, *Hegel* (Cambridge, 1975), p. 7.

responsible for its constitution was taken by Freud.[22] He described his own achievement in the following (less than modest) terms: 'In the course of centuries the naive self-love of man has had to submit to two major blows at the hands of science,' namely Copernicus's demonstration that the earth is not the centre of the universe, and Darwin's theory of evolution by natural selection, which demoted man from his self-appointed place at the head of the orders of living beings. Nevertheless: 'Human megalomania will have suffered its third and most wounding blow from the psychological research of the present time which seeks to prove to the ego that it is not even master in its own house but must content itself with scanty information of what is going on in its mind.'[23]

The theory of the human mind which Freud formulated is significant chiefly because it represents the most powerful and influential formulation of the concept of the unconscious. In other words, the existence of conscious mental states presupposes that of unconscious ones. It is important to appreciate that Freud conceives the unconscious to be as much an intentional phenomenon – consisting therefore of beliefs and desires – as are conscious mental states. Although the unconscious is marked by the effects of bodily drives, it is not a biological entity. Thus what goes on in the unconscious 'has a sense': 'By "sense" we understand "meaning", "intention", "purpose" and "position in a continuous psychical context".'[24]

Freud came to the idea of the unconscious as a result of his treatment of patients suffering from neuroses, and in particular hysteria. He and his colleague Joseph Breuer came to believe the delusions identified as the main symptoms of hysteria could not be treated, as medical orthodoxy held, as simply the consequences of physical states. These delusions, they argued, had to be treated as having a meaning: their content typically referred to some past event. Freud and Breuer concluded: '*our hysterical patients suffer from reminiscences*'. There thus evolved what Breuer's patient 'Anna O.' called 'the talking cure', the interchange between doctor and patient designed to elicit the painful memories from which the neurotic symptoms arose which constitutes the essence of psychoanalysis as a therapeutic practice.[25]

The fact that such an effort was required to draw out these memories implied

[22]   Sigmund Freud (1856–1939): born in Freiburg, Bohemia (now Příbor, Czech Republic); when he was 3, anti-Semitic riots forced his family to flee first to Leipzig and then to Vienna; studied science and medicine at the University of Vienna, 1873–80; qualified as a doctor of medicine, 1881; worked at General Hospital of Vienna, 1883–5; studied under the neurologist Jean Charcot at Salpêtrière Hospital, Paris, 1885–8; started private practice, 1886; *Studies in Hysteria* (1895), written jointly with Joseph Breuer, represented the first formulation of psychoanalysis; awarded a chair at the University of Vienna, 1902; International Psychoanalytical Association founded, 1910; after the German annexation of Austria, fled to London in June 1938.

[23]   S. Freud, *The Complete Introductory Lectures on Psychoanalysis* (London, 1971), pp. 284–5.

[24]   Ibid., p. 61.

[25]   J. Breuer and S. Freud, *Studies in Hysteria* (Harmondsworth, 1974), pp. 58, 83.

the existence of a force – what Freud called repression – seeking to deny the conscious mind access to them. This implied, first, the development of an interpretive practice calculated to draw out the meanings hidden by repression. Freud developed various techniques, of which the most important was presented in perhaps his greatest work *The Interpretation of Dreams* (1900). Freud indeed claimed: '*The interpretation of dreams is the royal road to a knowledge of the unconscious activities of the mind.*'[26]

Dreams must be treated as meaningful phenomena formed according to the rules of a language, albeit one very different from that employed by the conscious mind. Grasping this language requires that we distinguish between the manifest and latent content of the dream, that is, between how it immediately presents itself to the dreamer, and its actual, but concealed, meaning. The latent content of a dream is always, Freud claims, the fulfilment of a wish. But powerful forces of resistance seek to prevent the expression of this wish, so that the manifest content distorts the latent content. Thus 'the dream as a whole is a distorted substitute for something else, something unconscious'.[27]

Freud calls the process through which the latent content is transformed into the manifest content the 'dream work'. It consists of two main mechanisms – condensation and displacement – which break up the elements of the latent content and reshuffle them, sometimes fusing them, sometimes relating them to one another through misleading allusions. Moreover, they transform thoughts into sensory images, reversing the developmental process through which individual humans learn to use concepts. This '*archaic* or *regressive*' mode of expression provides the key to the latent content of dreams. The thoughts which dream-work seeks to censor usually involve repressed memories of childhood: '*A dream might be described as an infantile scene modified by being transferred onto a recent experience*. The infantile scene is unable to bring about its own revival and has to be content with returning as a dream.'[28] Indeed, Freud claims that '*all* dreams are children's dreams . . . they work with the same infantile material, with the same mental impulses and mechanisms of childhood'.[29]

But why do dreams take the form of a regression to childhood, and why does this process have to be concealed from the conscious mind? Positing the existence of the unconscious required not merely the development of the hermeneutic techniques required to elicit its contents, but some account of what is concealed by the forces of repression. Freud's answer, elaborated in *Three Essays on the Theory of Sexuality* (1905), was provided by what is still his most controversial theory, that of infantile sexuality. In other words, the great secret that dreams and neurotic symptoms seek to deny is that children from the very early stages

---

[26]   S. Freud, *The Interpretation of Dreams* (New York, 1972), p. 647.
[27]   Freud, *Introductory Lectures*, p. 114.
[28]   Freud, *Interpretation*, p. 585.
[29]   Freud, *Introductory Lectures*, p. 213.

of infancy are sexually active. Indeed, they are 'polymorphously perverse', experiencing desires which do not conform to the norm of heterosexual genital sexuality, and which indeed initially have no object at all. Freud distinguishes a succession of stages of infantile sexual organization in which the child commences as a bundle of fragmentary desires which gradually focus on an object – first itself, and then the mother. Finally, in what he calls the genital stage, the child develops the 'normal' desire for a member of the other sex (though the attainment of this orientation is then subject to a period of 'latency' till adolescence).

The critical phase in this process immediately precedes this happy outcome. Here both male and female children desire their mother. In the phallic stage, male children form the Oedipus complex. They wish to emulate the Greek tragic hero and kill their father, whom they hate as a rival for the mother's affection. The Oedipus complex is dissolved through the castration complex, when the boy comes to fear the loss of his penis, and therefore to fear the father as a potential castrator. This fear leads the child to abandon his Oedipal desire, in the expectation that he too will one day be the father and possess the mother. In the case of female children, the process is the reverse: 'The castration complex prepares for the Oedipus complex insteading of destroying it.' The recognition that she lacks a penis leads the girl to identify with the mother and to desire the father: in that way she can get a penis (or a child as a penis-substitute). This option involves 'substituting activity for passivity'. For girls the Oedipus complex is 'a haven of refuge' which is much more gradually overcome than in boys.[30]

This emotional history of early childhood provides Freud with his explanation of his patients' sufferings. Should the process leading to the Oedipus complex and its resolution go wrong, and he believes it never goes entirely right, the result is mental illness. More specifically, the 'transference neuroses', hysteria and obsessional neurosis, arise when some instinct or instinctual component is fixated at an earlier stage of infantile development. Repression is unable to prevent 'the return of the repressed', when the individual regresses to the stage of libidinal development where the fixation occurred. Mental illness thus has a regressive character: the patient suffers from a repressed desire which is denied satisfaction. Neurotic and hysterical symptoms are 'compromise formations' arising from the struggle between this desire and the forces of repression. They emerge from processes employing the same mechanisms of condensation and displacement as are involved in the dream-work. Psychoanalytic therapy therefore consists in the gradual reconstruction, in the face of powerful unconscious resistance, of the particular history to which the patient's dreams and symptoms are distorted allusions.

Freud's account of the formation of the individual subject and of the nature of mental illness is still fiercely contested. Viewed with respect to our theme, the development of social theory, it nevertheless has enormous significance. In

[30]   Ibid., pp. 593, 592.

the first place, the distinction between normality and abnormality – so important, for example, to Durkheim's sociology – is relativized. Repression is a universal phenomenon, at work in the healthy and the ill alike. If repressed desire does not return in the form of neurotic symptoms, it does so in dreams, and, as we have seen, the same processes of censorship are at work in both. Secondly, gender differences are not simply the result of the biological constitution of male and female human beings – or rather, the effects of this constitution are mediated by the process through which, within male-dominated family structures, girls and boys are prepared for their future roles in these same structures. Thirdly, the conscious self turns out to be the result of a history, a complex assemblage of desires and dispositions whose internal tensions both conceal and allude to a vast, unknown hinterland in which many of the most important effects of the process through which it was constructed lie hidden.

In his later writings Freud developed a more elaborate model of the mind than he had posited in works such as *The Interpretation of Dreams*. This model is based on the contrast between ego, id, and superego. The id is the seat of sexual desires. Initially, the mind is all id; individual mental development thus consists in a process of differentiation through which the ego and superego separate out from the id. The ego is the site of the conscious self, but Freud believes it is also the source of repression, and so certain aspects of ego, like the id once repression takes root, are unconscious. Finally, the superego is the introjected father, the heir of the Oedipus complex, and the representative of social morality: it is manifested in what everyday discourse calls the conscience, and also plays a role in abnormal conditions such as paranoia.

This complex anatomy of mind reflected Freud's growing interest in repression – not so much with what is repressed (infantile sexual desires) as with the forces responsible for its repression. This shift involved a series of attempts to conceptualize the drives or instincts (*Triebe*) – the biologically determined dispositions which underlie mental life, conscious and unconscious alike. Initially, Freud saw repression as the outcome of a conflict between what he called the reality and the pleasure principles, which in turn reflect the struggle between two kinds of drive – the libido, the urge for sexual satisfaction which finds expression in the desires, and the instinct for self-preservation. Roughly speaking, the libido's demand for immediate gratification runs up against the requirement that desires are repressed and pleasures deferred if the individual is to survive in an inhospitable world.

Freud came, however, to doubt the autonomy of what what he called the 'ego-instincts' oriented on self-preservation. According to the theory of 'primary narcissism' which he formulated in 1914, the self was the first sexual object; the ego was thus able to draw on the libido in order to defend itself. This argument implied that the drives were solely sexual, but Freud did not leave the matter there. In *Beyond the Pleasure Principle* (1920), seeking to explain a number of phenomena ranging from sadism and masochism in individuals to the collective aggressions recently displayed in the First World War, he postulated the existence of a death instinct.

Pain, he argued, arose from the accumulation of tension and pleasure from its release. The satisfaction gained from discharge, from the release of tension, arises from '*an urge inherent in organic life to restore an earlier state of things* which the living entity has been obliged to abandon under the pressure of external disturbing forces; that is, it is . . . the expression of the inertia inherent in organic things'. This 'earlier state of things' can only be the absence of life itself. Organisms aspire to die, 'to become . . . inorganic again'. Thus '*the aim of all life is death*'.[31] While the death instinct and the libido are in the first instance in conflict, they are at the same time closely related since both are an attempt to release tension. The death instinct is the libido taken to its limit – the ultimate outcome of the drive to seek pleasure and avoid pain. Moreover, both instincts operate together: hence the close association of loving and destructive urges in sexual relationships.

This highly speculative biology recalls that of Nietzsche, as do various specific ideas (for example, a stress on the functional role of forgetting, and the suggestion that sexual desires can be sublimated into cultural creation). But the overall tenor of Freud's theory of drives is very different from Nietzsche's doctrine of the will to power. The latter posits a dynamic tendency inherent in things bringing about transformations in which values are creatively refashioned. But, according to Freud, the drives are 'exclusively conservative': 'forces tending towards change and progress' are 'a deceptive appearance'.[32]

These reflections pose very sharply the question (raised, of course also, by nineteenth-century evolutionism) of the relationship between the social and the biological. Freud's general view is that human beings' biological constitution is quite directly responsible for a variety of social phenomena: thus, aggression, whether manifested in personal relationships or on the battlefield, is the death instinct turned outwards. This does not mean that he is a biological determinist or an opponent of social reform, but he believes that repression is a necessary condition of the existence of civilization, which will exert a high price in unhappiness whatever the form of society. Thus he thinks the Russian Revolution of October 1917 premature:

> a sweeping alteration of the social order has little prospect of success until new discoveries have increased our control over Nature and so made easier the satisfaction of our needs. Only then perhaps may it become possible for a new social order not only to put an end to the material need of the masses but also to give a hearing to the cultural demand of the individual. Even then, we shall still have to

---

[31] S. Freud, *On Metapsychology* (Harmondsworth, 1984), pp. 331, 311.
[32] Ibid., p. 310.

struggle for an incalculable time with the difficulties which the untameable character of human nature presents every kind of social community.[33]

At one level, psychoanalysis appears to represent a major blow to the Enlightenment project. The Cartesian subject is cracked open, revealing hidden
desires and drives as the main source of human motivation. Yet Freud regarded
his own discoveries as a great victory for scientific reason and an enlargement
of its domain. Moreover, he believed that therapy guided by them could help
individuals to gain control over their suffering by allowing them to understand
its origins in the secret course of their own personal history. This is a thoroughly Stoic conception of reason, consisting as it does in the recognition of
the necessary patterns traced by the human passions, and in the acceptance of
the unhappiness that these make inevitable, but it marks a major extension, and
not the abandonment, of the Enlightenment project.
   Even for those sympathetic to Freud's achievement, there remains the question of whether he unduly restricted the scope of social transformation by, in
effect, eternizing the privatized, male-dominated family structures of the modern West. Two of his most perceptive critics, Gilles Deleuze and Félix Guattari,
make the point very forcefully:

> Freud's greatness is to have determined the essence or the nature of desire . . . as
> an abstract subjective essence, libido or sexuality. Only, he still relates this es-
> sence to the family as the last territoriality of the private man . . . Everything
> happens as if Freud forgives himself for his profound discovery of sexuality by
> saying to us: at least it stays in the family! . . . He mobilizes all the resources of
> myth, of tragedy, of dream, to re-enchain desire, this time in the interior: an
> intimate theatre.[34]

Others would, however, read Freud's work as representing more than the
confinement of desire within a family drama: the Frankfurt School, for example, sought to forge out of historical materialism and psychoanalysis a broader
theory of human liberation (see §10.3 below).

8.4   Memories of underdevelopment: Russian intellectuals and capitalism

In their different ways Nietzsche and Freud, Weber and Simmel, are representative of the increasing doubts the most gifted members of the European
intelligentsia came to entertain about historical progress as the nineteenth century drew to a close. Living in societies which had experienced the recent and

---

[33]   Freud, *Introductory Lectures*, p. 645.
[34]   J. Deleuze and F. Guattari, *L'Anti-Œdipe* (Paris, 1972), pp. 322, 323.

apparently definitive triumph of industrial capitalism, they highlighted the historical contingency, the fragility, and the individual and collective costs of this
process. Yet, in this period, the modernization that they sought to question was
largely a west and central European and North American phenomenon. The
very rapidity with which Western societies were transformed by the onset of
industrial capitalism underlined the growing gap between them and the rest of
the world, at the very time, in the second half of the nineteenth century, that
much of Asia, Africa, and Latin America was incorporated into the formal and
informal empires of the European powers, and – by 1900 – of the United States
as well. The meaning of industrialization and colonization for the peoples now
subject to Western domination would become an increasingly pressing question for both social theory and political practice.

The society where this question was first systematically thematized was tsarist Russia. An important member of the European state system, it was at the
same time the most backward of the Great Powers, a society which entered the
twentieth century largely composed of smallholding peasants who lived mostly
in conditions of medieval poverty and squalor, under an imperial autocracy
which claimed to rule absolutely by divine right. The pressure of military competition with its more advanced rivals forced the Romanov monarchy from the
reign of Peter the Great (1682–1725) onwards to import social and technical
innovations from abroad. This process of authoritarian modernization promoted
the development of an intelligentsia, often recruited from the landed gentry but
largely employed in the imperial civil and military bureaucracy, which drew on
Western ideas in order to throw critical light on its own society, and to press for
much more extensive changes than the tsarist regime was willing to contem-
plate. The unsuccessful Decembrist rising of 1825 was the first in a series of
revolutionary challenges which radical intellectuals mounted against the
autocracy.

The specific situation of the Russian intelligentsia posed a dilemma which
became increasingly acute as the nineteenth century wore on. The model by
which they judged Russian society was provided by the most advanced forms
of Western thought. The Hegelian circles of the 1830s and 1840s (see §4.1
above) are merely one example of the eagerness with which *intelligenty* con-
sumed the latest ideas from abroad; in the 1860s and 1870s, Spencer and John
Stuart Mill replaced the German idealists. Initially, like their counterparts elsewhere in Europe in the era of the Holy Alliance (1815–48), their political demands were modelled on those of the Great French Revolution. Thus the more
radical wing of the Decembrists, led by Pavel Pestel, drew up a draft constitution which provided for the abolition of serfdom and of the feudal estates, land
redistribution, universal male suffrage, centralized republican government, Polish
independence, and Jewish self-determination.

Yet the Western literature which the Russian intelligentsia read so avidly
painted an increasingly sombre picture of the society emerging in post-

Revolutionary Europe. The Petrashevsky circle in the 1840s drew heavily on the French Utopian socialists; later radicals read Marx's *Capital* (translated into Russian in 1872), and learned that Western 'progress' had produced a capitalist society based on class exploitation and inherently liable to crises. Should Russia seek to copy a course of development that was producing such unattractive consequences? This question stimulated an extraordinarily rich debate, not merely expressed in theoretical analyses and political polemics, but also acted out in the novels of Gogol, Turgenev, Tolstoy, and Dostoevsky. The positions first staked out here were to be taken up again in many later controversies in other developing countries.

Initially, argument polarized between global acceptance and rejection of the Western course of development. The Westernizers' greatest representative was the critic Vissarion Belinsky. He argued that the transformation of Russia depended on the emergence of a Westernized elite: 'it has become obvious that the process of internal civic development will begin in Russia only when our gentry become transformed into a bourgeoisie'.[35] The other side to this programme was a fear of the predominantly peasant masses, who were conceived as a brute, irrational obstacle to progress.

This espousal of Western individualism was fiercely opposed by the Slavophiles. They denounced the atomizing effects of the kind of 'progress' western Europe was experiencing, and argued that these arose from a corrosive rationalism whose roots could be traced back to pagan Rome and which corrupted both Catholicism and Protestantism alike. The individual could find genuine expression only within the 'spiritual hierarchy' of the Orthodox Russian Church, which integrated all believers into an organic unity. Andrzy Walicki comments: 'Slavophile criticism of Western Europe was therefore essentially, though not solely, a critique of capitalist civilization from a romantic conservative point of view . . . it was less defence of the present than romantic nostalgia for a lost ideal.'[36] This form of Romantic anti-capitalism was not necessarily convenient for the autocracy, which sought selectively to import Western institutions and practices. Its ambivalence is brought out in Dostoevsky's later writings, which hold up the Russian Church as the cure to the suffering caused by Western rationalism and individualism, but which characterize this solution in terms derived from the Fourierist Utopian socialism he had learned in the Petrashevsky circle during the 1840s.

Many radical intellectuals sought a third way between simply endorsing or rejecting the Western pattern of capitalist development. Starting with the Petrashevtsy and Aleksandr Herzen, they found this in the idea of a distinctively 'Russian' socialism. This took as its starting-point the peasant village

---

[35] Quoted in A. Walicki, *A History of Russian Thought from the Enlightenment to Marxism* (Stanford, 1979), p. 146.
[36] Ibid., p. 107

community (*mir* or *obshchina*) which the Slavophiles had already idealized as part of the systematic contrast they drew between Russia and the West. The survival of communal institutions would allow Russia to bypass the Western pattern, and thus to avoid the suffering attendant on capitalist industrialization by moving directly to socialism. Most fully developed in the Populist movement from the 1870s onwards, this analysis put a premium on the rapid overthrow of the tsarist autocracy. Thus Piotr Tkachev argued that social revolution must take place 'now, or in a very remote future, perhaps never'.[37]

If the revolutionaries did not seize the opportunity offered by the crisis of the old regime, capitalism would entrench itself, and Russia would have to undergo all the miseries of bourgeois life. Since efforts to mobilize the masses proved unsuccessful, most notably in the attempt by the *intelligenty* to 'go to the people' in 1873–4, Tkachev and others, influenced by the French examples of the Jacobins and Auguste Blanqui's communist conspiracies, concluded that the revolution could only take the form of a minority insurrection. The most celebrated attempt to pursue this strategy, by Narodnaia Volya (People's Will), led to the assassination of Tsar Alexander II in 1881.

As Marx's *Capital* gained a widespread readership, his theory provided the main reference-point for the debate over whether capitalist development was inevitable in Russia. Marx himself denied that it was, attacking interpretations which 'turned my historical sketch of the genesis of capitalism in Western Europe into a historico-philosophical theory of general development, imposed by fate on all peoples, whatever the circumstances in which they are placed'. He argued that 'in Russia, thanks to a unique combination of circumstances, the rural commune, still established on a nationwide scale, may gradually detach itself from its primitive features and develop directly as an element of collective production on a nationwide scale'. The most important of these circumstances could be a revolution which, if it acted as 'the signal for a proletarian revolution in the West', might enable the commune to become 'the starting point for communist development'.[38]

These reflections show Marx at his most cautious and conditional, and cast doubt on interpretations of historical materialism as a teleological theory of inevitable change. Plekhanov, the founder of Russian Marxism, falls much more easily into this stereotype.[39] Rejecting the voluntarism and elitism of Narodnaia Volya, he espoused Marx's conception of the self-emancipation of the working class: 'The Social Democrat wants the worker *himself to make* his revolution, the Blanquist demands that the worker should *support* the revolution, which

---

[37]   Quoted in G. V. Plekhanov, *Selected Philosophical Works* (5 vols, Moscow, 1977), I, p. 322.
[38]   K. Marx and F. Engels, *Collected Works* (50 vols, London, 1975–   ), XXIV, pp. 200, 349, 426.
[39]   G. V. Plekhanov (1856–1918): trained as a mining engineer; initially active in the Populist movement; spent most of his life in exile in Switzerland where he formed the first Russian Marxist group, Emancipation of Labour, in 1883; broke with Lenin after 1903; opposed the October Revolution.

has been begun and led for him and in his name.' But this revolution would be a long time coming. What the Populists had feared was coming about; as a result of the development of capitalism, the rural commune was disintegrating. Indeed: 'By the inherent character of its organization, the rural community tends first and foremost to give place to bourgeois, not communist, forms of life.'[40] This process would gradually form a working class capable of carrying through a socialist revolution; in the meantime, Social Democrats (as, following the German example, Russian Marxists initially called themselves) should concentrate on the political education of workers, and on supporting the efforts of the liberal bourgeoisie to achieve a democratic constitution comparable to those increasingly prevalent in the West.

Plekhanov, unlike Kautsky, the other leading theoretician of Second International Marxism (see §5.2), was a careful student of Hegel. He enthusiastically embraced the latter's teleology, declaring: *'The irresistible striving to the great historical goal, a striving which nothing can stop – such is the legacy of the great German idealist philosophy.'*[41] Walicki suggests that Plekhanov required such a philosophical viewpoint in order to justify his acceptance of the inevitability of capitalist development, with all the suffering he believed this would entail:

> The necessity to which he appealed could not be a simple necessity of facts; to endorse such sacrifice merely for facts would be nothing more than simple opportunism. Therefore, it had to be conceived as an ontological necessity, a necessity inherent in the rational structure of the universe . . . To become reconciled with such a necessity was, indeed, something inspiring and lofty; it gave a powerful feeling of historical mission and a certainty of victory.[42]

The next generation of Russian Marxists – who were to play a leading role in the revolutions of 1905 and 1917 – rebelled against Plekhanov's determinism. His analysis implied that the revolutionary process would pass through two stages in Russia – first, a bourgeois-democratic revolution comparable to that of France in 1789, and then, once capitalist development had worked itself out, the socialist revolution in which social democracy would finally come into its own. This was a normative conception of history in which every society must undergo the same series of modes of production, each succeeding its predecessor by iron necessity. It also seemed to make the socialist movement itself redundant. Petr Struve and the 'Legal Marxists' drew what seemed to him the obvious inference that radicals should unequivocally welcome the triumph of capitalism: 'Let us conclude that we lack culture and take lessons from capitalism.'[43]

---

[40]   Plekhanov, *Selected Philosophical Works*, I, pp. 341–2, 373.
[41]   Ibid., I, p. 483.
[42]   A. Walicki, *Marxism and the Leap to the Kingdom of Freedom* (Stanford, 1995), pp. 233–4.
[43]   Quoted in Walicki, *History*, p. 437.

Yet the actual course of events in Russia tended to undermine this historical schema. From the 1890s onwards the tsarist regime sought to modernize the economy in order to provide the necessary industrial base to sustain the arms race into which all the Great Powers were increasingly drawn. An alliance of the imperial state and foreign capital promoted the rapid industrialization of the country based on the wholesale importation of advanced plant and technology. A small but highly concentrated industrial proletariat took shape; its economic and political grievances brought it into conflict with both the Russian business class and the autocracy itself. The implications of this development became clear during the 1905 Revolution: mass strikes by factory workers drove capitalists, initially supportive of liberal reforms, into the arms of the regime. The bourgeoisie, rather than play its appointed role of leading a democratic revolution against tsarism, allied itself to the autocracy.

The difficulty this development caused Russian Marxists contributed to growing divisions among them. Some, usually known after the 1903 split in Russian social democracy as the Mensheviks, held on to the orthodox schema. After the fall of the autocracy in February 1917, they supported the efforts of the Provisional Government to turn Russia into a Western-style liberal polity. The Bolsheviks under Lenin took a more nuanced position.[44] Lenin accepted that Russia would have to undergo a period of capitalist development before socialism could come onto the political agenda. His first major work, *The Development of Capitalism in Russia* (1899), was a theoretically and empirically sophisticated attempt to refute Populist arguments by demonstrating the extent to which the spread of commodity relations and of wage-labour had already eroded the peasant commune. Even here, however, as Walicki points out, 'he placed the emphasis on the question of the prevailing relations of production and the nature of the fundamental class contradictions', rather than on the development of the productive forces. 'Lenin treated history not as a reified process whose driving force is an impersonal necessity, but as a battleground, a scene with human actors whose participation implies conscious or unconscious identification with a specific class and therefore the conscious or unconscious choice of certain values.'[45]

Lenin accordingly modified the orthodox analysis of Russian society. He argued that the overthrow of tsarism would indeed be the work of a bourgeois-democratic revolution. The integration of the capitalists into the tsarist state, however, meant that it would be led, not by them, but by the working class. The result would be 'the revolutionary-democratic dictatorship of the proletariat and peasantry', which would, particularly by destroying the great landed estates of the gentry, achieve the thoroughgoing democratization of Russian society, and create conditions favourable to a rapid move towards socialist revolution

[44]   V. I. Lenin, *né* Ulyanov (1870–1924): active in the revolutionary movement from *c*.1890 onwards; in exile in the West for most of the years after 1900; founder and leader of the Bolshevik Party, 1903–24; chairman of the Council of People's Commissars, 1917–24.
[45]   Walicki, *History*, pp. 444, 443.

proper. This conception of a kind of 'bourgeois revolution from below' implied a recognition of the possibility of historical alternatives.

Thus after the defeat of the 1905 Revolution, Lenin feared that the promotion of individual peasant landholdings by the last tsarist minister of any ability, Piotr Stolypin, could open the way to a 'Prussian' road to capitalism, in which the gentry and the bourgeoisie would agree gradually to modernize the economy, leaving most of the political institutions of Russian absolutism intact. If history was therefore a relatively open process, with more than one possible outcome to any major crisis, then consciously undertaken political action by a revolutionary party could play a decisive part in tipping the balance one way or the other. Lenin belaboured the Mensheviks for 'ignoring the active, leading, and guiding part which can and must be played in history by parties which have realized the material prerequisites of a revolution and have placed themselves at the head of the progressive classes'.[46]

Trotsky developed an even more radical critique of Russian Marxist orthodoxy.[47] He argued that the conception of a revolutionary process passing of necessity through distinct stages ignored the tendency of capitalism to establish itself on a global scale. This gave rise to a process of uneven and combined development. The 'law of combined development' represented the 'drawing together of the different stages of the journey, a combining of separate steps, an amalgam of archaic and more contemporary forms'.[48] Backward societies such as Russia need not repeat the same patterns as capitalist pioneers such as Britain and France had undergone. By virtue of 'the privilege of historical backwardness', they could import the latest technologies and social institutions. In Russia some of the most advanced factories in the world were surrounded by the most primitive peasant agriculture.

This meant that the revolution in Russia would necessarily have a combined character. The peasants would seize and divide up the estates, promoting a vast extension of petty commodity production. Meanwhile, the workers would confront their capitalist exploiters. Proletariat and peasantry should certainly ally themselves against the old regime: indeed, history showed that the peasants could only take effective revolutionary action under the leadership of an urban class. But the workers should not (as Bolshevik strategy implied) restrain their demands in order to avoid antagonizing their petty bourgeois partners: such a 'self-denying ordinance' would, in all likelihood, lead only to demoralization

---

[46] V. I. Lenin, *Collected Works* (45 vols, Moscow, 1972), IX, p. 44.

[47] L. D. Trotsky, *né* Bronstein (1879–1940): president of the St Petersburg Soviet of Workers' Deputies 1905; escaped from Siberia to the West after the defeat of the revolution; president of the Petrograd Soviet in 1917; Commissar of Foreign Affairs, 1917–18; Commissar of War, 1918–25; founded the Left Opposition to Stalin's leadership of the Communist Party of the Soviet Union, 1923; expelled from the USSR, 1929; founded the Fourth International, 1938; murdered by a Soviet agent.

[48] L. D. Trotsky, *The History of the Russian Revolution* (3 vols, London, 1967), I, p. 23.

and defeat. Instead, the working class should unleash a process of 'permanent revolution', helping the peasants in their struggle against the gentry, but also expropriating the capitalists as well. This combined socialist and democratic revolution could, however, only succeed if, as Marx had suggested, it acted as a stimulus for proletarian revolution in the more advanced industrial countries of the West. As Trotsky later put it, generalizing his original analysis of Russian society: 'The socialist revolution begins on the national arena, it unfolds on the international arena, and is completed on the world arena. Thus, the socialist revolution becomes a permanent revolution in a newer and broader sense; it attains completion only in the final victory of the new society in the entire planet.'[49]

The Russian Revolution of October 1917, bringing to a culmination nearly a century of controversy and agitation, was undertaken by the Bolsheviks on the basis of a strategy essentially identical to that outlined by Trotsky. In its aftermath, the new revolutionary regime found itself facing the apparently uncompromising hostility of the Great Powers. The Bolsheviks' situation required, among other things, a theoretical understanding of the global context in which their revolution had occurred and now struggled to survive. The basis of such an understanding was provided by the theory of imperialism popularized by Lenin but most rigorously formulated by the Bolshevik economist Nikolai Bukharin. This asserted that the development of 'organized capitalism' had led to two crucial innovations: first, the concentration of economic power within individual countries was leading to a tendency for the nation-state and private capital to fuse; secondly, the growing international integration of capital meant that these emerging 'state-capitalist trusts' were now competing on a global stage. Hence the formal or informal subordination of economically backward countries to one or other of the Great Powers; hence also the tendency for economic competition increasingly to take the form of diplomatic and military rivalries.

The Lenin–Bukharin theory of imperialism provided an explanation of the global conflicts which, together with the contradictions of Russian society, had made possible the breakdown of the tsarist regime and the October Revolution itself. But no theory could remove the dilemma presented by the hostile international state system confronting the Bolsheviks. Should they continue their initial strategy of encouraging revolutions in the more advanced economies of the West, as the theory of permanent revolution suggested, or should they, in effect, adapt to that system by transforming Russia into an industrialized Great Power capable of holding its own in the global arena? It was, of course, the latter strategy, expressed in the slogan of 'Socialism in One Country', which prevailed in the Soviet Union from the mid-1920s onwards, as Josef Stalin consolidated his hold on power against, most notably, Trotsky's opposition.

---

[49]   L. D. Trotsky, *Permanent Revolution and Results and Prospects* (New York, 1969), p. 279.

By then, however, the debates among Russian intellectuals had attained an exemplary quality in more than one sense. First, the same positions they had staked out – acceptance of Western modernity and the capitalist social structures in which it was imbricated; rejection in the name of an idealized, organic past; and the avoidance of these choices through social revolution – were to be taken up by their counterparts in many countries more directly subject to Western domination than Russia had ever been. Secondly, the October Revolution offered a model of socialist transformation which became one of the main reference-points – whether negative or positive – in subsequent reflection on the future of the modern world. The dilemmas and polemics of the Russian intelligentsia were thus universalized.

9

Revolution and Counter-Revolution

9.1 Hegelian Marxism: Lukács and Gramsci

With the outbreak of war in August 1914 the tensions which social theorists had been exploring for the previous century finally burst out into the open. Arno Mayer called the era which this event ushered in 'the Thirty Years War of the general crisis of the twentieth century'.[1] The First World War (1914–18), the Great Depression of the 1930s, and the Second World War (1939–45) formed an interconnected whole: together they marked the closest to a systemic crisis that bourgeois society has yet experienced. Global wars and economic slump placed in question the viability of the existing social order. The end of the First World War was accompanied by revolutions in Russia and Germany, and by serious upheavals in other European states. The brutalizing effect of four years of trench warfare helped to introduce a new violence into political conflict: ex-frontline fighters contributed many of the cadres of the fascist movements which sought to combat the revolutionary challenge with what seemed often to be revolutionary means.

The postwar crisis decisively shaped the politics of the following decades. The extreme polarization between left and right during the German Revolution of 1918–23 meant that from its inception the Weimar Republic had a relatively narrow social and political base. It was therefore highly vulnerable to the onset of economic depression and renewed class conflict at the end of the 1920s. The outlook of the National Socialist regime which emerged amid Weimar's ruins was permeated by an ideology of crisis and struggle which provided the authoritarian right with an interpretation of the disasters Germany had undergone. The Soviet Union, which under Stalin developed into an authoritarian regime

[1]   A. J. Mayer, *The Persistence of the Old Regime* (New York, 1981), p. 3.

ruling domestically by terror and pursuing a relatively cautious foreign policy, remained for the Nazis the embodiment of the revolutionary threat to which Germany had nearly succumbed after the war. For the Nazis the invasion of the USSR in June 1941 launched a *Vernichtungskrieg* – a war of extermination against Bolshevism, in which the German master-race would seize the *Lebensraum* (living room) it needed from the 'inferior' Slavs. It was, of course, in this context that the Nazis committed the crowning atrocity of this, and indeed of any, era in human history, when they attempted systematically to murder the European Jews.

It would have been incredible if this extreme political polarization had not found its theoretical accompaniment. The 1920s and 1930s saw the reinterpretation of Marxism as a theory of revolutionary subjectivity; they also saw some sophisticated attempts, considered in the next section, to justify the politics of the authoritarian, anti-parliamentary right. These developments did not arise from nowhere. The radical questioning of modernity which we have traced in the past few chapters helped to prepare many intellectuals for the idea that some kind of political revolution was necessary to resolve the crisis they were experiencing. But, certainly in the case of Marxism, this necessity seemed to imply a rethinking of accepted theoretical structures.

The Marxism of the Second International (1889–1914) was far from stagnant intellectually. The publication of the third volume of Marx's *Capital* in 1894 helped to stimulate a series of major treatises in economic theory. Kautsky's *The Agrarian Question* (1899), Lenin's *The Development of Capitalism in Russia* (1899), Rudolf Hilferding's *Finance Capital* (1910), Rosa Luxemburg's *The Accumulation of Capital* (1913), and Nikolai Bukharin's *Imperialism and World Economy* (1917) together represent a remarkable achievement which sought to extend Marx's analysis by, in the case of the first two works, applying it systematically to agriculture, or, as the others did, seeking to theorize the specific characteristics of the organized capitalism taking shape at the beginning of the twentieth century. Attempts were also made to interpret cultural phenomena apparently resistant to historical materialism – for example, in Otto Bauer's *Social Democracy and the National Question* (1907), and in Kautsky's *The Foundations of Christianity* (1908).

Together these works and others like them form an important part of the intellectual heritage of classical Marxism. Yet the dominant note in the Marxism of the Second International was provided by the determinism developed in somewhat different forms by both Kautsky and Plekhanov (see §§5.2 and 8.4 above). This seemed in practice to imply political fatalism: already under challenge within the SPD by Luxemburg and the radical left before 1914, this strategy was discredited for many socialist activists by the impotence of the Second International in the face of the war itself, and its disintegration into national parties mostly supporting their own governments against other belligerents. 'Nothing has corrupted the German working class so much as the notion that it was moving with the current', Walter Benjamin later wrote.[2]

The Russian Revolution of October 1917 represented a dramatic contrast with Kautsky's and Plekhanov's fatalism. By seeking to carry through a socialist revolution in a relatively backward country, the Bolsheviks challenged the doctrine that every society must pass through a preordained sequence of modes of production. Gramsci, writing in December 1917 and filled with youthful enthusiasm, called the October Revolution 'the revolution against Karl Marx's *Capital*'.[3] Gramsci went on to explain that the Bolsheviks had broken with Second International determinism, 'contaminated with positivist and naturalist incrustations', rather than with Marx's own thought:

> This thought sees as the dominant factor in history, not raw economic facts, but man, men in societies, men in relation to one another, reaching agreements with one another, developing through these contacts (civilization) a collective, social will; men coming to understand economic facts, judging them and adapting them to their will until this becomes the driving force of the economy and moulds objective reality, which lives and moves and comes to resemble a current of volcanic lava that can be channelled wherever and in whatever way men's will determines.[4]

The most important contemporary Marxist interpretation of the October Revolution, by Trotsky, did not in fact treat it as a rebellion against economic objectivity. Rather, the workings of the law of uneven and combined development had led in Russia to a fusion of social processes so that the overthrow of the tsarist regime could only be accomplished by expropriating capital (see §8.4 above). Moreover, Trotsky argued that the Revolution remained subject to definite material limits: indeed, he came to believe that the economic pressures arising from the Bolshevik regime's isolation after 1917 in a relatively backward country were responsible for its transformation into what he denounced as Stalin's counter-revolutionary dictatorship. Nevertheless, the challenge which the Bolsheviks represented to previous Marxist 'orthodoxy', particularly after

---

[2]   W. Benjamin, *Illuminations* (London, 1970), p. 260.

[3]   Antonio Gramsci (1891–1937): son of a minor Sardinian functionary; studied at the University of Turin, 1911–15; from 1915 onwards a writer in the socialist press; a leading member of the Ordine Nuovo group associated with the Turin factory councils' movement, 1919–20; with the other leaders of the socialist left launched the Communist Party of Italy (PCdI) in January 1921; worked with the Communist International in Moscow, 1922–3; elected as a parliamentary deputy in 1924; in this role led the Communist opposition to Mussolini's dictatorship; appointed general secretary of the PCdI in January 1926; arrested in November 1926; sentenced to twenty years' imprisonment in 1918: 'We must stop that brain working for twenty years', the prosecutor declared; nevertheless, Gramsci's *Prison Notebooks* represent his main intellectual achievement.

[4]   A. Gramsci, *Selections from the Political Writings 1910–1920*, ed. Q. Hoare (London, 1977), pp. 34–5.

they launched the Third (or Communist) International (Comintern) in 1919 as an alternative to the discredited Second International, encouraged the formulation of a version of Marxism in which class subjectivities assumed a greater importance than objective economic structures.

The master-work of this Hegelian Marxism (as it is often described) was Lukács's *History and Class Consciousness* (1923).[5] Both Gramsci and Lukács were heavily influenced by the great current of anti-naturalism which swept through European thought at the end of the nineteenth century (see §7.2 above). The main philosophical influence on Gramsci was the Italian neo-Hegelian Benedetto Croce. Lukács drew heavily on the German variants of anti-naturalism. Late in his life he declared: 'I do not at all regret that I took my first lessons in social science from Simmel and Max Weber.'[6] Indeed, his most striking intellectual achievement was to take over their interpretations of modernity as a process of, respectively, objectification and rationalization, and integrate them into the Marxist critique of the capitalist mode of production.

Weber's analysis often seems to run parallel to such a critique. Thus he writes of 'the impersonal and economically rationalized (but for this very reason ethically irrational) character of purely commercial relationships', and declares: 'The growing impersonality of the economy on the basis of association in the market place follows its own rules, disobedience to which entails economic failure and, in the long run, economic ruin.'[7] Lukács radicalized this analysis. Every social relationship under capitalism, whether economic, political, cultural, or intellectual, has been transformed according to the requirements of instrumental rationality. But this is only a *formal* rationalization, which does not penetrate the substance of the relationships which have been subsumed under it:

---

[5]   Georg Lukács (1885–1971): son of a leading Hungarian Jewish banker; studied jurisprudence at the University of Budapest, 1902–6; spent much of the subsequent few years in Berlin, where he studied under Simmel; studied at the University of Heidelberg, becoming a member of Weber's circle; already emerging as an important philosopher and literary critic before outbreak of the First World War; joined the Hungarian Communist Party in December 1918; People's Commissar for Culture in the Hungarian Soviet Republic, 1919; after its fall fled to Vienna, where he became an important figure in the Communist movement; at the Marx–Engels–Lenin Institute in Moscow, 1929–31; lived in Berlin, 1931–3, returning to Moscow after the Nazi seizure of power, where he took an active part in aesthetic debates; arrested briefly as 'Trotskyist agent', 1941; returned to Hungary in 1945 and became parliamentary deputy and Professor of Aesthetics and Philosophy of Culture at Budapest University; at the height of the Cold War in 1949–52 he was the object of intense attack from cultural apparatchiks; Minister of Culture in Imre Nagy's government during the Hungarian Revolution of 1956; deported to Romania, 1956–7; allowed in his last years to write and speak fairly openly.

[6]   Quoted in D. Frisby, introduction to G. Simmel, *The Philosophy of Money* (London, 1978), p. 43 n. 78.

[7]   M. Weber (1992), *Economy and Society,* ed. G. Roth and C. Wittich (2 vols, Berkeley, 1978), I, pp. 584, 586.

This rationalization of the world appears to be complete, it seems to penetrate the very depths of man's physical and psychical nature. It is limited, however, by its own formalism, that is to say, the rationalization of isolated aspects of life results in the creation of – formal – laws. All these things do join together into what seems to the superficial observer to constitute a unified system of 'general laws'. But the disregard of the concrete aspects of the subject-matter of these laws . . . makes itself felt in the incoherence of the system in fact. This incoherence becomes particularly egregious in times of crisis.[8]

This contrast between partial rationality and global irrationality is a consequence of the nature of the commodity itself. According to Lukács, 'the problem of commodities' is 'the central, structural problem of capitalist society in all its aspects'.[9] The general 'reification' of social relations is a consequence of what Marx had called commodity fetishism (see §§4.2 and 4.3 above): the exchange of the products of labour on the market leads to the transformation of social relations among human beings into apparently natural relations among things. The division of labour and the worker's subordination to the capitalist reproduces itself in every aspect of life: society is experienced as an incoherent collection of fragments. In the great essay 'Reification and the Consciousness of the Proletariat' Lukács explores what he calls 'The Antinomies of Bourgeois Thought', seeking to show how modern Western philosophy has been crippled by a series of oppositions – between form and content, 'is' and 'ought', part and whole – which it has been unable to overcome, and which arise from the process of reification.

In his pre-Marxist writings, notably *The Theory of the Novel* (1916), Lukács had already analysed what he regarded as the inherently antinomical nature of modern culture. But to qualify this condition as globally irrational implied some perspective from which this judgement could be made, and which could itself be shown to be rational. Thus when Weber says that 'purely commercial relationships' are instrumentally rational, but 'ethically irrational', he means that they are irrational relative to some value-rational religious ethic; but he does not believe that the rationality of the ultimate values at the basis of such a religious ethic can itself be demonstrated (see §§7.2 and 7.3 above). Lukács's solution to this problem is to argue that the rational vantage-point from which to view society conceives it as an integrated whole: '*The primacy of the category of totality is the bearer of the principle of revolution in science.*'[10]

Lukács had also drawn a contrast between fragmentation and totality before he became a Marxist. But there the whole was an absence, the ideal of an integrated culture to which one nostalgically alludes but is unable to attain. In *History and Class Consciousness*, however, he treats such a totalizing under-

[8]   G. Lukács (1923), *History and Class Consciousness* (London, 1971), p. 101.
[9]   Ibid., p. 83.
[10] Ibid., p. 27.

standing as eminently possible. It consists in particular in grasping the mediations through which different institutions, beliefs, and practices are interconnected with each other in such a manner as to form a whole. This understanding, moreover, is given a definite social location, in the proletariat. These steps are made possible by Hegel: 'reality can only be understood and penetrated as a totality, and only a subject which is itself a totality is capable of this penetration. It was not for nothing that the young Hegel erected his philosophy upon the principle that "truth must be understood and expressed not merely as substance but also as subject".' We are therefore indebted to German classical idealism for 'the grandiose conception that thought can only grasp what it has itself created': the 'identical subject–object of history' simultaneously creates society through its actions and is solely capable of understanding it.[11]

Even Hegel, however, grasped this truth in a mystified form: failing to understand the real nature of history as a social and material process, he can only conceptualize the identical subject–object as Absolute Spirit coming to consciousness through the retrospective contemplation of this process. The working class, by contrast, provides the standpoint from which a genuine understanding of capitalist society is possible because the transformation of labour-power into a commodity is the real basis on which that society is built:

> The worker can only become conscious of his existence in society when he becomes aware of himself as a commodity . . . his immediate existence integrates him as a pure naked object into the production process. Once this immediacy turns out to be the consequence of a multiplicity of mediations, once it becomes evident how much it presupposes, then the fetishistic forms of the commodity system begin to dissolve: in the commodity the worker recognizes himself and his own relations with capital. Inasmuch as he is incapable of raising himself above the role of object his consciousness is the *self-consciousness of the commodity*; or in other words it is the self-knowledge, the self-revelation of the capitalist society founded upon the production and exchange of commodities.[12]

The position of the proletariat within capitalist relations of production thus represents a vantage-point from which the nature of the social whole can be rationally understood. Historical materialism is the theoretical articulation of proletarian class consciousness, and therefore 'the self-knowledge . . . of the capitalist society'. This does not mean that every worker necessarily attains such an understanding. Indeed, the immediate appearance of capitalist society to the individual worker is as fragmentary and reified as it is to everyone else. Reification 'can be overcome only by *constant and constantly renewed efforts to disrupt the reified structure of existence by concretely relating to the concretely manifested contradictions of the total development, by becoming*

---

[11] Ibid., pp. 39, 121–2.
[12] Ibid., p. 168.

conscious of the immanent meanings of these contradictions for the total development'. What is distinctive about the role of the proletariat in this process is that any effort on its part to understand its own situation drives it towards an understanding of the whole. This understanding is, moreover, not purely intellectual, but develops through a series of class struggles in which workers both literally 'disrupt the reified structure of existence', and attain a deeper insight into the nature of this structure. The socialist revolution which is the culmination of this process is not the 'irresistible necessity' Kautsky and Plekhanov claimed it to be:

> History is at its least automatic when it is the consciousness of the proletariat that is at issue . . . The objective economic evolution could do no more than create the position of the proletariat in the production process. But the objective evolution could only give the proletariat the opportunity and the necessity to change society. Any transformation can only come about as the product of the – free – action of the proletariat itself.[13]

History and Class Consciousness is a philosophical *tour de force*. It provides a theoretical rationale for an activist, non-determinist Marxism based on a careful and innovative reading of German idealist philosophy, the classical Marxist tradition, and the sociology of Weber and Simmel. Most (though not all) later Marxist theorists have been heavily in its debt. Yet the very ambition of the work is a source of serious difficulties. In the first place, Lukács claims that the standpoint of the proletariat permits an objective understanding of the nature of capitalism. But how is this claim justified? The answer seems to be that the working class has an interest in getting rid of class society altogether: 'The proletariat cannot liberate itself as a class without simultaneously abolishing class society as such. For that reason its consciousness, the last class consciousness in the history of mankind, must both lay bare the nature of society and achieve an increasingly inward fusion of theory and practice.'[14] The bourgeoisie, by virtue of its interest in perpetuating capitalist exploitation, can only develop a partial and limited understanding of society.

Lukács thus reformulates the Marxist theory of ideology as an account of how an individual's perspective on the world is a consequence of his or her social position, and in particular place in the class-structure. This perspectival conception of ideology was further developed by Lukács's fellow Hungarian Karl Mannheim in *Ideology and Utopia* (1929). Mannheim sought to avoid the potentially relativistic implications of seeking to account for actors' beliefs in terms of their social position by arguing that the 'free-floating intelligentsia' is able, by virtue of its relative detachment from the class structure, to integrate particular perspectives into a provisionally valid whole. But for Lukács it is the

[13]   Ibid., pp. 229, 197, 209.
[14]   Ibid., p. 70.

very rootedness of the proletariat at the heart of the commodity structure which gives it the capacity to understand capitalism as a totality.

Even if we were to grant this, some criteria are required in order to determine which theorization (say, within Marxism, Lenin's or Kautsky's) best captures the nature of social reality. Hegel is able to avoid this problem because he conceives the dialectic as self-validating, since the movement of its categories both generates their own content, and provides an immanent justification both of each individual step and of the process as a whole. But, as we saw in chapter 2 above, this conception of the dialectic rests on assumptions that are simply too speculative and teleological to be consistent with the procedures of the modern sciences. Marxists, just like everyone else who claims to use these procedures, must be able to show that the results of their researches can be defended according to some plausible theory of scientific rationality. Lukács claims that Marxist 'orthodoxy refers exclusively to *method*', and that it would not be invalidated if 'recent research had disproved once and for all every one of Marx's individual theses'.[15] This formulation is intended to open Marxism up to the possibility of being recast in the light of research, but the idea of a method that is immune to empirical refutation looks suspiciously like the most dubious aspect of the Hegelian dialectic.

Secondly, making history the creation of a subject which is ultimately able to see through and transform the reified structures arising from its own transformation into an object seems to have dramatically idealist implications. This is most obviously true with respect to the physical world. Lukács declares: 'Nature is a societal category. That is to say, whatever is held to be natural at any given stage of social development, however this nature is related to man and whatever form his involvement with it takes, i.e. nature's form, its content, its range and its objectivity are all socially conditioned.'[16] This view of nature, which seems to treat it as entirely socially constructed, sits ill with Marx's conception of labour as the basis of the interaction between humankind and nature, where neither term of the relationship is reducible to the other. But, as Lukács later acknowledged, this concept of labour is absent from *History and Class Consciousness*. Particularly after he became, in Moscow in the late 1920s, one of the first to read Marx's *Economic and Philosophic Manuscripts*, he considerably revised his basic theoretical scheme. Later works such as *The Young Hegel* (1948) and the posthumously published *Ontology of Social Being* advance a version of the dialectic based on Marx's account of the metabolic interchange between humans and nature through the intermediary of labour.

Finally, how can the working class actually attain the rational understanding of society of which it is objectively capable? Lukács draws a famous distinction between 'actual' and 'imputed' class consciousness: 'Class consciousness

---

[15]   Ibid., p. 1.
[16]   Ibid., p. 234

consists in fact of the appropriate and rational reactions "imputed" to a particular typical position in the process of production. This consciousness is, therefore, neither the sum nor the average of what is thought or felt by the single individuals who make up the class.' Imputed class consciousness bears some resemblance to a Weberian ideal type. This concept is nevertheless intended not merely as an intellectually stimulating stylization of reality but rather as a representation of the actual consciousness to which the proletariat will eventually attain. But how? Lukács only offers some very general and abstract formulations suggesting that the development of revolutionary class consciousness is a process rather than an instantaneous act. For example: 'proletarian thought is in the first place merely a *theory of practice* which only gradually (and indeed spasmodically) transforms itself into a *practical theory* that overturns the real world'. Consequently 'there can be no single act that will eliminate reification in all of its forms at one time'.[17]

Some critics, for example, Leszek Kolakowski, argue that Lukács overcomes this difficulty by tacit appeal to the idea of the vanguard party which sets itself up as the representative of imputed class consciousness: *History and Class Consciousness* is therefore a theoretical legitimation of Stalinism.[18] This interpretation is hard to sustain. Lukács only addresses the question of the revolutionary party in the very last of the essays (composed at different times) which make up the book. Here he argues: 'Organization is the form of mediation between theory and practice.'[19] Whatever one thinks of this view, it does not accord the party the epistemologically privileged status suggested by Kolakowski. *History and Class Consciousness* was written before the process of 'Bolshevization' of the Third International which made possible the general imposition of the Stalinist model of party organization on the Communist movement; indeed, it was one of the casualties of this process, being picked out for attack on the grounds on 'revisionism' by the Comintern president, Grigori Zinoviev, at the movement's Fifth Congress in 1924. Lukács's own (always qualified) accommodation with Stalinism was accompanied by the adoption of his later, much more objectivistic version of historical materialism.

Gramsci developed a much more elaborated theory of class consciousness from within a philosophical framework not dissimilar to Lukács's. Indeed, he owes to Croce a radically pragmatist conception of truth, according to which '[o]ur knowledge of things is nothing other than ourselves, our needs and interests.' This epistemology allows him to think of theory and practice as intimately related. Thus Gramsci takes up a formula of Croce's: 'Everyone is a philosopher, though in his own way and unconsciously, since even in the slightest manifestation of any intellectual activity whatever, in "language", there is con-

---

[17]   Ibid., pp. 51, 205, 206 (translation modified).
[18]   L. Kolakowski, *Main Currents of Marxism* (3 vols, Oxford, 1978), III, pp. 280–3.
[19]   Lukács, *History*, p. 299.

tained a specific conception of the world.' Each conception of the world is 'a response to certain specific problems posed by reality', one that represents a more or less theoretically rationalized articulation of the practice of a particular class. But more than one conception of the world may be present in the same consciousness:

> When one's conception of the world is not critical and coherent but disjointed and episodic, one belongs simultaneously to a multiplicity of mass human groups. The personality is strangely composite: it contains Stone Age elements and principles of a more advanced science, prejudices from all past phases of history and intuitions of a future philosophy which will be that of a human race united the world over.[20]

Gramsci believes the ideological domination of the capitalist class operates through the coexistence in the consciousness of the working class of elements of both socialist and bourgeois conceptions of the world, inducing a condition of paralysis which allows the existing order to carry on:

> The active man-in-the-mass has a practical activity, but has no clear theoretical consciousness of his practical activity, which nonetheless involves understanding the world insofar as it transforms it. His theoretical consciousness can indeed be historically in opposition to his activity. One might almost say that he has two theoretical consciousnesses (or one contradictory consciousness): one that is implicit in his activity and which in reality unites him with all his fellow workers in the practical transformation of the real world; and one, superficially explicit or verbal, which he has inherited from the past and uncritically absorbed. But this verbal conception is not without consequences. It holds together a specific social group, it influences moral conduct and the direction of will, with varying efficacity but often powerfully enough to produce a situation in which the contradictory state of consciousness does not permit of any action, any decision or any choice, and produces a condition of moral and political passivity.[21]

Bourgeois ideological domination is therefore a consequence not of the indoctrination of a largely passive mass, but of the relative balance of rival conceptions of the world within the composite consciousness of the working class. Similarly, the attainment of revolutionary class consciousness involves strengthening and articulating the socialist conception of the world implicit in workers' everyday practice within the process of production:

> Thus the unity of theory and practice is not just a matter of mechanical fact, but a part of the historical process, whose elementary and primitive phase is to be found

[20] A. Gramsci, *Selections from the Prison Notebooks*, ed. Q. Hoare and G. Nowell-Smith (London, 1971), pp. 368, 323, 324.
[21] Ibid., p. 333.

in the sense of being 'different' and 'apart', in an instinctive feeling of independence, and which progresses to the level of real possession of a single and coherent conception of the world.[22]

The development of class consciousness is thus a process, in which workers progress from an instinctive sense of solidarity and of antagonism to the employer to an elaborated understanding of their interests and capacities. This process depends crucially on the relatively spontaneous development of mass struggles in which the underlying conflict between capital and labour comes to the surface. But, to become effective, class consciousness must be institutionalized; its elaboration depends on the construction of forms of organization through which it is articulated and strengthened: 'A human mass does not "distinguish" itself, does not become independent in its own right without, in its widest sense, organizing itself; and there is no organization without intellectuals, that is, without organizers and leaders.'[23]

Gramsci sets Lenin's conception of the revolutionary party as the vanguard of the proletariat in the context of this theory of class consciousness. The party's chief function is that of developing the 'organic intellectuals' of the working class: 'Every social group, coming into existence on the original terrain of economic production, creates together with itself, organically, one or more strata of intellectuals which give it homegeneity and an awareness of its own function not only in the economic but also in the social and political fields.'[24] Gramsci conceives this party as 'the result of a dialectical process, in which the spontaneous movement of the revolutionary masses and the organizing and directing will of the centre converge'. He is hostile to the rival view, put forward within the Communist Party of Italy (PCdI) by Amadeo Bordiga, as 'something suspended in the air; something with its own autonomous and self-generated development; something which the masses will join when the situation is right . . . or when the party centre decides to initiate an offensive and stoops to the level of the masses'.[25]

Gramsci most fully developed his conception of the interaction between the revolutionary party and the working class in his theses for the Lyons Congress of the PCdI in January 1926:

We assert that the capacity to lead the class is related, not to the fact that the party 'proclaims' itself its revolutionary organ, but to the fact that it 'really' succeeds, as a part of the working class, in linking itself with all the sections of that class and in impressing upon the masses a movement in the direction desired and

[22]   Ibid.
[23]   Ibid., p. 334.
[24]   Ibid., p. 5.
[25]   A. Gramsci, *Selections from the Political Writings 1921–1926*, ed. Q. Hoare (London, 1978), p. 198.

favoured by objective conditions. Only as a result of its activity among the masses, will the party get the latter to recognize it as 'their' party (winning a majority); and only when this condition has been realized can it presume that it is able to draw the working class behind it.[26]

Socialist revolution thus requires extensive ideological and organizational preparation: in semi-industrialized countries like Italy, it may, indeed, involve the development of class alliances such as that Gramsci envisaged between the northern proletariat and the southern peasantry. It is against this background that he formulates, in his *Prison Notebooks*, his well-known theory of hegemony. The thought here essentially is that classes rule by securing consent as well as by coercively imposing their will. Thus

> the supremacy of a social group manifests itself in two ways, as 'domination' and as 'intellectual and moral leadership'. A social group dominates antagonistic groups, which it tends to 'liquidate', or even to subjugate perhaps even by armed force; it leads kindred and allied groups. A social group can, and indeed must, already exercise 'leadership' before winning governmental power (this indeed is one of the principal conditions for the winning of such power); it subsequently becomes dominant when it exercises power, but even if it holds it firmly in its grasp, it must continue to 'lead' as well.[27]

Gramsci seeks in the *Prison Notebooks* to identify the conditions under which such 'intellectual, moral and political hegemony' is established. It is with this in mind that he distinguishes between the state and civil society, conceived respectively as the coercive institutions of state power and as a range of cultural institutions – for example, churches and schools – through which the dominant ideology is disseminated. In the advanced capitalist countries, ' "civil society" has become a very complex structure and one which is resistant to the catastrophic "incursions" of the immediate economic element (crises, depressions, etc.)'.[28] The conquest of this structure would require what Gramsci called a 'war of position', which he conceived on analogy with the trench warfare of 1914–18 – the gradual capture of individual positions – as opposed to 'war of manoeuvre', the direct frontal assault through which the Bolsheviks were able to overwhelm the much weaker civil society of tsarist Russia and seize state power.

The precise strategic implications of this analysis have attracted considerable controversy. The conditions of prison censorship in which Gramsci wrote forced him to express himself in metaphorical and allusive language which contributes to the ambiguity of some of the key concepts and theses of his

[26] Ibid., p. 368.
[27] Gramsci, *Prison Notebooks*, pp. 57–8.
[28] Ibid., pp. 58, 235.

Notebooks. In particular, certain formulations can be taken to imply that the gradual conquest of civil society in Western liberal democracies obviates the need for a revolutionary overthrow of the capitalist state. Contrary though such an implication almost certainly would be to Gramsci's own views, there is enough conceptual looseness in his writings to license such a reformist interpretation, which was especially fashionable during the 1970s when the Italian and other European Communist parties embraced 'Eurocommunism'. Nevertheless, his own fate – death in one of Mussolini's prisons – certainly confirmed the capacity of bourgeois institutions to resist the ' "catastrophic" incursions' of world war and economic crisis.

9.2   Heidegger and the conservative revolution

The writings of the Hegelian Marxists – above all, *History and Class Consciousness* – were, among other things, a sophisticated attempt to integrate the critique of modernity developed especially by central European intellectuals into the framework of historical materialism. But other ideologies provided a means of interpreting the widespread sense of malaise in early twentieth-century Europe. Ernst Nolte has called fascism '[r]evolutionary reaction'.[29] The fascist movements indeed represented a response to the revolutionary upheavals in which the First World War ended. Hitler described himself as the 'smasher of Marxism'; it was on this basis that he was able to win the support of German industrialists, bankers, and landowners fearful of Communism and organized labour. But National Socialism projected itself as not a conservative but a revolutionary movement which would transform German society, creating a *Volksgemeinschaft* – national community – in which native capital and labour would be reconciled the better to wage war against rival races for living room.

Nazi ideology was in formal terms crude, eclectic, and derivative. Joachim Fest writes of Hitler: 'Nationalism, anti-Bolshevism, and anti-Semitism, linked by a Darwinist theory of struggle, formed the pillars of his world-view and shaped his utterances from the very first to the very last.'[30] Extreme vulgarizations of Nietzsche and Social Darwinism fused with biological racism and anti-Semitism to constitute the core of National Socialist ideology. But under the Weimar Republic (1918–33), a group of intellectuals, the so-called 'conservative revolutionaries' – notably Ernst Jünger, Arthur Moeller van den Bruck, Carl Schmitt, and Oswald Spengler – sought to offer considerably more subtle theorizations of far-right politics.

In doing so, they were able to draw on the critique of modernity already present in existing German conservative thought. By the late nineteenth cen-

---

[29]   E. Nolte, *Three Faces of Fascism* (New York, 1969), p. 81.
[30]   J. C. Fest, *Hitler* (Harmondsworth, 1977), p. 206.

tury, German intellectuals were already accustomed to drawing a distinction between civilization (*Zivilisation*) and culture (*Kultur*). The first, characteristic of France and Britain, is superficial, rationalistic, commercial; the second, authentically German, is organically integrated, intuitive, and oriented towards living. In other words, the contrast which, for example, Tönnies drew between pre-modern *Gemeinschaft* (community) and modern *Gesellschaft* (association) – between, that is, two phases of social development – is redrawn as a representation of national differences, with the implication that German *Kultur* contains within it the means of overcoming the atomization and disharmony of modernity.

Spengler developed the idea further in *The Decline of the West*, which appeared at the end of the First World War. He argued that world history consists of a plurality of Cultures, each representing a valid solution to the problems of human existence, and each displaying the pattern of development characteristic of individual organisms – namely, birth, youth, growth, maturity, decay, and death. As part of this pattern, each Culture inevitably develops its own Civilization, 'the progressive exhaustion of forms that have become inorganic or dead'. The identity of the the great Cultures – Spengler believed there were only eight in the whole of world history – is racially determined. Indeed: 'Race, like Time and Destiny, is a decisive element in every question of life, something which everyone knows clearly and definitely so long as he does not try to set himself to comprehend it by way of rational – i.e. soulless – direction and ordering.'[31]

This philosophy of history bears some resemblance to Gobineau's race theory (see §3.3 above), though Spengler is not obsessed by racial 'mixing'. Both lend themselves to various sorts of cosmic pessimism. Spengler indeed believes that the West made the transition from Culture to Civilization in the nineteenth century, and he finds much evidence of exhaustion in contemporary intellectual life. Nevertheless, the dominant note struck by the conservative revolutionaries is neither melancholy reflection on inevitable decline nor the kind of nostalgia for an idealized past characteristic of the more conservative versions of Romantic anti-capitalism. They respond to the crisis of modernity in a way that is as activist as that of the Hegelian Marxists. Jeffrey Herf calls them 'nationalists who turned the romantic anti-capitalism of the German Right away from backward-looking pastoralism, pointing instead to the outlines of a beautiful new order replacing the formless chaos due to capitalism in a united, technologically advanced nation'.[32]

Thus Jünger celebrates the experience of total war between 1914 and 1918 with the peculiar exaltation of frontline fighting, the effort of each belligerent state to mobilize all the resources of its society for victory, and the breakdown

---

[31]   O. Spengler, *The Decline of the West*, abbr.edn, ed. H. Werner and A. Helps (New York, 1991), pp. 25, 257.

[32]   J. Herf, *Reactionary Modernism* (Cambridge, 1984), p. 4.

of the traditional distinction between combatants and civilians. These developments exposed the brutal core of contemporary reality:

> It suffices simply to consider our daily life, with its inexorability and merciless discipline, its smoking, glowing districts, the physics and metaphysics of its commerce, its motors, airplanes, and burgeoning cities. With a pleasure-tinged horror, we sense that here, not a single atom is not in motion – that we are profoundly inscribed in this raging process. Total Mobilization is far less consummated than it consummates itself; in war and peace, it expresses the secret and inexorable claim to which our life in the age of the masses and machines subjects us. It thus turns out that each individual life becomes, ever more unambiguously, the life of a worker; and that, following the wars of knights, kings, and citizens, we now have wars of *workers*. The first great twentieth-century conflict has offered us a presentiment of both their rational structure and their mercilessness.[33]

For this 'reactionary modernism', as Herf calls it, advanced technology is not one symptom of decadent *Zivilisation*: it is an embodiment of the will to power, the potential instrument of a revivified German nation of 'workers' (understood broadly so as to embrace managers, entrepreneurs, and small producers as well as wage-labourers) in the struggle for existence. Though the conservative revolutionaries had a complex and ambivalent relationship to Nazism as an actual movement, they did articulate one of its main tendencies. The historian Detlev Peukert has argued that, far from representing a simple rejection of modernity, or arising from the 'special path' (*Sonderweg*) of German history, as some influential interpretations suggest, 'National Socialism demonstrated, with heightened clarity and murderous consistency, the pathologies and seismic fractures of the modern civilizing process':

> Consistent in its rejection of the legacy of 1789, National Socialism envisaged a society with modern technologies and institutions but owing nothing to the ideals of equal rights, emancipation, self-determination and common humanity. It pushed the utopian belief in all-embracing 'scientific' solutions of social problems to the ultimate logical extreme, encompassing the entire population in a bureaucratic racial-biological design and eradicating all sources of nonconformity and friction. It demonstrated the destructive power of modern technology by waging world war; in everday life it offered a foretaste of a depressing, atomized form of society abjuring social, political and moral responsibilities and deriving its coherence solely from bureaucratic procedures and institutions of incorporation and from the vapid specious forms of mass consumption.[34]

The conservative revolutionaries provide the ideological milieu from which the writings of one of the major philosophers of the twentieth century

---

[33]   E. Jünger (1930), 'Total Mobilization', in R. Wolin, ed., *The Heidegger Controversy* (Cambridge, Mass., 1993), p. 128.
[34]   D. Peukert, *Inside Nazi Germany* (London, 1989), p. 248.

emerged. Heidegger's relationship to Nazism is a matter of enormous controversy.[35] Nevertheless, the basic facts are now well established thanks especially to the research of Hugo Ott. Heidegger voted for Hitler in the 1932 presidential election, joined the Nazis after the seizure of power in January 1933, and assumed the post of Rector of the University of Freiburg the same April. While in that post he made a number of speeches unequivocally identifying himself with the National Socialist regime, and indeed declaring on several occasions: 'The Führer alone *is* the present and future German reality and its law.'[36]

During his term as Rector Heidegger enthusiastically sought to transform the university along Nazi lines, arguing, for example, that it should 'be *integrated again into the Volksgemeinschaft* [national community] *and be joined together with the state*'.[37] He also participated in the academic persecution of Jews and liberals. Forced out of the rectorate in April 1934 by one of the intrigues endemic to the Hitler regime, he did not disavow Nazism. After 1945 Heidegger consistently refused to apologize for his record under the Third Reich. For example, in a letter to his former pupil Herbert Marcuse he explained his decision to support the Nazis thus: 'I expected from National Socialism a spiritual renewal of life in its entirety, a reconciliation of social antagonisms and a deliverance of Western *Dasein* [human existence] from the dangers of communism.' Claiming that he had soon recognized his 'political error', he nevertheless refused to condemn the extermination of the Jews, comparing it to the expulsion of Germans from areas annexed by Poland, Czechoslovakia, and the Soviet Union at the end of the Second World War.[38]

Despite the efforts of Heidegger's apologists, notably in France, to extenuate his behaviour, this is undeniably the most shameful political record of any major twentieth-century thinker. It is open to various interpretations. Victor Farias argues that Heidegger identified himself with the radical Nazi faction led by Ernst Röhm advocating an anti-conservative 'Second Revolution' which would, for example, supplant the regular army with the party's stormtroopers (the SA) under Röhm's command; his removal from the rectorship must be seen as one in the series of concessions which Hitler made to traditional German military and economic elites, and which culminated in the massacre of the

---

[35] Martin Heidegger (1889–1976): born in Messkirch, Baden, the son of a master cooper; after an unsuccessful attempt to join the Jesuits, studied first theology and then Christian philosophy at Freiburg University, 1909–15; teaching assistant to the philosopher Edmund Husserl at Freiburg, 1920–3; Professor of Philosophy, University of Marburg, 1923–8; Professor of Philosophy, University of Freiburg, 1928–46; University Rector, 1933–4; forced to retire as part of the denazification process, 1946.

[36] For example, M. Heidegger (1933), 'German Students', in Wolin, ed., *Heidegger Controversy*, p. 47.

[37] M. Heidegger (1933), 'The University in the New Reich', in Wolin, ed., *Heidegger Controversy*, p. 44.

[38] Letter to Marcuse, 20 Jan. 1948, ibid., p. 162.

SA leadership on the Night of the Long Knives, 30 June 1944.[39] Ott, somewhat more charitably, portrays the philosopher as less a consistent National Socialist revolutionary than, throughout his career, an opportunist strongly motivated by his hatred of the Catholic Church. Even an admirer like Richard Rorty calls Heidegger 'a pretty nasty character', 'a Schwarzwald redneck' who never broke with the prejudices of the south German petty bourgeoisie from which he sprang.[40]

Perhaps more interesting is the question of the relationship between Heidegger's Nazism and his philosophical writings. These texts constitute one of the most complex, obscure, and influential intellectual achievements of the twentieth century. Plainly, any detailed discussion of Heidegger's philosophy would be out of place here. It may nevertheless be useful to identify certain themes connecting the critique of modernity he offers with his involvement in National Socialism. Indeed, Pierre Bourdieu argues:

> Heidegger is close to the spokesmen of the 'conservative revolution', many of whose words and theses he consecrates philosophically, but he distances himself from it by imposing a form which sublimates the 'crudest' borrowings by inserting them in the network of phonetic and semantic resonances which characterizes the Hölderlin-style *Begriffsdichtung* [conceptual poetry] of the academic prophet.[41]

Heidegger's peculiar oracular style, which became more pronounced in the course of his life, is indeed an obstacle to the understanding and the critical assessment of his writings. This does not, however, alter the importance of his most famous work, *Being and Time* (1927). Lukács, in *History and Class Consciousness*, had thrown down a challenge to traditional philosophy. The Kantian attempt to treat the world as the construction of a transcendental subject (an enterprise continued by Heidegger's teacher Husserl) seemed unable to avoid counterposing the formal structures of scientific rationality to the actual substance of physical and social life. How to reintegrate form and content without collapsing into some kind of naturalism which reduces mind either to sense-experience or to matter itself? Lukács's solution was to identify the working class as the identical subject–object of history. But, quite aside from the political unpalatability of Marxism, this strategy seemed to represent a further radicalization of German idealism, in which social reality is the creation of a macro-subject, the proletariat.

In *Being and Time* Heidegger takes up the challenge. He seeks to recommence Western philosophy outside the dichotomy of subject and object which had formed its starting-point since Descartes. He does so, in the first place, by arguing that the philosophical tradition has obscured the fundamental question

[39]   V. Farias, *Heidegger et le nazisme* (Paris, 1987), pp. 229–45.
[40]   R. Rorty, *Contingency, Irony, and Solidarity* (Cambridge, 1989), p. 111 (inc. n. 11).
[41]   P. Bourdieu, *The Political Ontology of Martin Heidegger* (Cambridge, 1991), p. 54.

of the nature of Being (*Sein*) as such, as opposed to that of particular entities or beings. The question of Being (*Seinsfrage*) is the preoccupation which runs through Heidegger's thought in all its variations and modifications. *Being and Time*, however, offers an analysis of *Dasein*, by which he means the Being of human beings, which is distinguished by the fact that 'Being is an issue for it'.[42]

One reason why Heidegger uses the term *Dasein* to refer to human existence is that he believes that it has to be understood in terms that transcend the subject–object dichotomy. His analysis of *Dasein* begins with 'Being-in the-world', which is 'a *unitary phenomenon*', so that 'Subject and Object do not coincide with *Dasein* and the world'. Being-in-the-world, in other words, cannot be broken down into subject and object connected primarily by the former's effort to know the latter. It consists rather in the various ways in which human beings are practically engaged in the world, particularly in work. 'The kind of dealing which is closest to us is . . . not a bare conceptual cognition, but rather that kind of concern which manipulates things and puts them to use; and this has its own kind of "knowledge".'[43]

In these practical involvements, the world – both natural and social – is disclosed to us. Human interpretations of this world are not somehow imposed on it by the subject. Our engagement with things in everyday life involves a tacit understanding of their role as 'ready-to-hand', available for our practical purposes. This understanding depends on a 'for-having' (*Vorhabe*) of things which precedes and makes possible their explicit interpretation: 'In every case interpretation is grounded in *something we see in advance* – in a *fore-sight* (*Vorsicht*). This foresight "takes the first cut" out of what has been taken into our fore-having, and it does so with a view to a definite way in which this can be interpreted', giving rise to a '*fore-conception*' of the thing that is articulated in interpretation. Therefore: 'An interpretation is never a presuppositionless apprehending of something presented to us.'[44] Our knowledge of things develops within the framework of our practical involvements in the world.

Heidegger no sooner offers this stunning analysis of Being-in-the-world, one of the great philosophical achievements of the twentieth century, than he radically undercuts it. Our relationship to the world is not that of a subject separate from it; nor is it that of an isolated individual: 'the world is always the one that I share with Others . . . Being-in is always *Being-with* Others.' Intersubjectivity is thus constitutive of human existence: 'So far as *Dasein* is at all, it has Being-with-one-another as its kind of Being. This cannot be conceived as a summative result of the occurrence of several "subjects".' But 'Being-with' (*Mitsein*) is in fact a relationship of '*subjection* to others': 'This Being-with-one-another dissolves one's own *Dasein* completely into the kind of Being of

---

[42]   M. Heidegger, *Being and Time* (Oxford, 1967), p. 32.
[43]   Ibid., pp. 78, 86, 95.
[44]   Ibid., pp. 191–2.

"the Others", in such a way, indeed, that the Others, as distinguishable and explicit, vanish more and more. In this inconspicuousness and unascertainability, the real dictatorship of the "they" [*das Man*] is unfolded.' Individuality vanishes in this inauthentic mode of Being, where '[e]veryone is the other, and no one is himself':

> The Self of everyday *Dasein* is the *they-self*, which we distinguish from the *authentic Self* – that is, from the Self that has been taken hold of in its own way. As the they-self, the particular *Dasein* has been dispersed into the 'they', and must first find itself . . . If *Dasein* is familiar with itself as the they-self, this means at the same time that the 'they' itself prescribes that way of interpreting the world and Being-in-the-world which lies closest.[45]

The public sphere is thus the realm of 'idle talk', of the empty, the mediocre, the second-hand. As remarks such as the following suggest, Heidegger is offering a political critique here: 'Distantiality, averageness, and levelling down, as ways of Being for the "they", constitute what we know as "publicness".'[46] This diagnosis echoes in far more abstract form the kind of critique of liberal democracy developed by Carl Schmitt during the 1920s which focuses precisely on the absence of the genuine public debate required for the viability of parliamentary institutions:

> The situation of parliamentarism is critical today because the development of modern mass democracy has made argumentative public discussion a formality. Many norms of contemporary parliamentary law . . . function as a result like a superfluous decoration, useless and even embarrassing, as [if] someone had painted the radiator of a modern central heating system with red flames in order to give the appearance of a blazing fire. The parties . . . do not face each other discussing opinions, but as social or economic power-groups calculating their mutual interests and opportunities for power, and they actually agree compromises and coalitions on this basis. The masses are won over through a propaganda apparatus whose maximum effect relies on an appeal to immediate interests and passions. Argument in the real sense that is characteristic for genuine discussion vanishes.[47]

Heidegger portrays a social world as alienated as that evoked by Lukács in his theory of reification. But, unlike Lukács, he finds no agency internal to this world that offers an escape. Rather it is anxiety (*Angst*), understood as a generalized sense of oppression caused by the world itself, that tears *Dasein* out of its absorption in the 'they' and in 'ready-to-hand' objects. 'Anxiety individualizes *Dasein*'; it forces us to confront the fact that we are not, after

---

[45] Ibid., pp. 155, 163, 164, 165, 167.
[46] Ibid., p. 165.
[47] C. Schmitt (1923–6), *The Crisis of Parliamentary Democracy* (Cambridge, Mass., 1985), p. 6.

all, 'at home' in the everyday and in 'publicness', and makes us aware of our incompleteness, of the potentialities through which we are free.[48] This awareness realizes itself in the fundamental recognition of human finitude that is the knowledge that we will all die. Spengler had already written: 'In the knowledge of death is originated that world outlook which we possess as being men and not beasts.'[49] The 'they' flee from this knowledge. In Being-towards-death, Heidegger believes, we have the possibility of an authentic mode of Being. This takes the form of 'resoluteness' (*Entschlossenheit*). Here anticipation of death leads to an orientation towards the future which accepts the finitude and contingency – the 'thrownness' – of human existence, and makes this the basis of action.

Richard Wolin observes that this analysis of 'resoluteness' offers the 'gateway to Heideggerianism as a political philosophy': 'once the inauthenticity of all traditional social norms has been existentially unmasked, the only remaining basis for moral orientation is a *decision ex nihilo*, a *radical assertion of will*'; a will, moreover, that is pure and unconstrained by the impediments of social convention'.[50] There is, as Wolin suggests, a close correspondence between this conception of authenticity as resoluteness, and Schmitt's 'decisionism', according to which in a political world constituted by the ever-present possibility of conflict, sovereignty attaches to he who, in a situation of crisis, to which legal principles designed to govern normal situations cannot by definition apply, decides what must be done.

'Every general norm demands a normal, everyday frame of life to which it can be factually applied and which is subjected to its regulation', Schmitt writes. The exception, where the very existence of the state may be under threat, demands a decision which cannot be derived from such norms. 'Looked at normatively, the decision emanates from nothing'; there is no general principle in terms of which it can be justified.[51] The Enlightenment developed a rationalism of universal laws from which the exception and the decision are banished, but Schmitt seeks to reinstate them, in order, radicalizing Weber's theory of plebiscitary democracy, to justify the dictatorship of the Reich President in Weimar Germany (see §7.4 above).

There is another point of contact between *Being and Time* and conservative-revolutionary thinking. Reflecting on the experience of total war, Jünger writes:

> Wherever we confront efforts of such proportions, possessing the special quality of 'uselessness' – say the erection of mighty constructions like pyramids and cathedrals, or wars that call into play the ultimate mainsprings of existence – economic explanations, no matter how illuminating, are not sufficient. This is

---

[48] Heidegger, *Being and Time*, p. 233.
[49] Spengler, *Decline*, p. 229.
[50] R. Wolin, *The Politics of Being* (New York, 1990), p. 39.
[51] C. Schmitt (1922), *Political Theology* (Cambridge, Mass., 1985), pp. 13, 31–2.

why the school of historical materialism can only touch the surface of the process. To explain efforts of this sort, we ought rather to focus our first suspicions on phenomena of a cultic variety.[52]

Jünger thus suggests that the real matter of world history is too profound to be understood in terms of anything as mundane as material interests. On a much broader scale, Heidegger argues that history as we normally understand it is not a fundamental dimension of *Dasein*. It is what is past 'in our Being-with-one-another, and which at the same time has been "handed down to us" and continuingly effective'. History is thus an incomprehensible burden we inherit from the past. Historicality (*Geschichtlichkeit*), by contrast, is constitutive of *Dasein*. It arises from the fundamental structure of temporality, which consists in the orientation towards the future inherent in authentic Being-towards-death. Thus 'when historicality is authentic, it understands history as the "recurrence" of the possible, and knows that a possibility will recur only if existence is open to it fatefully, in a moment of vision, in resolute repetition'.[53] So the real meaning of history lies in the structures inherent in human existence through which free action is possible. Bourdieu calls this a 'verbal somersault which allows escape from history by asserting the essential historicity of the existing, and inscribing history and temporality within Being, that is, within the ahistorical and the eternal': Heidegger thus uses 'the eternalization of temporality and of history in order to avoid the historicization of the eternal'.[54]

Heidegger's extraordinarily abstract and convoluted analysis of *Dasein* thus repeats in a philosophical register many of the political themes of the conservative-revolutionaries. From this perspective, his adhesion to National Socialism becomes intelligible. In the early 1930s he took part in a discussion group on Jünger's writings. He later wrote: 'What Ernst Jünger thinks with the thought of the rule and shape of the worker and sees in the light of this thought, is the universal rule of the will to power within history, now understood to embrace the planet. Today everything stands in this historical reality, no matter whether it is called communism, fascism, or world democracy.'[55] It is against this background that we must understand Heidegger's notorious remark, made in a lecture first given in 1935, that 'the inner truth and greatness' of National Socialism lie in 'the encounter between global technology and modern man'.[56]

In the same text Heidegger portrays Europe as caught 'in a great pincers, squeezed between Russia on the one side and America on the other. From a metaphysical point of view, Russia and America are the same; the same dreary

---

[52] Jünger, 'Total Mobilization', p. 129.
[53] Heidegger, *Being and Time*, pp. 431, 444.
[54] Bourdieu, *Political Ontology*, pp. 62, 63.
[55] M. Heidegger, 'The Rectorate 1933/34: Facts and Thoughts', *Review of Metaphysics*, 38 (1985), p. 485.
[56] M. Heidegger (1953), *An Introduction to Metaphysics* (New York, 1979), p. 199.

technological frenzy, the same unrestricted organization of the average man.'
Faced with 'the darkening of the world, the flight of the gods, the destruction of
the earth, the transformation of men into a mass, the hatred and suspicion of
everything free and creative', he sees in Nazism the hope of a heroic assertion
of will that, in the face of 'global technology', has, as Luc Ferry and Alain
Renaut put it, 'the *capacity to respond to it effectively by forestalling its dangers*'.[57] Repeating a longstanding theme of nationalist ideologues that Germany
is the centre of Europe, and the potential politico-economic capital of a
Mitteleuropa stretching from the Rhine to the Urals, Heidegger declares: 'If the
great decision concerning Europe is not to bring annihilation, that decision must
be made in terms of new spiritual energies unfolding historically from out of
the centre.'[58]

This embrace of a nationalist decisionism does not lead Heidegger to accept
biological racism. Nevertheless the writings of his Nazi period display what
Jacques Derrida calls a 'massive voluntarism', marked by the emphatic use of
the term 'spirit' and 'spiritual'.[59] Thus in his Rectorship Address, Heidegger
declares:

> spirit is the determined resolve to the essence of Being, a resolve that is attuned to
> origins and knowing. And the *spiritual world* of a Volk . . . is the power that
> comes from preserving at the most profound level the forces that are rooted in the
> soil and blood of a Volk, the power to arouse most inwardly and to shake most
> extensively the Volk's existence. A spiritual world alone will guarantee our Volk
> greatness. For it will make the constant decision between the will to greatness
> and the toleration of decline the law that establishes the pace for the march upon
> which our Volk has embarked on its way to future history.[60]

Here the formal analysis of resoluteness and historicality in *Being and Time*
is invoked to conceptualize the collective decision through which the German
Volksgemeinschaft will reverse Europe's decline. It is not surprising that
Heidegger's endorsement of conservative-revolutionary voluntarism leads to a
sustained engagement with Nietzsche. But his main texts on Nietzsche, written
between 1936 and 1946, record a progressive disillusionment. Heidegger reads
Nietzsche in the light of what he calls the '*grounding question*', namely that of
'the Being of beings'. Western philosophy since Plato has obscured this question by making '*one* region of being . . . *definitive* for our survey of being as
a whole'.[61] Nietzsche brings this process to a culmination: his critique of

---

[57] Ibid., pp. 37, 38; L. Ferry and A. Renaut, *Heidegger and Modernity* (Chicago, 1988), p. 61.
[58] Heidegger, *Introduction*, pp. 38–9.
[59] J. Derrida, *Of Spirit* (Chicago, 1989), p. 37.
[60] M. Heidegger (1933), 'The Self-Assertion of the German University', in Wolin, ed., *Heidegger Controversy*, pp. 33–4.
[61] M. Heidegger, *Nietzsche* (4 vols, San Francisco, 1991), II, pp. 193, 194, 197.

European nihilism, of the systematic devaluation of all values characteristic of modernity, reveals the dead-end that is the ultimate consequence of the forgetfulness of Being definitive of Western metaphysics.

Initially Heidegger seems to think that Nietzsche also offers us the re- sources with which to overcome metaphysics, and thereby to resolve Eu- rope's crisis. But he comes to believe that Nietzsche is part of the problem, rather than part of the solution. Nietzsche understands that 'nihilism is the covert, basic law of Western history'. But in seeking to overcome nihilism in actuality he fulfils it by developing 'a metaphysics of the will to power'. This metaphysics draws out what was implicit from the start in the effort of West- ern philosophy since Descartes to make subjectivity the foundation of know- ledge. Modern thought progressively absolutizes the subject, and turns everything else – including human beings – into its raw material. Thus 'Nietzsche's doctrine, which makes everything that is, and as it is, into the "property and product of man", merely carries out the final development of Descartes' doctrine, according to which truth is grounded in the self- certainty of the human subject', thereby articulating conceptually the drive for 'supreme and absolute self-development of all capacities of mankind for absolute dominion over the earth'.[62]

This reassessment of Nietzsche's philosophy as 'a *metaphysics of the absol- ute subjectivity of the will to power*' leads Heidegger to reassess his earlier views. He now dismisses the total mobilization for modern warfare celebrated by Jünger as 'the organization of unconditional meaninglessness by and for the will to power'. Indeed, '[t]he essence of modernity is fulfilled in the age of consummate meaninglessness', which is also the fulfilment of metaphysics. But the oblivion of Being as such that is constitutive of metaphysics does not arise from any human error or choice. 'The highest decision that can be made and that becomes the ground of all history' which consists in the concealment of Being 'is never first made and executed by a human being. Rather, its di- rection and perdurance decide *about* man and, in a different way, about the god.'[63]

The decision which can set history on a new path thus no longer depends on any merely human resoluteness. '*Being itself stays away*': it withdraws from us by allowing the question of Being to be concealed behind that of the nature of beings at the start of Western metaphysics. The entire development of this thought, culminating in Nietzsche, is thus not an accident or a mistake. Rather, it is the form in which Being discloses itself to us through its very concealment. Indeed, '[t]hrough its withdrawal, which nonetheless remains a relationship to beings, in which form "Being" appears, Being releases itself into the will to power.' The history of metaphysics, which Heidegger, like Hegel,

---

[62]   Ibid., IV, pp. 27, 52, 86, 99.
[63]   Ibid., IV, p. 147; III, pp. 174, 178, 5.

believes to be the essence of European history, is thus 'the self-veiled truth of Being'. What is left to us at the end of this history is to reflect upon 'the history of Being' – conceived as this process of self-disclosure through withdrawal – and of 'the provenance of metaphysics' within it.[64]

Being for Heidegger is thus somewhat like Hegel's Absolute Spirit; it seems to be a divinity that is not separate from its creation, but is immanent in the being to which it reveals (or conceals) itself – man, *Dasein*, the being for which Being is an issue. Thus: 'The essence of Being itself does not take place behind or beyond beings, but – provided the notion of such a relationship is permissible here – *before* the being.'[65] But whereas for Hegel history is the process through which the Absolute comes to self-consciousness through human thought and action, history becomes for Heidegger after his abandonment of the conservative revolution that of a humankind from whom God has hidden himself. His later writings relentlessly deny the subject the sovereign position which Descartes had accorded it. 'Man is not the lord of beings,' he declares; 'Man is the shepherd of Being.'[66] Similarly: 'Man acts as though he were the shaper and master of language, whereas in fact language remains the master of man . . . Strictly, it is language that speaks', not man.[67]

Heidegger's anti-humanism made his later thought attractive to French post-structuralists also eager to reject the philosophy of the subject (see §11.3 below). But, after the 'resoluteness' of National Socialism had failed to provide an effective response to modern technology, and in the face of 'the age of consummate meaninglessness', Heidegger counselled a kind of passive waiting on Being. 'Only a god can save us', he told the weekly *Der Spiegel* in a 1966 interview published after his death ten years later. 'The sole possibility that is left for us is to prepare a sort of readiness, through thinking and poetizing, for the appearance of the god or for the absence of the god in the time of foundering [*Untergang*]; for in the face of the god who is absent we founder.'[68]

Heidegger is the most important thinker since Nietzsche who has unconditionally rejected modernity. Imbued with the ideology of the radical right, this rejection led him to believe that fascism could reverse the process of European decline. The failure of this gamble left him ruminating on a hidden god somehow present in his very absence. His career does not simply demonstrate the ability of even the most gifted intellectuals to compromise with, even to embrace, evil. It also dramatizes the oscillation between voluntarism and fatalism with which thinkers of the left as well as the right responded to the Thirty Years

64   Ibid., IV, pp. 214, 231, 233, 244.
65   Ibid., IV, p. 238.
66   M. Heidegger (1947), 'Letter on Humanism', in *Basic Writings*, ed. D. F. Krell (London, 1978), p. 221.
67   M. Heidegger, *Poetry, Language, Thought* (New York, 1975), pp. 215–16.
68   M. Heidegger, 'Only a God Can Save Us', in Wolin, ed., *Heidegger Controversy*, p. 107.

War of the twentieth century. Lukács, whose record of resisting Stalinism was incomparably more principled and courageous than anything to be found in Heidegger's political history, first sought to rethink Marxism as a theory of class subjectivity before, as the revolutionary tide receded, embracing a more objectivist version of historical materialism. Perhaps this itinerary anticipated the demolition of the subject characteristic of social theory in the second half of the century.

10

The Golden Age

10.1 Theorists of capitalism: Keynes and Hayek

Following the convulsions of the first half of the twentieth century, the advanced industrial countries enjoyed a strange remission after 1945. As Eric Hobsbawm puts it, the 'Age of Catastrophe' – the era of the two world wars and the Great Depression – was succeeded by the 'Golden Age': 'the world, and particularly the world of developed capitalism . . . passed through an altogether exceptional phase of its history; perhaps a unique one'.[1] After the Second World War, capitalism experienced the longest and most sustained economic boom in its history. Between 1948 and 1973 world gross national product rose by three and a half times. For most of these years the advanced economies enjoyed full employment; furthermore, high growth-rates made it possible to finance substantial social reforms which reduced most citizens' vulnerability to the vicissitudes of the market, at least when it came to meeting their most basic needs. Prosperity greatly strengthened the political structures of liberal democracy. Threatened even in their heartlands of the United States, Britain, and France during the inter-war years, these structures rooted themselves much more firmly in continental Europe and Japan as the boom increasingly transformed these countries into societies of city-dwelling wage-earners. Politically and militarily integrated under American leadership through a nexus of Cold War alliances against the Soviet bloc, the Western liberal democracies increasingly emerged as the centre of gravity of world politics.

This process of economic expansion and political stabilization did not silence social criticism, though this tended (as we shall see in §10.3 below) to take on a much more despairing note. But the boom itself required explanation: did it, as Hobsbawm suggests, represent an exception, a deviation from the normal course of capitalist development, or did it mark rather a breakthrough to

---

[1] E. J. Hobsbawm, *Age of Extremes* (London, 1994), pp. 257–8.

a fundamentally different form of capitalism (if one could still call it that) in which political regulation could effectively abolish the trade cycle and guarantee uninterrupted economic growth? There were plenty willing to make the latter case. Tony Crosland, the main theoretician of postwar social democracy, argued that, while 'socialist thought has been dominated by the economic problems posed by capitalism', this need no longer be the case: 'Capitalism has been reformed almost out of recognition. Despite occasional minor recessions and balance of payments crises, full employment and at least a tolerable degree of stability are likely to be maintained . . . The prewar reasons for a largely economic orientation are therefore steadily losing their relevance.'[2]

Crosland and others sharing his analysis tended to give much of the credit for this transformation to one man – Keynes – and to his book *The General Theory of Employment Interest and Money* (1936).[3] Consider, for example, this assertion by an economist, made as the long postwar boom was drawing to a close: 'the basic fact is that with the acceptance of the *General Theory*, the days of uncontrollable mass unemployment in advanced industrial countries are over. Other economic problems may threaten; this one, at least, has passed into history.'[4] Such statements have, of course, been overtaken by events – in particular, by the return of serious economic crises accompanied by mass unemployment at the end of the 1960s, and by the subsequent intellectual revival of *laissez-faire* economics. These developments do not, however, alter the significance of Keynes's theory (even if they cast doubt on its more simplistic interpretations): it remains the most important challenge to certain basic assumptions of the economic orthodoxy created by the marginalist revolution to have been made from within its framework.

Keynes did not develop this critique from a standpoint hostile to capitalism as a social and economic system. He declared that 'the *class* war will find me on the side of the educated bourgeoisie'. Contemptuously dismissing Marxism in 1925, he wrote:

> How can I accept a doctrine which sets up as its bible, above and beyond criticism, an obsolete economic textbook which I know to be not only scientifically erroneous but without interest or application to the modern world? How can I adopt a creed which, preferring the mud to the fish, exalts the boorish proletariat

[2]   C. A. R. Crosland, *The Future of Socialism* (London, 1956), p. 517.
[3]   John Maynard Keynes (1883–1946): the son of a Cambridge don, of middle-class Nonconformist background; educated at Eton and at King's College, Cambridge, 1902–5; civil servant at the India Office, 1906–8; elected Fellow of King's, 1909; worked at the Treasury, 1915–19; *The Economic Consequences of the Peace* (1919), which denounced the harsh treatment of Germany in the Versailles Treaty, made his international reputation; served on the Macmillan Committee on Finance and Industry, 1929–30; adviser to the Treasury, 1939–46; chief British negotiator with US over Lend Lease, the 1944 Bretton Woods settlement establishing the postwar financial system, and the 1945 American loan to the UK; created a peer in 1942.
[4]   M. Stewart, *Keynes and After* (Harmondsworth, 1972), p. 299.

above the bourgeois and the intelligentsia who, with whatever faults, are the quality of life and surely carry the seeds of all human advancement?[5]

In fact Keynes's general outlook bears some resemblance to Weber's. Both defended the liberal bourgeois civilization in which they had grown up, but both did so acutely aware that the traditional justifications of that civilization were no longer available. Keynes could not sustain his Nonconformist forebears' faith in the Christian God. But utilitarianism, the most influential secular moral theory in nineteenth-century Britain, seemed to him too blunt an instrument. In particular, the maximization of the general welfare enjoined by Bentham did not seem to have a place for the cultivation of exceptional experiences by a cultural elite – for example, the pursuit of aesthetic and sexual experimentation by the Bloomsbury Group of writers and artists in which Keynes enthusiastically participated, notably in the years immediately before and during the First World War.

His biographer Robert Skidelsky comments: 'Keynes's life was balanced between two sets of moral claims. His duty as an individual was to achieve good states of mind for himself and for those he was directly concerned with; his duty as a citizen was to help achieve a happy state of affairs for society . . . He was thus both an aesthete and a manager.'[6] How close a connection there was between Keynes's personal outlook and his economics is open to argument (during the Thatcher era a famous leader in *The Times* effectively blamed the inflation of the 1970s on Keynes's homosexuality and aestheticism: 'there may be a parallel between his emotional resentment of the monetary rules which prevented inflation, and in particular the gold standard, and his need to reject the conventional sexual morality of his period'[7]). What is undeniable is that both are informed by a faith in an intellectual elite, the 'educated bourgeoisie', in whom the capacity to innovate both culturally and economically resided. Writing in 1931, as the Great Depression overwhelmed the world economy, Keynes declared: 'The economic problem . . . the problem of want and poverty, and the economic struggle between classes and nations, is nothing but a frightful muddle, a transitory and an *unnecessary* muddle.'[8] He regarded himself as having been called to resolve it.

At the heart of this 'muddle' was the belief, constitutive of mainstream economics since *The Wealth of Nations*, that the market is a self-equilibrating system. If shifted from its equilibrium point, at which both human and material resources are fully employed, the economy would tend to return to this point through adjustments in output and in relative prices. Keynes systematically attacks this belief, directing his fire particularly at Say's Law. Already a matter of controversy between Ricardo and Malthus after the Napoleonic Wars,

[5] J. M. Keynes, *Essays in Persuasion* (London, 1972), pp. 297, 258.
[6] R. Skidelsky, *John Maynard Keynes* (2 vols, London, 1983, 1992), I, p. 157.
[7] 'Mr Robinson and Mr Blunt', *Times*, 22 Nov. 1979.
[8] Keynes, *Essays*, p. xviii.

this proposition asserts that 'supply creates its own demand; – meaning by this in some significant, but not clearly defined sense that the whole of the costs of production must necessarily be spent in the aggregate, directly or indirectly, on purchasing the product'.[9] Goods cannot therefore go unsold, since the income required to purchase them is generated, in the form of wages and profits, in the course of producing them. Crises of overproduction, where commodities fail to find buyers, are, on this view, a consequence of some distortion of the market rather than (as Marx argued) being an inherent feature of capitalism.

Aggregate wages and profits constitute what Keynes calls the effective demand for goods and services. He points out that Say's Law depends on the assumption that any income that is saved rather than spent immediately on consumption will automatically be invested, and thereby spent to purchase plant and machinery. But saving and investment are distinct activities governed by different variables. Investment is determined by the marginal efficiency of capital (i.e. the expected return on an asset) and the rate of interest. Saving depends on the propensity to consume; economic actors may decide to hang on to their money rather than to spend or invest it. What Keynes calls liquidity preference, or the propensity to hoard, is a consequence of various motives – the need for cash in everyday transactions, the search for security, or the desire to hold money in case some opportunity for speculation turns up; its effect is to prevent the operation of Say's Law, since the greater the level of hoarding the less income is spent on consumption or investment goods. Effective demand is then insufficient to purchase all the goods and services produced.

Money plays a crucial part in Keynes's analysis. Skidelsky writes: 'If Marx is the poet of commodities, Keynes is the poet of money.'[10] The quantity theory of money first formulated by Hume treated it as, in principle, a neutral medium behind which lies the 'real economy' where goods and services are produced and exchanged. For Keynes, however, '[t]he interposition of this veil of money [through the banking system] between the real asset and the wealth owner is a specially marked characteristic of the modern world.'[11] He believes '*the importance of money flows from its being a link between the present and the future*'.[12] Economics, rather than being (as neo-classical orthodoxy held) concerned with the rational allocation of scarce resources to individuals, is about decisions taken in a condition of radical uncertainty about the future. As Will Hutton puts it,

> for Keynes, money transformed the dynamics of the economy . . . For it means
> that consumers and producers have the means of acting upon their expectations

[9]   J. M. Keynes, *The General Theory of Employment Interest and Money* (London, 1970), p. 18.
[10] Skidelsky, *Keynes*, II, p. 543.
[11] Keynes, *Essays*, p. 151.
[12] Keynes, *General Theory*, p. 293.

of the future. If they are optimistic, they can borrow and bring forward their purchases, investment, and production; if they are pessimistic they can defer
purchases and investment till tomorrow.[13]

The effects of actors' inescapable uncertainty about the future are most clearly
expressed in the case of investment decisions, which involve calculations of
expected return over relatively lengthy periods of time. 'The outstanding fact is
the extreme precariousness of the basis of knowledge on which our estimates of
prospective yield have to be made.' Financial markets develop to organize investment on a social scale, starting from the convention that existing patterns
can be projected into the future. But these are subject to 'mass psychology' – to
the irrational surges in opinion at work in stock-market bubbles and panics.
The professionals – stockbrokers and the like, meanwhile, are motivated chiefly
to anticipate shifts in sentiment which will lead to changes in the 'conventional
valuation' of assets: 'The social object of skilled investment should be to defeat
the dark forces of time and ignorance which envelop our future. The actual,
private object of the most skilled investment today is "to beat the gun" . . . to
outwit the crowd and pass on the bad, or depreciating, half-crown to the next
fellow.' This analysis of financial markets (which has lost none of its apposite-
ness since 1936) leads Keynes to conclude: 'Speculators may do no harm as
bubbles on a steady stream of enterprise. But the position is serious when enterprise becomes the bubble of a whirlwind of speculation. When the capital development of a country becomes the by-product of a casino, the job is likely to
be ill-done.'[14]
   The tendency of financial markets to be driven by speculation and herd behaviour is particularly serious because of the dependence of the overall level of
economic activity on the rate of investment: 'The traditional analysis has been
aware that saving depends on income but it has overlooked the fact that income
depends on investment in such fashion that, when investment changes, income
must necessarily change in just that degree which is necessary to make the
change in saving equal the change in investment.' It follows that, if savings rise
to a level higher than investment, the effective demand for goods and services
will fall, bringing down output and employment till savings and investment are
back in balance. So 'there is only one level of employment consistent with
equilibrium . . . But there is no reason in general for expecting it to be *equal* to
full employment.' Indeed, 'the mere existence of an insufficiency of effective
demand may, and often will, bring the increase of employment to a standstill
before a level of full employment has been reached'.[15] Moreover, governments
which responded to crises by cutting public spending and restricting credit, as

[13]   W. Hutton, *The State We're In* (London, 1995), p. 240.
[14]   Keynes, *General Theory*, pp. 149, 155, 159.
[15]   Ibid., pp. 184, 28, 30–1.

laissez-faire doctrine enjoined, would precipitate their economies into a vicious downward spiral in which declining demand and confidence forced up unemployment.

Keynes's economics was a peculiar mixture of conservatism and radicalism, both theoretically and politically. Luigi Pasinetti argues that the *General Theory* marks 'Keynes's clear break with the sixty-year-old tradition of marginal economic theory and his return to the methods of analysis of the earlier Classical economists of the beginning of the nineteenth century'.[16] Thus Keynes focuses on macro-economic aggregates rather than individual actors, and seeks to establish the causal relations between them, largely eschewing the reliance on systems of simultaneous equations that had become entrenched in neo-classical economics. Yet Keynes's eclectic and intuitive intellectual style involved the continued use of many marginalist concepts. This made possible his recuperation by, and reintegration into, orthodox economics, especially after the Second World War.

Keynes's practical remedies were directed towards the stabilization rather than the replacement of capitalism. Rather than cut spending in times of slump, governments should be willing to run quite substantial budget deficits in order to maintain effective demand. Furthermore, the dysfunctional nature of financial markets could be compensated for by 'the State, which is in a position to calculate the marginal efficiency of capital-goods on long views and on the basis of the general social advantage, taking an ever greater responsibility for directly organizing investment'. Keynes believed that 'a somewhat comprehensive socialization of investment will prove the only means of securing an approximation to full employment'. But these measures could be introduced piecemeal, and would stop well short of 'a system of State Socialism which would embrace most of the economic life of the community'.[17]

The political and economic context in which the *General Theory* appeared in 1936 was highly favourable to the acceptance of such measures. The era of the Thirty Years War (1914–45) saw a further development of the tendencies towards 'organized capitalism' already visible before 1914. Total war and world depression encouraged states increasingly to intervene in, direct, and even replace markets, a trend reflected in the spectacular rise of public expenditure as a proportion of national income. The slump of the 1930s was greatly exacerbated by governments' resort to protectionist policies, which caused a collapse of world trade. The disintegration of the international finance system – symbolized by Britain's departure from the gold standard in 1931 – allowed governments far greater freedom in formulating their domestic economic policies. The Stalinist Five-Year Plans, the Nazi Four-Year Plan, and Roosevelt's New Deal in the US were all symptoms of a universal movement towards the national,

---

[16] L. L. Pasinetti, *Growth and Income Distribution* (Cambridge, 1974), p. 42.

[17] Keynes, *General Theory*, pp. 164, 378.

state-directed organization of economic life. These changes – together with technical innovations such as the development of national-income accounting – made Keynes's policies of demand management both organizationally feasible and politically acceptable.

It is therefore not surprising that Keynes posthumously received the credit for the long boom of the 1950s and 1960s. From a historical point of view, this is as just (or unjust) as the tendency to blame him for the shift at the end of the 1960s towards 'stagflation' – in other words, the return of serious recessions combined with accelerating inflation. The most visible attack on Keynesian economics took the form of a revival of Hume's quantity theory of money, according to which price rises are caused exclusively by an increase in the amount of money in the economy.

Monetarism, chiefly associated with the Chicago economist Milton Friedman, enjoined on the basis of this diagnosis a return to *laissez faire*, in which governments should confine their activities to keeping the money supply constant, thereby creating a stable policy environment within which market actors could freely pursue their private goals. This doctrine was notable for reinstating both the distinction between the 'real economy' and money which Keynes had sought to dismantle, and the idea that public policy could not prevent the former from gravitating towards a 'natural' rate of unemployment. Keynesian economists such as Nicholas Kaldor were able to expose the theoretical and practical defects of monetarism, but this did not prevent it legitimizing the pursuit by British governments from 1976 onwards of policies that devastated the economy.

A far more powerful *laissez-faire* riposte had already been formulated during the 1930s and 1940s by Keynes's younger contemporary Hayek, who outlived him by nearly fifty years to see the apparent triumph of market capitalism at the end of the 1980s.[18] Hayek was a product of the Austrian tradition of marginalist economics which had always been far more sceptical than its counterparts elsewhere about the theory of perfect competition – the attempt to define the conditions under which a market economy will attain an equilibrium at which resources are optimally allocated. The definition of perfect competition typically involves highly restrictive, and indeed unrealistic, conditions – notably that no individual consumer or producer can influence the price of any commodity, and that actors are perfectly informed about the future.

Hayek directs especial criticism at the latter condition: 'it is assumed that the data for the different individuals are fully adjusted to each other, while the problem which requires explanation is the nature of the process by which

[18] Friedrich August von Hayek (1899–1992): born in Vienna, son of a municipal official; studied law and economics at the University of Vienna, 1918–23; director, Austrian Institute of Business Cycle Research, 1927–32; Tooke Professor of Economic Science and Statistics, London School of Economics, 1932–50; Professor of Social and Moral Sciences, University of Chicago, 1950–62; Professor of Economic Policy, University of Freiburg, 1962–8; Professor of Economics, University of Salzburg, 1968–77; awarded the Nobel Prize for Economics in 1974.

the data are thus adjusted'. Equilibrium theory, which models markets through a set of simultaneous equations, ignores the fact that economic processes unfold over time, with actors constantly adjusting to each other through a series of initiatives which prevents the attainment of perfect equilibrium: 'competition is by its nature a dynamic process whose essential characteristics are assumed away by the assumptions underlying static analysis'.[19]

These arguments recall the stress laid by Keynes on time and uncertainty. But Hayek's overall analysis is radically different. Far from depending for their proper functioning on actors having perfect information, markets are the most effective way of *acquiring* information: 'I propose to consider competition as a procedure for the discovery of such facts as, without resort to it, would not be known to anyone, or at least would not be utilitized.'[20] Information, to be useful in addressing the central economic problem of how to respond to change, must be specific, reflecting the peculiar circumstances of time and place. Such information is, by the nature of the things, dispersed among individual economic actors.

The market, through the fluctuations of the relative prices of commodities, acts as a mechanism for transmitting these scattered bits of knowledge. These prices reflect the preferences attached to goods and services by individual actors; in the marginal utility of every commodity is 'condensed its significance for the whole means–end structure'. 'The whole acts as one market,' therefore, 'not because any of its members survey the whole field, but because their limited individual fields of vision sufficiently overlap so that through many intermediaries the relevant information is communicated to all.' Thus 'the real function' of 'the price system' is 'as such a mechanism for communicating information'.[21]

This theory allowed Hayek to argue that any system of central planning would necessarily lead to a less than optimal allocation of resources. The statistical summaries on which planning decisions were based 'would have to be arrived at precisely by abstracting from minor differences by lumping together, as resources of one kind, items which differ as regards location, quality and other particulars in a way which may be very significant for the specific decision'.[22] Only the market, as a decentralized system of communication, could mobilize the inherently dispersed pieces of information required for economically rational decisions. This argument was Hayek's contribution to a debate initiated by the Austrian economist Ludwig von Mises, who claimed that socialist planning was a logical impossibility. But it also struck home at Keynes's mandarin

---

[19]   F. A. von Hayek, *Individualism and the Economic Order* (London, 1949), p. 94.
[20]   F. A. von Hayek, *New Studies in Philosophy, Politics, Economics and the History of Ideas* (London, 1978), p. 179.
[21]   Hayek, *Individualism*, pp. 85, 86.
[22]   Ibid., p. 83.

belief that an enlightened state bureaucracy was more likely to make well-informed decisions – for example, about the marginal efficiency of capital – than individual economic actors.

Following Adam Smith, Hayek believes that capitalism, or, as he prefers to call it, 'the extended order of human co-operation', 'resulted not from human design or intention but *spontaneously*'. But he does not think that the logic of the market economy arises from tendencies inherent in human nature such as Smith's 'propensity to truck, barter and exchange' (see §1.3 above). On the contrary, human instincts were formed during an evolutionary process spanning several million years during which successive species of hominids lived in small bands whose members relied heavily on one another for survival. 'These modes of co-ordination depended decisively on instincts of solidarity and altruism – instincts applying to the members of one's own group but not to others . . . The primitive individualism described by Thomas Hobbes is hence a myth. The savage is not solitary, and his instinct is collectivist. There was never a "war of all against all".'[23]

The 'extended order' thus developed *against* this 'instinctual order', in particular through the gradual evolution of systems of learnt rules such as legal and moral codes, among whose unintended consequences was, over time, the formation of private property and markets, and the differentiation of the individual from his or her social context. Thus: 'The [extended] order is even "unnatural" in the common meaning of not conforming to man's biological endowment.'[24] Socialism and less extreme forms of collectivism such as the postwar Keynesian welfare state are therefore atavistic, politically and economically disastrous attempts to return to the narrow solidarity of the band societies in which human nature acquired, through natural selection, its biological constitution.

In their effort to combat collectivism, Hayek and his fellow Austrian, the philosopher of science Karl Popper, further elaborated the doctrine of methodological individualism which Carl Menger and Max Weber had already championed, according to which social structures are the unintended consequences of individual actions. Ernest Gellner, like Hayek and Popper a central European intellectual who found refuge in Britain from the horrors of the mid-century, speculates that the embattled, anxious tone of what he calls 'the Viennese Theory' may have been 'inspired by the fact that, in the nineteenth century, the individualistic, atomized, cultured bourgeoisie of the Habsburg capital had to contend with the influx of swarms of kin-bound, collectivistic, rule-ignoring migrants from the eastern marches of the Empire, from the Balkans and Galicia'.[25]

Whether or not this *aperçu* is correct, Hayek's economics represents

[23] F. A. von Hayek, *The Fatal Conceit* (London, 1988), pp. 6, 12.
[24] Ibid., p. 19.
[25] E. Gellner, *Plough, Sword and Book* (London, 1988), p. 28.

the most serious defence of the market yet mounted. But this defence involves
a crucial inconsistency. Hayek's use of the term 'order' to characterize the social cohesion achieved by the market reflects his desire to distance himself from
equilibrium analysis: 'While an economic equilibrium never really exists, there
is some justification for asserting that the kind of order of which our theory
describes an ideal type, is approached in a high degree.' But this raises the
question, central to Keynes's critique of neo-classical orthodoxy, of the nature
and extent of the economic stability attained by this 'order': in particular, do
recessions and the mass unemployment they produce arise from the normal
functioning of markets or from their distortion? In selecting the latter alternative, Hayek tends to fall back on the idea that the market economy is self-
equilibrating. Thus, rejecting Keynes's explanation of recessions as a
consequence of insufficient aggregate demand, he restates the traditional *laissez-
faire* view: 'The cause of unemployment . . . is a deviation of prices and wages
from their equilibrium position that would establish itself with a free market
and stable money.'[26]

Hayek's own theory of crises, developed in *Prices and Production* (1931),
treated them as a consequence of over-investment made possible by the creation of money through the credit system. As Skidelsky observes, 'his conclusion, like Keynes's, was that a credit-money capitalist system is violently
unstable – only with this difference, that nothing could be done about it'.[27] It is
little wonder that John Strachey, a leading Marxist economist in the 1930s,
made extensive (though critical) use of *Prices and Production*, calling it 'a
theory of capitalist crisis and of the trade cycle that made sense'.[28] Yet it seems
as though Hayek's commitment to the 'extended order' led him to combine this
esoteric doctrine, which came close to admitting that crises are an endemic
feature of capitalism, with the exoteric, and indeed apologetic, view that they
arise from some maladjustment of the market.

Another Austrian economist, Joseph Schumpeter, was more willing to acknowledge the implications of rejecting the theory of perfect competition. He
argued that capitalism is 'incessantly revolutionized *from within* by new enterprise, i.e., by the intrusion of new commodities or new methods of production
or new commercial opportunities into the industrial structure as it exists at any
moment. Every situation is being upset before it has had time to work itself
out.' The regular oscillations of output and employment characteristic of the
business cycle are a consequence of '[t]his process of Creative Destruction',
which is 'the essential fact about capitalism'.[29]

Schumpeter gives Marx the credit for having first formulated this analysis in

[26]   Hayek, *New Studies*, pp. 184, 200.
[27]   Skidelsky, *Keynes*, II, p. 457.
[28]   J. Strachey, *The Theory of Capitalist Crisis* (London, 1935), p. 58.
[29]   J. A. Schumpeter (1942), *Capitalism, Socialism and Democracy* (London, 1976), pp. 31–2, 83.

his theory of capital accumulation. Indeed, despite the disdain Keynes expresses for Marx, and Hayek's loathing for him, many of their arguments are anticipated in *Capital*. The schemes for the reproduction of capital in Volume II provide the formal means for developing the kind of analysis for which Keynes used the concept of effective demand. In Part V of Volume III Marx analyses the development of the credit system, stressing its contribution to crises of overproduction, and noting the destructive consequences of attempts by central banks to cure such crises by restricting the money supply. In sum, the most sophisticated theorizations of the capitalist economy, whether by the neo-liberal Hayek, the reformer Keynes, or the revolutionary Marx all highlight its inherent instability.

10.2 Functionalist sociology: Talcott Parsons

The most influential social theory produced in the Western world in the mid-century, by contrast, focused on social stability. For Parsons, the tendency of a given social system to maintain itself is 'the first *law of social process*'.[30] His first major work, *The Structure of Social Action* (1937), was a systematic critical survey of European social theory concentrating on Pareto, Durkheim, and Weber. Pierre Bourdieu has rather contemptuously dismissed this work – and indeed Parsons' overall achievement – as that of a mediocre vulgarizer: 'In some ways, Parsons was to the European sociological tradition what Cicero had been to Greek philosophy; he takes the original authors and retranslates them into a rather limp language, producing a syncretic message, an academic combination of Weber, Durkheim and Pareto – but, of course, not Marx.'[31]

Parsons is, however, a more interesting thinker than this harsh judgement suggests. He was indeed very hostile to Marx, participating in the anti-Marxist 'Pareto Circle' at Harvard during the 1930s, at a time when Marxism was exerting a powerful attraction on young intellectuals in Depression America. During his studies in Germany in the 1920s, he had been heavily influenced by the critique of Marxism offered by Weber and by Werner Sombart. Alvin Gouldner suggests: 'Much of Parsons' theoretical work is shaped by these two powerful impulses clearly manifested in his earliest work: (1) by his effort to *generalize* the anti-Marxist critique, and (2) at the same time, by his effort to overcome the *determinism*, the pessimism, and indeed the anti-capitalism of these critics of Marxism.'[32]

[30] T. Parsons, *The Social System* (London, 1951), p. 205. Talcott Parsons (1902–79): born in Colorado Springs, son of a Congregationalist minister; majored in biology at Amherst College, 1920–4; studied at the London School of Economics, 1924–5, and the University of Heidelberg, 1924–6; member of the Faculty of Harvard University, 1926–73; founder member of the Department of Sociology, 1931; chairman of the Department of Social Relations, 1946–56; first social scientist to be elected president of the American Academy of Arts and Sciences, 1967.
[31] P. Bourdieu, *In Other Words* (Cambridge, 1990), p. 37.
[32] A. Gouldner, *The Coming Crisis of Western Sociology* (London, 1971), p. 183.

The central theme of *The Structure of Social Action* is indeed the development of a 'voluntaristic theory of action' first clearly formulated by Weber. Parsons contrasts this theory with what he calls the 'positivistic theory of action' which informs the utilitarian tradition (understood very broadly). Utilitarianism is essentially defined by its modelling all action on what Weber calls instrumentally rational action (see §7.2 above). Instrumentally rational actors select the most effective means to achieve their chosen ends. But,

> though the conception of action as consisting in the pursuit of ends is fundamental, there is nothing in the theory dealing with the relations of the ends to each other, but only with the character of the means–end relationship . . . the failure to state anything positive about the relation of means and ends to each other can then have only one meaning – that there are no significant relations, that ends are random in the statistical sense.[33]

Parsons then proceeds to demonstrate that utilitarianism thus understood is unable to account for the existence of social order. In particular, Hobbes's state of nature (see §1.3 above) depicts the inevitable consequence of a state of affairs where instrumentally rational actors pursue their 'random' ends in circumstances of scarcity: 'A purely utilitarian society is chaotic and unstable, because in the absence of limitations on the use of means, particularly force and fraud, it must, in the nature of the case, resolve itself into an unlimited struggle for power.' Hobbes's achievement was to identify 'the problem with a clarity that has never been surpassed', but he offers no satisfactory solution to it. Much subsequent social theory, disabled by its reliance on the deeply embedded assumptions of the positivistic theory of action, has been unable even to pose the problem. Parsons casts the net wide in his critique of utilitarianism. Thus Marx has the merit of reintroducing 'the factor of differences of power into social thinking, which had been so important in Hobbes's philosophy and so neglected since', but historical materialism is, 'fundamentally, a version of utilitarian individualism'.[34]

Parsons traces the gradual emergence of the solution to 'the Hobbesian Problem of Order', the voluntaristic theory of action, through two parallel processes: the disintegration of the positivistic tradition, in which Pareto and Durkheim, along with the marginalist economist Alfred Marshall, play a major role; and the development from German idealism of Weberian sociology. This intellectual evolution makes possible the formulation of 'the action frame of reference'. This involves distinguishing four 'structural elements' of action – 'end, means, conditions, and norms'.[35] The first three of these elements are also present in the positivistic theory of action. Instrumentally rational actors select

---

[33]   T. Parsons, *The Structure of Social Action* (2 vols, New York, 1968), I, p. 59.

[34]   Ibid., I, pp. 93–4, 109, 110.

[35]   Ibid., II, p. 732; see also I, pp. 43ff.

efficacious means for achieving their ends relative to conditions representing the objective context of their action. The introduction of norms, however, constitutes a radically new element. It is their role in specifying and reconciling the ends of individual actors, and integrating them with the ends of other actors which provides the solution to the problem of order.

Parsons can therefore legitimately be regarded as offering a version of what David Lockwood calls 'normative functionalism', according to which 'society is a moral and ultimately a religious entity whose intrinsic nature is a set of commonly held values and beliefs'.[36] He declares, for example: 'The problem of order, and thus of the nature of stable systems of social interaction, that is, of social structure, thus focuses on the integration of the motivation of actors with the normative cultural standards which integrate the action system, in our context interpersonally.'[37] Though in *The Structure of Social Action* Parsons lays great stress on Weber's contribution to the development of the voluntaristic theory of action, his approach to social theory seems in fact much closer to Durkheim's. Indeed, he declared in 1967: 'My own inclination is to refer above all to Durkheim (*The Division of Labour in Society*, especially) as the fountainhead of the primary fruitful trend.'[38]

It would nevertheless be a mistake to see Parsons' theory as a kind of sociological idealism in which social structures are somehow an expression of norms and values. 'Action must be thought of as involving a state of tension between two different orders of elements, the normative and the conditional', he writes in 1937. 'As process, action is, in fact, the process of alteration of the conditional elements in the direction of conformity to norms.' Ignoring the normative dimension leads to utilitarianism; getting rid of the objective conditions of action leads to what he calls 'idealistic emanationism'.[39] After the Second World War, Parsons sought to construct a rigorous sociological theory by, in particular, analysing the *systematic* properties of societies that allow them to maintain and reproduce themselves. Commentators are divided over the extent to which this shift in focus represents a conceptual break with Parsons' earlier writings, which follow Weber and the German neo-Kantian tradition in stressing the intentional character of human action and its irreducibility to causal processes.

In fact, Parsons' postwar writings involve a series of conceptual recastings, all of which bear an intelligible relationship to the problem-situation defined in *The Structure of Social Action*: namely, what theory of action can account for the existence of social order? His growing preoccupation with social systems reflects a succession of attempts to address this problem in a manner consistent with the the fact that societies are (among other things) complex articulations

---

[36] D. Lockwood, *Solidarity and Schism* (Oxford, 1992), pp. 7–8.
[37] Parsons, *Social System*, pp. 36–7.
[38] Quoted in Gouldner, *Coming Crisis*, p. 163 n. 27.
[39] Parsons, *Structure*, II, p. 732.

of social structures (Parsons has no time for methodological individualism). Running through all the different versions is an emphatic conception of *theory*. From the 1930s onwards Parsons conducts a relentless critique of empiricism, which he argues fails to distinguish how we experience the world from the analytical concepts required to explain that world. This privileging of theory represents one strategy for the professionalization of sociology: rather than being driven by different forms of empirical research, the development of the discipline depends on the formulation of rigorous concepts that can provide research with the appropriate guidance. It is presumably because of this conception of social enquiry, which is plainly modelled on theoretical physics, that Parsons tends to rely on an arcane technical vocabulary that achieves rigour, often at the price of rendering his writings opaque to the uninitiated reader.

The Social System (1951) represents the first full statement of what Parsons himself calls his 'structural functionalism'. He defines a social system as 'a mode of organization of action-elements relative to the persistence or ordered processes of change of the interactive patterns of a plurality of individual actors'. It is not the only systematic feature of human action: 'The other two are the personality systems of individual actors and the cultural system which is built into their actions.'[40] (Parsons later adds a fourth, the 'behavioural organism'.) The social system is thus crucially concerned with the problem of how human interactions are stably integrated. A determinate pattern of social interaction involves a differentiated structure of roles involving specific powers and rewards to which actors are allocated.

How then can the reproduction of a particular social system with its differential rewards be secured? 'The basic condition on which an interaction system can be stabilized is for the interests of the actors to be bound to conformity with a shared system of value-orientation standards.' These standards offer a particular way of defining the ends of action, and more specifically of offering the actor a set of expectations about the roles he or she can legitimately hope to occupy. They originate in the cultural system, but social stability depends on their institutionalization. Parsons develops an elaborate classification of the 'pattern-variables of role-definition', but concedes that there are in fact two historically significant combinations of value-orientations which are permutations of just two pattern variables – 'Universalism vs. Particularism', and 'Achievement vs. Ascription'. The first concerns the justification of social roles – are they legitimized by some universally applicable standard such as scientific rationality or human rights, or by the traditions specific to a given society? Secondly, are social roles filled on the basis of the status ascribed to actors, typically through the position inherited from their parents, or may the individual legitimately aspire to the place in society that corresponds to the achievements reflecting his or her own abilities? Parsons says that 'the great majority

[40]   Parsons, *Social System*, pp. 24, 6.

of known societies' are instances of 'the Particularistic-Ascription Pattern'; modern industrial societies, notably the United States, exemplify the 'Universalistic-Achievement Pattern'.[41]

The institutionalization of such value-orientations represents the point of interface between the cultural and the social systems. Each is irreducible to the other, but securing the 'functional prerequisites' of the social system requires a minimum degree of compatibility between the two. 'It is a cardinal principle of the theory of action that culture . . . becomes directly constitutive of personalities', Parsons holds. This occurs through the 'internalization' of norms and beliefs by individual actors. Consequently: 'It is only by virtue of the internalization of institutionalized values that a genuine motivational integration of behaviour in the social structure takes place.' This occurs primarily through 'the *mechanisms of socialization*', a series of learning processes, crucially in the stages of infancy and childhood (society is constantly subject to a 'barbarian invasion' by babies unschooled in its ways) located in the household, school, etc., which 'tend to bring about . . . the internalization of certain patterns of value-orientation' which shape individuals' expectations about the social roles they can legitimately expect to occupy.[42]

Any partial failure of socialization is likely to give rise to deviance, 'a disturbance of the equilibrium of the interaction system' arising from 'a motivated tendency for an actor [or actors] to behave in contravention of one or more institutionalized normative patterns'. This gives rise to various mechanisms of social control, whose role is to restore equilibrium, either through some form of direct repression or, more subtly, through the development of 'secondary institutions' which permit limited forms of deviant behaviour in contexts where they are insulated from the rest of society: gambling and the rituals of 'American youth culture' are examples of such safety-valves for the expression of alienation.[43]

This analysis of deviance indicates that Parsons does not, as critics sometimes claim, simply ignore or deny the existence of social conflict. He makes it clear that '[e]xact coincidence' between 'the interests of the collectivity and the interests of its individual members' is 'a limiting case' rather than a condition that is likely actually to obtain. Nevertheless his functionalism does presume that societies are self-equilibrating systems: thus he calls the proposition that 'the stabilization of the processes of mutual orientation within complementary roles is a fundamental "tendency" of interaction . . . *a theoretical assumption, not an empirical generalization*'. Societies by definition will tend to a condition of stability. Deviance therefore evokes mechanisms of social control whose effect is to counter and contain it. Its existence and that of 'social strains' are

---

[41] Ibid., pp. 38, 66–7, 181, 182ff.
[42] Ibid., pp. 34, 42, 205, 208–9.
[43] Ibid., pp. 250, 360ff.

secondary phenomena rather than being constitutive of social life. Contrary to Marx's belief that structural contradictions and class struggle are responsible for social change, '[s]train is not itself a "prime mover"'.[44] For example, Parsons argues that the McCarthyite witch-hunts of the 1950s are 'best understood as a symptom of the strains attendant on a deep-seated process of change in our society', namely the transformation of the US into both an industrial society and a global superpower.[45]

The extent of Parsons's commitment to a functionalist conception of the social is demonstrated in his writings subsequent to *The Social System*. Thus he rejects C. Wright Mills' thesis that American society is dominated by a 'power-elite' of the corporate rich and the military and civilian bureaucracies as not simply empirically mistaken, but conceptually flawed. Mills relies on 'the "zero-sum" concept of power; power, that is to say, is power *over* others. The power A has in a system is, necessarily and by definition, at the expense of B.' So if public and private bureaucrats have more power, then others must have less. This concept of power thus builds conflict into its very definition: it thereby 'elevate[s] a secondary and derived aspect of a total phenomenon into the central place'. This 'total phenomenon' is in fact concerned with the achievement of common goals, not the pursuit of social and political conflict:

> Power is a generalized facility or resource in the society. It has to be divided or allocated, but it also has to be produced and it has collective as well as distributive functions. It is the capacity to mobilize the resources of society for the attainment of goals for which a general 'public' commitment has been made, or may be made. It is mobilization, above all, of the action of persons and groups, which is *binding* on them by virtue of their position in society.[46]

Parsons develops this conception of power as part of his attempt further to refine his theory of the social system. From *Economy and Society* (1956) onwards, he argues that the social system is differentiated into four 'sub-systems': the economy, the polity, 'pattern maintenance', through which culture provides the values governing action, and the 'societal community', the normative order necessary for integration.[47] Thus the polity is 'an analytically defined, a "functional" sub-system of a society'. Its 'value-reference' is effectiveness, just as the economy's is utility. Both involve a 'generalized medium' which offers 'a "measure" of the relevant values' – in the economy, money, in the polity, power. Parsons takes the comparison so far as to argue that just as (in the days of the gold standard) gold acted as the ultimate linchpin of monetary systems which normally dealt in paper and credit, force underpins consent in the realm of

---

[44]   Ibid., pp. 42, 42 n. 11, 481, 493.
[45]   T. Parsons, *Politics and Social Structure* (New York, 1969), p. 181.
[46]   Ibid., pp. 199, 200.
[47]   T. Parsons, *The System of Modern Societies* (Engelwood Cliffs, NJ, 1971) p. 11, table 2.

political power. 'Force, therefore, is in the first instance important as the "ulti-mate deterrent". It is the means that . . . can be assumed to be "intrinsically" the most effective in the context of deterrence, where means of effectiveness which *are* dependent on an institutionalized order are insecure or fail.' Like gold, it is always present, but, outside crises, rarely used to secure stability.[48]

The concept of differentiation also plays a critical role in Parsons's theory of social change. In *The Social System* he declares: 'We do *not* in the present state of knowledge possess a general theory of the processes of change in society as a whole.'[49] But by the 1960s he is offering a theory not simply of social change but of evolution: 'Socio-cultural evolution, like organic evolution, has proceeded by variation and differentiation from simple to progressively more complex.' By contrast with his earlier endorsement of Weber's anti-naturalism, Parsons now treats 'man as integral to the organic world and human society as properly analysed in the general framework appropriate to the life-process'. He lays prime emphasis on 'the process of *differentiation*. A unit, sub-system, or category of units or sub-systems having a single, relatively well-defined place in the soci-ety divides into units or systems (usually two) which differ in *both* structure and functional significance for the wider system.'[50] For example, the key to the Industrial Revolution lay in 'the differentiation of labour from the diffuse matrix in which it had been embedded. This differentiation involved distin-guishing the work-role complex from the family household and also increasing the mobility of "labour".'[51]

Parsons sees the polity as the locus of differentiation, but this process has implications for all the other sub-systems. Differentiation usually involves '*adapt-ive upgrading*', whereby the new structures perform their function more effect-ively than the old one did, typically through the economy's increased ability to meet agents' needs and wants. The society's normative order is also likely to change: integrating the more differentiated system of roles 'requires that specialized functional capacities be freed from ascription within more diffuse structural units'. Finally, the greater complexity of the new structure implies that 'its value-pattern must be couched at a higher level of *generality* in order to legitimize the wider variety of goals and functions of its sub-units'.[52]

Now this is all rather familiar. Spencer after all developed a theory of social evolution as a process of progressive differentiation culminating in the indus-trial societies of modern Europe and North America (see §5.2); this theory provided Durkheim with a crucial dimension of his problem-situation, espe-cially in *The Division of Labour*. We seem to have come full circle. This is

[48]   Parsons, *Politics*, pp. 354, 355, 365–6.
[49]   Parsons, *Social System*, p. 537.
[50]   T. Parsons, *Societies: Evolutionary and Comparative Perspectives* (Englewood Cliffs, NJ, 1966), pp. 2, 22.
[51]   Parsons, *System*, p. 77.
[52]   Parsons, *Societies*, pp. 22, 23.

especially ironic since *The Structure of Social Action* famously begins with a quotation from Crane Brinton: 'Who reads Spencer now?'[53] As Gouldner observes, 'the answer in the 1960s must be, Parsons himself'.[54]

Of course, Parsons' late, evolutionary social theory is not a simple reprise of Spencerian sociology. It is a development of a theory of action which is intended precisely to avoid the impasses of the utilitarian tradition of which Parsons sees Spencer as a late representative. He owes to biology rather than to any sociological predecessor the concept of a self-maintaining system. Moreover, the distinction he draws between the cultural system and the social system introduces a distinctive tension into his social theory. The values which provide the basis for the norms forming the basis of social integration and socialization derive from outside the social system itself. As Habermas puts it, this 'makes it possible for him to import the Kantian dualism of values and facts into systems functionalism'.[55] Had Parsons, like Weber before him, thematized the impossibility of rationally justifying ultimate values, he might have offered a very different perspective on societies, one which highlighted their dependence on rationally indefensible clusters of values.

As it is, Parsons' account of social evolution concentrates on portraying modern Western societies as the culmination of a historical process which he regards as essentially beneficent. His conception of differentiation implies that the drift of development is in the direction of the 'Universalistic-Achievement Pattern' which already in *The Social System* he claims to be characteristic of industrial societies, especially the US. As for the rest, '[i]nsofar as an action system is highly primitive . . . it will be highly *undifferentiated* at the social, cultural, and personality levels'.[56] We need not fear the movement away from primitive diffuseness. Weber exaggerated the dangers of rationalization: 'the main trend is not actually towards increased bureaucracy . . . but rather towards associationism'. Modern liberal democracies have highly pluralistic structures which impede the illegitimate concentration of power. Meanwhile: 'The main direction of modern societal development is towards an essentially new pattern of stratification.' No longer can inequalities be justified on the basis of ascribed status. For 'the new egalitarianism' inequalities are legitimate only when '*functional* to the society conceived as a system'. Furthermore, this 'trend towards modernization has now become worldwide'.[57]

Parsons' functionalist sociology is reminiscent of the great theological system constructed by St Thomas Aquinas in the thirteenth century. Aquinas developed subtle distinctions and sometimes illuminating arguments in order to defend a core of Christian doctrine which included dogmas such as that of the

---

[53] Parsons, *Structure*, I, p. 3.
[54] Gouldner, *Coming Crisis*, p. 357.
[55] J. Habermas, *The Theory of Communicative Action*, II (Cambridge, 1987), p. 226.
[56] Parsons, *Societies*, p. 33.
[57] Parsons, *System*, pp. 116, 119, 137.

Trinity. Similarly, Parsons elaborated a complex set of concepts and propositions at whose centre is a hard nugget of irrationality. This does not derive simply from the way in which the values on which the social system depends for its functioning are givens produced by the cultural system. Parsons' evolutionary theory involves an implicit teleology. Stephen P. Savage writes: 'Socio-cultural evolution is more than a process of increasing efficiency in social relations – it is a developmental process . . . It is the passage from an "animal existence" . . . to the highest level of human existence – the form of socio-cultural organization represented in Western societies.'[58] Little wonder, then, that Parsonian sociology provided the conceptual framework within which American theorists of 'modernization' sought to persuade newly independent countries to adopt a Western model of development. Where Weber had surveyed the formation of modernity with deep forebodings, Parsons now suggested we sit back and enjoy the ride.

10.3 Despairing critique: the Frankfurt School

Parsonian sociology enjoyed an enormous international influence during the 1950s and 1960s. Alvin Gouldner wrote at the end of the latter decade: 'More than any other academic sociologist of any nationality, Parsons is a world figure.'[59] No doubt his status was to some extent a consequence of the new-found position of the US as the leading power in the international state system. Moreover, from mid-century onwards, the vast and wealthy American university system began to exert a growing gravitational pull on Western intellectual life (though, paradoxically, this has often taken the form of the promotion of imported theories). In any case, Parsons' basically optimistic view of the trajectory taken by modernity could claim support from the actual experience of societies which were experiencing unprecedented prosperity and stability.

This does not mean that structural functionalism ever went unchallenged. There were dissenters even within American sociology. Thus from a methodological point of view, Robert K. Merton sought to specify and thereby to rein in the ambitions of functional analysis; he also argued that what he called 'theories of the middle range' – theories, that is, constructed to guide empirical research – were more likely than Parsonian grand theory to produce results.[60] C. Wright Mills, a Texan prairie rebel who identified strongly with American radical movements such as the Populists and the Wobblies, poured scorn on Parsons' opaque verbiage in *The Sociological Imagination* (1959), and waged

---

[58] S. P. Savage, *The Theories of Talcott Parsons* (London, 1981), pp. 232–3.
[59] Gouldner, *Coming Crisis*, p. 168.
[60] R. K. Merton, 'Manifest and Latent Functions', and 'Sociological Theories of the Middle Range', in id., *Social Theory and Social Structure* (New York, 1968).

relentless war in books such as *The Power Elite* (1956) on what he regarded as the inequality and alienation endemic in US society.

But the most systematic critique of the apparently pacified and contented Western societies during the Long Boom came from elsewhere. The Frankfurt School is the collective name given to a group of German intellectuals who sought to continue Marxist theory in an idiosyncratic form and in unfavourable conditions. It originated in the Institute for Social Research set up at Frankfurt University in 1923. The finance came (as it was to do for many years) from Felix Weil, the son of a wealthy grain merchant. Weil later described himself as having been a 'salon Bolshevik' in the early 1920s; the establishment of the Institute reflected the influence of different variants of Marxism – the rival orthodoxies of the Social Democratic and Communist Parties and the heresies of Hegelian Marxism – on a substantial section of the Weimar intelligentsia. The first director of the Institute was the Austrian economist and historian Carl Grünburg. At the opening ceremony in June 1924 he expressed a commitment to an optimistic Kautskyan determinism, declaring himself to be among those who were 'firmly, scientifically convinced that the emerging order will be a socialist one, that we are in the midst of a transition from capitalism to socialism and are advancing toward the latter with gathering speed'.[61]

Under Grünberg's directorship, the Institute pursued research of a broadly orthodox Marxist character. Its staff included the economist Henryk Grossman, the author of an important work on crisis theory, and the Orientalist Karl Wittfogel, in the 1920s and early 1930s an active member of the German Communist Party (KPD). The Institute's character changed radically after Grünberg was incapacitated by a stroke, and replaced as director in 1930 by Max Horkheimer.[62] The change occurred along two dimensions.

In the first place, Horkheimer, as a philosopher, intellectually reoriented the Institute. In his inaugural lecture in January 1931, he proposed a programme of collective research directed at specific social groups, particularly the working class, that could elucidate the problem of the relationship between reason and history. This would be 'a dictatorship of planned work in place of the mere juxtaposition of philosophical construction and empirical research in social enquiry'.[63] Martin Jay observes: 'If it can be said that in the early years of its history the Institut concerned itself primarily with the analysis of bourgeois society's socio-economic substructure, in the years after 1930 its prime interest

[61] Quoted in R. Wiggershaus, *The Frankfurt School* (Cambridge, Mass., 1994), pp. 13, 25.

[62] Max Horkheimer (1895–1973): born in Stuttgart, son of a rich Jewish textile manufacturer; studied philosophy at Frankfurt University; Professor of Social Philosophy, Frankfurt University, 1930–3; restored to his chair in 1949; Rector of Frankfurt University, 1951–3; after retiring in 1959 moved to Switzerland.

[63] M. Horkheimer, *Between Philosophy and Social Science*, ed. G. F. Hunter (Cambridge, Mass., 1995), p. 11.

lay in its cultural superstructure.'[64] This preoccupation with cultural questions is related to the Institute's receptiveness to psychoanalysis and its various attempts to integrate the thought of Marx and Freud. Others during the inter-war years were similarly minded – for example (in very different ways), Trotsky, Wilhelm Reich, and André Breton – but the Frankfurt School represented the first attempt systematically to hitch together the apparently very different conceptual structures of historical materialism and psychoanalysis.

Horkheimer's assumption of leadership also marked a change in the Institute's relationship with the workers' movement. Hitherto, the Institute had been in a very loose sense a fellow-traveller of the international Communist movement. Many of its staff were members of the KPD or of dissident Communist groups. Some were activists: in 1931 Wittfogel abandoned his studies to throw himself into political work aimed at preventing the Nazis coming to power. Horkheimer shared these pro-Moscow political sympathies, at least till the late 1930s. In 1930 he called 'events in Russia . . . a continuation of the agonizing attempt to overcome horrifying injustices'.[65] But he nevertheless sought systematically to distance the Institute from any association with the organized left and to present it as a purely academic enterprise. The very name 'Marxism' was bowdlerized as 'Critical Theory'.

This relocation of Marxism into the academy represented a major shift. Hitherto leading Marxist intellectuals had typically worked for the political movement: this was true, for example, of Kautsky, Lenin, Luxemburg, Trotsky, Lukács, and Gramsci. This was partly a function of the universities' discrimination against the left (thus Robert Michels, while a Marxist, was unable to obtain an academic position in Germany), but, more fundamentally, it reflected Marx's rejection of a contemplative conception of theory divorced from political practice. Perry Anderson sees Horkheimer's attempt to give the Institute an essentially academic identity as symptomatic of a more universal process, the emergence of a 'Western Marxism' divorced from the working-class movement and dominated by academic philosophers: 'After the Second World War . . . Marxist theory had migrated virtually completely into the universities – precincts at once of refuge and of exile from the political struggles in the world outside.'[66]

Anderson stresses the importance of the political context in this development: 'The hidden hallmark of Western Marxism is thus that it is a product of *defeat*.'[67] The isolation of the Russian Revolution made possible the transformation of Bolshevism into Stalinism. By the late 1920s, Marxism could no longer be pursued in the Soviet Union as critical intellectual enquiry but had been transformed into the state ideology of 'Marxism–Leninism'. Meanwhile,

---

[64]   M. Jay, *The Dialectical Imagination* (London, 1973), p. 21.
[65]   Quoted in Wiggershaus, *Frankfurt School*, p. 63.
[66]   P. Anderson, *Considerations on Western Marxism* (London, 1976), pp. 59–60
[67]   Ibid., p. 42.

the 1930s were marked by a series of stunning defeats for the European left: the Nazi seizure of power in 1933; the destruction of the Austrian workers' movement in 1934; and Franco's victory in the Spanish Civil War (1936–9). These events represented for the members of the Institute more than a demoralizing experience. All of them were Jews: the triumph of fascism therefore constituted for them the most deadly of threats. They were forced to flee into exile. Horkheimer moved in May 1934 to New York, where he re-established the Institute in loose association with Columbia University.

In Horkheimer's case the natural fear engendered by the victories of the Nazis and their allies took an almost pathological form. Soon after his arrival in New York, he wrote: 'things are much worse here than I had thought. We must expect rapid developments in the aggravation of the economic situation. Precisely on that account I'd like to get to know Canada.'[68] After the outbreak of the Second World War, he moved to Los Angeles, even further from the scene of the European drama. Rolf Wiggershaus, in his monumental history of the Frankfurt School, has documented Horkeimer's obsession with conserving Weil's dwindling capital in order to allow him to continue his researches in comfort and safety.

After an exploratory trip to the West Coast, Horkheimer wrote: 'On the whole journey I kept seeing it come up in front of my eyes: "Money is the best protection, money is the best protection, money is. . ."'[69] This obsession led him continually to manipulate the other members of the Institute, all exiles dependent on his financial patronage and eager to enjoy the unique intellectual environment he offered. Some were kept on low salaries or dropped; others were the victims of a strategy of divide-and-rule. Horkheimer, for example, continually played Adorno and Marcuse off against each other, helping to create lasting enmities.[70] This pathological timidity long outlasted its cause: in the late 1950s,

---

[68] Letter to Pollock, 27 May 1934, quoted in Wiggershaus, *Frankfurt School*, p. 143.

[69] Letter to Lowenthal, 25 July 1940, quoted ibid., p. 250.

[70] Theodor Wiesengrund-Adorno (1903–69): born in Frankfurt, son of a Jewish wine-merchant and a Catholic opera singer (he later adopted his mother's surname, Adorno); studied at Frankfurt University; pursued musical studies with Alban Berg and Eduard Steuermann in Vienna (where he was also part of Schoenberg's circle), 1925–8; appointed Extraordinary Professor of Philosophy, Frankfurt University, 1931; after the Nazi seizure of power obtained a research studentship at Merton College Oxford, thanks to the good offices of Keynes, a friend of his father's; moved to New York, 1938: only now formally a member of the Institute; returned to Frankfurt, 1949; only appointed to a full professorship of philosophy and sociology in 1957 after bitter resistance from conservative academics was overcome.

Herbert Marcuse (1898–1979): born in Berlin, son of a Jewish builder and architect; active in the Soldiers' Councils in Berlin during the 1918 Revolution; studied philosophy at Berlin and Freiburg universities; after reading *Being and Time* returned to Freiburg in 1929 to study under Heidegger and Husserl; left Germany, December 1932; joined Institute in 1933; moved to US in 1934; after being gradually squeezed out of the Institute by Horkheimer and Adorno, worked for the Office for Strategic Studies (precursor of CIA), 1942–50; did not return to Germany after the war; taught at Brandeis University 1954–65; temporary appointments at the University of California, San Diego, 1965–70.

now firmly established in conservative West Germany as a notable of Frankfurt University, Horkheimer stopped Adorno (who, although much cleverer, always deferred to him) from supervising Jürgen Habermas's research into what became *The Structural Transformation of the Public Sphere* because he thought the latter was too left-wing.

Fear and exile are not necessarily obstacles to creativity. The timorous Hobbes, faced with the English Revolution of the 1640s, fled to France, and produced a masterpiece, *Leviathan*. The intellectual achievement of the Frankfurt School during the 1930s and 1940s was formidable. I concentrate here on a few leading themes. The theoretical starting-point for the Institute under Horkheimer's leadership was provided by Lukács's *History and Class Consciousness* (see §9.1 above). The central essay, 'Reification and the Consciousness of the Proletariat', demonstrated that it was possible for Marxist philosophy to be conducted at as great a level of sophistication as that of mainstream philosophy. It also offered a new analytical strategy, in which bourgeois society was conceived as a totality unified by the structure of reification: every aspect of social life reflected the commodity fetishism arising from, at the core of the capitalist mode of production, the transformation of the worker into a marketable object.

Lukács was forced to abjure this strategy in order to remain a member of the Communist movement. He told Adorno when they met in Vienna in 1925 'that in his conflict with the Third International his opponents are right, but that concretely and dialectically his own absolute approach to dialectics was necessary'.[71] But how to pursue this project of 'absolute dialectics' which so fascinated left-wing Weimar intellectuals like Adorno and Benjamin?[72] Doing so posed two particular problems for the Frankfurt School.

In the first place, for Lukács the unity of the social totality depended on the role of the proletariat as the identical subject–object of history. But the idea, central to classical Marxism, that the working class is the agent of social emancipation is quite absent from the thought of the Frankfurt School. Summarizing Horkheimer's position in the late 1920s and early 1930s, Wiggershaus writes:

> What was lacking in Horkheimer was the audacious theoretical construction produced by Marx and Lukács, and their view that the proletarian class was driven by the development of history to become a class for itself, and to continue, with self-confidence and under its own leadership, what it was already doing in an alienated form – that is, carrying out the reproduction of society. Horkheimer's

---

[71] Adorno to Kracauer, 17 June 1925, quoted in Wiggershaus, *Frankfurt School*, p. 76.

[72] Walter Benjamin (1892–1940): born in Berlin, son of a wealthy Jewish art-dealer; studied at Freiburg, Berlin, Munich, and Bern universities, 1912–20; active in youth movement; his *Habilitationsschrift* (a post-doctoral thesis required to qualify as a university teacher in Germany) was rejected by the philosophy faculty of Frankfurt University; lived as a writer and translator; after 1933 moved to Paris, where he became an associate of the Institute; committed suicide at Portbou in September 1940 while trying to flee from Vichy France to Spain.

emphasis was on establishing that those living in misery had a right to material egoism and that it was not base to think that 'the improvement of material existence by a more useful restructuring of conditions' was 'the most important thing in the world' . . . It was as if an awareness of the finiteness and transitoriness of human existence was being given a historical-materialist backbone.[73]

This position implied a commitment to the method of Lukácian Marxism, but not to the conception of proletarian self-emancipation which Lukács had inherited from the classical tradition. During the last days of Weimar, the Institute conducted a study of working-class attitudes, from which it concluded that, as Jay puts it, 'the German working class would be far less resistant to a right-wing seizure of power than its militant ideology would suggest'.[74] In a key essay, 'Traditional and Critical Theory' (1937), Horkheimer contrasts what remains a relatively conventional conception of the Marxist method to 'traditional theory', which reflects the intellectual fragmentation caused by the division of labour. Yet he denies that 'critical theory' can, as Lukács argued, simply articulate working-class consciousness:

> Even the situation of the proletariat is, in this society, no guarantee of correct knowledge. The proletariat may indeed have experience of meaninglessness in the form of continuing and increasing wretchedness and injustice in its own life. Yet this awareness is prevented from becoming a social force by the differentiation of the social structure which is still imposed on the proletariat from above and by the opposition between personal [and] class interests which is transcended only at very special moments. Even to the proletariat the world superficially seems quite different than it really is.[75]

This demotion of the working class from the position assigned it by Lukács gave rise to a second problem. The comprehension of society as a totality depends in *History and Class Consciousness* on the role of the proletariat as the identical subject–object. In the absence of this absolute subject, can critical theory still aspire to totalize? As early as his 1931 inaugural lecture Adorno renounced any such totalizing ambition: 'The mind is indeed not capable of producing or grasping the totality of the real, but it may be possible to penetrate the detail, to explode in miniature the mass of merely existing reality.'[76]

This view reflects the influence on Adorno of Benjamin's *The Origin of German Tragic Drama* (1928). Here (grossly to oversimplify) Benjamin argues that in an unredeemed, inherently fragmented world, knowledge consists in the conceptual organization of empirical phenomena into specific constel-

---

[73] Wiggershaus, *Frankfurt School*, p. 51.
[74] Jay, *Dialectical Imagination*, p. 117.
[75] M. Horkheimer, *Critical Theory* (New York, 1972), pp. 213–14.
[76] T. W. Adorno, 'The Actuality of Philosophy', *Telos*, 31 (1977), p. 133.

lations or configurations. These constellations operate like montage in film or like Cubist collages – they are apparently random combinations of images which somehow manage to evoke an idea that is not present in experience. This idiosyncratic conception of method reflects Benjamin's peculiar synthesis of neo-Kantian philosophy, Jewish messianic thought, and avant-garde Modernism. From the late 1920s onwards, he mobilizes this method in an effort, inspired by *History and Class Consciousness*, to arrive at an understanding of bourgeois society at its apogee. In the *Passagen-Werk*, Benjamin's unfinished study of Paris under the Second Empire (1851–70), he orchestrates a vast collection of facts and observations. The thoroughly commodified society they portray is permeated with images of a mythologized past which represent what Susan Buck-Morss calls 'a *re*enchantment of the social world'.[77] These 'dialectical images' are ambiguous: they serve both to legitimize existing society, and to evoke memories of the primitive communism of prehistoric humankind. In their latter aspect they can have a revolutionary potential.

Adorno was in many ways strongly attracted towards what Habermas calls Benjamin's method of 'redemptive critique'. He believed, as he argued in his major philosophical work, *Negative Dialectics* (1966), that the German idealist tradition, culminating in Hegel, had systematically denied any validity to what he called the non-identical – the individual, the particular, the material, the empirical. Everything is instead reduced to the product of absolute, self-constituting subjectivity. One can see how Lukács's concept of the identical subject–object would seem to Adorno a continuation of this tradition rather than a break from it. Benjamin's 'micrological' approach, his preoccupation with tiny details, offered an alternative model for the relationship between thought and its content, one that did not simply efface that content by making it an exemplification of the conceptual, but allowed it its freedom. By constructing constellations one could simultaneously demonstrate the antagonistic character of the existing social world and evoke a genuinely reconciled condition which might come about in the future.

Adorno was, however, highly critical of Benjamin's use of dialectical images in the drafts for the *Passagen-Werk*, and particularly of his tendency to juxtapose cultural and economic phenomena. Adorno objects that it is 'methodologically unfortunate to give conspicuous individual features from the realm of the superstructure a "materialistic" turn by relating them immediately and perhaps even causally to corresponding features of the superstructure. Materialist determination of cultural traits is only possible if it is mediated through the *total social process*.'[78] Benjamin's 'theological' method can thus collapse into vulgar materialism. To ward off this danger, Adorno invokes the Lukacian

---

[77] S. Buck-Morss, *The Dialectics of Seeing* (Cambridge Mass., 1989), p. 253.
[78] Letter to Benjamin, 10 Nov. 1938, in E. Bloch et al., *Aesthetics and Politics* (London, 1977), p. 129.

concepts of totality and mediation. He is able to do so despite his rejection of the 'identitarian' tradition of German idealism because he believes that the effect of commodity fetishism is precisely to transform society into a totality. Thus he writes: 'Even in the theory of the conceptual mediation of all being, Hegel envisaged something decisive in real terms . . . The act of exchange implies the reduction of the products to be exchanged to their equivalents, to something abstract.'[79] The suffocating self-identity of the Absolute Idea thus corresponds to the way in which the exchange of commodities transforms the concrete activities engaged in by human producers into mere quantities of abstract social labour. Idealism thus has a certain historical truth which permits the use of Marxist theory to provide a totalizing view of society.

This is, to say the least, a position that contains within it substantial tensions. These become clear with the later development of the Frankfurt School. The outbreak of the Second World War in September 1939 and the Nazi conquest of western Europe the following summer proved a turning-point. This catastrophe was all the greater because it was preceded by the Hitler–Stalin non-aggression pact: the USSR's betrayal of the anti-fascist movement had a devastating effect on the international left. It was in this context that Benjamin wrote his 'Theses on the Philosophy of History' in which he depicts 'the angel of history' staring aghast at 'the one single catastrophe' that is the past, while 'a storm . . . . from Paradise' blows him willy-nilly into the future. 'This storm is what we call progress.'[80]

The 'Theses' are a powerful critique of the idea of historical progress, and in particular of the complacent determinism shared by both Communist and Social Democratic Parties in the face of fascism. Benjamin himself, even though he was soon to fall victim to Hitler's *Blitzkrieg*, did not abandon his own peculiar version of revolutionary socialism. Thus in the prepatory materials for the 'Theses', he wrote: 'Three moments must be made to penetrate the foundations of the materialist view of history: the discontinuity of historical time; the destructive power of the working class; the tradition of the oppressed.'[81] In the 'Theses' he conceives revolution as a sudden irruption into the 'homogeneous, empty time' of bourgeois society, 'a tiger's leap into the past', in which the memories both of past exploitation and of primitive communism are activated to demolish the existing order.[82]

For the core of the Frankfurt School, however, the catastrophe of 1939–40 finally marked the moment, from their American vantage-point, to say farewell, for the foreseeable future, to the prospect of socialist transformation. In an essay originally published in a private memorial volume for Benjamin in

[79]   T. W. Adorno, 'Sociology and Empirical Research', in Adorno et. al., *The Positivism Dispute in German Sociology* (London, 1976), p. 80.

[80]   W. Benjamin, *Illuminations* (London, 1970), p. 260.

[81]   Quoted in R. Wolin, *Walter Benjamin: An Aesthetic of Redemption* (New York, 1982), p. 261.

[82]   Benjamin, *Illuminations*, p. 263.

1942, Horkheimer argues that the 'authoritarian state', whether Stalinist or fascist, is a form of state capitalism, in which what Marx called the anarchy of the market is overcome, but on a basis that perpetuates exploitation. Any future social revolution will be 'not a further acceleration of progress, but a qualitative leap out of the dimension of progress', for '[a]s long as world history follows its logical course, it fails to fulfil its human destiny.'[83] In the absence of even Benjamin's theory of dialectical images, revolution no longer has any social anchorage, and is thus reduced to a mere hope.

This despairing outlook was reinforced by the move to Los Angeles. The Frankfurt School found themselves part of the community of exiled German intellectuals who took refuge in the city. Horkheimer, living in Pacific Palisades, had the novelists Thomas Mann and Leon Feuchtwanger among his neighbours. There is something ineffably comic in the thought of such immensely refined products of the extraordinarily sophisticated intellectual culture of early twentieth-century Mitteleuropa coming to rest in southern California, the home of Hollywood, capital of what Horkheimer and Adorno were soon to call the 'culture industry'. They experienced Los Angeles as a nightmare of banal consumerism. Mike Davis acerbically comments:

> Exhibiting no interest in the wartime turmoil in the local aircraft plants nor inclined to appreciate the vigorous nightlife of Los Angeles's Central Avenue ghetto, Horkheimer and Adorno focused instead on the little single-family boxes that seemed to absorb the world-historic mission of the proletariat into family-centred consumerism under the direction of radio jingles and magazine ads.[84]

Dialectic of Enlightenment (1947), the collaborative work that was the main intellectual fruit of these years in California, and companion texts, radicalize the earlier Frankfurt School analysis in two fundamental respects. First of all, Horkheimer and Adorno argue that the tendency, characteristic of authoritarian states, to absorb the individual into the social is also present in liberal bourgeois societies. The individual subject of nineteenth-century competitive capitalism no longer exists. 'Late capitalism' has broken it open, and subordinated its conscious and unconscious mental life directly to the impersonal rhythms of mass production and consumption. This claim is most fully developed in Horkheimer's and Adorno's analysis of the 'culture industry' – an oxymoronic expression from the standpoint of German intellectual tradition which symbolizes the way in which the creation of meaning has become, in the modern mass media, an industrial process. 'In the culture industry the individual is an illusion not merely because of the standardization of the means of production. He is tolerated only so long as his complete identification with the generality is unquestioned.' This

---

[83]   M. Horkheimer, 'The Authoritarian State', in A. Arato and E. Gebhard, eds, *The Frankfurt School Reader* (Oxford, 1978), pp. 107, 117.

[84]   M. Davis, *City of Quartz* (London, 1990), p. 48.

process goes much deeper than the mere concession of improved material conditions to the working class: 'The unleashed colossi of the manufacturing industries did not overcome the individual by granting him full satisfaction but by eliminating his character as a subject.'[85]

The abolition of the individual subject is paradoxically the outcome of a process which involves the systematic subordination of nature to humankind. This is the second great theme of *Dialectic of Enlightenment*. Exploitation, class struggle, and crisis, the features of capitalist society on which Marxist critique has traditionally focused, pit human beings against each other. But the fundamental contradiction is not that between classes, but that between humankind and nature. Here we must confront the contradictory character of enlightenment itself. 'Enlightenment is as totalitarian as any system.' It seeks systematically to know and to control nature. This implies the destruction of nature as an order of being of which human beings are merely one aspect. Thus in the subjective conception of reason characteristic of modern Western thought, '[a]ll the power of nature was reduced to mere indiscriminate resistance to the abstract power of the subject.'[86] Classical German idealism expresses a hatred of nature in its effort to eliminate anything outside the absolute subject: 'The system is the belly turned mind, and rage is the mark of each and every idealism.'[87]

Enlightenment justifies itself by claiming that it is a liberating force; the spread of scientific knowledge breaks the hold of myth on humankind. But in fact it erects a 'second nature', the fetishized social world of capitalism which escapes from human control or comprehension. Thus: 'The more the machinery of thought subjects existence to itself, the more blind its resignation in reproducing existence. Hence enlightenment returns to mythology, which it never really knew how to elude.' Consequently, '[c]ivilization is the victory of society over nature which changes everything into pure nature.' Fascism is not simply the negation of enlightenment, but the price it pays for having sought to efface nature. Desires and drives which the subject is unable to acknowledge as its own burst out in the barbaric destruction of the other. 'Fascism is also totalitarian in that it seeks to make the rebellion of suppressed nature against domination directly useful to domination.'[88]

There seems to be little space for resistance, let alone revolution, in the airless world of what Horkheimer and Adorno increasingly call the 'totally administered society'. The problem goes deeper than politics, however. From what vantage-point is critical theory able to conduct its interpretation of world history as the triumph of myth masked as enlightenment? Rationality is deeply implicated in this process: 'Reason is the organ of calculation, of planning; it is

[85]   M. Horkheimer and T. W. Adorno, *Dialectic of Enlightenment* (London, 1973), pp. 154, 205.
[86]   Ibid., pp. 24, 90.
[87]   T. W. Adorno, *Negative Dialectics* (London, 1973), p. 23.
[88]   Horkheimer and Adorno, *Dialectic*, pp. 27, 186, 185.

neutral in regard to ends; its element is co-ordination.'[89] This is plainly Weber's instrumental rationality, which serves the selection of efficacious means but is unable to determine the values guiding the ends of action. His pessimistic view of the course of Western history stemmed largely from his belief that the process of rationalization which is that history's inner meaning involves the ineluctable triumph of instrumental rationality (see §§.7.2 and 7.3 above).

Horkheimer and Adorno often express views that seem little different. The assertion, for example, that '[r]eification is a process that can be traced back to the beginning of organized society and the use of tools', reverses Lukács's attempt in *History and Class Consciousness* to represent rationalization as a historically specific feature of capitalism that socialist revolution would remove.[90] As Habermas observes, 'Horkheimer and Adorno anchor the mechanism that produces the reification of consciousness in the anthropological foundations of the history of the species, in the form of the existence of a species that has to reproduce itself through labour.'[91] Labour, for Marx the central activity through which humans realize themselves, is thus the inevitable cause of domination. A few months before his death, Adorno told Martin Jay that 'Marx wanted to turn the whole world into a giant workhouse.'[92]

Horkheimer and Adorno do indeed sometimes counterpose 'subjective reason', 'the ability to calculate probabilities and thereby to co-ordinate the right means with the right end', to 'objective reason', which is concerned with 'a comprehensive system, or hierarchy, of all beings, including man and his aims'.[93] Objective reason would thus determine the ends as well as the means of action. But Horkheimer and Adorno offer nothing like a systematic account of this conception of rationality. While they were working on *Dialectic of Enlightenment*, Adorno admitted:

> It often seems as though we were professing objective reason 'dogmatically' to a certain extent, having previously determined that subjective reason is ineluctable. In reality, two things must be made clear: first, that there is no positive 'solution' in the sense of providing a philosophy which could simply be contrasted to subjective reason; secondly, that the critique of subjective reason is only possible on a dialectical basis, i.e. by demonstrating the contradictions in its own course of development and transcending it through its own determinate negation.[94]

In the absence of a 'positive "solution"', critical theory in fact became the abstract negation of the present. For Adorno, dialectics could no longer take the

[89] Ibid., p. 88.
[90] M. Horkheimer, *Eclipse of Reason*, (New York, 1947), p. 41.
[91] J. Habermas, *The Theory of Communicative Action*, I (London, 1984), p. 379.
[92] Jay, *Dialectical Imagination*, p. 57.
[93] Horkheimer, *Eclipse of Reason*, pp. 40, 4, 5.
[94] Letter to Lowenthal, 3 June 1945, quoted in Wiggershaus, *Frankfurt School*, p. 332.

form that it had in Marx, of identifying the tendencies inherent in the existing order that are leading to its transformation. Since these tendencies have been destroyed or absorbed in late capitalism, dialectics could only be negative, 'the consistent sense of nonidentity', whose task was to show 'the untruth of identity, the fact that the concept does not exhaust the thing conceived'.[95] Intimations of an emancipated society could only come indirectly, Adorno argued, through philosophical reflection on the most austere forms of Modern art: the plays of Beckett and the music of Schoenberg, in their formal, fractured structures, were both a reproach to the suffering secreted within the totally administered society, and an allusion to a redeemed social existence beyond its limits where humankind and nature could finally be reconciled.

Not all the members of the Frankfurt School drew such gloomy conclusions. Though Marcuse's best-known book, *One-Dimensional Man* (1964), was essentially a popularization of *Dialectic of Enlightenment*, as Habermas says, there is 'an affirmative feature of Herbert Marcuse's negative thinking'.[96] The chief influences on him were Lukács and Heidegger. From both he took the idea of an integration of subject and object – something which, as we have seen, both Adorno and Horkheimer emphatically rejected. In his early writings on Hegel and Marx, Marcuse saw life as the force unifying subject and object. This theme recurs in his most original work, *Eros and Civilization* (1955). Here he seeks to reconcile Marx and Freud, arguing that in class society men and women are subordinated to the 'performance principle', which exacts from them a 'surplus-repression' that, like surplus labour, reflects the exigencies of exploitation rather than the minimal repression and sublimation of desires without which human survival would be impossible. Socialist revolution will thus be a liberation of the instincts as well a social and political emancipation. Recalling some of the speculations of the Utopian socialists, Marcuse imagines an emancipated society where the difference between work and play has been transcended, and where men and women could finally escape from the relentless drive to produce, and enjoy the easygoing existence evoked in popular conceptions of a lost golden age.

Even though Marcuse was as sceptical as the rest of the Frankfurt School about the revolutionary potential of the Western working class, his philosophy of history made him highly receptive to the radical student movements which developed in the United States and western Europe in the late 1960s. Horkheimer and Adorno were, by contrast, highly embarrassed, especially when the youthful revolutionaries invoked their own writings to justify their rebellion. Horkheimer, who had by this time settled for Western liberal capitalism as the best society on offer, was genuinely hostile to the student movement; Adorno

[95]   Adorno, *Negative Dialectics*, p. 5.
[96]   J. Habermas, 'Psychic Thermidor and the Rebirth of Rebellious Subjectivity', in R. Pippin et al., *Marcuse: Critical Theory and the Promise of Utopia* (South Hadley, Mass., 1988), p. 3.

was privately sympathetic, but afraid of the conservative backlash that public support might attract against the Institute (it happened anyway). Marcuse welcomed the students with open arms. He told Adorno: 'We cannot ignore the fact that these students have been influenced by us (and not least by you) . . . this situation is so horrible, so suffocating and humiliating, that rebellion against it forces you into a biological, physiological reaction: you can no longer bear it, you're suffocating and you have to get out.'[97]

The Frankfurt School indeed offered an explanation of this sense of suffocation, by portraying the enclosure of human potential within the narrow, all-encompassing structures of late capitalism. But it was too good an explanation, since it offered no escape, either theoretical or practical, from these structures. Moreover, as Habermas observes of *Dialectic of Enlightenment*, 'this description of the self-destruction of the critical capacity is paradoxical, because in the moment of description it still has to make use of the critique that has been declared dead. It denounces the Enlightenment's becoming totalitarian with its own tools.'[98] In struggling with what Habermas calls 'this performative contradiction' Adorno and Horkheimer anticipated one of the main dilemmas of social theory at the end of the twentieth century.

---

[97] Letter, 5 Apr. 1969, quoted in Wiggershaus, *Frankfurt School*, pp. 633–4.
[98] J. Habermas, *The Philosophical Discourse of Modernity* (Cambridge, 1987), p. 119.

11

Crack-Up?

11.1 The 1960s and after

The meaning of the 1960s is a matter of intense political and cultural debate. It nevertheless seems undeniable that (whether or not one thinks it a good thing) the decade represented for the developed countries a profound shift in consciousness that has had long-term consequences. Eric Hobsbawm argues that the long boom of the 1950s and 1960s was responsible for 'the most dramatic, rapid and profound revolution in human affairs of which history has the record'.[1] The crux of this transformation was the extension of the process of capitalist industrialization, which had begun in Britain in the late eighteenth century, to much larger portions of the globe; even the end of the boom in the early 1970s did not bring this process to halt, as, for example, a cluster of new capitalisms emerged in East Asia. Features of the original industrializations in north-western Europe and the United States now became a global experience – the decline of the peasantry, the movement to the cities, transcontinental flows of migrants. The intensive character of the industrialization under way was, furthermore, indicated by several phenomena which were either novel or marked accelerations of earlier trends – the increasing incorporation of women into the labour market, the extraordinary expansion of secondary and higher education, and a tendency for the commodification of every aspect of social life.

The effect of these changes was to put increasing pressure on existing social and political structures. The resulting conflicts involved a peculiar mixture of changed lifestyles and political movements. Most obviously, the demand of growing numbers of women for political, economic, and social equality with men entailed both struggles for institutional reform and a fiercely contested reordering of personal relationships that was highly ambiguous in its consequences. The significance of the 1960s is that it represents the moment at

---

[1]   E. J. Hobsbawm, *Age of Extremes* (London, 1994), p. 286.

which the pressures for both socio-political and personal transformation came to consciousness. Typically the trigger was provided by political issues. In the United States, the racial oppression of African-Americans and moral outrage at the Vietnam War together stimulated movements which sought, in however confused a way, social revolution, but within which all sorts of other demands were raised – for example, for a more expressive and less instrumentally rational culture, and for the liberation not merely of blacks, but of women, lesbians and gays, and Native Americans.

While many of the same issues also came up in western Europe, they did so in a notably different context. Here the tension between authoritarian social and political structures, developed to govern predominantly peasant populations, and societies that had been transformed by the spectacular growth-rates achieved by continental Europe from the late 1940s onwards produced a succession of major class confrontations. Student movements, like their American counterparts opposing the Vietnam War and demanding a liberated lifestyle, served as the detonator of mass strikes in France in May–June 1968 and in Italy in the 'hot autumn' of 1969. The terminal crises of the dictatorships in Portugal, Spain, and Greece in the mid-1970s similarly unleashed large-scale mobilizations of working classes whose power and numbers had been vastly increased by rapid industrialization.

The same pattern has been repeated elsewhere, as societies in the so-called 'periphery' underwent crises reflecting their own transformation as a result of accelerated capital accumulation. South Africa, for example, experienced its equivalent of the 1960s during the 1980s, when the structures of apartheid finally cracked under the combined impact of the political rebellion of a black working class that had become too powerful simply to repress and of long-term socio-economic trends that made many racial laws simply unenforceable. For South Korea, the most important of the East Asian 'Tiger' economies, the 1960s began in 1987, when a revolt by students and workers brought nearly thirty years of military dictatorship to an end.

The political aspirations raised in the movements of the 1960s were, for the most part, unrealized. At most, different forms of authoritarian capitalism were replaced by closer approximations to the free-market version prevailing in the US. Indeed for some commentators, for example, Régis Debray, the inner meaning of May 1968 in France and its counterparts elsewhere is reduced to this largely unintended consequence.[2] This seems an unnecessarily determinist way of looking at such events, one that implies that their actual outcome was the only possible one. Nevertheless, the political radicalization produced by the eruptions of the 1960s was followed in western Europe and North America – above all in Britain and the US – by a reaction which was marked by a series of

[2]   R. Debray, 'A Modest Contribution to the Rites and Ceremonies of the Tenth Anniversary', *New Left Review*, 115 (1979).

serious defeats for organized labour and by the revival of the *laissez-faire* economic policies which Keynes had so scornfully demolished in the inter-war years.

These political reversals did not prevent Hobsbawm's 'social revolution' from continuing to work its way through as a long-term process expressed in an immense variety of different general trends and specific alterations. But – as confidence in any project of collective transformation dwindled in an ideological climate dominated by the neo-liberalism of the American New Right and the Thatcherite wing of British Toryism – the decline of many traditional structures was often experienced as having produced a fragmented, thoroughly commodified social world from which moral guidelines for individual action were absent. The political response took diverse forms: descending into cynicism and indifference (probably the most common reaction); making some identity – revived from the past or adopted in pursuit of personal liberation – the basis of collective action; seeking to restore a fictional past when communal reference-points were clear and unambiguously authoritative; eagerly embracing the present as the beginning of a new era of unprecedented structural fluidity, social mobility, and individual choice.

The claim that this condition (dubbed that of 'postmodernity' by the French philosopher Jean-François Lyotard) is radically novel is historically dubious. Quite aside from the question (touched on in ch. 12 below) of whether the characteristic structures of capitalism have undergone a fundamental transformation over the past thirty years, the kind of cycle of political radicalization and disillusionment which very large numbers of intellectuals have experienced since the 1960s proper (or their own local version of the 1960s) is far from being unprecedented. Radical intellectuals who came of political age in Europe during the 1840s experienced a period of exciting social and artistic experimentation centred on Paris that was followed, after the defeat of the revolutions of 1848, by one of reaction and disillusionment. Flaubert's great novel *Sentimental Education* is, among other things, a reflection on that experience. More recently, for many young American intellectuals the 1930s was a decade when Marxist theory, working-class politics, and Modernist art opened new vistas that were all too rapidly closed in the 1940s, especially after the onset of the Cold War. At most, this cycle has been globalized, so that, for example, South African and Korean radical intellectuals experienced in the early 1990s the kind of political let-down their Western counterparts had suffered on earlier occasions.

In any case, how have the social transformations and the political upheavals of the past few decades affected the development of social theory? The most obvious consequence concerned Marxism. The radical movements of the 1960s stimulated a renaissance of Marxist theory that was significant especially because it sought to liberate this tradition from its confining association with the official Communist parties aligned to Moscow. This involved the systematic scrutiny of the entire corpus of Marx's own writings, including those texts (for example, the *Economic and Philosophic Manuscripts of 1844*) which Communist orthodoxy found unpalatable; the rediscovery of earlier, heretical currents of thought – for example, the Hegelian Marxism of the 1920s, and the Frankfurt School; and the development of a number of new variants, of which the most influential was probably Althusser's 'anti-humanist' Marxism (see §11.2 below).

This revival of Marxism produced an explosion of new literature in the 1970s, much of it 'applied' work seeking to deploy theoretical concepts in empirical research. Even the English-speaking countries, whose universities had hitherto been strongly resistant to any Marxist intrusions, witnessed the spectacular development of scholarship inspired by different versions of socialist theory; indeed the 1980s saw the emergence of a short-lived school of 'analytical Marxism', which sought to use the conceptual tools of the tradition of analytical philosophy dominant in the English-speaking world to clarify and correct the central propositions of historical materialism.

Like earlier versions of Western Marxism, this new 'Social-Scientific Marxism', as Göran Therborn dubbed it, was located primarily in the universities rather than in the working-class movement.[3] Whether or not for that reason, it proved vulnerable to the swing of the political pendulum back to the right which developed from the late 1970s onwards. The most spectacular reversal took place in France, where Marxism in some version had dominated intellectual life since the German Occupation. In the mid-1970s, a group of young ex-Maoists collectively dubbed the *nouveaux philosophes* succeeded, with considerable backing from the mass media and from the leadership of the Socialist Party, in portraying Marxism as a philosophy of domination from which atrocities such as the Gulag Archipelago of labour camps in Stalinist Russia ineluctably flowed.

The ensuing abandonment of Marxism by the French intelligentsia – encouraged by political events such as the outbreak of the so-called Second Cold War in the late 1970s and the suppression of the Solidarność trade union by the Polish regime in December 1981 – was repeated in less dramatic form elsewhere in continental Europe and Latin America. The process of retreat was slower in the English-speaking world, but by the beginning of the 1990s, under the impact of postmodernism and the collapse of 'existing socialism' in eastern Europe and the Soviet Union, Marx was a dead dog for most intellectuals there as well.

Nevertheless, the crisis which Marxism underwent from the mid-1970s onwards did not produce an intellectual relapse into social theories implicitly celebrating the status quo. Thus various critiques of Parsonian sociology had been gaining strength through the 1960s. These tended to concentrate on its failure

---

[3] G. Therborn, 'Problems of Class Analysis', in B. Matthews, ed., *Marx: A Hundred Years On* (London, 1983), p. 161.

to thematize historical change and social conflict which they often linked to what they argued were apologetic tendencies which privileged an idealized version of Western capitalist development. Such criticisms could easily be made the basis of the attempt to develop a Marxist alternative to Parsonian orthodoxy: thus Therborn argues that the 'Social-Scientific Marxism' which emerged in the 1970s had undertaken a 'Critique of Sociology' that continued Marx's 'Critique of Political Economy' and Western Marxism's 'Critique of Philosophy'.

Nevertheless, many theorists pursued a third alternative. They sought to develop a version of sociology whose frame of interpretation was provided by historical transformation rather than by social stability, but which, in dialogue with Marxism, continued themes to be found particularly in Weber's thought. A founding text of this tradition of historical sociology is Norbert Elias's *The Civilizing Process* (1939). Elias offers a new slant on the process of rationalization which preoccupied Weber. He seeks systematically to connect the development of centralized bureaucratic states in the early modern era to the gradual transformation of personal behaviour and psychic structures which he traced in European court society in particular. Elias describes how individuals were encouraged to regulate their interpersonal relations, table manners, bodily hygiene, and conduct in the bedroom in a process whose unforeseen long-term results are now taken for granted, certainly by the Western middle classes, but which represented a drastic change from what was considered appropriate in feudal society. When his book was republished in the late 1960s, Elias explicitly contrasted his own approach to the ahistorical version of sociology practised by Parsons and his followers (though his explanatory framework relies heavily on the concept of social differentiation central to evolutionary theory since Comte and Spencer).

Other sociologists took this emphasis on history further by linking it explicitly to the theme of class conflict. Barrington Moore Jr, offered in *The Social Origins of Dictatorship and Democracy* (1966) an explanation of the different routes to modern industrialized society taken by various societies in which the historically variable outcomes of worldwide struggles between lord and peasant played the decisive role. Moore's analysis had a more or less explicit critical dimension, since he challenged Parsonian theories of modernization, arguing that the degree to which a society had developed genuinely democratic political structures depended on the thoroughness with which it had settled accounts, by revolutionary means, with its agrarian past. It was thus no accident that those countries which succumbed to fascism in the inter-war years had grafted capitalist industrialization onto social structures dominated by pre-modern landowning classes.

Moore cultivated a relationship of studied ambiguity towards both Marxism and liberalism (in the preface to *Social Origins* he thanks Marcuse and another alumnus of the Frankfurt School, Otto Kirchheimer[4]). Others who sought to develop further the approach he had pioneered were often members of a younger generation radicalized by the 1960s – for example, Theda Skocpol, whose *States and Social Revolutions* (1979) sought to develop Moore's pursuit of comparative historical analysis within a theoretical framework which attached equal importance to domestic class-structures and inter-state competition.[5] A dramatic further extension of historical sociology took place in the 1980s, when several large-scale theories of history appeared. These were the work, in the main, of British social theorists – Ernest Gellner, Anthony Giddens, Michael Mann, and W. G. Runciman.

Mann and Runciman in particular produced very ambitious, theoretically articulated and historically wide-ranging multi-volume works, respectively *The Sources of Social Power* (two volumes so far, published in 1986 and 1993) and *A Treatise on Social Theory* (three volumes, published between 1983 and 1997). There are considerable differences between the individual theories each offers. Runciman, for example, has tried to develop a version of evolutionary social theory which eschews the teleology and the Lamarckianism of earlier variants for a more strictly Darwinian account of social selection: individual social practices are selected when they enhance the power of a specific social group (or 'systact') in its competition with others. Giddens and Mann, by contrast, express a strongly anti-evolutionary bias, and tend to highlight the contingency of historical outcomes.

All, however, belong recognizably to the tradition founded by Weber in rejecting historical materialism and arguing that events and processes are caused by the interaction of several irreducibly distinct forms of power – (at least) political, economic, and ideological domination. Probably the most influential theme in their writings was the stress they laid, following some hints of Weber's, on military competition as an autonomous social reality and, consequently, on the role played by the early modern inter-state system in creating the conditions for the emergence of contemporary capitalism. Weberian historical sociology is thus a version of social theory which, like Marxism, studies societies from the perspective of their transformation, which it explains in terms of the conflicts constitutive of them. The difference between the two traditions lies in the fact that the Weberian theorists insist that social divisions are inherently plural in nature, and that there is no prospect of their being abolished. The main political reference-point for this form of historical sociology is classical social democracy as traditionally represented by the British Labour Party.

After the watershed of the 1960s, structural functionalism was therefore much less plausible than it had been earlier. But the political upheavals of that decade were also associated with an expansion of the scope of social theory. New,

---

[4]   B. Moore Jr, *Social Origins of Dictatorship and Democracy* (Harmondsworth, 1969), p. xv.
[5]   T. Skocpol, 'An "Uppity Generation" and the Revitalization of Macroscopic Sociology', *Theory and Society*, 17 (1988).

previously marginalized subjects – in the double sense of areas of study and collective agents – were now thematized. Two books may serve to illustrate this development. Michel Foucault's *Histoire de la folie* (1961), an abridged version of which was translated into English under the title of *Madness and Civilization*, sought to trace the history of the constitution of madness, through a series of social practices (notably the institution of confining those classified as mad in asylums) that developed in the eighteenth century, as the 'other' of reason, a voice that has been silenced and excluded. While situated within the French 'epistemological' tradition which, stemming from Comte, sought to reconstruct the conceptual history of particular sciences (in this case psychiatry), Foucault's book was also an attempt to render visible

> The space, at once empty and populated, of all those words without a language which allow the person who lends an ear to hear a muffled voice from below history, the stubborn murmuring of a language which seems to speak quite by itself, without a speaking subject and without an interlocutor, huddled in on itself, a lump in its throat, breaking down before it has achieved any formulation and lapsing back into the silence from which it was never separated.[6]

There is the thought here, not so much of speaking for the silenced, but perhaps of helping to create the conditions in which they can speak for themselves. The efflorescence of political movements addressing particular forms of oppression (for example, those suffered by women, blacks, lesbians and gays) encouraged the idea that the marginal and excluded give themselves a voice through various forms of writing – fictional, autobiographical, historical, and analytical. A book that far more explicitly articulates the politics of such writing than the *Histoire de la folie* is Edward Said's *Orientalism* (1978). Here Said, a Palestinian Arab trained and working in American universities, systematically analyses the literary and scholarly discourse of Orientalism ostensibly developed by Westerners in order to know the East as what Foucault in works somewhat later than the *Histoire* calls an apparatus of power-knowledge (see §11.3 below): representations of an essentialized East as stagnant, sensual, and irrational thus function as a means of dominating the actual East. *Orientalism* marked the beginning of what is now known as postcolonial theory, which focuses on the relationship between Western societies and those formally or informally colonized by them, and in particular on how this relationship structures various kinds of writing.

---

[6]   Quoted in D. Macey, *The Lives of Michel Foucault* (London, 1994), p. 93. Paul-Michel Foucault (1926–84): born to a rich bourgeois family in Poitiers; studied philosophy at the École Normale Supérieure (ENS) in Paris, 1946–50; taught at the University of Lille and ENS, 1952–5; director, Maison de France, Uppsala, 1955–8; director, Centre Français, University of Warsaw, 1958–9; director, Institut Français, Hamburg, 1959–60; taught at the universities of Clermont-Ferrand, 1960–6, Tunis, 1966–8, and Vincennes, 1968–9; elected Professor in the History of Systems of Thought at the Collège de France, 1969; died of AIDS.

These and related developments plainly mark a major expansion in the *extension* of social theory. It is much more open to argument whether they have brought about a radical transformation of its conceptual structures. The idea, for example, that the various forms of oppression are irreducibly plural, and represent distinct sites of struggle which cannot somehow be incorporated (as orthodox Marxists would claim) into an all-embracing movement centred on the working class can be formulated in terms that derive directly (post-structuralism) or indirectly (Weberian historical sociology) from Nietzsche's doctrine of the will to power. Novel content does not necessarily entail comparable conceptual innovation. Thus Said's critique of Orientalism is expressed in terms which, as his critics point out, rather eclectically combine Foucault's variant of post-structuralism with a more traditional liberal humanism. Or again, the feminist theorist Nancy Fraser describes her attempt to distinguish between two kinds of injustice, that of distribution, arising from material inequalities, and that of recognition, which refuses to acknowledge the existence of different identities such as those of gender, race, and sexuality as 'a quasi-Weberian dualism of status and class'.[7]

Perhaps the best way of determining if contemporary social theory has broken through the boundaries set for the debate on modernity after the collapse of Hegel's system (see §2.3 above) is to consider some individual cases. The theorists discussed in the rest of this chapter are selected from a wide array of potential candidates for inclusion (it is more difficult to see the wood for the trees when dealing with one's rough contemporaries). They have been chosen because of their influence, exemplary value, and intrinsic merit, in somewhat varying combinations. I have chosen to concentrate largely (though not exclusively) on French thinkers partly because of their enormous international influence since the Second World War, and partly because doing so makes it easier to extract a coherent narrative from the immense diversity of different theories.

11.2   Structure and subject: Lévi-Strauss and Althusser

Perhaps the most important novelty about social theory since the 1960s has been the importance that language – conceptualized in often divergent ways – has come to assume. Foucault suggests this is one example of a more pervasive characteristic of Western culture in the twentieth century:

> When we consider the extraordinary destiny of formalism in painting or formal research in music, or the importance of formalism in the analysis of folklore and legend, in architecture or its application to theoretical thought, it is clear that formalism has probably been one of the strongest and at the same time one of the most varied currents in 20th-century Europe.[8]

[7]   N. Fraser, 'Heterosexism, Misrecognition and Capitalism', *New Left Review*, 228 (1998), p. 142; see also id., 'From Redistribution to Recognition?', ibid., p. 212 (1995).
[8]   M. Foucault, 'Structuralism and Post-Structuralism', *Telos*, 55 (1983), p. 196.

Certainly Modernism's preoccupation with questions of form and with the process of artistic creation brought the nature of language itself into focus. 'The real metaphysical problem today is the word', Eugene Jolas declared in 1929 in an essay devoted to James Joyce.[9] Language has indeed become a preoccupation for philosophers, a phenomenon worthy of investigation in its own right, where once Western thought tended to take it for granted as either a transparent medium for, or an obstacle to, the expression of thoughts. The resulting philosophies of language have been of markedly different character.

In the analytical tradition, for example, the early and later writings of Ludwig Wittgenstein have encouraged two quite distinct approaches, one of which identifies meaning with abstract logical form while the other consists in the description of specific linguistic practices; more recently, the work of American philosophers such as W. V. Quine, Donald Davidson, and Saul Kripke has offered contrasting versions of this first approach. A gulf separates almost all English-speaking philosophers of language from Hans-Georg Gadamer's attempt to develop Heidegger's remarks on the subject into a theory of the hermeneutic interpretation of texts in which understanding is conceived as a relationship between two speakers sharing the same tradition. Meanwhile, challenging any such consensual view of language is the approach developed in Russia during the 1920s by Mikhail Bakhtin and his pupils: while they make dialogue between speakers the paradigm situation, they treat the utterance as impregnated with the social conflicts that constitute its context.

What Richard Rorty calls 'the linguistic turn' has thus taken very different forms.[10] Plainly the implications of this development for social theory will therefore depend heavily on which particular philosophy of language is taken up in order to elucidate the nature of society. The most influential such philosophy has proved to be that of the Swiss linguist Ferdinand de Saussure: the reception of his thought in France constituted one of the starting-points of what has come to be known as structuralism and therefore also of post-structuralism (see §11.3 below). In order to understand this reception something must be said about its context, in particular in the structural anthropology of Lévi-Strauss.[11]

The French sociological tradition had already highlighted the role of systems of concepts in 'primitive' societies. In their 1903 essay *Primitive Classification* Durkheim and his nephew, the anthropologist Marcel Mauss, declared: 'Every

---

[9]   E. Jolas, 'The Revolution of Language and James Joyce', in S. Beckett et al., *Our Exagmination Round his Factification of Work in Progress* (London, 1972), p. 79.

[10]   R. Rorty, ed., *The Linguistic Turn* (Chicago, 1967).

[11]   Claude Gustave Lévi-Strauss (1908–   ): born in Brussels, into a family of French Jewish painters; studied philosophy at the University of Paris, 1927–32; schoolteacher, 1932–4; Professor of Sociology, University of São Paulo, 1934–7; undertook field research among Indians of Matto Grosso, 1938–9; taught at New School for Social Research, New York, 1941–5; associate director, Musée de l'Homme, Paris, 1949; director of studies, École Pratique des Hautes Études, 1948–74; elected Professor of Social Anthropology at the Collège de France, 1958.

mythology is fundamentally a classification, but one which borrows its principles from religious beliefs, not from scientific ideas.' They also argued that there was a direct continuity between 'primitive' systems of categories, which constitute 'a first philosophy of nature', and the logical structure of modern scientific rationality.[12] This analysis must be seen against the background of Durkheim's later sociology, according to which the actual referent of religious representations is society itself (see §6.3). Moreover, *Primitive Classification* offers nothing in the way of a philosophy of language that would explain how mythical categories acquire meaning, or how they function in relation to each other and to the social and physical worlds.

Lévi-Strauss sought to continue the tradition of Durkheim and Mauss in which the concepts of classification and of exchange (notably in the latter's essay *The Gift* [1925], which seeks to uncover the logic of reciprocity governing transfers of goods in 'primitive' societies) are set to work. He filled the gap left in their account of primitive classification with Saussure's theory of language. For our purposes, this theory, expounded in the *Course in General Linguistics* (1915), has two crucial features. First, Saussure argues that 'the linguistic sign unites, not a thing and a name, but a concept and a sound-image'. Signification, the production of meaningful utterances, thus consists in the relationship between signifiers and signified, that is, between the sounds which form the basic elements of language, and the concepts which they can be combined to signify. Secondly, words succeed in signifying by means of the differences between them. It is because signifiers consist in a set of contrasting sounds that they are able to locate concepts that are similarly identified through the differences between them. Language thus consists of two parallel structures, the signifiers and the signified, sounds and concepts, each of which is defined by the relations of difference between its constituent items. Indeed:

> In language there are only differences. Even more important: a difference generally implies positive terms between which a difference is set up; but in language there are only differences *without positive terms*. Whether we take the signified or the signifier, language has neither ideas nor sounds that existed before the linguistic system, but only conceptual and phonic differences that issue from the system. The idea or phonic substance that a sign contains is less important than the other signs that surround it.[13]

Saussure's holist theory of meaning thus brackets the question of the natural and social context in which utterances are made, and that of reference, that is, of their relationship to the items in the world to which they refer. Saussure himself never denied the importance of context and reference, but by focusing on the internal relationship between signifiers and signified he made it possible to conceive of language as an autonomous system. Fredric Jameson observes:

[12] E. Durkheim and M. Mauss (1903), *Primitive Classification* (London, 1963), pp. 77–8, 81.
[13] F. de Saussure, *Course in General Linguistics* (New York, 1966), pp. 66, 120.

The lines of flight in his system are lateral, from one sign to another, rather than frontal, from word to thing, a movement already interiorized in the sign itself as the movement from signifier to signified. Thus, implicitly, the terminology of the sign tends to affirm the internal coherence and comprehensibility, the autonomy of the system of signs itself, rather than the constant movement outside the symbol system to the things themselves.[14]

Lévi-Strauss, in taking over Saussurian linguistics, drew out this potential. He argues that there is 'a superabundance of the signifier, relative to the signifieds'. This is a consequence of the fact that, since it consists of two parallel *systems*, 'language can only be born at once', rather than develop piecemeal. But the signifieds, the concepts to which the system of signifiers points, can only acquire their content gradually, as a result of the development of knowledge. So: 'Man from his origin disposes of an integral system of signifiers to which he must allocate a signified, given as such without thereby being known. There is always a discrepancy between the two', reflected in the existence of 'floating signifiers' which, themselves lacking any sense, serve to take on any meaning that is given them. Lévi-Strauss, in thus giving the signifier primacy over the signified, explicitly asserts the autonomy of language. Indeed: 'Like language, the social *is* an autonomous reality (the same, moreover); the symbols are more real than that which they symbolize, the signifier precedes and determines the signified.'[15]

Thus in *The Elementary Structures of Kinship* (1949) Lévi-Strauss treats kinship systems as linguistic structures, sets of binary oppositions in which the exchange of women functions as the transmission of messages. J. Q. Merquior argues that 'his entire anthropological approach' consists in 'Standing Durkheim on his Head': 'Durkheim's method always moved *from the mental to the social*: from belief to social structure . . . With Lévi-Strauss it is the other way round. In structuralism we move *from the social to the mental*; from social relations or cultural constructs, like kinship systems or myths, to intellectual structures.'[16] This contrast is somewhat overstated, since Durkheim came to think that social facts consisted primarily of collective representations (see §6.2 above). Nevertheless, it is undoubtedly the case that Lévi-Strauss conceives the unconscious structures he seeks to detect as essentially mental. Thus he says he is 'guided by the search for the constraining structures of the mind', and declares: 'Starting from ethnographic experience, I have always aimed at drawing up an inventory of mental patterns, to reduce apparently arbitrary data to some kind of order, and to attain a level at which some kind of necessity becomes apparent, underlying the illusions of liberty.'

[14] F. Jameson, *The Prison-house of Language* (Princeton, 1974), p. 32.
[15] C. Lévi-Strauss, 'Introduction à l'œuvre de Marcel Mauss', in M. Mauss, *Sociologie et anthropologie* (Paris, 1950), pp. xlix, xlvii, xlix, xxxii.
[16] J. Q. Merquior, *From Prague to Paris* (London, 1986), p. 38.

Thus 'myths signify the mind that evolves them by making use of the world of which it is part'.[17]

The philosopher Paul Ricoeur called Lévi-Strauss's structural anthropology 'a Kantianism without a transcendental subject', a description which the latter accepted.[18] In other words, he seeks to uncover the unconscious conceptual structures presupposed by conscious experience, but without ascribing these to the activity of a self that itself underlies experience. This approach has two important implications.

First, taking over a contrast drawn by Saussure, Lévi-Strauss privileges the study of synchrony, of the universal structures underlying concrete sets of beliefs and social institutions, over that of diachrony, of historical transformations. In a celebrated polemic in *The Savage Mind* (1962), he demolishes Jean-Paul Sartre's attempt in his *Critique of Dialectical Reason* to conceptualize history as a process in which individual subjects are, in some cases at least, able collectively to act and to change the 'practico-inert' structures that normally weigh down on them. Lévi-Strauss dismisses this attempt to read the whole of human history in terms of Western experience since the French Revolution as a ethnocentric attempt to make the concept of a collective subject 'the last refuge of a transcendental humanism: as if men could regain the illusion of liberty on the plane of the "we" merely by giving up the "I"s that are too obviously wanting in consistency'.[19] Elsewhere he declares history itself to be the domain of 'irreducible contingency'.[20]

Secondly, therefore, Lévi-Strauss' adaptation of Saussure assigns to the subject, either individual or collective, a secondary and constituted rather than a primary and constitutive place: 'I believe the ultimate goal of the human sciences to be not to constitute, but to dissolve man'.[21] This anti-humanism is one of the common features of what (somewhat misleadingly) came to be known as structuralism, the most influential intellectual trend in France during the 1960s. Jacques Lacan used Saussurian linguistics in his attempt to restate Freud in terms which avoided either the reduction of the unconscious to biological instincts or the transformation of psychoanalysis into a therapy of adaptation to reality. The slogan of Lacan's self-proclaimed 'return to Freud' was thus 'the unconscious is structured like a language'. Freud had shown that the subject is 'decentred', since underlying and shaping its conscious life is the record of its formation in the unconscious, to which it is denied access. Inverting Descartes's *cogito ergo sum* ('I think therefore I am'), Lacan declared: 'I think where I am not, therefore I am where I do not think.'[22]

[17] C. Lévi-Strauss (1964), *The Raw and the Cooked* (London, 1970), pp. 10, 341.

[18] C. Lévi-Strauss, 'A Confrontation', *New Left Review*, 62 (1970), p. 61.

[19] C. Lévi-Strauss, *The Savage Mind* (London, 1972), p. 262.

[20] C. Lévi-Strauss, *From Honey to Ashes* (London, 1973), p. 475.

[21] Lévi-Strauss, *Savage Mind*, p. 247.

[22] J. Lacan, *Écrits: A Selection* (London, 1977), p. 166.

Lacan's reinterpretation of Freudian theory was one of the main influences on perhaps the most systematic attempt to formulate an anti-humanist social theory, Althusser's reconstruction of historical materialism.[23] Indeed, invoking Freud's description of his own 'Copernican Revolution' (see §8.3 above), Althusser draws a parallel between his achievement and that of Marx, arguing that both have contributed to the displacement of the subject from the central role hitherto claimed for it: 'Since Marx, we have known that the human subject, the economic, political or philosophical ego is not the "centre" of history – and even, in opposition to the Philosophers of the Enlightenment and Hegel, that history has no "centre" but has a structure which has no necessary "centre" except in ideological misrecognition.'[24]

Althusser's version of Marxism is thus radically different from the theory of class subjectivity which Lukacs and Gramsci conceived it to be (see §9.1 above). For him, 'history is *a process without a subject*'.[25] Each social formation is a complex structured totality consisting of a plurality of distinct 'instances' – the economy, politics, ideology, and theory (the sciences). None of these, even the economy, constitutes the centre of the social formation. Each has its own distinctive internal logic which allows it to develop according to a particular dynamic, and even its own 'differential temporality'.

The economy is 'determinant in the last instance'. In other words, economic causality operates indirectly, less through immediately affecting specific political or cultural events than by selecting a particular instance to play the role of directly shaping the other instances (the 'structure in dominance'). Therefore historical events – say, the Russian Revolution – do not have a single, economic cause. Althusser invokes a Freudian concept to bring out what is involved here. They are 'overdetermined': many different factors come together, fusing into a single complex formation that produces a historical rupture:

> The economic dialectic is never active in *the pure state*; in History, these instances, the superstructures, etc., are never seen to step respectfully aside when their work is done, or when the time comes, as his pure phenomena, to scatter before His Majesty the Economy as he strides along the royal road to the Dialectic. From the first moment to the last, the lonely hour of the 'last instance' never comes.[26]

---

[23]   Louis Pierre Althusser (1918–90): born in Algeria, the son of a banker; prisoner of war, 1940–5; studied philosophy at the École Normale Supérieure, 1945–7; joined the Communist Party in 1948; *caïman* (philosophy tutor) at the ENS, 1949–80; suffered repeated bouts of mental illness (probably a manic-depressive psychosis); murdered his wife, Helene Rytman, November 1980; declared unfit to stand trial; spent most of his remaining years in mental institutions; in 1985 wrote a confessional memoir, *The Future Lasts a Long Time*, published in 1992, after his death.

[24]   L. Althusser, *Lenin and Philosophy and Other Essays* (London, 1971), p. 201.

[25]   L. Althusser, *Politics and History* (London, 1972), p. 183.

[26]   L. Althusser (1965), *For Marx* (London, 1969), p. 113.

Althusser's interpretation of Marx implies a radical difference between the latter's dialectic and that of Hegel. Althusser challenges the traditional formulation (inherited from Engels) according to which Marx kept Hegel's dialectical 'method' while abandoning his idealist 'system'. Method and system are too closely intertwined for such an operation to succeed: to retain one is to retain both. More specifically, Hegel's conception of totality is an 'expressive' one, in which each individual part reflects the structure of the whole. If social formations are viewed in this way, the effect is economic reductionism: every social phenomenon is treated as replicating the central economic contradiction, as, for example, in *History and Class Consciousness* every aspect of social life reproduces the structure of reification.

Hegelian Marxism (or 'historicism', as Althusser rather confusingly calls it) thus conceives itself as a rebellion against the fatalism of the Second International; but the conception of social totality that it employs leads it to collapse into another kind of economic reductionism. As a messianic young Stalinist in the late 1940s, Althusser had espoused a particularly extreme form of Hegelian Marxism. But in his most influential works, *For Marx* and the collectively written *Reading Capital* (both published in 1965), he argues that Marx, in breaking with the Young Hegelians in the mid-1840s, also abandoned his own earlier 'humanist' works, for example, *The Economic and Philosophic Manuscripts of 1844*. This shift constituted an 'epistemological break', in which Marx replaced the ideological and (indeed, because) humanist problematic of his early writings for a new scientific problematic first present in *The German Ideology* and the 'Theses on Feuerbach'.

Althusser's theory of overdetermination implies the relative autonomy of the politico-ideological superstructure. This result was important to him for several, primarily political, reasons. In the first place, it offers him a means of explaining Stalinism: the Great Terror of the 1930s is to be seen as a consequence of the presence in the superstructure of 'survivals' from the past which, because the different aspects of the social whole develop unevenly with respect to one another, could continue to have effects despite the fact that the economic base had been transformed along socialist lines.

Secondly, along with the superstructure, theory also gains relative autonomy. As a member of the French Communist Party (PCF), Althusser had experienced during the height of the Cold War at the end of the 1940s and the beginning of the 1950s what he later called 'the period of intellectuals in arms, hunting out error from all its hiding places'.[27] Throughout the Communist movement, party apparatchiks enforced on its intellectual supporters the idea that every aspect of cultural life was polarized along class lines, and that in every field of research two sciences – 'proletarian' and 'bourgeois' – confronted one another: this 'theory of the two sciences' legitimized the Lysenko affair in the USSR, the persecution of Mendelian genetics as 'bourgeois science'.

---

[27]   Althusser, *For Marx*, p. 21.

In reaction to what he described in retrospect as this 'madness', Althusser argued that 'theory is a practice' – in other words, each science has its own specific logic irreducible to that of any other, let alone to that of other instances of the social whole, and must be appraised according to its own internal criteria of validity. This argument reflected the influence on him of the French 'episte-mological' tradition, whose leading practitioners were Gaston Bachelard and Georges Canguilhem. Rejecting the tendency of English-speaking philosophers of science to treat theories as generalizations from sense-experience, both treated sciences as historically constituted and developing systems of concepts. The political effect of Althusser's version of this philosophy of science, the 'theory of theoretical practice' was, he later claimed, 'to justify the thesis of the relative autonomy of theory and thus the right of Marxist theory not to be treated as a slave to tactical political decisions, but to be allowed to develop, in alliance with political and other practices, without betraying its own needs'.[28]

This attempt to create a certain distance between theory and practice did not mean that Althusser had no interest in politics. On the contrary, between the early 1960s and mid-1970s he more or less openly expressed his sympathy with the Chinese Communist leader Mao Zedong's critique of the Soviet Union's 'revisionist' policies. Indeed, many of his pupils abandoned the PCF, whose leadership remained loyal to Moscow, in the mid-1960s to set up independent Maoist groups. Althusser himself never left the party, on the grounds that it was the main political organization of the French working class. This situation – member of a highly disciplined mass party with whose policies he strongly disagreed – helps to explain the often ambiguous and elusive nature of his political pronouncements. When the left suffered a humiliating defeat in the legislative elections of March–April 1978, he launched an open polemic against the PCF leadership, denouncing in particular the lack of internal party democ-racy, but this was soon overtaken by the extraordinary tragedy in which Althusser strangled his wife, an event inevitably followed by his disappearance from pub-lic life.

The loosening of the tight connection which Marx had established between theory and practice must be seen in the context of Althusser's theory of ideol-ogy. He conceives the economic structure of capitalist society rather as Heidegger did Being – as present only in its own absence (the influence of Heidegger on postwar French philosophy was pervasive, though Althusser claims to have read him mainly in the 1980s[29]). Thus:

> *Capital* . . . exactly measures a distance and an internal dislocation in the real, inscribed in its *structure*, a distance and a dislocation such as to make their own

---

[28]   L. Althusser, *Philosophy and the Spontaneous Philosophy of the Scientists and Other Essays*, ed. G. Elliott (London, 1990) p. 208.

[29]   L. Althusser, *Sur la philosophie* (Paris, 1994), pp. 98–9, 112, 116.

effects themselves illegible, and the illusion of an immediate reading of them the ultimate apex of their effects: *fetishism* . . . Only from history in thought, the theory of history, was it possible to account for the historical religion of reading: by discovering that the truth of history cannot be read in its manifest discourse, because the text of history is not a text in which the Logos speaks, but the inaudible and illegible notation of the effect of a structure of structures.[30]

Thus 'theoretical practice' is necessary because social reality is complex and opaque and so must be decoded. Althusser takes this idea to the length of developing a theory of reading. Texts, like dreams, have a manifest content which conceals their latent content, the 'problematic' or system of questions underlying the surface discourse which can only be wrested from the text's gaps and silences by a theoretically informed reading. The complexity of the text exemplifies the complexity of the social itself. Marx in his theory of commodity fetishism argued that there is a systematic discrepancy between the surface appearance and the underlying reality of capitalist society (see §§4.2 and 4.3 above), but Althusser takes this idea much further.

Individuals must be seen as 'bearers' or 'supports' of the prevailing relations of production, not as agents capable of initiating action. The category of the subject does not merely mislead us about the real nature of individual human beings. It also plays a critical role in the structure of ideological misrecognition through which individuals are prepared for their role as 'supports' by, so Althusser claims, subsuming them under the form of subjects: '*The category of the subject is only constitutive of all ideology insofar as all ideology has the function (which defines it) of "constituting" concrete individuals as subjects.*'[31] By 'interpellating' individuals as subjects ideology encourages them to conceive themselves as independent agents for whom reality exists, and thereby secures the performance of their actual role as supports. This function – performed in capitalist society through the 'Ideological State Apparatuses' (for example, churches, schools, universities, trade unions, political parties) – would be necessary in any society: '*Ideology (as a system of mass representations) is indispensable if men are to be formed, transformed and equipped to respond to the demands of their conditions of existence.*' Indeed, '*historical materialism cannot conceive that even a communist society could ever do without ideology*', for '[h]uman societies secrete ideology as the very element and atmosphere indispensable to their functioning.'[32]

Practice is thus necessarily mystified. This seems a long way from Marx's theory of working-class self-emancipation, where collective action is precisely the process through which human beings come both to understand and to transform their situation. Critics have suggested that Althusser's theory of ideology

---

[30] L. Althusser and E. Balibar, *Reading Capital* (London, 1970), p. 17.

[31] Althusser, *Lenin and Philosophy*, p. 160.

[32] Althusser, *For Marx*, pp. 264, 232.

bears a close resemblance to Parsonian functionalist sociology, in which the mechanisms of socialization form individuals for their place in the system of roles (see §10.2 above). Nevertheless, despite the austere distance it took up from political practice, Althusserian Marxism had an enormous influence on young intellectuals radicalized by the political upheavals of the 1960s, both in France and elsewhere. To understand its sudden collapse in the 1970s we must consider the rise of post-structuralism, which displaced it as the main form of avant-garde theorizing.

11.3   Nietzsche's revenge: Foucault and post-structuralism

Under the impact of the writings of Lévi-Strauss, Lacan, Althusser, and others (for example, the literary critic Roland Barthes), the belief developed that they represented a single current in French thought, 'structuralism', and it was under this label that they were received elsewhere. In fact, there were considerable differences among the leading figures identified with structuralism: thus Althusser, though he subsequently criticized himself for having 'flirted' with structuralism, was consistently hostile to what he called Lévi-Strauss's 'bad Formalism'.[33] Nevertheless, around the middle of the 1960s the idea that Saussure's conception of language offered a general model for the 'human sciences' generally did influence even thinkers who were later to deny any connection with structuralism. So Foucault in *The Order of Things* (1966) divides intellectual history into periods each of which is governed by a single *episteme*, an implicit conceptual structure which provides the horizon of thinking across different disciplines.

The structuralist moment proved all the same to be a short-lived one. This reflected tensions inherent in the philosophy of language which Lévi-Strauss and others had extracted from Saussure's *Course*. They tended to think of structure as a series of permutations of a finite set of elements from which an infinite number of binary oppositions could be generated. Thus myths for Lévi-Strauss represent variations of a very small number of basic themes. There was always a tension between this essentially closed conception of structure and the primacy which he gave to signifiers over signified. The decisive step in constituting *post*-structuralism lay in resolving this tension by, in effect, using the infinite movement of signification to disrupt the stability of structures.

The clearest example of this move is provided by Jacques Derrida. In a famous essay, 'Structure, Sign and Play in the Discourse of the Human Sciences' (1967), he counterposes the concept of 'centred structure' to that of 'play'.

---

[33]   L. Althusser, 'Sur Lévi Strauss', in id., *Écrits philosophiques et politiques* (2 vols, Paris, 1994–5), II.

The latter term refers to the tendency of every binary opposition to subvert itself, generating a new one which is in turn subverted, and so on to infinity. 'The concept of centred structure is in fact the concept of a play based on a fundamental ground, a play constituted on the basis of a fundamental immobility, and a reassuring certitude, which itself is beyond the reach of play.' But the nature of the signifying process undermines this notion of structure. Each signifier points towards a signified which is itself another signifier. In other words, signification is itself a process of infinite play. The only way in which this movement could be halted would be if one could posit a 'transcendental signified' outside language which is immediately 'present', that is, to which we somehow have direct access without the mediation of language. But to imagine such a possibility is to commit a philosophical error by falling into what Derrida calls 'the metaphysics of presence'. The collapse of the transcendental signified 'was the moment when, in the absence of a centre or origin, everything became discourse . . . that is to say, a system in which the central signified, the original or transcendental signified, is never absolutely present outside a system of differences. The absence of the transcendental signified extends the domain and the play of signification infinitely.'[34]

'Everything became discourse.' Derrida famously expressed the same thought elsewhere: '*There is nothing outside the text* . . . There have never been anything but supplements, substitutive significations, which could only come forth in a chain of differential references, the "real" supervening and being added only when taking on meaning from a trace and from an invocation of the supplement, etc. And thus to infinity.'[35] The most influential way in which post-structuralism has been received in the English-speaking world is indeed as a form of linguistic idealism, what Richard Rorty calls 'textualism', according to which the world, rather than existing independently of the ways we talk about it, is constructed in discourse.[36] This is, however, misleading, and indicates the problematic way in which the work of what in many ways are quite different thinkers – notably Derrida, Foucault, and the philosopher Gilles Deleuze – has been marketed, especially in the United States, under the labels 'post-structuralism' and 'postmodernism'.

The significance of post-structuralism is less that Derrida or Foucault wish to deny that tables and trees exist when we are not talking about them than that the subversion of the Saussurian model of language created a space within which certain themes deriving from Nietzsche could be pursued. Thus if history no longer has a structure, then chance and contingency can assume a far greater importance. Similarly, if discourse does not mirror the world, but in some sense constitutes it, then maybe scientific theories could be seen as elements in

---

[34] J. Derrida, *Writing and Difference* (London, 1978), pp. 279, 280.

[35] J. Derrida, *Of Grammatology* (Baltimore, 1976), pp. 158–9.

[36] R. Rorty, *The Consequences of Pragmatism* (Brighton, 1982), p. 141.

strategies of domination. A Nietzschean preoccupation with power also helped to express the political concerns of many French intellectuals. Disillusionment with the failure of May 1968 and its aftermath to produce any fundamental social transformation, and the remarkably belated discovery of the crimes committed by the Stalinist regimes in the USSR, China, Cambodia, and elsewhere, promoted the view that history is a succession of forms of domination.

Althusserian Marxism proved highly vulnerable to this change in the political and intellectual climate. This was partly because Althusser and his followers tended to give only very superficial explanations of Stalinism, which they traced back to ideological deformations. But Althusser's reconstruction of Marxism also contained within it major conceptual tensions. For one thing, his conception of totality is thoroughly ambiguous. On the one hand, as we saw above, it seems to imply a version of structural functionalism, in which self-perpetuating structures shape individuals according to their needs; on the other hand, Althusser offers only the most formal of explanations of how his 'structure of structures', as a plurality of relatively autonomous instances, constituted a genuine totality rather than a mere aggregate of independent factors. For another thing, he insists that each science has its own internal criteria of validity. He denies, in other words, that there can be what Karl Popper calls a 'demarcation criterion' on the basis of which one can discriminate between scientific and non-scientific theories. The difficulty is that we therefore have no way of telling whether a theoretical problematic is scientific or ideological. Why not then give way to the temptation of denying that any such difference exists, and claim that all theoretical discourses are constituted by extra-scientific interests?

The conceptual flaws of Althusserian Marxism thus meant that it was liable to collapse into something much closer to the kind of Nietzschean social theory which began to gain ground in the mid-1970s. The key figure in effecting this shift was Foucault (though, as what he called 'a Nietzschean Communist', he was briefly a PCF member in the early 1950s, he never claimed to be a Marxist[37]). His influence was chiefly expressed through a series of texts which, though they formally belonged to the genre of intellectual history, in actuality represented a novel form of historical writing. Foucault himself said: 'My books aren't treatises in philosophy or studies in history: at most they are philosophical fragments put to work in a historical field of problems.'[38] He later elaborated:

> recourse to history – one of the great facts of French philosophical thought for at least twenty years – is meaningful to the extent that history serves to show how that-which-is has not always been; i.e., that the things which seem most evident to us are always formed in the confluence of encounters and chances, during the course of a precarious and fragile history.[39]

[37] M. Foucault, *Remarks on Marx* (New York, 1991), p. 51.
[38] M. Foucault, 'Questions of Method', *I&C* 8 (1981), p. 4.
[39] Foucault, 'Structuralism', p. 207.

Foucault's writings of the 1960s were, as we saw above, influenced by the general structuralist preoccupation with language. By the end of that decade, however, he came to think of himself as engaged in a practice he called 'archaeology', whose task 'consists of not – of no longer – treating discourses as groups of signs (signifying elements referring to contents or representations) but as practices that systematically form the objects of which they speak'.[40] 'Discursive practices' consist of articulations of particular discourses and the institutional contexts from which they gain their identity in which neither term – neither the discursive nor the non-discursive – is reducible to the other. Thus, even at this stage, Foucault was moving beyond the idea of the autonomy of language.

Coming up with a satisfactory account of the relationship between the discursive and the non-discursive turns out to require resort to Nietzsche. In a key text, 'Nietzsche, Genealogy, History' (1971) , Foucault embraces the doctrine of the will to power: 'Humanity does not gradually progress from combat to combat until it arrives at universal reciprocity where the rule of law finally replaces warfare; humanity installs each of its violences in a system of rules and thus proceeds from domination to domination.' He also espouses Nietzsche's critique of scientific reason:

> In appearance, or rather, according to the mask it bears, historical consciousness is neutral, devoid of passions, and committed solely to truth. But if it examines itself and if, more generally, it interrogates the various forms of scientific consciousness in its history, it finds that all these forms and transformations are aspects of the will to knowledge: instinct, passion, the inquisitor's devotion, cruel subtlety, and malice.[41]

Archaeology, the historical description of discursive practices, thereby becomes genealogy, whose object is 'power-knowledge'. In *Discipline and Punish* (1975) Foucault declares: 'There is no power-relation without the correlative constitution of a field of knowledge, nor any knowledge that does not presuppose and constitute at the same time power-relations.'[42] Instead of trying to reconstruct the *episteme*, the underlying conceptual structure, constitutive of any historical epoch, we should look for the prevailing 'apparatus' (*dispositif*) of power-knowledge, 'a thoroughly heterogeneous ensemble consisting of discourses, institutions, architectural forms, regulatory decisions, laws, administrative measures, scientific statements, philosophical, moral and philanthropic propositions – in short, the said as much as the unsaid'.[43]

For our purposes, Foucault's theory of power-knowledge has three decisive elements. First, there is his concept of power. Power consists of a multiplicity

---

[40] M. Foucault, *The Archaeology of Knowledge* (London, 1972), p. 49.
[41] P. Rabinow, ed., *The Foucault Reader* (Harmondsworth, 1986), pp. 85, 95.
[42] M. Foucault, *Discipline and Punish* (London, 1977), p. 27.
[43] M. Foucault, *Power-Knowledge*, ed. C. Gordon (Brighton, 1980), p. 194.

of specific, localized relationships which together constitute the social body. It is not the attribute of any subject either individual or collective, nor does its exercise depend on the pursuit of a global strategy. Rather, a multiplicity of local tactics combine, unintentionally, in a way that is functional to a particular apparatus of power-knowledge. Furthermore, power is not negative: it does not act by repressing or controlling the initiatives of independently formed subjects. On the contrary, power is productive: in particular, acting directly on human bodies, rather than relying on the intermediary of ideology, it transforms them into individuals and allocates them to their position within the social body. Finally, '[w]here there is power, there is resistance.' Power-relations generate 'points of resistance' which are necessary conditions of their functioning.[44]

Secondly, this theory of power continues the anti-humanist critique of the subject. Thus Foucault acknowledges that one position he shares with Lévi-Strauss, Lacan, and Althusser is 'the calling into question of the theory of the subject'.[45] He takes this challenge even further than they did:

> It is already one of the prime effects of power that certain bodies, certain gestures, certain discourses, certain desires come to be identified and constituted as individuals. The individual, that is, is not the *vis-à-vis* of power; it is, I believe, one of its prime effects. The individual is an effect of power, and at the same time, or precisely to the extent to which it is that effect, it is the element of its articulation. The individual which power has constituted is at the same time its vehicle.[46]

Thus *Discipline and Punish* traces the emergence at the beginning of the nineteenth century of a new apparatus of power-knowledge. This is exemplified in changes in the nature of punishment. Power no longer relies on spectacular public executions which serve to demonstrate in the pulverized body of the criminal the sovereignty of the absolute monarch. Imprisonment implies the application of a comprehensive body of rules which, enforced by means of the continual surveillance of the inmates, seeks to regulate and transform their behaviour. The prison is one of a series of new institutions – schools, factories, barracks, and hospitals are other examples – in which the 'disciplinary society' takes shape:

> The historical moment of the disciplines was the moment at which an art of the human body was born, which was directed not only at the growth of its skills, nor at the intensification of its subjection, but at the formation of a relation that in the mechanism itself makes it more obedient as it becomes more useful, and conversely. What was then being formed was a policy of coercions that act upon the

[44] M. Foucault, *The History of Sexuality*, I (Harmondsworth, 1981), p. 95.
[45] Foucault, *Remarks*, p. 58.
[46] Foucault, *Power-Knowledge*, p. 98.

body, a calculated manipulation of its elements, its gestures, its behaviour . . . it defined how one may take a hold on others' bodies, not only so that they may do what one wishes, but so they may operate as one wishes, with the techniques, the speed and the efficiency that one determines. Thus discipline produces subjected and practised bodies, 'docile bodies'.[47]

Thirdly, Foucault's genealogy implied a fundamental critique of modernity. To begin with, the emergence of modern society in the epoch after the French Revolution represented not even the beginnings of a process of liberation, but merely the installation of another apparatus of power-knowledge in the shape of the disciplines. Not only liberal capitalism, but also its supposed other, Marxism, was implicated in the resulting form of domination. Foucault argued that 'what has happened since 1968, and arguably what made 1968 possible, is something profoundly anti-Marxist'.[48] He believed that the explosion of movements contesting specific forms of oppression could not be contained within the framework of historical materialism with its totalizing focus on class exploitation. Foucault was personally active in one such movement, concerned with the prison system, in the early 1970s; this involvement is an important part of the background to *Discipline and Punish*. It took place during a period when Foucault was a fellow-traveller of the Maoist group Gauche Prolétarienne. Many of the intellectuals attracted towards this milieu moved rightwards in the second half of the 1970s, thereby giving birth to the *nouvelle philosophie* which claimed that the Gulag Archipelago was the logical consequence of Marx's own thought (see §11.1 above). Foucault followed this general drift, declaring:

Stalinism was the truth, 'rather' naked, admittedly, of an entire political discourse which was that of Marx and of other thinkers before him. With the Gulag, one sees not the consequences of an unfortunate error but the effect of the most 'true' theories in the order of politics. Those who helped to save themselves by opposing Marx's real beard to Stalin's false nose are wasting their time.[49]

But Foucault's critique of modernity extended to scientific reason itself. His concept of power-knowledge was not a crude instrumentalism: the relationship between power-relations and forms of knowledge is a two-way one. Nevertheless, it does commit him to a version of Nietzsche's perspectivism according to which every body of knowledge must be scrutinized for the particular will to power which it embodies. More specifically, it was the claim to objectivity of modern scientific rationality which he challenged, that is,

---

[47] Foucault, *Discipline*, pp. 137–8.

[48] Foucault, *Power-Knowledge*, p. 57.

[49] M. Foucault, 'La Grande Colère des faits', *Le Nouvel Observateur*, 9 May 1977, p. 84.

a rationality that has been historically and geographically defined in the West, starting from the sixteenth century on. The West could never have attained the economic and cultural effects that are unique to it without the exercise of that specific form of rationality. Now, how are we to separate that rationality from the mechanisms, procedures, techniques, and effects of power that determine it, which we no longer accept and which we point to as the form of oppression typical of capitalist societies, and perhaps of socialist societies too. Couldn't it be concluded that the promise of *Aufklärung* (Enlightenment), of attaining freedom through the exercise of reason, has been overturned within the domain of Reason itself, that it is taking more and more space away from freedom?[50]

This is, of course, a version of the problem with which both Weber and the Frankfurt School struggled. Towards the end of his life Foucault acknowledged their importance. He said, for example: 'if I had been familiar with the Frankfurt School [in the 1950s and 1960s] . . . I would not have said a number of stupid things that I did say and I would have avoided many of the detours which I made while trying to pursue my humble path – when, meanwhile, avenues had been opened up by the Frankfurt School.'[51] Yet this comparison indicates the main contradiction in Foucault's genealogy. Like Adorno and Horkheimer, he takes up a critical stance towards the history of domination which he reconstructs. Like them also, he lacks a vantage-point from which to take up this stance (see §10.3 above). What will to power do his genealogical histories articulate?

Sometimes Foucault tries to evade this question by denying that his texts have any truth-value: 'I am well aware I have never written anything but fictions.' But these assertions are contradicted by the labour of historical research and narrative construction which he puts into his books. And if they are fictions, how are they to be of any political use, as he plainly hopes they will be? He says that genealogy is 'based on a reactivation of local knowledges . . . in opposition to the scientific hierarchization of knowledges and the effects intrinsic to their power'.[52] This suggests some connection between genealogy and particular localized forms of resistance. But resistance is itself a mystery.

Foucault asserts that 'where there is power, there is resistance'. What, however, are the sources of resistance? Other thinkers have answers to this question. For Marx, the antagonistic relationship between exploiter and exploited necessarily gives rise to class struggle. Nietzsche thinks that reality is composed of nothing but rival centres of power. But Foucault claims that power constitutes the individuals through which it then operates. There is, moreover, no escape from it: 'It seems to me that power is "always already there", that one is never "outside" it, that there are no "margins" for those who break with the

50   Foucault, *Remarks*, pp. 117–18.
51   Foucault, 'Structuralism', p. 200.
52   Foucault, *Power-Knowledge*, pp. 193, 85.

system to gambol in.'[53] It seems hard to see how the subjects of power can resist it – except when it wants them to. And indeed Foucault's discussions of particular forms of resistance are often pretty functionalist, depicting them as opportunities for the prevailing apparatus to restructure and modernize itself. He does at one point say that 'against the apparatus of sexuality' which is one aspect of the modern apparatus of power-knowledge one must counterpose 'bodies and pleasures'.[54] But this seems to invoke Rousseau's idea of a natural man repressed by civilization – a conception totally at odds with the rest of Foucault's writings.

It is nevertheless in the second and third volumes of his *History of Sexuality*, published very shortly before his death in June 1984, that Foucault begins to indicate a way out of the closed system of power-knowledge. He began this *History* in the mid-1970s. Initially his aim was to undermine the idea, which he attributed to Freud, that sexuality is a kind of natural essence to which we have till recently been denied access by repression. He argues that sexuality is not a natural substance, but a historical construct, formed in a specific context of power-knowledge. Secondly, he seeks to show that the attempt to discover our inner nature by exploring sexuality is not something which we owe to psychoanalysis, but can be traced back to the early Christian centuries, and thereby to establish 'how it comes about that people are taught that the secret of their truth lies in the region of their sex'.[55]

In the event, Foucault found it necessary to go back ever further, into the history of classical antiquity. In doing so he refined the nature of his theoretical enterprise. Thus he announces: 'My objective . . . has been to create a history of the modes by which, in our culture, human beings are made into subjects . . . Thus it is not power, but the subject, which is the general theme of my research.'[56] As Thomas R. Flynn observes, 'at each spiral of his research. Foucault has read the previous turn as dealing with what the next professed to study'.[57] Thus in the second and third volumes of the *History* he introduces the concept of 'technologies of the self', that is, 'techniques which permit individuals to effect, by their own means, a certain number of operations on their own bodies, their own souls, their own thoughts, their own conduct, and this in a manner so as to transform themselves, modify themselves, and to attain to a certain state of perfection, happiness, purity, supernatural power'.[58] The main example

---

[53]   Ibid., p. 141.

[54]   Foucault, *History*, p. 157 (translation modified).

[55]   Foucault, *Power-Knowledge*, p. 214.

[56]   M. Foucault, 'The Subject and Power', appendix to H. Dreyfus and P. Rabinow, *Michel Foucault* (Brighton, 1982), pp. 208–9.

[57]   Thomas R. Flynn, 'Truth and Subjectivation in the Later Foucault', *Journal of Philosophy*, 82 (1985), p. 532.

[58]   M. Foucault and R. Sennett, 'Sexuality and Solitude', in *London Review of Books: Anthology One* (London, 1981), pp. 171–2.

Foucault gives of such a technology is the practice of *enkrateia* (mastery) performed by the citizens of ancient Athens in order to develop the self-control necessary to rule over non-citizens – women, children, and slaves – in both the city and the household.

The account which Foucault provides of this 'aesthetics of existence' in *The Use of Pleasure* (1984) is strongly reminiscent of Nietzsche's descriptions of the practices of 'self-overcoming' necessary if the 'overman' is to arise from amid the dreary mediocrity of the 'last men' (see §5.3 above). But what is significant for our purposes is that Foucault treats these as processes of *self-constitution*, through which subjects act on and form themselves. At the very least this represents a marked shift of emphasis compared to the writings of his 'middle' period in the 1970s. Another sign of this shift is a late text where Foucault takes up the question first posed by Kant: 'What is Enlightenment?' He rejects what he calls 'the "blackmail" of the Enlightenment', in other words, the idea that 'one has to be "for" or "against" the Enlightenment'. But at the same time he argues that humanism (which he continues to oppose) and the Enlightenment are not the same thing, and suggests that the Enlightenment project is best continued as 'an attitude, an ethos, a philosophical life in which the critique of what we are is at one and the same time the historical analysis of the limits that are imposed on us and an experiment with the possibility of going beyond them'.[59] This suggests, once again, a convergence between Foucault and the Frankfurt School, and one in which Nietzsche's reduction of reason to an expression of the will to power is no longer simply taken for granted.

11.4   Carrying on the tradition: Habermas and Bourdieu

Foucault's writings are a particularly distinguished example of the kind of critique of modernity now apparently indissociable from the label 'postmodernism' (however much he and other supposed exemplars of this current might reject such a description[60]). The difficulties he encounters – in particular those of specifying the theoretical and political vantage-point from which this critique is conducted – are representative ones: one can see them recurring, for example, in much cruder and less interesting examples of the genre, for example, the work of the cultural theorist Jean Baudrillard. But theories which can, without too much violence to their content, be packaged as postmodernist do not exhaust the contemporary intellectual scene. A number of thinkers have sought to continue what one might call the classical tradition of social theory – represented above all by Marx, Durkheim, and Weber – in a way that is responsive to the 'revolution of language' characteristic of so much twentieth-century thought.

---

[59]   Rabinow, ed., *Foucault Reader*, pp. 42, 43, 50.
[60]   See, for example, Foucault, 'Structuralism', pp. 204–5.

Some of these are Marxists; others, however, are more difficult to classify. Among the latter are two of the most interesting contemporary social theorists, Jürgen Habermas and Pierre Bourdieu. I conclude, therefore, with a discussion of some of the main themes in their work.

(1) *The healing powers of reason: Habermas.* Habermas is the chief intellectual heir of the Frankfurt School.[61] But he is in no sense an uncritical pupil of Horkheimer and Adorno. He points to what he calls the 'performative contradiction' inherent in the *Dialectic of Enlightenment*: 'If they . . . still want to *continue with critique,* they will have to leave at least one rational criterion intact for their explanation of the corruption of *all* rational criteria.'[62] Interestingly, in their correspondence, Horkheimer and Adorno adumbrated precisely the kind of resolution of this paradox that Habermas was to pursue. Thus Horkheimer writes: 'Language intends, quite independently of the psychological intentions of the speaker, the universality of the speaker, the universality that has been ascribed to reason alone. Interpreting this universality necessarily leads to the idea of a correct society.' Thus:

> To speak to someone basically means recognizing him as a possible member of the future association of free human beings. Speech establishes a shared relation towards truth, and is therefore the innermost affirmation of another existence, indeed of all forms of existence according to their capacities. When speech denies any possibilities, it necessarily contradicts itself.[63]

Though Adorno endorsed this idea, it appears in neither his nor Horkheimer's published writings. It became, however, the leitmotif of Habermas's theory of communicative action. 'Our first sentence expresses unequivocally the intention of universal and unconstrained consensus', he says.[64] Every speech-act involves the speaker undertaking to provide the hearer with good reasons for accepting whatever assertion, command, etc. he or she is making. Understanding consists of the hearer's acceptance of this 'redeemable validity-claim'. Implicit in every utterance, therefore, is an orientation towards the achievement of

---

[61]   Jürgen Habermas (1929–   ): born in Düsseldorf and brought up in Gummersbach, where his father was director of the Chamber of Commerce; studied at Göttingen, Zurich, and Bonn universities, 1949–54; joined the Frankfurt Institute for Social Research in 1956 as Adorno's research assistant; after Horkheimer prevented him pursuing his *Habilitation* at Frankfurt, completed it under the supervision of Wolfgang Abendroth at Marburg University; Extraordinary Professor of Philosophy at Heidelberg University, 1961–4; Professor of Philosophy and Sociology at Frankfurt University, 1964–71 ; director of Max Planck Institute, Starnberg, 1971–82; Professor of Philosophy, Frankfurt University, 1982–   .

[62]   J. Habermas, *The Philosophical Discourse of Modernity* (Cambridge, 1987), pp. 119, 126–7.

[63]   Letter to Adorno, 14 Sept. 1941, quoted in R. Wiggershaus, *The Frankfurt School* (Cambridge Mass., 1994), p. 505.

[64]   J. Habermas, *Knowledge and Human Interests* (London, 1972), p. 314.

an uncoerced agreement between speaker and hearer. It is this orientation, not some ungrounded moral aspiration or obsolete philosophy of history, which entitles us to pursue an emancipated society whose basis would be precisely the kind of freely undertaken consensus which is the telos of every speech-act: 'The Utopian perspective of reconciliation and freedom is ingrained in the conditions for the communicative sociation of individuals; it is built into the linguistic mechanism of the reproduction of the species.'[65]

This philosophy of language, which is a development of the speech-act theory developed by J. L. Austin, H. P. Grice, and John Searle, and is most fully expounded in *The Theory of Communicative Action* (1981), provides Habermas with what he believes to be the solution to the dilemmas of the early Frankfurt School. Horkheimer's and Adorno's error was, in effect, to equate reason in general with what they call 'subjective reason', Weber's instrumental rationality, which is oriented towards selecting the most effective means to achieve ends that are, as Parsons puts it, 'random' (see §10.3 above). This reductive conception of reason reflects the fact that they were operating within the framework of the 'philosophy of consciousness' which has dominated Western thought since Descartes. Here subjectivity is conceived as 'monologic', isolated from other subjects and confronting a world of things which it seeks to use and control: from this perspective, reason is necessarily instrumental, a means to allow the subject to dominate nature. Classical Marxism (or what Habermas calls 'praxis philosophy') bases itself on this conception of subjectivity: the 'production paradigm' depicts human beings as constituted through their interaction with nature through the intermediary of labour.[66]

We can escape from this framework, which denies us a vantage-point from which to criticize the work of instrumental rationality,

> only if we give up the paradigm of the philosophy of consciousness – namely a
> subject that represents objects and toils with them – in favour of the paradigm of
> linguistic philosophy – namely that of intersubjective understanding or commun-
> ication – and put the cognitive-instrumental aspect of reason in its place as part of
> a more encompassing *communicative rationality*.[67]

Habermas is therefore as critical as Foucault of any attempt to make the self-certain individual subject the foundation of knowledge, but he believes that Foucault's solution – the attempt to continue Nietzsche's critique of reason – ends up in precisely the same kind of performative contradiction that wrecks *Dialectic of Enlightenment*. What is required, then, is 'a *different* way out of the philosophy of the subject'.[68] The theory of communicative action offers a broader

[65]   J. Habermas, *The Theory of Communicative Action*, I (London, 1984), p. 398.
[66]   Habermas, *Philosophical Discourse*, pp. 75–82.
[67]   Ibid., p. 390.
[68]   Ibid., p. 301.

conception of rationality, one which treats instrumental rationality as merely one form of rationality, pertinent to 'action oriented to success', which is fundamentally different from communicative action, where 'the actions of the agents involved are co-ordinated not through egocentric calculations of success but through acts of reaching understanding'.[69]

This philosophy of language allows Habermas to identify what he argues is the critical weakness of Weber's theory of rationalization, namely that it relies on a one-sided and narrow conception of reason which, like that of the Frankfurt School after him, equates it with instrumental rationality:

> Weber's intuitions point in the direction of a selective pattern of rationalization, a jagged profile of modernization. Yet Weber speaks of paradoxes and not of the partial character of societal rationalization. In his view, the real reason for the dialectic of rationalization is not an unbalanced institutionalization of available cognitive potentials; he locates the seeds of destruction of the rationalization in the very differentiation of independent value-spheres that released that potential and made that rationalization possible.[70]

Modernity thus represents a *partial* realization of the potential inherent in communicative rationality; it is 'an incomplete project'.[71] Habermas follows Weber and Parsons in seeing modernization as essentially a process of differentiation. This crucially affects what he calls the 'lifeworld' (*Lebenswelt*). This concept derives from the idea, found in different forms in both Husserl and Heidegger, that understanding presupposes certain tacit *pre*-understandings which allow us, without being consciously aware of it, to interpret the actions and utterances of others (see §9.2 above). The lifeworld is 'a culturally transmitted and linguistically organized stock of interpretive patterns'; it 'circumscribes action situations in the manner of a preunderstood context that, however, is not addressed'.[72] It forms the background which we take for granted when seeking through our utterances to reach agreement among ourselves.

With the formation of modernity, the lifeworld undergoes rationalization, in two respects. First of all, we see a 'a differentiation of independent cultural value spheres' – science, law and morality, and art emerge as distinct practices regulated by their own specific procedures. It is this development which Weber portrays as the 'war of gods', the struggle of rival values each making incommensurable claims on our obedience (see §7.2 above). This interpretation involves a failure to understand that rationality consists precisely in the formal procedures through which claims in the different value-spheres are assessed:

---

[69]   Habermas, *Theory*, I, pp. 285–6.

[70]   Ibid., I pp. 241–2.

[71]   J. Habermas, 'Modernity—An Incomplete Project', in H. Foster, ed., *Postmodern Culture* (London, 1985).

[72]   J. Habermas, *The Theory of Communicative Action*, II (Cambridge, 1987), pp. 124, 132.

> Weber goes too far when he infers from the loss of the substantial unity of reason
> a polytheism of gods and demons [*Glaubensmächte*] struggling with one another,
> with their irreconcilability rooted in a plurality of competing validity-claims. The
> unity of rationality in the multiplicity of all value-spheres rationalized according
> to their inner logics is secured precisely at the formal level of the argumentative
> redemption of validity-claims.[73]

Secondly, modernization involves the differentiation of system and lifeworld. Here Habermas draws heavily on the tradition of normative functionalism whose chief representatives are Durkheim and Parsons. In order to exist, every society requires social integration, through which the orientations of actors are harmonized in the medium of communicative action. But the imperatives of material reproduction, which receive full expression with the development of capitalism, require the formation of 'systemic mechanisms that stabilize nonintended consequences of action by way of functionally intermeshing action *consequences*'. The two main examples of these mechanisms which Habermas discusses are the bureaucratic state and the market economy. His analysis of them follows Parsons' theory of the 'sub-systems' of polity and economy quite closely (see §10.2 above). Thus, with the development of the market and the state, '[d]elinguistified media of communication such as money and power, connect up interactions in space and time into more and more complex networks that no one has to comprehend or be responsible for.' And so, '[f]ollowing Parsons, we can conceive the integration of society as a continuously renewed compromise between two series of imperatives', those of the essentially communicative understanding of actors rooted in a shared lifeworld (social integration), and those involved in the functional interdependence of sub-systems operating according to logics which we cannot fully control (system integration).[74]

Habermas argues that the differentiation of system and lifeworld is inevitable and, up to a point, desirable. 'Marx's error stems in the end from dialectically clamping together system and lifeworld.' In consequence, 'he fails to recognize the *intrinsic* evolutionary *value* that media-steered sub-systems possess . . . the differentiation of the state apparatus and the economy also represents a higher level of system differentiation, which simultaneously opens up new steering possibilities and forces a reorganization of the old feudal class relationships'.[75] Late capitalism involves an 'institutionalization' of class conflict between capital and labour through the development of structures and policies – parliamentary democracy, the welfare state, and Keynesian demand-management – which represent forms of normative regulation of the sub-systems.

---

[73] Habermas, *Theory*, I, pp. 243, 249.
[74] Ibid., II, p. 150, 184, 233.
[75] Ibid., II, pp. 340, 339.

This appraisal does not mean that Habermas follows Parsons in believing that basically all is well with modernity. On the contrary, he argues that 'capitalist modernization follows a pattern such that cognitive-instrumental rationality surges beyond the bounds of the economy and the state into other, communicatively structured areas of life and achieves a dominance there at the expense of moral-political and aesthetic-practical rationality'. This amounts to 'a *colonization of the lifeworld* . . . the imperatives of the sub-systems make their way into the lifeworld from outside – like colonial masters coming into a tribal society – and force a process of assimilation upon it'.[76] As a result, 'processes of monetarization and bureaucratization penetrate the core domains of cultural reproduction, social integration, and socialization'. These processes represent the rational core of Weber's and the Frankfurt School's critique of modernity. But we should not, like them, despair of reason. Habermas's more differentiated conception of rationality allows us to see that 'it is a question of building up restraining barriers for the exchanges between system and lifeworld and of building in sensors for the exchanges between lifeworld and system'.[77]

Habermas's theory of communicative action represents an extraordinarily impressive attempt to pursue the questions which have been constitutive of social theory since Hegel. How plausible one finds it will depend heavily on one's assessment of the way in which at every level of his system, from his theory of meaning to his analysis of late capitalism, Habermas privileges a tendency towards intersubjective understanding or consensus. As Perry Anderson puts it, 'where, we might say, structuralism and poststructuralism developed a kind of diabolism of language, Habermas has unruffledly produced an angelism'.[78] As I seek to show in the final chapter, whether this is a sustainable approach to a social world riven by every kind of conflict is, to say the least, open to question.[79]

(2) *Competition and finitude: Bourdieu*. Certainly, Habermas's social theory represents a dramatic contrast with Bourdieu's.[80] The latter offers a vision not of a movement towards uncoerced agreement, but of unremitting struggle:

> Every state of the social world is thus no more than a temporary equilibrium, a moment in the dynamics through which the adjustment between distributions and incorporated or institutionalized classifications is constantly broken and restored.

[76] Ibid., II, pp. 304, 355.
[77] Habermas, *Philosophical Discourse*, pp. 355, 364.
[78] P. Anderson, *In the Tracks of Historical Materialism* (London, 1983), p. 64.
[79] See also A. Callinicos, *Against Postmodernism* (Cambridge, 1989), ch. 4.
[80] Pierre Bourdieu (1930–): born in the Béarn area of south-eastern France; son of a civil servant; studied philosophy at the École Normale Supérieure; schoolteacher, 1955–6; served as French conscript in Algeria, 1956–8; from this experience wrote *Sociologie d'Algérie* (1958); taught at the University of Algiers, 1958–60; taught at universities of Paris and of Lille, 1960–4; Director of Studies at École Pratique des Hautes Études, 1964–81; director of Centre de Sociologie Européene, 1968– ; elected Professor of Sociology at the Collège de France, 1981.

> The struggle which is the very principle of the distributions is inextricably a struggle to appropriate rare goods and a struggle to impose the legitimate way of perceiving the power-relations manifested by the distributions, a representation which, through it own efficacy, can help to perpetuate or subvert these power-relations.[81]

Bourdieu, like Lévi-Strauss, is a philosopher turned anthropologist (and, later, sociologist). He started out employing the tools of structural analysis, but his research among the Kabyle Berbers of Algeria uncovered a systematic discrepancy between 'official' kinship structures and actual practice. He concluded that

> the logical relations of kinship, which the structuralist tradition almost completely autonomizes with respect to economic determinants, exist in practice only through and for the official and unofficial uses made of them by agents whose inclination to keep them in working order and to make them work more intensively . . . rises to the degree to which they actually or potentially fulfil useful functions, satisfying material or symbolic interests.[82]

Talk of interests reintroduces agency into social theory. Axel Honneth suggests that 'Bourdieu is guided by utilitarian motifs in overcoming structuralism. He proceeds from the assumption that symbolic constructions . . . should also be conceived as social activities performed from the point of view of utility maximization.'[83] And indeed the idea that any given state of society is the product of 'a struggle to appropriate rare goods' is a generalization of the economic model the marginalist tradition (drawing on utilitarianism) constructed, where competing actors seek to make the best use of scarce resources. Bourdieu goes so far as to claim that '[t]here is an economy of practices, a reason immanent in practices,' that is 'constitutive of the structure of rational practices, that is, the practice most appropriate to achieve the objectives inscribed in the logic of the particular field at the lowest cost'. One such objective is 'the maximization of monetary profit, the only one recognized by economism'.[84]

In proposing 'a general theory of the economy of practices' of which the 'theory of strictly economic practices is a particular case', Bourdieu does not totally break with structuralism.[85] Thus he toys with the formulations '*genetic structuralism*', or '*constructivist structuralism*' in order to characterize his own position. He believes that 'there exist in the social world itself, and not merely in symbolic systems, language, myth, etc., objective structures which are independent of the consciousness and desires of agents and are capable of guiding or constraining their practices or their representations'.[86]

---

[81] P. Bourdieu (1980), *The Logic of Practice* (Cambridge, 1990), p. 141.

[82] Ibid., p. 35.

[83] A. Honneth, 'The Fragmented World of Symbolic Forms', *Theory Culture & Society*, 3/3 (1986), p. 56.

[84] Bourdieu, *Logic*, p. 50.

[85] Ibid., p. 122.

[86] P. Bourdieu, *In Other Words* (Cambridge, 1990), pp. 14, 123.

Social structure is in fact, according to Bourdieu, a Saussurian system of differences in which agents' positions are defined by their antagonistic relations to one other:

> These objective relations are relations between the positions occupied in the distribution of resources which are or may become active, effective, like trumps in a game of cards, in the competition for the appropriation of the rare goods of which this social universe is the locus. These fundamental social powers are, according to my empirical researches, economic capital, in its different forms, and cultural capital, and also symbolic capital, a form which is assumed by different kinds of capital when they are perceived and recognized as legitimate.[87]

Bourdieu's general theory of economic practices thus involves a generalization of the concept of capital to embrace more than narrowly 'economic' capital. Although he pays homage to Marx's formula that 'capital is a social relation', in fact, as Craig Calhoun points out, 'Bourdieu . . . consistently sees capital as a resource (that is, a form of wealth) which yields power'.[88] Thus cultural capital is the degree of mastery one has of the cultural practices which a given society recognizes as legitimate. Educational capital – the formal qualifications an individual acquires – is one index of the amount of cultural capital, but the two are not equivalent. Cultural capital is, for example, present in 'the paradoxical relationship to culture made up of self-confidence amid (relative) ignorance and of casualness amid familiarity, which bourgeois families hand down to their offspring as if it were an heirloom'.[89]

The different forms of capital are mutually convertible. For example, the bourgeoisie may undertake the 'reconversion of economic capital into educational capital', investing in the acquisition of academic qualifications by their offspring so that the latter may gain access to a share of profits in the form of salaries and other kinds of 'earned income'.[90] The most important such conversion involves symbolic capital. Drawing on Marcel Mauss's analysis of 'primitive' exchange in *The Gift*, Bourdieu argues that in pre-capitalist societies the generosity of the rich serves as a means through which the economically dominant class can secure the consent of the dominated in the shape of gratitude, respect, and a sense of obligation:

> In an economy which is defined by the refusal to recognize the 'objective' truth of 'economic' practices, that is, the law of 'naked self-interest' and egoistic calculation, even 'economic' capital cannot act unless it succeeds in being

---

[87] Ibid., p. 128.
[88] C. Calhoun, 'Habitus, Field, and Capital', in C. Calhoun et al., eds, *Bourdieu: Critical Perspectives* (Cambridge, 1993), p. 69. Compare P. Bourdieu (1979), *Distinction* (London, 1984), p. 113.
[89] Bourdieu, *Distinction*, p. 66.
[90] Ibid., p. 137.

recognized through a conversion that can render unrecognizable the true principle of its efficacy. Symbolic capital is this denied capital, recognized as legitimate, that is, misrecognized as capital (recognition, acknowledgement, in the sense of gratitude aroused by benefits, can be one of the foundations of this recognition).[91]

This mechanism of 'symbolic violence' – 'the conversion of economic capital into symbolic capital, which produces relations of dependence that have an economic basis but are disguised under a veil of moral relations' – operates in capitalist societies as well.[92] Indeed, it is the process through which a given social structure is reproduced:

> By virtue of the fact that symbolic capital is nothing more than economic or cultural capital which is acknowledged or recognized, when it is acknowledged in accordance with the categories of perception that it imposes, the symbolic power-relations tend to reproduce and to reinforce the power-relations which constitute the structure of the social space.[93]

It follows, Bourdieu believes, that a proper account of social class must take into account the dimension of symbolic capital: 'A class is defined by its *being-perceived* as by its *being*, by its consumption . . . as much as by its position in the relations of production (even if it is true that the latter governs the former).' His best-known book, *Distinction* (1979), pursues this project in loving detail. An empirical study of the judgements of taste, particularly (though not exclusively) with respect to art, made by the bearers of different class positions, it allows Bourdieu to explore the endless struggle for classification which permeates and constitutes modern societies. Modern art presupposes the autonomy of cultural production which in turn privileges 'that of which the artist is master, i.e., form, manner, style rather than the "subject", the external referent, which involves subordination to functions'. Responding appropriately to art of this kind requires 'a specific cultural competence' which 'is, for the most part, acquired simply by contact with works of art'.[94]

This 'aesthetic disposition' is differentially distributed throughout society. It is directly opposed to the 'the "popular aesthetic"', which is 'based on the affirmation of continuity between art and life, which implies the subordination of form to function'. The capacity to respond appropriately to autonomously produced art thus allows its bearer to distinguish herself from the working class. Indeed: 'The pure aesthetic is rooted in an ethic, or rather, an ethos of elective distance from the necessities of the natural and social world.' Such a stance presupposes the possession of economic capital, for '[e]conomic power is first

---

[91]   Bourdieu, *Logic*, p. 118.
[92]   Ibid., p. 123.
[93]   Bourdieu, *In Other Words*, p. 135.
[94]   Bourdieu, *Distinction*, pp. 483, 3, 4.

and foremost a power to keep economic necessity at arm's length.' But the aesthetic disposition does not simply reflect the conversion of economic into cultural capital. Both the 'dominant' and the middle class are internally differentiated between a fraction which possesses considerable economic capital (employers at the higher level, craftsmen and shopkeepers at the intermediate level) and a fraction that is materially poorer but has plentiful cultural capital (university and secondary-school teachers in the 'dominant class', primary-school teachers in the middle class). Therefore 'the structure of the distribution of economic capital is symmetrical and opposite to that of cultural capital'.[95]

The uneven distribution of cultural and economic capital both between and within classes therefore gives rise to a relentless struggle in which the contestants each seek to take advantage of the resources in which they are relatively wealthy in order to impose their definition of the social and in particular of their position within it on the others: 'The struggle of classifications is a fundamental division of class struggle. The power of imposing a vision of divisions, that is the power of making visible and explicit the social divisions that are implicit, is the political power *par excellence*: it is the power to make groups, to manipulate the objective structure of society'.[96]

If *Distinction* offers an account of the demand side of cultural production – the consumption of works of art – Bourdieu's more recent *The Rules of Art* (1992) portrays the supply side. Here he traces the origins of the idea of autonomous art, particularly in the fiction and criticism of Flaubert under the Second Empire, but also develops a theory of the field of cultural production, which is in turn one instance of a more general theory of fields. The concept of a field is a specification of Bourdieu's 'relational' view of society. Every field consists of a set of positions defined by their mutually antagonistic relations; it exists, therefore, in the continuous struggles among the bearers of these positions. The constitution during the nineteenth century of an autonomous field of cultural production in both painting and literature took the form of competition among producers for symbolic capital where the decisive claim is that of the aesthetic innovator who is able to gain recognition for his claim to novelty.

The artistic field is defined by its antagonistic relationship to the 'economic' field in the narrow sense, represented in this case by commercial publishing, art-dealers, etc. Within the artistic field, the commercially successful writer or painter can claim far less symbolic capital than the 'pure' artist. But, in a process that has the structure of Weber's dialectic of charisma and routine, the artists who are successful within the artistic field tend to gain 'consecrated' status. This allows them to convert symbolic capital into economic capital; but it also makes their works more commonplace and less scarce, and so renders them vulnerable to the challenge of new innovators. The further the autonomous

---

[95] Ibid., pp. 32, 5, 55, 120.
[96] Bourdieu, *In Other Words*, p. 138.

development of the aristic field goes, the more writers and painters internalize the whole history of the field, defining themselves negatively with respect to both their predecessors (who may, as the process of innovation speeds up, be only a few years older) and their contemporaries.

Distinction and *The Rules of Art* are major works by any standard. Yet reading them one is struck by the extent to which Bourdieu is influenced by the classical structuralism of Saussure and Lévi-Strauss. Thus, when presenting a complex set of diagrams depicting the relationships between the different forms of capital and the dispositions and strategies of its bearers, he says that his aim is to show 'the homologies between systems of difference'.[97] Or, again, he writes of the 'structural and functional homology between the space of authors and the space of consumers (and of critics) and the correspondence between the social structures of spaces of production and the mental structures which authors, critics, and consumers apply to their products (themselves organized according to these structures'.[98] Direct or inverse homologies between structures defined by the differential relations among their terms play a central explanatory role in Bourdieu's analyses.

Bourdieu nevertheless expresses his vehement opposition to 'structuralism and its strange philosophy of action which, implicitly in the Lévi-Straussian notion of the unconscious and avowedly among the Althusserians, made the agent disappear by reducing it to the role of supporter or bearer . . . of the structure'.[99] One of the main purposes of his best-known concept, the *habitus*, is to transcend the opposition between structuralism, which reduces agents to the effects of structures, and the methodological individualism of Sartre and rational-choice theorists such as Jon Elster who treat structures in turn as merely the unintended consequences of individual actors.

By *habitus* Bourdieu means a particular set of dispositions, consisting especially in the practical abilities required to apply categories that are means of perceiving and of appreciating the world, appropriate to a specific objective position within the class structure. Thus:

> The conditionings associated with a particular class of conditions produce conditions of existence, produce *habitus*, systems of durable, transposable dispositions, structuring structures predisposed to function as structuring structures, that is, as principles which generate and organize practices and representations that can be objectively adapted to their outcomes without presupposing a conscious aiming at ends or an express mastery of the operations necessary in order to attain them. Objectively 'regulated' and 'regular' without being in any way the product of obedience to rules, they can be collectively orchestrated without being the product of the organizing action of a conductor.[100]

[97]   Bourdieu, *Distinction*, p. 126.
[98]   P. Bourdieu (1992), *The Rules of Art* (Cambridge, 1996), p. 162.
[99]   Ibid., p. 179.
[100] Bourdieu, *Logic*, p. 53.

The *habitus* constitutes the means through which individual actors are adapted to the needs of specific social structures. It must therefore be seen as 'a virtue made of necessity'; each class's *habitus* reflects its adjustment to the possibilities defined by its access to the different kinds of capital. Thus in the case of the working class 'necessity includes for them all that is usually meant by the word, that is, an inescapable deprivation of material goods'. The relative 'modesty' of working-class tastes reflects a tacit recognition that any more expansive aspirations do not correspond to the distribution of social power. Accordingly: 'Social class is not defined solely by a position in the relations of production, but by the class *habitus* that is "normally" (i.e. with a high statistical probability) associated with that position'.[101]

Bourdieu does not think of the *habitus* as anything resembling a set of consciously held beliefs. For one thing, it is quite literally embodied – 'social necessity turned into nature, converted into motor schemes and bodily automatisms', present in, for example, tastes for different kinds of food, and in the way in which people hold and orient themselves physically, dress, and so on.[102] For another, it consists not in anything resembling the grasp of an explicit proposition, but a kind of tacit competence implicit in actors' practical ability to cope with a wide range of situations in ways that are predictable without being reducible to the conscious observance of a set of rules. Bourdieu's analysis here reflects the influence of Heidegger and the later Wittgenstein, both of whom see social conduct as consisting in the mastery of practical skills unamenable to formal representation. Philosophers sympathetic to these thinkers have therefore welcomed Bourdieu's social theory.[103]

It is nevertheless unclear whether he has succeeded in transcending the opposition between structuralism and methodological individualism. The *habitus* represents the effect of social conditioning on agents which adapts them to the requirements of the field in which they operate. Bourdieu believes that such a pre-established harmony (he even invokes Leibniz, the author of this concept), or 'spontaneous orchestration of dispositions', legitimizes the idea of 'objective strategies', that is, of

> those strings of 'moves' which are objectively organized as strategies without being the product of a genuine strategic intention . . . If each stage in the sequence of ordered and oriented actions that constitute objective strategies can appear as determined by anticipations of the future, and in particular, of its own consequences (which is what justifies the use of the concept of strategy), it is because the practices that are generated by the *habitus* and are governed by the past conditions of production of their generative principles are adapted in advance to the

---

[101] Bourdieu, *Distinction*, p. 372.
[102] Bourdieu, *Logic*, p. 68.
[103] For example, H. Dreyfus and P. Rabinow, 'Can There be a Science of Existential Structure and Social Meaning?'; C. Taylor, 'To Follow a Rule . . .', both in Calhoun et al., eds, *Bourdieu*.

objective conditions whenever the conditions in which the *habitus* functions have remained identical, or similar, to the conditions in which it was constituted.[104]

This argument looks very much like a form of functionalism, in which a phenomenon is explained by its beneficial consequences (in this case the reproduction of social structures) without the mechanism responsible for this process being specified.[105] Bourdieu has vehemently repudiated this criticism, without, however, more than restating his original claim.[106] It is true that, as the passage just cited implies, he admits the possibility of situations where *habitus* and field are not mutually adjusted because the present objective situation is different from that in which the *habitus* was formed. He calls this 'the Don Quixote effect', which arises 'in cases of discordance between the conditions of acquisition and conditions of use, i.e., when the practices generated by the *habitus* appear as ill-adjusted because they are attuned to an earlier state of the objective conditions'.[107]

Yet the constant reiteration, notably but not solely in *Distinction*, of the phrase 'everything takes place as if' suggests that society is objectively oriented towards goals even if no individual or collective agent has adopted or pursued them. Similarly, though the various fields are constituted by the struggles among agents, these struggles serve primarily to reproduce the existing structure of the fields rather than to transform them. Thus, Bourdieu comments on struggles over classification in which educational qualifications become more widely available, leading to the development of new, more exclusive qualifications which preserve the existing structure of social differences, 'what the competitive struggle makes everlasting is not different conditions, but the difference between conditions'. This shows that 'social contradictions and struggles are not all, or always, in contradiction with the perpetuation of the established order'.[108]

Bourdieu does not claim that social struggle always reproduces the existing order. Indeed: 'Competitive struggle is the form of class struggle which the dominated classes allow to be imposed on them when they accept the stakes offered by the dominant classes.' His overall conception of class structure, though very sketchily outlined (the boundaries of the 'dominant class', for example, are set very wide), plainly does bear some kinship to Marx's, since both view class as a set of antagonistic relationships. Yet the classification struggles on which he concentrates seem very close to the picture Weber paints of status groups competing in order to increase their social prestige. Bourdieu's sympathies are plainly with the 'dominated', as is evident, for example, in his

---

[104]   Bourdieu, *Logic*, pp. 59, 62.
[105]   See J. Elster, *Sour Grapes* (Cambridge, 1984), pp. 69ff., 103–7.
[106]   For example, Bourdieu, *In Other Words*, pp. 10–12.
[107]   Bourdieu, *Distinction*, p. 109.
[108]   Ibid., p. 164.

description of the 'ethic of convivial indulgence' involved in forms of working-class consumption that prize the immediate pleasures of eating and drinking, and thereby challenge 'the new ethic of sobriety for the sake of slimness, which is most recognized at the highest levels of the social hierarchy'.[109] Yet he does not offer those at the bottom of society any prospect of a collective escape from the structures of class domination and cultural distinction.

That this is not merely a consequence of the particular focus of Bourdieu's published writings but is an inherent feature of his social theory is suggested by this remarkable passage from his inaugural lecture at the Collège de France, in which Durkheim's deification of society meets Heidegger's analysis of Being-towards-death:

> What is expected of God is only ever obtained from society, which alone has the power to justify you, to liberate you from facticity, contingency and absurdity; but – and this is doubtless the fundamental antinomy – only in a differential, distinctive way: every form of the sacred has its profane complement, all distinction generates its own vulgarity, and the competition for a social life that will be known and recognized, which will free you from insignificance, is a struggle to the death for symbolic life and death.[110]

So the only way to give human finitude a meaning is (to use one of Bourdieu's favourite metaphors) to play the game, and throw oneself into the perpetual struggle to transmute one's resources into symbolic capital. For all Bourdieu's undoubted originality, and his determined effort to liberate himself from an intellectual context dominated by the heritage of structuralism, he offers another restatement of the theme common, despite all their differences, to Lévi-Strauss, Althusser, and Foucault, that human beings are fated to be prisoners of the structures of domination.

---

[109] Ibid., pp. 165, 179.
[110] Bourdieu, *In Other Words*, p. 196.

12

In Place of a Conclusion

Evidently this overview of the development of social theory over the past 200 years cannot end, as does Hegel's *Phenomenology of Spirit*, in a moment of reconciliation in which the various contending viewpoints are integrated as partial insights into a single, total truth. As the preceding chapter should have made clear, the debate about modernity goes on. The different positions staked out in that debate – the revolutionary transformation, critical acceptance, or outright rejection of modernity – may be reformulated, they may gain strength as a result of wider intellectual developments or historical transformations, or they may go into temporary eclipse or find only weak or oblique expression. But the struggle between them is still unresolved.

Rather than pretend an impossible impartiality or seek the chimera of absolute knowledge, in this final chapter I merely offer a series of remarks about some of the key issues raised by the current state of the debate. No doubt these observations will make more explicit my own views about the best way to carry on social theory, but their aim is not to close off controversy, but to identify some of the questions which it is particularly urgent to address.

(1) *Postmodernity?* The first of these questions concerns the issue which has come to dominate cultural debate since the end of the 1970s. Has the dialectic of modernity been transcended thanks to our entry into a postmodern condition constituted by the collapse of the 'grand narratives' which offer comprehensive interpretations of the totality of human history? The short answer to this question is 'No.' Many reasons could be offered in support of this response, but two are particularly relevant here. The first is that versions of what we now call the postmodernist critique of modernity have been around for a long time – at least since Nietzsche.

French post-structuralism has since the 1960s reformulated this critique, detaching it from the biologistic cosmology of *The Will to Power*, and situating it with respect to issues arising from, among other things, Saussure's theory of language and Heidegger's philosophy of Being. In the process, the Nietzschean position has been enriched, and we have a much better idea of both its potential and its limitations. But only historical ignorance or rhetorical exaggeration can explain the claims made for the radical novelty of the kind of critique of modernity developed by Foucault, Deleuze, and Derrida in particular. Thus, as we have seen, towards the end of his life Foucault began to realize that his problematization of the Enlightenment had been largely anticipated by the Frankfurt School. Post-structuralism reactivated and redeployed a set of arguments that have been around for over a century.

Secondly, these arguments have not definitively resolved the debate on modernity. The mere existence of social theories as powerful and sophisticated as Habermas's and Bourdieu's which stake out positions at odds with postmodernism should make this clear. Habermas's *The Philosophical Discourse of Modernity* – by far the most powerful theoretical critique of postmodernism – has gone without serious answer. The fact that postmodernism has nevertheless become entrenched as the unchallengeable orthodoxy in many parts of the Western academy invites a sociological explanation. Ideas that spoke to the sense of political disillusionment of many members of the 1960s generation (see §11.1 above) have now become institutionalized in many university departments, providing the basis on which courses are set and assessed, degrees awarded, appointments made, and book contracts awarded. To that extent, postmodernism has become the Parsonian sociology of our *fin de siècle*.[1]

This is no reason to give way to the pressures to accept postmodernist definitions of the issues confronting social theorists (as well as the rest of us). To do so is to risk the enormous intellectual impoverishment that would follow from ignoring the resources offered by the traditions which represent the other positions in the debate about modernity – for example, Weberian historical sociology and those versions of Marxism which have survived the debacle of Stalinism. Parodoxically, despite postmodernists' claims to represent intellectual openness and plurality, it is only by resisting their attempts to close this debate that social theory is likely to retain its vitality.

(2) *Modernity and capitalism.* This then raises the question of the terms on which the debate should be conducted. The concept of modernity is in fact highly ambiguous. It can be understood first of all as a philosophical idea – as the historical realization of the Enlightenment's conception of a present which justifies itself by its difference from the past it leaves behind and by the indefinite progress it will achieve in the future (see §1.2 above). This is Habermas's 'incomplete project'. Secondly, and more concretely, modernity can be thought of as a particular kind of society, typically specified in terms of an evolutionary social theory which treats it as a stage in human history – the concept of industrial society which Durkheim inherited from Comte and Saint-Simon is an

---

[1]   See A. Callinicos, 'Postmodernism as Normal Science', *British Journal of Sociology*, 46 (1995).

example. Thirdly, modernity can be identified with the particular kind of experience associated with this kind of society; Marshall Berman has given a brilliant account of this type of experience:

> There is a mode of vital experience – experience of space and time, of the self and others, of life's possibilities and perils – that is shared by men and women all over the world today. I will call this body of experience 'modernity'. To be modern is to find ourselves in an environment that promises us adventure, power, joy, growth, transformation of ourselves and the world – and, at the same time, that threatens to destroy everything we have, everything we know, everything we are. Modern environments and experiences cut across all boundaries of geography and ethnicity, of class and nationality, of religion and ideology: in this sense modernity can be said to unite all mankind. But it is a paradoxical unity, a unity of disunity: it pours us into a maelstrom of perpetual disintegration and renewal, of struggle and contradiction, of ambiguity and anguish. To be modern is to be part of a universe in which, as Marx said, 'all that is solid melts into air'.[2]

These three concepts of modernity – as philosophical idea, form of society, and historical experience – are not equivalent to one another. In the famous passage from the *Manifesto* which Berman cites, Marx treats '[c]onstant revolutionizing of production, uninterrupted disturbance of all social conditions, everlasting uncertainty and agitation' as distinguishing features, not of modernity, but of 'the bourgeois epoch' (see §4.2 above). One might say that he explains what Berman calls the experience of modernity in terms of the laws of motion of a specific socio-economic system, the capitalist mode of production, and in particular of its peculiarly dynamic and destabilizing character.

This then poses the question of whether the concepts of capitalism and modernity represent alternative ways of theorizing the distinctive form of society which might be seen as both a historical realization of the philosophical idea of modernity and the context in which the specifically 'modern' experience analysed by Berman becomes possible. To put it another way, is modernity (as idea and experience) a response to and a consequence of capitalism, or is capitalism merely one of the dimensions of modernity (conceived as the social form produced by Hobsbawm's dual revolution)? Anthony Giddens selects the latter alternative. He argues that modernity has four 'institutional dimensions' – capitalism, industrialism, surveillance, and war. Each of these dimensions is irreducible to the others; there is, therefore, no sense in which capitalism, for example, can be responsible for the general characteristics of modernity.[3]

The issues involved here are plainly more than the verbal one of whether 'capitalism' or 'modernity' is a better label. In particular, there is, first, the methodological question of whether or not any form of social power should be

---

[2] M. Berman, *All That Is Solid Melts Into Air* (London, 1983), p. 15.
[3] A. Giddens, *The Consequences of Modernity* (Cambridge, 1990), pp. 55–63.

accorded explanatory primacy over the others. Weberian historical sociologists like Giddens are committed to explanatory pluralism, and therefore answer this question in the negative. Michael Mann writes of the formation of classes and nation-states during the 'long nineteenth century' (1760–1914):

> they actually arose together, and this created a further unresolved problem of ultimate primacy: the extent to which social life was to be organized around, on the one hand, diffuse, market, transnational, and ultimately capitalist principles or, on the other hand, around authoritative, territorial, national, and statist ones . . . By 1914, no simple choice had been made – nor has one yet been made. These considerations remain the key ambivalence of modern civilization.[4]

There is, secondly, the related, but logically independent and substantive, question of whether modernity has, as it were, transcended capitalism. The idea of 'high' or 'late' modernity developed by Giddens among others tends to imply that it has. Thus he writes: 'Rather than entering a period of postmodernity, we are moving into one in which the consequences of modernity are becoming more radicalized and universalized than before.'[5] Ulrich Beck has sought to conceptualize these consequences through what he calls 'the theory of reflexive modernization: at the turn of the twenty-first century the unleashed process of modernization is overrunning and overcoming its co-ordinate system'.[6]

Industrial society, Beck argues, is 'a *semi*-modern society', since it '*never* is and *never* was possible only as industrial society, but always as half industrial and half *feudal* society, whose feudal side is not a relic of tradition, but the *product* and *foundation* of industrial society'. Among these 'feudal' prerequisites are the class division of society between labour and capital, the nuclear family, the sexual division of labour, and large-scale public and private bureaucratic organizations. But the process of modernization, which in the nineteenth century swept away pre-industrial society, is now feeding on itself, thereby undermining the structures of industrial society. As a result, '*another modernity is coming into being*'.[7]

What are the decisive features of this 'other modernity'?

> In the welfare states of the West, reflexive modernization dissolves the traditional parameters of industrial society: class culture and consciousness, gender and family roles. It dissolves these forms of the conscience collective, on which depend and to which refer the social and political organizations and institutions in industrial society. These detraditionalizations happen in a *social surge of individualization*. At the same time the *relations* of inequality remain stable. How is

---

[4] M. Mann, *The Sources of Social Power*, II (Cambridge, 1993), p. 3.
[5] Giddens, *Consequences*, p. 3.
[6] U. Beck (1986), *Risk Society* (London, 1992), p. 87.
[7] Ibid., pp. 14, 89, 11.

this possible? Against the background of a comparatively high material standard
of living and advanced social security systems, the people have been removed
from class commitments and have to refer to themselves in planning their individual labour-market biographies.[8]

In this 'capitalism *without* classes, but with individualized social inequality
and all the related social and political problems', social conflict takes new forms.
Two are particularly important. First, '[i]n advanced modernity the social production of *wealth* is systematically accompanied by the social production of
risks.' The modernization process creates new hazards and uncertainties, largely
because of the unintended consequences of the use of scientific knowledge to
control nature: global warming and mad cow disease are two obvious examples. Risk transcends national borders and class divisions: '*poverty is hierar-
chic, smog is democratic*'. Therefore 'everything which threatens life on this
Earth also threatens the property and commercial interests of those who live
from the commodification of life and its prerequisites'. The conflicts that develop in this 'risk society' cut across class lines. They are '*doctrinal struggles*
within *civilization* over the proper road for modernity': at stake in them is the
status of science and the struggle to democratize it.[9]

Secondly, the process of 'individualization' affects in particular that 'modern counter-modernity' which is the nuclear family. This represents a form of
status hierarchy, in which roles are ascribed on the basis of birth. But 'these
inequalities contradict the principles of modernity, and become problematic
and conflictual in the continuity of reflexive modernization'. The result is reflected not simply in macro-processes such as the rebirth of feminism and the
progressive incorporation of women into the labour market, but also in the
micro-struggles between individual women and men as they seek to redefine
their personal relationships: 'In *all* forms of male–female cohabitation (before,
during and after marriage), the *conflicts of the century* break through. Here
they always show their private, personal face. But the family is *only the setting,
not the cause* of the events.'[10]

Beck's is perhaps the most systematically argued, and certainly one of the
most influential, attempts to articulate the widespread sense among contemporary social theorists that Western societies have experienced fundamental change
over the past thirty years. One might regard him and others, notably Giddens,
whose recent writings have developed along parallel lines, as seeking to identify the kernel of truth concealed amid the extravagances and fallacies of
postmodernism. Several Marxist writers, notably Fredric Jameson and David
Harvey, have attempted something similar, arguing that the emergence of
Postmodernist art must be understood as a consequence of the emergence of a

[8]   Ibid., p. 87.
[9]   Ibid., pp. 88, 19, 36, 39, 40.
[10]   Ibid., pp. 107, 104.

new phase of capitalist development, which they call respectively 'multi-national capitalism' and 'flexible accumulation'.[11]

The issues raised by this quite diverse body of writing are far too complex and wide-ranging properly to be addressed here. But it may nevertheless be helpful to make four points, all of which involve reservations about Beck's theory of reflexive modernization. The first concerns his conception of industrial society as a 'semi-modern' hybrid. Beck stresses that the 'feudal' aspects of this society – class structure, say, or the nuclear family – are not pre-industrial survivals, but arise from the modernization process itself: 'The bit of the Middle Ages that industrial society not just preserved but produced, is melting away.' The reason why this is happening is that there is 'a *contradiction* between the universal principles of modernity – civil rights, equality, functional differentiation, methods of argumentation and skepticism – and the exclusive structure of institutions, in which these principles can only be realized on a *partial, sectoral and exclusive* basis'.[12]

The nuclear family is thus 'feudal' because it is inegalitarian. This sets it in conflict with 'the universal principles of modernity', which are normatively defined essentially in terms of the aspirations of the Enlightenment. The implication is that modernization has a necessarily democratizing dynamic: hence its contemporary tendency to generate struggles over interpersonal relationships and the status of science. But it is not obvious why the development of industrial society should necessarily undermine inegalitarian social structures; there is at least as much evidence that it promotes the greater centralization of economic and political power. Beck notes (and overstates) contemporary trends towards 'the *dismantling* of hierarchically organized mega-bureaucracies and administrative apparatus'.[13] But these changes have not been accompanied by an increase in citizens' political control over their governments in liberal democracies, while at the economic level the decline of 'organized capitalism' caused by the increased dominance of national economies by multinational corporations and globally integrated financial markets has led to the strengthening of democratically unaccountable concentrations of economic power.

This suggests the importance of distinguishing between the explanatory theory of the capitalist mode of production as a socio-economic system with its distinctive dynamics and phases of development from the normative philosophical idea of modernity as the actualization of the ideals of the Enlightenment. Drawing this distinction then poses, secondly, the question of how novel are the tendencies towards 'individualization' on which Beck lays such stress. After all, such tendencies form one of the main themes of Tocqueville's analysis

---

[11] F. Jameson, *Postmodernism, or, the Cultural Logic of Late Capitalism* (London, 1991); D. Harvey, *The Condition of Postmodernity* (Oxford, 1989).

[12] Beck, *Risk Society*. pp. 118, 14.

[13] Ibid., p. 218.

of democratic societies. Both Lukács and the Frankfurt School used Marx's theory of commodity fetishism in order to conceptualize the atomization of social life under capitalism. Beck does indeed take these arguments further in that he claims that individualization is breaking down class identities. He predicts: 'Class society will pale into insignificance beside an *industrialized society of employees.*'[14]

The thought here is not so much that class inequalities are disappearing but that they are increasingly likely to be experienced as constituting individual problems to be solved through personal strategies. This raises a third question: to what extent is Beck extrapolating from relatively short-term trends? The 1980s, when he published his theory of reflexive modernization, were a time when, as noted in §11.1, the workers' movement throughout the Western world experienced severe setbacks as a result of a phase of brutal capitalist restructuring. These defeats cast doubt on the viability of working-class politics; at the same time, the hopes of many radical intellectuals focused on the so-called 'new social movements', one of whose main concerns is environmental destruction, notably in West Germany, where the Greens made some important electoral advances. How much, then, is the idea of 'risk society' a generalization of this political mood? Certainly, when confronted with the description by Beck and Elizabeth Beck-Gernsheim of 'the antagonisms between men and women over gender roles' as 'the "status struggle" which comes after the class struggle', it is hard not to feel that the life-experiences of a generation of Western intellectuals are being hypostatized into social trends.[15]

Other social theorists have been much more sceptical about the idea that Western modernity underwent an epochal transformation in the late twentieth century. For example, W. G. Runciman argues that 'English society did undergo an evolution from one to another sub-type of capitalist liberal democracy between 1915 and 1922', marked by a much higher level of state involvement in the economy and in the provision of welfare, the emergence of a more managerial capitalism, and the institutionalization of class conflict. Neither the social reforms introduced by Labour under Clement Attlee (1945–51) nor the free-market policies forced through by the Conservatives under Margaret Thatcher (1979–90) fundamentally altered this 'sub-type': 'The 1940s, like the 1980s, exemplify not a qualitative change in the relations between the economy and the state but rather the continuing disjunction between the rhetoric of politicians and journalists and the underlying processes of social evolution which only with hindsight can be seen for what they are.'[16] Runciman dismisses the so-called 'Thatcher revolution' as 'no more . . . than another swing in the pendulum', a mere phase in the constantly shifting balance between state and

---

[14] Ibid., p. 100.

[15] U. Beck and E. Beck-Gernsheim, *The Normal Chaos of Love* (Cambridge, 1995), p. 2.

[16] W. G. Runciman, *A Treatise on Social Theory*, III (Cambridge, 1997), pp. 11, 82.

market, and stresses 'the importance, in the study of the evolution of any soci-ety, of not mistaking a cycle for a trend'.[17]

Whether or not we agree with Runciman's specific arguments, his method-ological warning undoubtedly has a bearing on the various theories which an-nounce the emergence of 'another modernity' at the end of the twentieth century. To the extent that current trends towards 'individualization' and 'personaliz-ation' are bound up with a dramatic process of capitalist reorganization, they may generate their own reaction. Beck seems to believe that the welfare state will prevent social inequalities from giving rise to forms of collective action: 'Processes of individualization . . . can only become entrenched when material immiseration, as the condition of the formation of classes as predicted by Marx, has been *overcome*.'[18]

But contemporary trends involve not simply extensive economic restructur-ing – the decline of traditional manufacturing industries, the 'downsizing' of individual firms, and so on – but also the emergence of a public policy con-sensus on the need drastically to reduce the systems of social protection that were a fundamental feature of the postwar welfare state. The resulting situ-ation – chronic mass unemployment, unrelenting pressure on the earnings and working conditions of wage-earners, and continually eroded welfare provision – hardly suggests that 'material immiseration . . . has been *overcome*'. On the contrary, the available evidence points towards growing inequalities of wealth and income accompanied by increasing levels of absolute poverty. Why should these conditions not give rise to distinctively working-class forms of collective organization and action?

Developments in continental Europe during the 1990s suggest that this question is more than idle speculation. Here the wider policy consensus on the necessity of 'welfare reform' was brought into sharper focus by the obligation of governments seeking to meet the conditions for participation in the single European currency by sharply cutting public expenditure. The ensuing assault on the welfare state produced a number of major social confrontations, of which the most important to date has been the French public sector strikes in Novem-ber–December 1995. Ignacio Ramonet calls these 'the greatest social offensive since May 1968', and 'the first collective rebellion, on the scale of an entire country, against neo-liberalism'.[19]

The French strikes, which played a decisive part in creating the political climate in which the parties of the left won the legislative elections of May–June 1997, are simply the most spectacular instance of a more widespread trend towards class confrontation in the European Union. The development of this

[17]   W. G. Runciman, 'Has British Capitalism Changed Since the First World War?', *British Jour-nal of Sociology*, 44 (1993), pp. 64, 66.
[18]   Beck, *Risk Society*, pp. 95–6.
[19]   I. Ramonet, 'Le Retour de politique', in *Offensives du mouvement social*: articles originally published in *Le Monde diplomatique*; republished in *Manière de voir 35* (Sept. 1997), p. 6.

trend has been particularly marked in Germany, which has become a much more polarized society and polity since reunification in 1990 ushered in a more pronounced economic cycle of boom and bust than the Federal Republic had experienced since its foundation in 1949. One might then argue that advanced capitalist society generates tendencies towards *both* individualization *and* class-based collective action. Further, the relative strength of these tendencies at any given time depends on a variety of specific conditions – the economic conjuncture, patterns of industrial organization, states of political consciousness, broader cultural phenomena, etc. – which cannot simply be deduced from larger theoretical speculations.

My final reservation concerns the concept of 'risk society' itself. It is undeniable that the large-scale intervention in nature involved in industrialization has produced unintended consequences representing severe dangers for both humankind and the planet. Whether this justifies making such risks the constitutive feature of 'late modernity' is, however, another matter. More particularly, doing so may involve effacing the historical specificity of particular social relationships. Thus Giddens argues that modernity involves the development of 'disembedding mechanisms' through which social relations are stretched over 'indefinite spans of time-space'. These mechanisms take two forms – 'symbolic tokens', for instance, money, and 'expert systems', through which (for example, when travelling by air) we entrust ourselves to qualified professionals with whom we have no personal relationship. The emergence of these mechanisms helps to give rise to the 'specific risk profile of modernity', which includes both the kind of risk on which Beck focuses, arising from 'the infusion of human knowledge into the material environment', and those produced by the 'development of *institutionalized risk environments* affecting the life-chances of millions: for example, investment markets'.[20]

But there is an important difference between risks which arise from the unanticipated consequences of human intervention in nature and those caused by crashes on the financial market. The first are an inherent feature of human social life, and predate the advent of industrial capitalism, even though it has undoubtedly made them a pervasive feature of the modern world. Thus, rapid population growth and the resulting scarcity of land led to extensive deforestation in nineteenth-century China, and thereby contributed to a series of devastating floods during the century after 1850. Financial markets, on the other hand, are the distinctive form through which investment is organized in developed capitalist economies. Grouping the two kinds of risk together suggests that the irrationalities inherent in these markets, which Keynes so remorselessly depicted (see §10.1 above), are an unavoidable consequence of modernity. But this comes dangerously close to what Marx accused the classical political economists of doing – namely, naturalizing features of a historically specific form of society. It may

<hr>

[20] Giddens, *Consequences*, pp. 22ff., 124–5.

also encourage an underestimation of the extent to which even the first kind of risk might be reduced in a more democratically organized society.

(3) *Reason and nature.* Whatever the wider validity of Beck's theory of reflexive modernization, he is undoubtedly right to identify a contemporary trend towards the problematization of the natural sciences. As he puts it, '[s]cience is no longer concerned with "liberation" from *pre-existing* dependencies, but with the definition and distribution of errors which are *produced by itself.*'[21] Instead of freeing humankind from dependence on nature, science seems to have made it vulnerable to new forms of catastrophe arising from our interference in the physical world. Yet the issues posed here are particularly difficult for contemporary social theory to address.

Since Weber social theorists have tended to situate the physical sciences within the framework of instrumentally rational action. On this account scientific knowledge constitutes one of the most effective means of allowing social actors to achieve their ends, typically by enhancing human control of nature. Horkheimer and Adorno incorporated this interpretation into their critique of enlightenment as the process through which human beings, in seeking to control nature, erect forms of social domination in which they find themselves trapped. Foucault's Nietzschean conception of power-knowledge easily lends itself to a similarly instrumentalist conception of the physical sciences. Habermas, while challenging Weber's tendency to equate reason with instrumental rationality, does not reject this conception, but instead incorporates it into a multi-dimensional conception of reason in which communicative rationality provides the basis for the kind of interpretive understanding required for the study of society.

Yet this instrumentalist approach is quite inadequate as a basis for understanding the physical sciences. For one thing, it involves a hopelessly impoverished conception of scientific knowledge. Other traditions – notably the 'epistemological' history of the sciences pioneered by Gaston Bachelard and Georges Canguilhem, and the philosophy of science developed by Karl Popper – have displayed a much firmer grasp of what Imre Lakatos calls 'the *relative autonomy of theoretical science*'.[22] The history of sciences such as physics, Lakatos argues, consists in the development of research programmes – successive versions of theories constituted by a 'heuristic' which identifies the problems they are to address, indicates possible strategies, and rules out certain solutions. Such a picture of the development of sciences, in which theoretical research is powered by an internal dynamic, is hard to reconcile with the idea that the pursuit of scientific knowledge is primarily governed by instrumental considerations. One can accept this picture without ignoring the various ways in which scientific research is integrated into public bureaucracies and private corporations, but these forms of incorporation are likely to be far

---

[21] Beck, *Risk Society*, p. 158.
[22] I. Lakatos, *Philosophical Papers* (2 vols, Cambridge, 1978), I, p. 52

more complex and contradictory than the instrumentalist conception suggests.

The instrumentalist view of science also makes it very hard for social theory to conceptualize nature as a distinct reality. Partly in reaction to the tendency of ideologies to eternize various historically specific social relations by presenting them as natural, social theory tends to treat nature itself as a social construction. At best it figures as a raw material to be used by instrumentally rational actors. Sometimes this view of nature takes the form of a historical thesis. Thus Beck writes: 'At the end of the twentieth century, nature is *neither* given *nor* ascribed, but instead has become a historical product, the *interior* furnishings of the civilizational world destroyed or endangered in the natural conditions of its reproduction.'[23] Similarly Giddens asserts: 'Nature is increasingly subject to human intervention, and therefore loses its very character as an extrinsic source of reference.'[24]

Quite aside from the fact that such claims confuse nature with developments on one obscure planet, the idea of what Beck calls 'the societalization [*Vergesellschaftung*] of nature' tends to ignore the fact that the destructive consequences of human intervention in the physical world do not abolish the laws of nature. Indeed, they rather demonstrate that, contrary to the anthropomorphic arrogance sometimes implicit in instrumentalist views, human actions are subject to physical constraints which sometimes subvert the intentions with which they are performed. This tendency to see nature as merely the object of human action, lacking any structure or powers of its own, is associated with the propensity of many social theorists to efface those aspects of human beings which themselves partake of the physical. Habermas is a prime example: his purely procedural conception of rationality depends on, *inter alia*, the refusal to integrate into his theory of communicative action the inescapable reality that human beings are *embodied* agents whose physical structures and biological needs constitute inescapable parameters of and forces within social life.[25]

These remarks are far from being a plea for a return to the biologistic social theories which flourished with such disastrous consequences in the era of Social Darwinism. They amount rather to the suggestion that most versions of social theory would benefit from a dialogue with a naturalistic conception of the world which recognizes the continuities between both the physical and social worlds and the forms of scientific understanding appropriate to them, but which does not suppress or ignore the discontinuities between them. Such a dialogue might permit an escape from the false polarization between a conception of the social from which natural processes and constraints have been banished and various attempts to reduce the human and the social to the physical and the biological.[26]

[23]   Beck, *Risk Society*, p. 80.
[24]   A. Giddens, *Modernity and Self-Identity* (Cambridge, 1991), p. 166.
[25]   See A. Heller, 'Habermas and Marxism', in J. B. Thompson and D. Held, eds, *Habermas: Critical Debates* (London, 1982).
[26]   R. Bhaskar, *The Possibility of Naturalism* (Brighton, 1979); A. Collier, *Critical Realism* (London, 1994).

(4) *Theory and practice.* One reason why social theorists have been resistant to such a naturalism is that it might obscure the distinctive role of human agency in constituting and reproducing the social world. Yet, as we have seen, scepticism about human beings' ability to effect any large-scale transformation of social structures has become an increasingly powerful motif in twentieth-century social theory. Nor is this simply a consequence of the dissolution of the subject effected by French anti-humanists. Weberian historical sociologists ostensibly hostile to deterministic versions of social theory have evinced the same scepticism. Mann, for example, summarily dismisses Marx's 'view of the working class' as 'absurdly utopian – how unlikely that an exploited class could confound all of previous history and rise up to destroy all stratification'. So society may be what Mann calls a 'patterned mess', but it seems that there is enough pattern to rule out certain outcomes.[27]

Giddens is a particularly interesting case of this combination of voluntarism and fatalism. In works such as *The Constitution of Society* (1984) he seeks to restore individual subjectivity to its proper, formative role in the social world. He refuses to analyse modernity as constituted by alienation or reification. 'Modernity expropriates – that is undeniable', but some modernizing processes 'make possible forms of mastery over life-circumstances unavailable in pre-modern circumstances'. In particular, the self becomes 'a reflexive project, for which the individual is responsible'.[28] Individuals in 'high modernity', no longer constrained by tradition, are confronted with a wide range of genuine choices as to how to shape their lives, in particular with respect to what kind of personal relationships they should seek. Yet the expansion of individual choice is not accompanied by a commensurate increase in collective freedom. On the contrary, the development of new forms of risk which threaten environmental and economic catastrophe on a far larger scale than in the past suggests that we should think of modernity as a juggernaut – 'a runaway machine of enormous power which, collectively as human beings we can drive to some extent but which also threatens to rush out of our control and which could rend itself asunder'.[29] It was, of course, this sense of having lost control over central aspects of the social world that Marx sought to articulate by means of the concept of alienation.

One might argue that scepticism about the possibilities of social transformation, however articulated theoretically, is a reasonable inference from the historical experience of the twentieth century: we saw in chapter 9 how, at extreme opposites of the political spectrum, both Lukács and Heidegger moved from revolutionary voluntarism towards something much closer to fatalism (though I should stress that at every stage of this evolution Lukács's positions

---

[27] Mann, *Sources*, II, pp. 26–7, 4.

[28] Giddens, *Modernity and Self-Identity*, pp. 192, 75.

[29] Giddens, *Consequences*, p. 139.

were much more explicitly formulated, rationally justified, and politically defensible than were Heidegger's oracular and evasive pronouncements).

This may be so. It is nevertheless worth at least speculating about whether a connection exists between the political pessimism common to so many social thinkers over much of the past century and their increasingly marked tendency to take up residence in the academy. The biographies of individual theorists record, over the course of this book, a steady march deeper and deeper into the universities. Though academics were there from the start – think of Smith or Hegel – we see other social types, the man of letters, the journalist, the politician, even the revolutionary organizer, progressively replaced by the professor.

At the extreme, this transformation can help foster a state of affairs where particular academic institutions exercise an extraordinary influence on intellectual life. Astonishingly, with the exception of Lévi-Strauss, all the French theorists discussed in chapter 11, and indeed just about every twentieth-century French thinker of note from Durkheim onwards, studied philosophy at the École Normale Supérieure. The biographies of figures such as Althusser and Foucault turn out to be one long succession of *normaliens*, caught in lifelong relationships of friendship and competition as they ascend the academic ladder. One does not have to endorse Nietzschean perspectivism to recognize a particularly tight nexus of knowledge and power at work here.

Of course – as the case of the École Normale indicates – even the narrowest academic elites can produce extremely gifted theorists. Sometimes at least such milieux can give their denizens the intellectual self-confidence to cross the normal boundaries of intellectual specializations. Perhaps more than any other twentieth-century theorist, Maynard Keynes epitomized this confidence, as is indicated by this anecdote told by C. H. Rolph about Keynes in his role as chairman of the left-wing British weekly the *New Statesman*:

> Keynes . . . used to say that he could write the whole of a *New Statesman* issue himself and thoroughly enjoy the process, and that it was absurd to pay large fees for a pleasant exercise that was also a privilege. The trouble was, everyone knew that Keynes could have done precisely what he boasted (the only page that *might* have been a little below par, Raymond Mortimer told me, was the music page).[30]

For all such virtuosity, enclosure in an exclusively academic environment is likely to have consequences for the kind of social theory produced there. Russell Jacoby has noted the decline of 'public intellectuals, writers and thinkers who address a general and educated audience', in the United States since the Second World War.[31] He argues that a number of trends – for example, suburbanization, inner-city gentrification, university expansion – have destroyed the old urban

---

[30]   C. H. Rolph, *Kingsley* (Harmondsworth, 1978), pp. 175–6.
[31]   R. Jacoby, *The Last Intellectuals* (New York, 1987), p. 5.

Bohemias where such intellectuals had flourished, and made the academy their only refuge. In the self-contained university world, intellectual life is specialized and professionalized: academics, even those who think of themselves as political radicals, write for each other using an idiom which renders their work unintelligible to those outside.

Perhaps the itinerary of the Frankfurt School is emblematic of this larger process: Marxism becomes 'critical theory', a body of thought elaborated in the academy at long remove from any political practice, profoundly pessimistic about the possibility of social revolution, and expressed in allusive and arcane language. In what is, however, all too common a feature of cultural life at the end of the twentieth century, an avant-garde activity has now been massified, as innumerable academics engage in what Althusser called theoretical practice, matching Adorno and Horkheimer in obscurity of expression, but not, alas, in novelty of content.

Some theorists demonstrate an awareness of this situation and a desire to escape from it. Bourdieu, for example, frequently draws attention to the socially situated character of academic discourse and the class positions it tends to defend. And he argues for a specific political intervention by intellectuals, what he calls the *'Realpolitik of reason'*, 'a corporatism of the universal'.[32] This intervention is in response to the threat of neo-liberalism, 'a return to a sort of radical capitalism answering to no law except that of maximum profit'. Apart from the negative economic and social consequences which this represents, '[t]he autonomy enjoyed by the universes of cultural production in relation to the market, which had increased continuously through the struggles of writers, artists and scientists, is under increasing threat.'[33]

It is here that intellectuals have a particular role to play:

> Intellectuals are two-dimensional figures who do not exist and subsist as such unless (and only unless) they are invested with a specific authority, conferred by the autonomous intellectual world (meaning independent from religious, political or economic power) whose specific laws they respect, and unless (and only unless) they engage this specific authority in political struggles. Far from there existing, as is customarily believed, an antinomy between the search for autonomy (which characterizes the art, science or literature we call 'pure') and the search for political efficacy, it is by increasing their autonomy (and thereby, among other things, their freedom to criticize the prevailing powers) that intellectuals can increase the effectiveness of a political action whose ends and means have their specific logic of the fields of cultural production.[34]

---

[32] P. Bourdieu, *The Rules of Art* (Cambridge, 1996), p. 348.
[33] P. Bourdieu, 'A Reasoned Utopia and Economic Fatalism', *New Left Review*, 227 (1998), pp. 125, 127.
[34] Bourdieu, *Rules*, p. 340.

It is thus by virtue of the authority they gain from their position in autonomous fields of cultural production that intellectuals act politically. Moreover, 'it is especially urgent today that intellectuals mobilize and create a veritable *International of intellectuals* committed to defending the autonomy of the universes of cultural production'.[35] Paradoxically, then, intellectuals should cross the border separating theory and practice in order to secure it. Honourably intended though this position undoubtedly is, it serves to underline how deeply entrenched the idea of a radical disjunction between theory and practice has become even among those intellectuals who seek to situate it historically and sociologically.

(5) *Universal and particular.* The insulation of social theory from other activities poses the question of the particular interests it serves. Bourdieu's formula of 'a corporatism of the universal' proposes the intellectuals as Hegel's 'universal class', whose social position requires it to defend the general interests of society at large, and indeed those of reason itself. But ever since Marx and Nietzsche in their different ways subjected the Enlightenment to critical scrutiny, the very ideas of universality and rationality have been under suspicion for secreting within themselves hidden particularisms. As we saw in §1.5 above, the universal rights and happiness promised by the American and French revolutions tacitly excluded, among others, slaves, the poor, and women.

Postcolonial theory has been one common way in which in recent years the charge has been made that such implicit exclusions are inherent in the Enlightenment project. Thus the group of Indian social historians and theorists associated with the journal *Subaltern Studies* has increasingly come to argue, under the influence of postmodernism, that even apparently radical ideologies such as anti-colonial nationalism and Marxism are in fact particular forms of the 'colonial power-knowledge' which independent states in the Third World have come to perpetuate. A characteristic feature of this power-knowledge is its claim to be of universal application. Partha Chatterjee writes:

> If there is one great moment that turns the provincial thought of Europe into universal history, it is the moment of capital – capital that is global in its territorial reach and universal in its conceptual domain. It is the narrative of capital that can turn the violence of mercantilist trade, war, genocide, conquest and colonialism into a story of universal progress, development, modernization, and freedom.[36]

Counterposed to the narrative of capital is that of community. The accumulation of capital presupposes the destruction of communities; the viability of the modern nation-state requires a 'sanitized, domesticated form' of community as 'a shared subjective feeling that protects and nurtures'. Yet, Chatterjee argues,

---

[35]   Ibid., p. 344.
[36]   P. Chatterjee, *The Nation and its Fragments* (Delhi, 1995), p. 235.

> It is not so much the state/civil society opposition but rather the capital/com-munity opposition that seems to me to be the great unsurpassed contradiction in Western social philosophy . . . Community, which ideally should have been ban-ished from the kingdom of capital, continues to lead a subterranean, potentially subversive, life within it because it refuses to go away.[37]

Chatterjee insists that community 'is not an archaic idea buried in the re-cesses of history, nor is it part of a marginal subculture, nor can it be dismissed as a premodern remnant that an absent-minded Enlightenment has somehow forgotten to raise'.[38] Yet his argument slides all too easily into a version of Romantic anti-capitalism. The rights and traditions of communities are, of course, a burning issue in contemporary India, where a state whose doubtful and tarnished commitment to secularism is under challenge from the exclusivist nationalism of the Hindu right. Rejecting the liberal-left stance of seeking to de-fend and strengthen existing secularist traditions on the basis of a commitment to universal rights, Chatterjee argues that 'what is being asserted in a collective cultural right is in fact *the right not to offer a reason for being different*'. He sees such an assertion as going '*against governmentality*': in other words, a specific community's insistence on maintaining its own traditions is a form of resistance to the forms of disciplinary power constitutive of the modern state.[39]

The problem of how democratic societies can accommodate the existence of different groups with their distinctive conceptions of the good has become a major theme of contemporary liberal political philosophy. Addressing and re-solving this problem is, however, unlikely to be facilitated by effectively con-ceiving communities as self-enclosed entities, as Chatterjee does. For actually existing communities may contain highly unequal power structures which are legitimized by the dominant versions of their traditions. Recognition of the right of communal leaders not to have to justify these structures and traditions thus leaves untouched the position of those subordinated within the com-munity. Chatterjee's version of postcolonial theory seems to condemn one form of oppression – that represented by the modern bureaucratic state – while im-munizing those occurring within particular communities from scrutiny. This is a position little removed from a conservative Romantic condemnation of the capitalist present in the name of tradition.

This example illustrates the difficulties created by seeking simply to break with the Enlightenment. Abjuring appeal to universal principles restricts the scope of social criticism. The prevailing ideology within a specific community or a larger society is likely largely to endorse its existing institutions and pract-ices. Attempts to change these institutions and practices which seek to legit-imize themselves on the basis of beliefs having widespread acceptance within

---

[37]   Ibid., p. 236.
[38]   Ibid., p. 237.
[39]   P. Chatterjee, *A Possible India* (Delhi, 1997), pp. 254, 255.

that society or community are therefore likely to confine themselves to relatively limited adjustments. More radical criticism of the entire structure of the society or community will often be extrinsically based in the sense of appealing to beliefs other than those prevailing there – in the way that, for example, opponents of apartheid in South Africa tended to base themselves on liberal-democratic or socialist ideologies. Whether or not extrinsically based, such criticism characteristically appeals to beliefs not merely on the grounds that they are different from the prevailing ones but because they involve universal principles – thus racial segregation in South Africa was condemned not primarily because things were different elsewhere but because it denied black people rights common to all human beings. The 1955 Freedom Charter, the main programmatic document of the African National Congress, is written in the language of universal rights.

There are, then, two ways of responding to the tacit limitations to the Enlightenment's promise of universal emancipation. One is to conclude that these limitations demonstrate that *any* universal theory is necessarily a masked particularism. All that one can then do is decide which particularism one prefers. Chatterjee's attempt to defend communities from extrinsic criticism is, from this perspective, simply a logical consequence of his rejection of what he calls 'the tired slogans about the universality of discursive reason'.[40] The other is to respond to the failures of the Enlightenment project by striving for the achievement of a *genuine* universality – of a social and political order which has no 'others', from which no one is excluded. This is a programme for the permanent radicalization of the Enlightenment: as specific exclusions are overcome, others are identified and addressed. Indeed, it may turn out that, as I believe, the bulk of these exclusions constitutes an interdependent social whole, a complex of oppression and exploitation which can only be addressed through a single, comprehensive process of revolutionary transformation.

Here the philosophical idea of modernity, embodying a certain ethical conception of political and social life, which earlier I sought to distinguish from the analytical theory of capitalism as a distinctive social system, comes into its own. From this standpoint, capitalism might be condemned as an inadequate realization of the idea of modernity. Making this idea out requires the formulation of a satisfactory normative political theory. It is interesting that the recent renaissance of liberal political philosophy, which has typically taken the form of a search for egalitarian principles of social justice, should involve a certain opening up to social theory.

John Rawls's theory of justice as fairness – according to which inequalities are acceptable only in so far as they benefit the worst off in society (the famous Difference Principle) – is a case in point. The subject of justice is, he argues, 'the basic structure of society', 'understood as the way in which the major

---

40   Ibid., p. 261.

social institutions fit together into one system, and how they assign fundamental rights and duties and shape the division of advantages that arises through
social cooperation'. Therefore '[t]he role of the institutions that belong to the
basic structure is to secure just background conditions against which the actions
of individuals and associations take place.'[41] Brian Barry comments:

> Rawls's incorporation of this notion of a social structure into his theory repre-
> sents the coming of age of liberal political philosophy. For the first time, a major
> thinker in the broadly individualistic tradition has taken account of the legacy of
> Marx and Weber by recognizing explicitly that societies have patterns of inequal-
> ity that persist over time and systematic ways of allocating people to positions
> within their hierarchies of power, status, and money.[42]

The dialogue between social theory and political philosophy, furthermore,
goes in both directions, as is indicated by the recent exchange between Rawls
and Habermas, the outstanding living representative of 'the legacy of Marx and
Weber'.[43] Dialogue, however, is not the same as complete convergence. The
main thrust of contemporary liberal political philosophy has been remarkably
egalitarian: the principal disagreements among theorists such as Rawls, Barry,
Ronald Dworkin, Amartya Sen, and G. A. Cohen have concerned how to specify
the content, and how to justify principles, of justice in which the concept of
social equality plays a central role. The gulf, however, dividing abstract normative theory from social and political reality is enormous, and has grown wider
since Rawls's *A Theory of Justice* was originally published in 1971.

Rawls's own more recent work is generally seen as representing a retreat
from the universalistic ambitions of his first book. Yet consider his description,
written in 1995, of the conditions under which the liberties guaranteed by a
constitutional democracy cease to be merely formal:

> a. Public financing of elections and ways of guaranteeing the availability of pub-
> lic information on matters of public policy . . .
>
> b. A certain fair equality of opportunity, especially in education and training . . .
>
> c. A decent distribution of income and wealth . . . all citizens must be assured the
> all-purpose means necessary for them to take intelligent and effective advantage
> of their basic freedoms . . .
>
> d. Society as employer of last resort through general or local government, or
> other social and economic policies . . .
>
> e. Basic health care assured all citizens.[44]

---

[41] J. Rawls, *Political Liberalism*, expanded edn (New York, 1996), pp. 258, 266.
[42] B. Barry, *Justice as Impartiality* (Oxford, 1995), p. 214.
[43] J. Habermas, 'Reconciliation Through the Public Use of Reason', *Journal of Philosophy*, 92
(1995); J. Rawls, 'Reply to Habermas', ibid.
[44] Rawls, *Political Liberalism*, p. lviii.

To anyone familiar with contemporary political conditions in liberal capitalist societies such as the United States and Britain these requirements will seem wildly Utopian. Of course, as the Frankfurt School well understood, there are times when social reality is so demeaned and contemptible that to describe an idea as Utopian is to honour it. Nevertheless, some account is required of the relationship between abstract norms and the historical conditions of their realization. Not the least of Marx's contributions was, from *On the Jewish Question* onwards, to demand that the language of universal rights be put to the test of social practice, without abandoning the Enlightenment aspiration to what he called 'human emancipation'.

(6) *Taking sides*. This brings me, finally, to the question of whether any of the principal theorists discussed in this book offers the best vantage-point from which to view the social world. For it would be a misunderstanding of my argument to conclude from the fact that the debate about modernity is unresolved that it is irresoluble. Contemporary intellectual fashion, deeply influenced by different versions of philosophical scepticism, is in love with indeterminacy and incompleteness. But the soil from which the debate about modernity grows is not whatever philosophical difficulties there may be about the concepts of truth and knowledge but modernity itself. It is the concrete existence of a historically specific, uniquely dynamic and unstable form of society which has evoked various responses reducible to the three on which this book has concentrated – the self-conscious acceptance of modernity, its radical rejection, and the call for its revolutionary transformation. History has posed these alternatives; there is no reason, therefore, why history – in the sense of the future evolution of the modern world – should not ultimately settle the debate between them.

Many contemporary theorists and commentators indeed believe that history has spoken definitively on one fundamental issue – the contest between capitalism and its socialist critics. The most famous expression of this belief is Francis Fukuyama's thesis that the collapse of the Soviet Union and its east European dependencies marked the End of History: liberal capitalism had seen off its main ideological rival, and now constituted the inescapable horizon of all future human achievement.[45] While few were willing to encumber themselves with Fukuyama's Hegelian metaphysical baggage, or his neo-conservative politics, his conclusion – that there is no longer any historically feasible alternative to liberal capitalism – is very widely accepted.

A capitalist triumphalism has become deeply entrenched in public discourse, most notably in the United States. After the East Asian economies, widely perceived after 1989 as the main challenge to the 'Anglo-American model' of unregulated free-market capitalism, were shattered by the financial crash of

---

[45]   F. Fukuyama, *The End of History and the Last Man* (New York, 1992).

1997, Alan Greenspan, the normally cautious chairman of the US Federal Reserve Board, claimed victory: 'My sense is that one consequence of this Asian crisis is an increasing awareness in the region that market capitalism, as practised in the West, especially in the US, is the superior model; that is, it provides greater promise of producing rising standards of living and continuous growth.'[46]

The future will tell how much hubris there was in declarations of this kind. Nevertheless, the belief that we have nothing better to hope for than liberal capitalism has become one of the reigning dogmas. It has, in particular, allowed centre-left politicians on both sides of the Atlantic to proclaim a 'third way' beyond traditional left and right in which the policies of the neo-liberal right are ill concealed by talk of 'modernity' and 'community'. One consequence is that public policy increasingly redefines social problems as the outcome of defective individual behaviour. The inference is natural enough: if the structure of liberal capitalist societies is basically sound, then social dysfunctions are caused by maladjusted individuals. Contemporary social policy has effectively reinvented, beneath a language of 'empowerment', the Victorian concept of the undeserving poor, whose plight is caused by their own failure to acquire the skills and modes of conduct required of those who wish to enter the world of wage-labour. Constructing social problems as the consequence of personal faults legitimizes the coercion of recalcitrant individuals and sporadic campaigns to revive the 'values' whose loss is allegedly responsible for the moral decline reflected in the misbehaviour of the 'underclass'.

One can imagine how caustically Marx or Nietzsche would have expressed himself about this debasement of public discourse. But theoretical argument has, inevitably, been affected. Thus political philosophy is increasingly polarized in the lopsided debate between egalitarian liberals and their communitarian and postmodernist critics, who spurn the abstractions of normative theory in the name of a more or less nuanced rejection of modernity. Despite the quality of writing produced by, for example, Weberian historical sociologists such as Mann and Runciman, social theory itself has, as I remarked in the Introduction, been sidelined by cultural studies. (Though Runciman himself believes this development may in the long run strengthen sociology, declaring that '"postmodernism" has come and largely gone, taking with it those aspects of the study of human behaviour which properly belong to literature rather than science'.[47]) Once again, this shift in focus is intelligible enough: if the hope or threat of qualitative social transformation no longer haunts capitalism, would not time be better spent exploring the experiences and discourses through which individuals bearing various identities inhabit an increasingly commodified social world than exploring mechanisms of historical change unlikely to be operative in the future?

[46] *Financial Times*, 19 Apr. 1998.
[47] W. G. Runciman, *The Social Animal* (London, 1998), p. vii.

A necessary condition of the existence of this rather depressing intellectual conjuncture is the marginalization of Marx. It is this development, entailed by Fukuyama's proclamation of the End of History, which implies that our social horizons are inescapably defined by the existing liberal capitalist societies, and that this modernity may be contested only by a postmodernism that specifically eschews any project of comprehensive transformation. But can Marx be so easily forgotten?

The case for saying that he cannot rests above all on the fact that Marx provided a theorization of capitalism which has yet to be surpassed. Three aspects of this theorization especially bear stressing. First, the picture which he paints in the *Communist Manifesto* of a revolutionary mode of production that 'has given a cosmopolitan character to production and consumption' and 'creates a world after its own image' seems now less a description of the world in 1848 than an anticipation of tendencies which are only beginning fully to be realized today. The *Manifesto*, in depicting the processes through which industrial capitalism was beginning in the first half of the nineteenth century to dominate and transform the world, thereby captures what it has become a contemporary cliché to call 'globalization'. As Eric Hobsbawm puts it, 'what might in 1848 have struck an uncommitted reader as revolutionary rhetoric – or, at best, as plausible prediction – can now be read as a concise characterization of capitalism at the end of the twentieth century'.[48]

Secondly, as we have seen, it is capitalism's dynamic *instability* that forms the main theme of Marx's economic writings. In other words, the processes of what Schumpeter called 'creative destruction' unleashed by capitalism are inseparable from that mode of production's chronic tendency towards serious and profound slumps. Continuing to engage with Marx's theory of crises seems especially urgent at a time when vulgarized versions of neo-classical economics which dismiss recessions as minor interruptions of the market's ceaseless and benign expansion have become so deeply entrenched in policy-making and political debate. The fact that *laissez-faire* dogma should have been enthroned in a period when the world economy has experienced three major slumps as well as, in the 1990s, a succession of devastating financial crises in Mexico, Japan, and East Asia is another symptom of the debasement of public discourse referred to above, but it also underlines the importance of keeping alive the most powerful critique yet offered of capitalism's claim to have discovered the fairest and most rational way of meeting humankind's economic needs.

Thirdly, Marx argues that there is a necessary connection between the process of capital accumulation and the exploitation of wage-labour. In remaking the world, capitalism creates a class of workers who over time will develop the numbers, cohesion, and self-organization necessary to revolutionize society. It

---

[48]   E. J. Hobsbawm, introduction to K. Marx and F. Engels, *The Communist Manifesto: A Modern Edition* (London, 1998), p. 18.

is Marx's claim that this too is a tendency inherent in the capitalist mode of production which arouses the opposition even of many sympathetic to the rest of his theory. Thus Hobsbawm argues that '[t]he Manifesto's vision of the historical development of "bourgeois society", including the working class which it generated, did not *necessarily* lead to the conclusion that the proletariat would overthrow capitalism and, in so doing, open the way to the development of communism'.[49]

Here, of course, many issues arise. The development of capitalism has certainly led to the transformation of a growing proportion of the world's workforce into wage-labourers. Thus the entrenchment of industrial capitalism over the past generation in East and South Asia has greatly increased the size of the global industrial proletariat. The general (though uneven) decline in manufacturing's share of output in the advanced economies over the same period has undoubtedly reduced the size of the industrial workforce in these countries and sometimes (though far from universally) weakened unions based on this sector. But other developments – for example, the expansion of white-collar trade unionism, the growing insecurity which large-scale economic restructuring has caused among those in hitherto comfortable and well-rewarded professional and administrative jobs, the increase in manual employment of all kinds in service industries – suggests that the contraction of traditional industries must be set against the background of larger-scale processes of proletarianization.

What effect these structural tendencies have on the capacity of the working class to engage in collective action is another matter. At the very least, however, developments in the 1990s – for example, the strike waves referred to above in France and Germany, the bitter social conflicts which have developed in Canada's most important industrial region of Ontario, and the emergence of new labour movements in East Asia (for example, in South Korea) – all suggest that it would be foolish to write off the working class as a historical subject. Whether or not future class struggles fulfil Marx's expectations of socialist revolution raises, of course, formidable unresolved issues. Many are political and ideological: some concern the salience of non-class forms of identity such as nationality, race, and religion; others turn on the question of whether Marx's conception of socialism as self-emancipation can be successfully disengaged from the debacle of no longer 'existing socialism'.

It would therefore be quite unrealistic to expect these considerations successfully to close the gap indicated by Hobsbawm, and demonstrate that the historical evolution of capitalism leads inevitably to proletarian revolution and the construction of an authentic communist society (as opposed to its Stalinist caricature). But then this book should have shown that it is not at all clear that Marx needs such a conception of historical inevitability. Thus in the *Manifesto* he says that the crisis of a mode of production may result 'either in a

---

[49]   Ibid., p. 22.

revolutionary reconstitution of society at large, or in the common ruin of the contending classes'. This suggests that historical materialism is not required to guarantee that socialist revolution will necessarily happen, but rather to show that it is practically feasible and politically desirable.

I cannot claim to have achieved in these brief remarks even this latter, more modest goal. Such, in any case, has not been their purpose. My aim has rather been to establish that Marx's distinctive contribution to the debate on modernity cannot easily be effaced. It is interesting that even theorists the overall thrust of whose work is hostile to the classical Marxist tradition have in recent years paid more or less grudging tribute to it. Runciman, for example, endorses the judgement that 'Weber is not merely the greatest sociologist but *the* sociologist'. Yet, expounding his evolutionary social theory, he declares that 'at any given level of population, technology and resources, there are not that many different ways in which economic, ideological and coercive power can be distributed', a statement which seems suspiciously close to what Runciman calls a few pages later 'outdated "Historical Materialism"'.[50] More strikingly perhaps, Jacques Derrida, whose version of post-structuralism had an enormous influence in weaning the 1960s generation off Marxism, in his *Spectres of Marx* (1993), not merely affirms a characteristically ambiguous commitment to the 'spirit of Marxism', but links this to a vehement critique of Fukuyama and of the 'new world order' of triumphant liberal capitalism.

Marx has thus proved, not for the first time, to be a difficult customer to silence. I do not insist on the importance of keeping open the Marxist position in the debate on modernity simply because I think that it represents the right answer to the questions posed by the collapse of Hegel's system (though I do think this), but also because in its absence both social theory and political discourse will continue to be impoverished in ways some of which I have indicated above. Social theory, I have suggested, belongs to the heritage of the Enlightenment. It has lived in the field of tensions created by the different positions thinkers have taken over the meaning and the fate of the modern world. If one of the main interlocuters in that debate were permanently silenced, thinking about the social world might degenerate into a universalism too abstract to engage with the concrete forms taken by social injustice, and a particularism unable to conduct effective criticism of these forms. But, spurred on by the voice of the radicalized Enlightenment, social theory can become what the *philosophes* believed reason to be, a force for liberation.

---

[50] Runciman, *Social Animal*, pp. 49, 118, 140.

Further Reading

Introductory works are marked with an asterisk.

General

H. Barth, *Truth and Ideology* (Berkeley, 1976)
A. Callinicos, *Theories and Narratives* (Cambridge, 1995)
S. Collini et al., *That Noble Science of Politics* (Cambridge, 1983)
T. Eagleton, *Ideology* (London, 1991)
*A. Giddens, *Capitalism and Modern Social Theory* (Cambridge, 1971)
J. Habermas, *The Philosophical Discourse of Modernity* (Cambridge, 1987)
A. MacIntyre, *After Virtue* (London, 1981)
*C. W. Mills, *The Sociological Imagination* (Harmondsworth, 1970)
T. Parsons, *The Structure of Social Action* (2 vols, New York, 1968)
J. Rees, *The Algebra of Revolution* (London, 1998)
J. Roberts, *German Philosophy* (Cambridge, 1988)
M. Rosen, *Of Voluntary Servitude* (Cambridge, 1996)
I. I. Rubin, *A History of Economic Thought* (London, 1979)
*W. G. Runciman, *The Social Animal* (London, 1998)
J. A. Schumpeter, *History of Economic Analysis* (London, 1994)
G. Therborn, *Science, Class and Society* (London, 1976)

Introduction

W. G. Runciman, *A Treatise on Social Theory*, I (Cambridge, 1983)
J. Tully, ed., *Meaning and Context* (Cambridge, 1988)

1 The Enlightenment

L. Althusser, *Politics and History* (London, 1972)
I. Berlin, 'The Originality of Machiavelli', in id., *Against the Current* (Oxford, 1981)

H. Blumenberg, *The Legitimacy of the Modern Age* (Cambridge, Mass., 1983)

N. Bobbio, 'Gramsci and the Concept of Civil Society', in id., *Which Socialism?* (Cambridge, 1986)

J. B. Bury, *The Idea of Progress* (London, 1920)

E. Cassirer, *The Philosophy of the Enlightenment* (Boston, 1962)

P. Gay, *The Enlightenment: An Interpretation* (2 vols, London, 1973)

E. Halévy, *The Growth of Philosophical Radicalism* (London, 1949)

P. Hazard, *European Thought in the Eighteenth Century* (Harmondsworth, 1965)

J. Heilbron, *The Rise of Social Theory* (Cambridge, 1995)

A. O. Hirschmann, *The Passions and the Interests* (Princeton, 1977)

I. Hont and M. Ignatieff, eds, *Wealth and Virtue* (Cambridge, 1984)

R. Koselleck, *Critique and Crisis* (Oxford, 1988)

R. Koselleck, *Futures Past* (Cambridge, Mass., 1985)

Y. Lacoste, *Ibn Khaldun* (London, 1984)

R. L. Meek, *Economics and Ideology and Other Essays* (London, 1967)

R. L. Meek, *Smith, Marx and After* (London, 1977)

R. Pascal, 'Property and Society', *Modern Quarterly* (1938)

J. G. A. Pocock, *The Machiavellian Moment* (Princeton, 1975)

M. A. Screech, *Montaigne and Melancholy* (Harmondsworth, 1991)

A. S. Skinner, 'Economics and History: The Scottish Enlightenment', *Scottish Journal of Political Economy*, 12 (1965)

A. S. Skinner and T. Wilson, eds, *Essays on Adam Smith* (Oxford, 1975)

Q. Skinner, *The Foundations of Modern Political Thought* (2 vols, Cambridge, 1978)

Q. Skinner, *Machiavelli* (Oxford, 1981)

Q. Skinner, 'The Idea of Negative Liberty', in R. Rorty et al., eds, *Philosophy of History* (Cambridge, 1984)

E. Stokes, *The English Utilitarians and India* (Delhi, 1989)

C. Taylor, *Sources of the Self* (Cambridge, 1989)

K. Tribe, *Land, Labour and Economic Discourse* (London, 1978)

G. Wills, *Inventing America* (New York, 1978)

2 Hegel

L. Althusser, *The Spectre of Hegel* (London, 1997)

S. Avineri, *Hegel's Theory of the Modern State* (Cambridge, 1972)

J. Hyppolite, *Studies in Marx and Hegel* (New York, 1969)

A. Kojeve, *An Introduction to the Reading of Hegel* (New York, 1969)

K. Löwith, *From Hegel to Nietzsche* (London, 1965)

G. Lukacs, *The Young Hegel* (London, 1975)

H. Marcuse, *Reason and Revolution* (London, 1968)

H. Marcuse, *Hegel's Ontology and the Theory of Historicity* (Cambridge, Mass., 1987)

F. G. Nauen, *Revolution, Idealism and Human Freedom* (The Hague, 1971)

T. Pinkard, *Hegel's Phenomenology* (Cambridge, 1994)

R. Pippin, *Modernism as a Philosophical Problem* (Oxford, 1991)
M. Rosen, *Hegel's Dialectic and its Criticism* (Cambridge, 1982)
C. Taylor, *Hegel* (Cambridge, 1975)
A. W. Wood, *Hegel's Ethical Thought* (Cambridge, 1990)

3 Liberals and Reactionaries

I. Berlin, 'Joseph de Maistre and the Origins of Fascism', in id., *The Crooked Timber of Humanity* (London, 1991)
R. C. Boesche, 'The Strange Liberalism of Alexis de Tocqueville', *History of Political Thought*, II (1981)
P. Bourdieu, *The Rules of Art* (Cambridge, 1996), pt 1
J. Burrow, *Evolution and Society* (Cambridge, 1966)
J. Godechot, *The Counter-Revolution* (London, 1972)
J. Heilbron, *The Rise of Social Theory* (Cambridge, 1995)
F. Jacob, *The Logic of Living Systems* (London, 1974)
A. Jardin, *Tocqueville* (New York, 1988)
D. Johnson, *Guizot* (London, 1963)
A. Majeed, *Ungoverned Imaginings* (Oxford, 1992)
K. Mannheim, *Conservatism* (London, 1986)
L. Siedentop, 'Two Liberal Traditions', in A. Ryan, ed., *The Idea of Freedom* (Oxford, 1979)
L. Siedentop, *Tocqueville* (Oxford, 1994)
W. Thomas, *The Philosophical Radicals* (Oxford, 1979)
R. Williams, *Culture and Society 1780–1950* (Harmondsworth, 1968)

4 Marx

L. Althusser, *For Marx* (London, 1969)
C. J. Arthur, *Dialectics of Labour* (Oxford, 1986)
*I. Berlin, *Karl Marx* (Oxford, 1978)
*A. Callinicos, *The Revolutionary Ideas of Karl Marx* (London, 1983)
A. Callinicos, *Making History* (Cambridge, 1987)
A. Callinicos, ed., *Marxist Theory* (Oxford, 1989)
S. Clarke, *Marx's Theory of Crisis* (London, 1994)
G. A. Cohen, *Karl Marx's Theory of History* (Oxford, 1978)
G. A. Cohen, *History, Labour and Freedom* (Oxford, 1989)
D. Conway, *A Farewell to Marx* (Harmondsworth, 1987)
A. Cornu, *Karl Marx et Friedrich Engels* (4 vols, Paris, 1958–70)
H. Draper, *Karl Marx's Theory of Revolution* (4 vols, New York, 1977–90)
J. Elster, *Making Sense of Marx* (Cambridge, 1985)
B. Fine and L. Harris, *Rereading Capital* (London, 1979)
N. Geras, *Marx and Human Nature* (London, 1983)
A. Gilbert, *Marx's Politics* (Oxford, 1981)

S. Hook, *Towards an Understanding of Karl Marx* (London, 1933)

S. Hook, *From Hegel to Marx* (Ann Arbor, 1971)

K. Löwith, *From Hegel to Nietzsche* (London, 1965)

D. McLellan, *Karl Marx* (London, 1973)

R. Rosdolsky, *The Making of Marx's 'Capital'* (London, 1977)

I. I. Rubin, *Essays on Marx's Theory of Value* (Detroit, 1972)

P. M. Sweezy, *The Theory of Capitalist Development* (New York, 1968)

M. Wartofsky, *Feuerbach* (Cambridge, 1977)

J. Weeks, *Capital and Exploitation* (London, 1981)

5 Life and Power

*K. Ansell-Pearson, *An Introduction to Nietzsche as a Political Thinker* (Cambridge, 1994)

J. Burrow, *Evolution and Society* (Cambridge, 1966)

R. Dawkins, *The Blind Watchmaker* (London, 1991)

G. Deleuze, *Nietzsche and Philosophy* (London, 1983)

D. Dennett, *Darwin's Dangerous Idea* (London, 1995)

A. Desmond and J. Moore, *Darwin* (London, 1992)

M. Foucault, 'Nietzsche, Genealogy, History,' in P. Rabinow, ed., *The Foucault Reader* (Harmondsworth, 1986)

V. Gerratana, 'Marx and Darwin', *New Left Review*, 82 (1973)

S. J. Gould, *The Mismeasure of Man* (Harmondsworth, 1984)

M. Heidegger, *Nietzsche* (4 vols, San Francisco, 1991)

R. Hofstadter, *Social Darwinism in American Thought* (Boston, 1955)

F. Jacob, *The Logic of Living Systems* (London, 1974)

R. Jacoby and N. Glauberman, eds, *The Bell Curve Debate* (New York, 1995)

A. Kelly, *The Descent of Darwin* (Chapel Hill, 1981)

R. Levins and R. Lewontin, *The Dialectical Biologist* (Cambridge, Mass., 1985)

A. Nehemas, *Nietzsche: Life as Literature* (Cambridge, Mass., 1985)

M. Salvadori, *Karl Kautsky and the Socialist Revolution, 1880–1938* (London, 1979)

R. Schacht, *Nietzsche* (London, 1983)

E. Sober, *The Nature of Selection* (Chicago, 1993)

G. P. Steenson, *Karl Kautsky, 1854–1938* (Pittsburgh, 1991)

6 Durkheim

G. Canguilhem, *The Normal and the Pathological* (New York, 1991)

*A. Giddens, *Durkheim* (London, 1978)

J. Habermas, *The Theory of Communicative Action*, II (Cambridge, 1988)

I. Hacking, *The Taming of Chance* (Cambridge, 1990)

P. Q. Hirst, *Durkheim, Bernard and Epistemology* (London, 1975)

D. Lockwood, *Solidarity and Schism* (Oxford, 1992)

S. Lukes, *Émile Durkheim* (Harmondsworth, 1975)

R. K. Merton, 'Manifest and Latent Functions', in *Social Theory and Social Structure* (New York, 1968)

F. Pearce, *The Radical Durkheim* (London, 1989)

7 Weber

R. Bendix, *Max Weber* (New York, 1960)

D. Blackbourn and G. Eley, *The Peculiarities of German History* (Oxford, 1984)

R. Collins, *Weberian Sociological Theory* (Cambridge, 1986)

A. Giddens, *Politics and Sociology in the Thought of Max Weber* (London, 1972)

J. Habermas, *The Theory of Communicative Action*, I (London, 1984)

C. G. Hempel, *Aspects of Scientific Explanation* (New York, 1965)

W. Hennis, *Max Weber* (London, 1988)

K. Löwith, *Max Weber and Karl Marx* (London, 1993)

M. Löwy, 'Weber against Marx?', in id., *On Changing the World* (Atlantic Highlands, NJ, 1993)

H. Marcuse, 'Industrialization and Capitalism in the Work of Max Weber', in id., *Negations* (Harmondsworth, 1972)

G. Marshall, *In Search of the Spirit of Capitalism* (London, 1982)

W. J. Mommsen, *The Age of Bureaucracy* (Oxford, 1974)

W. J. Mommsen, *Max Weber and German Politics 1890–1920* (Chicago, 1984)

W. J. Mommsen, *The Political and Social Theory of Max Weber* (Cambridge, 1989)

W. J. Mommsen and J. Osterhammel, eds, *Max Weber and his Contemporaries* (London, 1988)

F. Parkin, *Marxism and Class Theory* (London, 1979)

*F. Parkin, *Max Weber* (London, 1982)

R. Pipes, 'Max Weber and Russia', *World Politics*, 7 (1954–5)

W. G. Runciman, *A Critique of Max Weber's Philosophy of Social Science* (Cambridge, 1972)

C. Taylor, 'Interpretation and the Sciences of Man', *Review of Metaphysics*, 25 (1971)

K. Tribe, ed., *Reading Weber* (London, 1989)

M. Weber, *Max Weber* (New York, 1975)

8 The Illusions of Progress

I. Berlin, *Russian Thinkers* (Harmondsworth, 1979)

D. Frisby, *Fragments of Modernity* (Cambridge, 1985)

E. Gellner, *The Psychoanalytic Movement* (London, 1983)

E. J. Hobsbawm, *The Age of Empire 1875–1914* (London, 1987)

J. Mitchell, *Psychoanalysis and Feminism* (Harmondsworth, 1975)

C. Schorske, *Fin-de-Siècle Vienna* (New York, 1980)

J. H. Seddon, *The Petrashevtsy* (Manchester, 1985)

T. Shanin, *The Roots of Otherness* (2 vols, Houndmills, 1985)

N. Stone, *Europe Transformed 1878–1919* (London, 1983)
V. N. Volosinov, *Freudianism* (Bloomington, 1987)
A. Walicki, *The Controversy over Capitalism* (Oxford, 1969)
A. Walicki, *The Slavophile Controversy* (Oxford, 1975)
A. Walicki, *A History of Russian Thought from the Enlightenment to Marxism* (Stanford, 1979)
R. Webster, *Why Freud Was Wrong* (London, 1996)
*R. Wolheim, *Freud* (London, 1971)

9 Revolution and Counter-Revolution

*P. Anderson, *Considerations on Western Marxism* (London, 1976)
P. Anderson, 'The Antinomies of Antonio Gramsci', *New Left Review*, 100 (1976–7)
A. Arato and P. Breines, *The Young Lukács and the Origins of Western Marxism* (London, 1979)
P. Bourdieu, *The Political Ontology of Martin Heidegger* (Cambridge, 1991)
A. Callinicos, *Marxism and Philosophy* (Oxford, 1983)
A. Davidson, *Antonio Gramsci* (London, 1977)
J. Derrida, *Of Spirit* (Chicago, 1989)
H. L. Dreyfus and H. Hall, eds, *Heidegger: Critical Perspectives* (Oxford, 1992)
V. Farias, *Heidegger et le nazisme* (Paris, 1987)
J. Femia, *Gramsci's Political Thought* (Oxford, 1981)
L. Ferry and A. Renaut, *Heidegger and Modernity* (Chicago, 1990)
D. Forgacs, 'Gramsci and Marxism in Britain', *New Left Review*, 176 (1989)
*C. Harman, *Gramsci versus Reformism* (London, 1983)
E. Laclau and C. Mouffe, *Hegemony and Socialist Strategy* (London, 1985)
M. Löwy, *Georg Lukács: From Romanticism to Bolshevism* (London, 1979)
H. Ott, *Martin Heidegger: A Political Life* (London, 1993)
G. Stedman Jones, 'The Marxism of the Early Lukács', *New Left Review*, 70 (1971)
R. Wolin, *The Politics of Being* (New York, 1990)
R. Wolin, ed., *The Heidegger Controversy* (Cambridge, Mass., 1993)

10 The Golden Age

S. Brittan, *How to End the 'Monetarist' Controversy* (London, 1982)
S. Buck-Morss, *The Origins of Negative Dialectics* (Hassocks, 1977)
S. Buck-Morss, *The Dialectics of Seeing* (Cambridge, Mass., 1989)
A. Gamble, *Hayek* (Cambridge, 1996)
A. Gouldner, *The Coming Crisis of Western Sociology* (London, 1971)
J. Habermas, *The Theory of Communicative Action*, II (Cambridge, 1987)
C. Harman, 'The Crisis in Bourgeois Economics', *International Socialism*, 2/71 (1996)
D. Held, *Introduction to Critical Theory* (London, 1980)
F. Jameson, *Late Marxism* (London, 1990)

M. Jay, *The Dialectical Imagination* (London, 1973)

M. Jay, *Adorno* (London, 1984)

Lord Kaldor, 'Memorandum of Evidence', *Treasury and Civil Service Committee: Memoranda on Monetary Policy* (London, 1980)

D. Lockwood, 'Some Remarks on *The Social System*', *British Journal of Sociology*, 7 (1956)

D. Lockwood, 'Social Integration and System Integration', in G. K. Zollschan and W. Hirsch, eds, *Explorations in Social Change* (London, 1964)

A. MacIntyre, *Marcuse* (London, 1970)

P. Mattick, *Marx and Keynes* (London, 1969)

R. Pippin et al., *Marcuse: Critical Theory and the Promise of Utopia* (South Hadley, Mass., 1988)

S. P. Savage, *The Theories of Talcott Parsons* (London, 1981)

R. Skidelsky, *John Maynard Keynes* (2 vols, London, 1983, 1992)

J. Tomlinson, 'Why Was There Never a "Keynesian Revolution" in Economic Policy?', *Economy and Society*, 10 (1981)

J. Tomlison, *Problems of British Economic Policy 1870–1945* (London, 1981) *Hayek and the Market* (London, 1990)

R. Wiggershaus, *The Frankfurt School* (Cambridge, Mass., 1994)

R. Wolin, *Walter Benjamin: An Aesthetic of Redemption* (New York, 1982)

11 Crack-Up?

P. Abrams, *Historical Sociology* (West Compton House, 1982)

L. Althusser, *The Future Lasts a Long Time* (London, 1993)

P. Anderson, *In the Tracks of Historical Materialism* (London, 1983)

P. Anderson, *A Zone of Engagement* (London, 1992)

P. Anderson, 'A Culture in Contra-Flow', in id., *English Questions* (London, 1992)

R. Bernstein, ed., *Habermas and Modernity* (Cambridge, 1985)

J. Bidet et al., 'Autour de Pierre Bourdieu', special issue of *Actuel Marx*, 20 (1996)

C. Calhoun et al., eds, *Bourdieu: Critical Perspectives* (Cambridge, 1993)

*A. Callinicos, *Althusser's Marxism* (London, 1976)

A. Callinicos, *Is There a Future for Marxism?* (London, 1982)

A. Callinicos, 'Foucault's Third Theoretical Displacement', *Theory, Culture & Society,* 3 (1986)

A. Callinicos, *Against Postmodernism* (Cambridge, 1989)

*V. Descombes, *Modern French Philosophy* (Cambridge, 1980)

P. Dews, *Logics of Disintegration* (London, 1987)

H. Dreyfus and P. Rabinow, *Michel Foucault* (Brighton, 1982)

G. Elliott, *The Detour of Theory* (London, 1987)

G. Elliott, ed., *Althusser: A Critical Reader* (Oxford, 1994)

D. Eribon, *Michel Foucault* (Cambridge, Mass., 1991)

C. Harman, *The Fire Last Time* (London, 1988)

A. Honneth, 'The Fragmented World of Symbolic Forms', *Theory Culture & Society*, 3/3 (1986)

D. C. Hoy, ed., *Foucault: Critical Perspectives* (Oxford, 1986)

E. A. Kaplan and M. Sprinker, eds, *The Althusserian Legacy* (London, 1993)
A. Kuper, *Anthropologists and Anthropology* (London, 1973)
D. Macey, *The Lives of Michel Foucault* (London, 1994)
J. G. Merquior, *From Prague to Paris* (London, 1986)
Y. Moulier Boutang, *Louis Althusser: Une biographie*, I (Paris, 1992)
M. Roberts, *Analytical Marxism* (London, 1996)
J. B. Thompson and D. Held, eds, *Habermas: Critical Debates* (London, 1982)

12 In Place of a Conclusion

A. Ahmad, *In Theory* (London, 1992)
P. Anderson, *The Origins of Postmodernity* (London, 1998)
S. Béroud et al., *Le Mouvement social en France* (Paris, 1998)
R. Brenner, 'Uneven Development and the Long Downturn: The Advanced Capitalist Economies from Boom to Stagnation, 1950–1998', *New Left Review*, 229 (1998)
A. Callinicos, *Against Postmodernism* (Cambridge, 1989)
A. Callinicos, *The Revenge of History* (Cambridge, 1991)
A. Callinicos, 'Postmodernism: A Critical Diagnosis', in J. Van Doren, ed., *The Great Ideas Today 1997* (Chicago, 1997)
L. Elliott and D. Atkinson, *The Age of Insecurity* (London, 1998)
R. Guha and G. C. Spivak, eds, *Selected Subaltern Studies* (New York, 1988)
C. Harman, 'Where is Capitalism Going?', *International Socialism*, 2/58 and 2/60 (1993)
C. Harman, 'France's Hot Autumn', *International Socialism*, 2/70 (1996)
C. Harman, 'Globalization: Critique of a New Orthodoxy', *International Socialism*, 2/73 (1996)
P. Hirst and G. Thompson, *Globalization in Question* (Cambridge, 1995)
W. Hutton, *The State We're In* (London, 1995)
D. Miliband, ed., *Reinventing the Left* (Cambridge, 1994)
M. Rustin, 'The Future of Post-Socialism', *Radical Philosophy*, 74 (1995)
S. Sarkar, 'The Decline of the Subaltern in *Subaltern Studies*', in id., *Writing Social History* (Delhi, 1997)
E. O. Wright, *Class Counts* (Cambridge, 1997)
R. Young, *White Mythologies* (London, 1990)

Index